FIELDS OF GLORY, PATHS OF GOLD

FIELDS OF GLORY, PATHS OF GOLD

The History of European Football

KEVIN CONNOLLY

AND

RAB MacWILLIAM

MAINSTREAM
PUBLISHING

EDINBURGH AND LONDON

This edition, 2006

First published in Great Britain in 2005 by
MAINSTREAM PUBLISHING COMPANY
(EDINBURGH) LTD
7 Albany Street
Edinburgh EH1 3UG

ISBN 1 84596 099 8

All internal illustrations © Cleva

A catalogue record for this book
is available from the British Library

Typeset in Univers and Times New Roman

Printed and bound in Great Britain by
Cox & Wyman Ltd

CONTENTS

INTRODUCTION

As I write the introduction for this updated paperback version, the knockout stages of the European Cup/Champions League will soon stir into life. Will we, though, ever see such an incredible comeback as Liverpool mounted in last season's final – the greatest in the 50-year history of the European Cup. Who, at half-time, would even have dreamt that they would pull back Milan's 3–0 lead, let alone ride their luck when Andriy Shevchenko seemed certain to score – and go on to win the penalty shootout? If West Germany's win over Hungary in the 1954 World Cup final (see Chapter 5) was the 'Miracle of Bern' then no wonder that Liverpool's victory has gone down as the 'Miracle of Istanbul'.

UEFA's archive noted: 'Liverpool's astounding victory evoked an era when open and attacking football dominated the continental game, with regular high-scoring matches.' Games like the first final in 1956, when Real Madrid (see Chapter 7) fought back from two goals down to beat Reims 4–3 in Paris.

Shevchenko, the 2004 European Player of the Year, was denied by Liverpool's Polish goalkeeper Jerzy Dudek, first in the dying minutes of extra time, then in the decisive kick of the shootout. He said, 'The match was in our hands and we let it slip away.' But it was indicative of how much football in the old Soviet bloc (see Chapter 18) has changed that the two actors in the drama's finale should come from Ukraine and Poland.

It was fitting, too, that, 20 years after the Heysel tragedy (see Chapter 13) – at a final also involving Liverpool – 60,000 visiting fans behaved with grace and decency. Most of them wore Liverpool colours.

Liverpool's amazing recovery was a tribute to their coach, Rafa Benitez, who emulated Jose Mourinho by winning the UEFA Cup (with Valencia) and the European Cup in successive seasons. Benitez was tactically canny and fostered a magnificent team spirit, as Liverpool's rally demonstrated. In the quarter-finals, semi-finals and final, Benitez outwitted three of the great generals of the Champions League (see Chapter 19): Fabio Capello of Juventus, Chelsea's Mourinho and Milan's Carlo Ancelotti. Now he is an honoured member of that elite band.

Mourinho, meanwhile, transmitted his own huge confidence to the players and duly delivered the Premiership title. He is on course to deliver another, bankrolled by Roman Abramovich's billions.

Yet Liverpool's victory illustrates the huge changes to the European Cup format (see Chapter 20) since they last won the trophy in 1984. Only the holders and national champions could take part then, and Liverpool entered as champions of England. They qualified for last season's competition by taking fourth place in the Premiership and finishing 30 points behind the champions Arsenal. In 2004–05, they finished fifth, 37 points behind champions Chelsea. And the competition that Joe Fagan's Liverpool won in 1984 was a straight knockout rather than an amalgam of (Champions) league and cup football.

The changes to the format have been the price that UEFA has paid to keep the G-14 group of leading western European clubs on board (see Chapter 20). The G-14, already hugely influential in European club football, are determined to expand their influence into the international game too. They were conspicuous in backing the Belgian club Charleroi's 2006 action against FIFA after the team's Moroccan player Abdelmajid Oulmers damaged ankle ligaments playing for his country against Burkina Faso. Oulmers was sidelined for eight months. Charleroi, supported by G-14, sued FIFA for compensation for his treatment – and sued the world governing body for forcing clubs to release players for internationals in the first place.

If Benitez was *the* European coach of 2004–05, he was run close by Guus Hiddink, who steered PSV Eindhoven to the Dutch Double and an unlucky European Cup semi-final defeat by Milan despite losing star forwards Mateja Kezman and Arjen Robben to Chelsea.

Hiddink has excelled himself in 2005–06, combining his PSV job with the role of Australia's part-time coach, guiding the Aussies to their first World Cup finals appearance since 1974.

Sven-Goran Eriksson made the headlines for different reasons. He was forced to announce that he would quit as England coach after the 2006 World Cup finals following a series of 'revelations' to a tabloid reporter disguised as a Middle Eastern sheikh. Perhaps Eriksson's most pointed comments were his allegations of corruption in the English game, following soon after Luton manager Mike Newell's claims about agents and bungs.

Chelsea continue to carry all before them in England. They virtually had the 2005–06 Premiership title in the bag by the end of January. In a different era, fans would have talked about the battle between Manchester United and Liverpool, or the revival of Tottenham while Arsenal went through a transitional season. Chelsea's dominance has killed all that.

Abramovich's massive investment has distorted Premiership competition. Chelsea have spent £280 million on new players in two years and their last accounts showed a loss of £140 million, figures that would sink any other club. Yet no English club can compete with them. Not even Manchester United, once the world's most formidable football brand, now weakened financially after the takeover by the Glazer family.

The ancient rivalry between Barcelona and Real Madrid (see chapters 7 and 21) continues to shape Spanish football – with the Catalans in the ascendancy. Barcelona, coached by Johan Cruyff's protégé Frank Rijkaard, defended their title impressively in the first half of the season. Barca's trump card, Ronaldinho, was deservedly named World Player of the Year for the second consecutive season. Their top scorer, Samuel Eto'o, came third in the poll. And the teenage Argentine forward Leo Messi looks like another Barca great in the making.

By February 2006, Madrid had achieved Florentino Perez's goal of overtaking Manchester United as the world's richest club. At the end of the month, though, Perez stood down as president. His decision to fire Vicente del Bosque in 2003 looked more and more misguided as Madrid lurched through five coaches in less than three seasons.

Felix Magath's rejuvenated Bayern Munich, the German champions, led the Bundesliga again at the 2005–06 winter break. But Magath must rebuild an ageing squad if the modern Bayern are to rival the great side of the 1970s (see Chapter 11).

The usual suspects – Juventus, Internazionale and Milan – dominate in Italy. Serie A has all but become a three-horse race with the clubs who benefit most from the Champions League reinforcing their superiority over the rest. In France, Lyon, another of the Champions League elite, are chasing their fifth successive title.

CSKA Moscow's victory in the 2005 UEFA Cup final was the exception that proved the rule about the sad decline of club sides in the old Soviet bloc (see Chapter 18). The Russian media hailed CSKA's win over Sporting Lisbon as a 'watershed'. But CSKA are hardly a typical eastern club, worrying about making ends meet while losing their best players to the west. Abramovich spent a small fortune on turning Chelsea into English champions. The £14 million he pumps into CSKA each season puts them several classes above their counterparts in the old east.

The European Cup/Champions League continues to overshadow all other club competitions, enriching already wealthy clubs and handing them even more resources to dominate their domestic competitions (see Chapters 20 and 22). In 2005–06, the last 16 was once again filled entirely by western European teams, with clubs from England, Italy and Spain each taking three places.

On the World Cup front, Zinedine Zidane came out of international retirement to inspire France to automatic qualification for the 2006 finals. The Czech Republic's talisman, Pavel Nedved, also ended his self-imposed exile to star in his team's play-off victories over Norway. Meanwhile, Shevchenko, typically, finished top scorer as Ukraine reached the finals for the first time.

Yet national teams continued to take a poor second place to club football, even as the 2006 World Cup finals loom. This is a concern to former greats such as Cruyff and Michel Platini, who remain concerned about the consequences of the Bosman judgement (see Chapter 22). Cruyff said: 'Take England. They seem to be a little confused there because now they have more foreign stars than English ones. It's not just an English problem, though. I can see the standard of the national teams of several countries deteriorating. National teams should become more important.'

Platini said: 'National sides risk being distorted. Is it OK that some sides don't even field two players from their own country? If I hadn't been given the chance to play for my local team when I was young, I would never have had the chance to turn pro.' He warned: 'If football fails to return to its core values over the new few years, its popularity will fade.'

It was against this Euro-background that *Fields of Glory, Paths of Gold* was first written. The title is meant to be double-edged. On one hand, this book is about great deeds on the pitch. On the other – especially in the closing chapters – it is about the impact of such phenomena as satellite TV, the changing format of the European Cup, the decline of club football in the old Soviet bloc and the effects of the Bosman judgement on domestic competition.

The results – as detailed above – have been the concentration of power and wealth in the hands of a handful of clubs in a handful of western European leagues.

Fields of Glory, Paths of Gold is not meant as a chronological history, or a reference book. There are already several good editions of those on the market, as well as books dedicated to particular competitions such as the World Cup and the European Cup.

This book is a thematic history which aims to explain how and why European football has developed the way it has. I have tried to write it from a European perspective rather than a British one. For instance, I would like to have devoted more space to Jock Stein's Celtic and Matt Busby's Manchester United team, which won the European Cup in 1968. But, in European terms, both were footnotes in between the decline of one dominant team, Internazionale (see Chapter 9) and the rise of another, Ajax (see Chapter 10) .

However, I have devoted a chapter (Chapter 9) to England's 1966 World Cup winners – because that was the only time that England have won the World Cup, and because they did it with revolutionary tactics.

The first two chapters set the scene. The rest of 'Part One: Teams, Themes and Issues' is a series of interlocking essays about great teams, players and figures: about Hugo Meisl, the driving force behind the Austrian '*Wunderteam*'; about Gabriel Hanot, whose vision created the European Cup; and Santiago Bernabeu, the president who turned Real Madrid into Europe's leading club.

It's about important issues in the game: the reaction to the disasters at Heysel, Hillsborough and Bastia; the effects of the collapse of Communism on football; the 'evolution' of the European Cup, from Hanot's dream to the Champions League.

It's about authoritarian governments, of left and right, trying to use football as a propaganda weapon.

It's about the role that immigrants have played in the success of French football.

It's about the bitter antagonism between Real Madrid and Barcelona (see Chapter 7), which dates back to 1916 – and was sharpened by the Spanish Civil War and its aftermath.

It's about mysteries, like the strange death of the great Austrian forward Matthias Sindelar and the bizarre accusations made against the England captain Bobby Moore before the 1970 World Cup finals.

It's about visionary coaches like Jimmy Hogan and Rinus Michels; controversial coaches such as Helenio Herrera and Sir Alf Ramsey; and Herbert Chapman, Vittorio Pozzo and Cruyff, who were both.

It's about Bob Paisley and Brian Clough, temperamental opposites, whose teams won five European Cups.

It's about their modern counterparts, that elite band, 'the generals of the Champions League.'

Most of all, *Fields of Glory, Paths of Gold* is about great players: Alex James of Chapman's Arsenal, Ferenc Puskas of the Magnificent Magyars, Alfredo Di Stefano at Madrid, Cruyff and Franz Beckenbauer – followed in the past 25 years by the two mercurial Frenchmen, Platini and Zidane, another Dutchman, Ruud Gullit, and the modern greats from the old east, Nedved and Shevchenko.

It's about great goal scorers too: Silvio Piola, the lethal finisher of Italy's 1938 World Cup winners, Marco van Basten whose career was sadly cut short by ankle injuries – and the greatest of the modern era: Gerd Muller.

Some names keep cropping up. In the early chapters, spot the influence of Hogan, who taught the Austrians and Hungarians how to play so beautifully. Then come Puskas – first with Hungary then with Madrid – and Herrera, an attacking coach at Barcelona and a dourly defensive one at Internazionale.

The later chapters are dominated by three towering figures of the modern game. The first is Cruyff, the greatest of all Dutch players, who inspired Ajax and Holland to glory, then became a hero to Catalonia, first as a Barcelona player – then as the only European Cup-winning coach in their history.

The second is Beckenbauer, who defined the role of attacking sweeper, won every honour in the game with Bayern Munich and West Germany, then returned to coach his country to World Cup victory in 1990. He was the unchallenged candidate to preside over Germany's World Cup 2006 organising committee.

The third is Platini, the great scorer from midfield, who imposed himself upon the 1984 European Championship finals in a way no player had done before or has done since – then went on to become co-president of France's World Cup '98 organising committee and a rising figure in FIFA and UEFA.

The second part of the book is 'European Competitions', which includes a resumé of all 50 European Cup finals, plus details of the UEFA Cup and Cup Winners' Cup and three chapters devoted to the history of the European Championship.

This book was written from many, many sources, which are detailed in the Bibliography. I've read several good books while researching this project, but two gave me particular pleasure: *Forty Years in Football* by the leading inter-war football writer Ivan Sharpe and the excellent *Tor! The Story of German Football* by Uli Hesse-Lichtenberger.

The website www.rsssf.com was a wonderful source for statistical material. At times, I could hardly believe the depth and breadth of the material there.

Thank you to my co-author Rab MacWilliam, to Alex Fynn – whose vast knowledge helped guide me through the maze of satellite TV and TV rights deals – and to Chris Lightbown, Keir Radnedge and Giles Watson.

Thank you, too, to the folks at Mainstream, and to all the kind people who supported the project.

Kevin Connolly
January 2006

NOTE ON THE TEXT: Kevin Connolly wrote chapters 8 to 22 alone. He expanded and rewrote chapters 3 to 7 from text by Rab MacWilliam. Rab wrote chapters 1 and 2. Rab wrote the text for the European Competitions section and Kevin compiled the statistical appendices.

NOTE ON TERMINOLOGY: Champions League/European Cup – when referring to matches, I have continued to use 'European Cup' to describe the knock-out stages of the competition.

PART ONE

TEAMS, THEMES AND ISSUES

CHAPTER 1

IN THE BEGINNING

The game of football has been enjoyed, in one form or another, for at least 2,000 years. One of the earliest examples comes from China and was seemingly intended to keep up the fitness levels of the Han Dynasty soldiers. Evidence exists that around 200 BC a game called *tsu chu* was played with two thirty-foot-high bamboo poles acting as goals and a ball made of leather and stuffed with hair and feathers.

The Greeks played a form of football as early as 4 BC. The game was known as *pheninda* or *episkyros* and consisted of kicking and throwing a ball. The Romans followed the Greeks' example and called their game *hapastum*. This was played on a rectangular field, between two teams, often each over a hundred strong, who defended the lines marking the ends of the field. The object of the game was to throw the ball from player to player, moving forward all the time, and eventually to throw it beyond the opponents' goal line. The defending side was allowed to tackle and kick.

There are other examples of early versions of the game evolving elsewhere around the world. In Kyoto, Japan, around the fifth century AD a game called *kemari* was played which involved players kicking the ball back to one another across a square pitch. In Italy, a similar game, called *calcio* (*calciare* means 'to kick' in Italian), was played in the fifteenth and sixteenth centuries. This was a regular occurrence in Florence on feast days and the rules were first published in 1491. Football is still known as calcio in Italy.

Although an apocryphal story has it that the first football game was played in the east of England – where the locals played 'football' with the severed head of a Danish warrior they had defeated in battle – the game in England appears to have had its roots in holy days. In the twelfth century, a game with a ball was played on Shrove Tuesday in Ashbourne, with the goals three miles apart. A similar game existed in Derby between two parishes in the town. The term 'derby' – meaning a game between two neighbouring clubs – has its origins in this local tussle. These games grew quickly in popularity in medieval times, with towns and villages taking on other towns and villages. They were normally played between gangs of hundreds of people, through streets, fields and bogs. They usually developed into dangerous, unruly mêlées, with kicking, punching and gouging permitted, leading often to rioting and serious injury.

So violent and lawless did these matches become that, over the centuries, many attempts were made by the authorities to ban football. In England, King Edward III passed legislation in 1331 and 1349 to try to suppress football. In 1414, Henry IV ordered his men to concentrate on archery and exhorted them not to play football. In Scotland, King James I, in 1424, proclaimed in Parliament 'That nae man play at the Fute-ball'. Elizabeth I passed a law that provided for football players to be 'jailed for a week and obliged to do penance in church'. The Puritans, too, attempted to suppress the game, partly because it was normally played on the Sabbath but also due to their fears of the social unrest and threat to the established order associated with football. The game, however, proved too popular for any of these interdicts and prohibitions to have lasting effect, and it proceeded in its various forms to be the main popular activity of the rural population.

However, by the early nineteenth century, football, although still the game of the working people, was beginning to lose its mass appeal. The Enclosure Acts between 1760 and 1830 meant that the open land necessary for the old, sprawling form of the game was much reduced. At the same time, the increasing development of industrialisation and urbanisation, and the general move of country folk into the cities, limited not only the space but also the time available for football. The factories and workplaces required their new employees to work regular and long hours, cutting back on the spare time, and indeed energy, necessary for leisure activities. And the emerging authority of local and central government created an increasingly efficient law enforcement system that was able to police those, such as the London apprentices, who still played the game on the streets. So by the mid-nineteenth century, the old form of the game was dying out. However, football as we know it today was being formed in the unlikely environment of the English public schools.

Football had been played at Oxford and Cambridge since the sixteenth century but it had never become an acceptable upper-class pastime until the public schools embraced the game with enthusiasm in the mid-nineteenth century. In keeping with the Victorian ethos of discipline, selflessness, the benefits of physical exercise and the submission of the individual to the team, the leading public schools saw in football a means of inculcating in their students the desired manly values of the age. The game, however, had to change from its amorphous, unregulated state in order to accommodate the demands about to be made on it.

The necessity for regulation was further complicated by the varying rules under which it was played at the individual schools, principally Westminster, Harrow, Eton, Charterhouse, Winchester, Uppingham, Shrewsbury and Rugby. The rules at each institution were partly formulated by the space and conditions allowed for the game at the particular school. For instance, at Charterhouse, players organised in teams of 20-a-side could dribble the ball but not handle; Eton had its own peculiar Wall Game; at Uppingham, the goal was the width of the pitch; and at Rugby, handling was permitted but running with it was penalised (until Rugby created the myth that one William Webb Ellis did just that in 1823 and laid the foundations for the game of rugby). Something had to be done to codify and simplify exactly what could and could not be done on a football pitch.

The first real attempt to do so was made in 1846 by J.C. Thring, an assistant master at Uppingham who published The Cambridge Rules, which outlawed violence, allowed the ball to be handled if then immediately placed on the ground and kicked, and did not allow players in front of the ball. Further codification occurred in the mid-1850s in Sheffield, where the world's first football club – Sheffield Football Club – was established in 1855. In 1863, the rules – now known as The Simplest Game – were published. Shortly after this, a momentous meeting took place in the Freemason's Arms in London on 26 October 1863, a meeting which effectively began the game of football as we now know it.

The meeting was held to establish 'a definite code of rules for the regulation of the game of football' and was presided over by old

Harrovian Charles Allcock with 11 clubs in attendance. These were No Names of Kilburn, the War Office, Barnes, Crusaders, Perceval House (Blackheath), Leytonstone Forest, Crystal Palace, Blackheath, Kennington School, Surbiton and Blackheath School, and the meeting led to the formation of the Football Association, the world's first organised football body. All the clubs except Blackheath were proponents of the kicking and dribbling game and by the time the rules were published in December that year, carrying the ball and hacking an opponent were declared illegal. Blackheath disagreed, withdrew their membership and formed a rugby club, which is still playing today.

Although Sheffield had drawn up its own set of rules, by 1866 the two codes were similar enough for the two cities to play each other in representative matches, incidentally the first game to be played over one and a half hours. The game, however, remained largely a gentlemen's sport based in the south of England. Indeed, when Allcock instigated the FA Challenge Cup in 1872, 13 of the 15 entrants came from the London area, with Wanderers defeating Royal Engineers 1–0 in the final. Only one Scottish team, Queen's Park, entered the competition on the grounds that they were far too good to get a decent game from any other Scottish club. Queen's Park became a catalyst for the formation of the Scottish Football Association and the Scottish Cup, which they won three times in succession between 1874 and 1876.

The success of the FA Cup saw a rapid increase in the number of entries, particularly from northern clubs, who were by now forming their own regional associations and who were embracing the game with enthusiasm. The hegemony of the southern clubs – who had won the FA Cup for the first 11 years of the competition's existence – was coming under threat from the north, and the new order was marked when Blackburn Olympic became the first northern winners when they defeated Old Etonians in 1883.

The divide between the two regions was, however, more than simply geographical. The north of England was a poorer, more deprived area, with many of the players employed in the factories and mills and having to suffer loss of essential income if they took time off to play football. Few northern footballers could rely on private incomes, as many could in the south, so under-the-counter payments became commonplace. Some of the northern clubs were also becoming dependent on Scots, who brought down with them their passing game and who had to be rewarded for their appearances. A de facto professionalism emerged, enraging the FA who frowned on the practice of payment.

In the season following Olympic's FA Cup win, the FA expelled Preston and Accrington from the competition on the grounds of their admitted professionalism, and Preston suggested the formation of a breakaway competing association of northern and midland clubs, a suggestion which received much support in the north. Rather than lose control of the game, the FA capitulated just before the beginning of the 1885 season and legalised professionalism.

Although clubs could now pay their players, the fairly chaotic jumble of friendlies and cup ties was not regular or consistent enough to draw in paying spectators. In March 1888, William McGregor, a director of Aston Villa, arranged a meeting in London to discuss the issue. A further meeting was held a month later in Manchester, as no southern clubs had bothered to turn up in London. The clubs decided that there were 22 free days in each season and, therefore, only 12 clubs could be admitted to the new Football League, to be played on a home and away basis. The 12 historic members of the world's oldest football league were Accrington, Aston Villa, Blackburn, Bolton, Burnley, Derby County, Everton, Notts County (formed in 1862 and the world's oldest league club), Preston North End, Stoke, West Bromwich Albion and Wolverhampton Wanderers.

In the League's first season, 1888–89, Preston North End, regularly fielding no fewer than eight Scots, took the title at a canter, winning the league without losing a game and failing to score on only one occasion. They also claimed the double, defeating Wolves 3–0 in the FA Cup final. To mark this remarkable achievement, they became known as 'the Old Invincibles'.

The 1890s were marked by the decline of Preston and the dominance of, first, Sunderland and then Aston Villa, who between them won the league eight times during the decade. Villa became the second team to win the double, in 1897, and it was to be another 64 years before this increasingly difficult and tantalising achievement was repeated.

Meanwhile, a similar process was occurring in Scotland. The Scottish League was formed for the 1890–91 season and consisted of 11 clubs – Abercorn, Celtic, Cowlairs, Cambuslang, Dumbarton, Hearts, Rangers, St Mirren, Renton, Third Lanark and Vale of Leven. The Scottish FA were even more intolerant of professionalism than their English counterparts and only five games into the first league season Renton were expelled for playing a game against Edinburgh Saints, a team deemed professional. However, the need to retain their best players in Scotland and to keep them out of the clutches of the wealthier northern English clubs could have had only one outcome. In 1893, the Scottish FA also legalised professionalism. Dumbarton won the first two league titles, and Celtic and Hearts vied for the league title throughout the rest of the decade. In 1899, Rangers, now ensconced in their palatial Ibrox stadium, won all 18 of their league games to set up a record never since beaten.

The game was also quickly developing at international level. In 1872, Queen's Park, representing Scotland, invited an English representative side to visit Glasgow for a match. A crowd of over 2,000 squeezed into the West of Scotland Cricket Club to witness a 0–0 draw. The profits made from this game allowed the Scottish FA to send a team to Kennington Oval in London the following year, where they lost 4–2. The oldest international fixture in world football had been established.

The Welsh FA was formed in 1875 and they played their first international against England five years later. In 1880, the Irish Football Association was established and when Scotland played Ireland in 1883, the Home International Championship was born. This annual tournament was to last for 100 years until it was killed off by hooliganism and political disagreements.

So, by the end of the nineteenth century, football was well established in the United Kingdom, its elegant simplicity, visceral excitement and appeal to tribal and local loyalties ensuring a healthy and expanding future for the game. But the sport could not be contained within the British Isles. The game had been introduced to the European continent by British sailors, travellers, businessmen, teachers and expatriates, and a whole new chapter in football was about to begin.

CHAPTER 2

THE FOOTBALL MISSIONARIES

The spread of football across Europe was speedy and dramatic. By the end of the nineteenth century, many countries on the Continent had established clubs, associations and leagues, with, in the majority of cases, the initial impetus provided by the British. British sailors, textile and railway workers, students and businessmen – all football fans – set about establishing or helping to establish football clubs wherever they travelled or worked in Europe.

Denmark was one of the first countries to adopt the game, with British residents and visiting sailors setting up the Continent's first club, Kjobenhavns Boldklub, in 1876. A Danish FA was set up in 1889 and the league in 1915. France's Le Havre, established by British sailors, also had an early beginning, in 1872, but played rugby – a more popular game than football in nineteenth-century France – until 1892. Up till the First World War, no less than five different organisations claimed the right to be the French national FA and this was not unified until 1918.

Sweden and Norway also took to the game early, with British engineers playing regularly in Gothenburg in the 1870s and British embassy staff playing in Stockholm's parks. The first league tournament was inaugurated in 1896 in Gothenburg and included two of the earliest teams, Orgryte (1887) and Gothenburg (1894). In 1900, the league was enlarged to include clubs from Stockholm. In Norway, four teams were established in the 1890s and the Norwegian FA was founded in 1902.

The physical proximity of the Low Countries to the United Kingdom was an important factor in the early development of the game in Belgium and Holland. In Belgium, there was a good-sized population of British students in Brussels and engineering and textile workers in Antwerp, Brugge and Liege, and they promoted the diffusion of football throughout the country, with the first club, Brugge, founded in 1891. Like Sweden, Belgium's league competition was begun in 1896 and the two countries share the distinction of having the oldest league competition outside the British Isles. Before the First World War, Belgian football was dominated by Racing Club de Bruxelles and Union St Gilloise, both based in Brussels.

In Holland, English textile workers in the late 1860s had helped popularise and spread the game. The first Dutch club, Haarlemse FC, was started in 1879 by a Dutch-born, English-educated journalist, Pim Mulier, and national league and cup tournaments sprang up ten years later. Holland's insistence on remaining amateur, however, was to relegate the country to minor footballing status until the arrival, first, of professionalism in 1956 and then the emergence of Ajax and 'Total Football' in the 1970s.

In Germany, although football was embraced in the late nineteenth century by the northern ports and the English students in Berlin, the sporting scene was dominated by gymnastics (*Turnen*), with its emphasis on individual health and fitness and overtones of militarism, and football was considered too anarchic and threatening (particularly with the British connection) to make an immediate impact. It was banned in the armed forces and in Prussian schools. However, Anglo-American FC was established in 1881, becoming Hamburg, Germany's oldest club, in 1887. Hertha Berlin was formed in 1892 and the first recorded German inter-city match was held in 1896, when Berlin thrashed Hamburg 13–0. In spite of authoritarian disapproval, the game gradually percolated through the country, with the German federation formed in 1900 and a national championship instituted in 1902. The ban was lifted in 1911 and the game became hugely popular.

Switzerland and Austria were also early football enthusiasts. Today the home of international football – hosting the headquarters of both UEFA and FIFA – Switzerland possessed a longer tradition of football than most other Continental countries, with football matches being played between English and Swiss students as early as the 1850s. The oldest Swiss club still in existence is FC St Gallen, formed in 1879, soon followed by Grasshoppers Zurich, again at the instigation of

British students, some seven years later. By the time the national championship began in 1897, such familiar names as FC Zurich, Servette and Young Boys Berne (the latter a clear reference to the club's English-speaking origins) were all in contention for the title, which was won by Grasshoppers.

The first two Austrian clubs, both coming from Vienna with its large British population, were established in 1894. The formation of First Vienna FC was inspired by football-loving English gardeners employed by the Rothschild family. The Vienna Cricket and Football Club was founded by an Englishman, John Gramlick, and the two clubs played each other in the first official Austrian game in 1894. Three years later, Gramlick instituted the Challenge Cup, a tournament between all the clubs in the Austro–Hungarian Empire, including the Hungarian trio MTK, Ferencvaros and Ujpest, all set up in the 1880s. An employee of the Thomas Cook Company, Englishman M.D. Nicholson, became the first president of the Austrian Football Union in 1904.

In 1912, Hugo Meisl, the father of Austrian football, invited English coach Jimmy Hogan to Vienna to teach the short passing game that became the national team's trademark. Hogan would later become an illustrious coach with Hungary.

In the Czech Republic (or Bohemia as it was then known), the two leading teams were Athletic Club King's Vineyard (soon to be renamed Sparta Prague) and Slavia Prague, founded in, respectively, 1893 and 1892. A Prague league was in existence by 1896.

Within two decades of its introduction, football had pervaded northern and central Europe, and the situation was no different in the Latin south. Italy had its own traditional folk form of football – calcio – but the north of the country soon adapted to the new association football. In Italy, Genoa Cricket and Football Club was formed in 1893 by James Richardson Spensley so that the Italian port's employees could have regular matches against visiting ships' crews. Spensley played in goal. No Italians were admitted into the club until 1897.

The Italian FA was established in 1898. Genoa became the first Italian champions and they won the title a further six times between then and 1904. Englishman Willy Garbutt was appointed manager in 1912 and he was to have a huge influence on the development of the Italian game. However, the last title won by the Genoese club was the Coppa Italia in 1937, which perhaps illustrates that first is not always best.

25

The other team to win the title in that turn-of-the-century, Genoa-dominated period was Milan Cricket and Football Club, established by British expatriate Alfred Edwards, which would soon become Athletic Club (AC) Milan. Another of today's famous Italian football clubs, Juventus, had been formed a year before AC Milan, in 1898, while Internazionale emerged as a breakaway club from AC Milan in 1908 as a protest about AC only playing Italians. Pro Vercelli, today in Serie C, dominated Italian football from 1908 till the First World War, with Roman side Lazio one of the few non-northern clubs to offer serious competition.

The first club to be formed in Spain was Recreativo Huelva in 1889. They played their first game in 1890 against a Seville select XI composed of British workers from the Seville Water Works. There were only two Spanish players on the pitch. The British workers team became Sevilla in 1905 and their bitter city rival Real Betis was created two years later as a reaction to Sevilla's hiring practices. In the northern Basque country, Atletico Bilbao was founded in 1898 by local traders, engineers from the north of England and British students. Their red and white strip is said to have been modelled on the dominant English team of the period, Sunderland. However, Phil Ball, in his entertaining book on Spanish football, *Morbo*, claims that the ubiquity of red and white striped shirts in Spain is because they were cheap to make from traditional bed sheets.

Founded by the Swiss Joan Gamper, Barcelona played their first match on Christmas Eve 1899, featuring England's Alfred Whitty as captain. Barca's distinctive maroon and blue strip is reputed to be based on the colours of Whitty's public school, Merchant Taylor's. The club's first president was an Englishman, Walter Wild. The following year, some local students established another club, Espanol, in the city in opposition to Barca's Catalan and foreign connections.

The first Spanish regional league began in Catalonia in 1901. The Spanish Cup was established in 1902, with Barcelona beating Madrid FC (to be renamed Real Madrid in 1920) 3–1 in this first meeting between the two clubs, and though it has undergone many name changes, it is one of the oldest football competitions in Europe. In 1913, under the presidency of King Alfonso XIII, the Real Federacion Espanola de Futbol (RFEF) was formed.

Portugal was also an important trading partner of Britain and English sailors founded Lisbon FC in 1875. Portuguese students returning from

England brought football back with them and in the first six years of the twentieth century, the country's biggest clubs – Benfica, Porto, Sporting Lisbon and Boavista – were formed. The British influence is evident in Boavista's original name, Boavista Footballers, the club being formed by British bosses and Portuguese textile workers in 1903.

The English origins of much of European football can also be traced further east, in Russia. Brothers Clement and Harry Charnock ran some textile mills around Moscow. Both Blackburn Rovers fans, the brothers founded a football club known as Orekhovo Sports Club (KSO) in 1887 and imported a set of Blackburn strips for their players. The new club won the first four Moscow championships. After the Russian Revolution, the club changed its name to Dynamo Moscow and became one of the Soviet Union's most famous clubs.

In other countries such as Tsarist Poland, Ottoman Turkey and northern Greece and Serbia, football was developing a grassroots base but was suppressed by the authorities, who were fearful of the destabilising effect of thousands of people gathering to watch football matches. Clubs were, however, being formed in all these countries and an unstoppable impetus was building up, fed by the visiting British, to formalise leagues and tournaments. In Turkey, for example, today's top sides – Fenerbahce, Galatasaray and Besiktas – had all been formed by the turn of the century but were forced by the Istanbul Caliphate to play in Jewish and Christian areas, as Muslims were banned from playing the game. As an indication of the growing Europeanisation of the game, Galatasaray toured Switzerland and came back with a Swiss song, '*Jim Bom Bom*'. To this day, the club's nickname is 'Cim Bom Bom'.

In southern Greece, English bankers established a club in Athens called Panhellenic, and it changed its name to Panathinaikos in 1908. The club badge retains the shamrock from the original club.

Developments were also occurring at the international level. The first international between two Continental European countries was held in Vienna in October 1902, with Austria defeating Hungary 5–0 in a game organised by Hugo Meisl. FIFA was founded in Paris in May 1904, the original members being Belgium, Denmark, Holland, Spain, France, Sweden and Switzerland. Although England had been invited to apply for membership, the English FA were disdainful of the embryonic organisation and prevaricated about joining until it was too late. They did, however, become members two years later.

English belief in their superiority over European countries had some justification. The 1908 Olympics, held in London, was the first tournament to recognise football as a competitive, as opposed to exhibition, sport. Only five countries entered – England, Denmark, France, Holland and Sweden – and an all-amateur England defeated an unlucky Denmark in the final. Denmark's early introduction to football, and the formation of the Danish FA in 1889, had contributed to Denmark's national side becoming one of the top teams in Europe but they still could not beat the 'fathers' of the game – despite beating France 17–1 in the first round of the tournament, with Nobel Prize-winner Nils Bohr in the Danish squad.

Earlier that year, England had embarked on their first international tour and asserted their dominance. They beat Austria 6–1 and 11–1 in Vienna, Hungary 7–0 in Budapest and Bohemia 4–0 in Prague. In 1909, they again travelled to Central Europe and defeated Hungary 4–2 and 8–2, and Austria 8–1. In the 1912 Olympics in Stockholm, 11 countries entered and England reached the final without conceding a single goal. They defeated Denmark, again, 4–2 in the final.

By the beginning of the First World War, it was clear that the British version of association football, and its league and cup structures, had become the model for virtually all European countries and that football had been established as the most popular sport on the Continent. It was equally clear that England considered itself some distance above the Continental upstarts and that, although the standard of the game was rising in Europe, there was some distance to go before the likes of Spain and Hungary could compete with any degree of equality with England on the football pitch. That day, however, would come.

Meanwhile, back in 'the home of football', the game was booming. In Scotland, the 'Old Firm' of Celtic and Rangers were, as usual, dominating the game, shrugging aside the occasional impertinence of the likes of Third Lanark and Hibernian winning the league title. Competition was much stiffer in England, with no fewer than eight different teams winning the league in the 1900–14 period. The Home Internationals were becoming enormously popular, and in 1914 Ireland finally broke England and Scotland's stranglehold on the title. However, with the exception of amateur teams such as Corinthians and Oxford University – and Arsenal, whose post-season tour of Europe in 1907 saw them win seven out of the eight games they played – British football remained insular, a situation that owed as much to ignorance as disdain.

When Britain went to war with Germany on 4 August 1914, all tournaments in Britain, except those in the Scottish First Division, were postponed until the end of hostilities. The post-war period was to witness the emergence of exceptional European clubs and national sides, and British football would no longer be able to claim undisputed mastery of the game.

CHAPTER 3

CHAPMAN'S ARSENAL – AND THEIR EUROPEAN COUNTERPARTS

Herbert Chapman created the Arsenal team that dominated a decade, built a dynasty and turned football upside down with his revolutionary tactics. He stands head and shoulders above every other British manager of the inter-war years.

Chapman made Arsenal. He laid the foundations for every success that they have achieved since. Without him, there would have been no marble halls of Highbury, no double in 1971 and no Arsene Wenger to redefine the club's image in a new century. As Martin Tyler and Phil Soar write in the club's official history, 'The history of Arsenal remains in essence a tale of the 1930s.'

Before Chapman's Arsenal, football in England had been a provincial game – dominated by teams from the industrial north, north-east and west midlands. The Gunners changed all that. They became the first London club to win the championship and only the second – after the Huddersfield side that Chapman built – to win the title three years in a row.

Chapman died in January 1934, while his team were on their way to the second of those consecutive titles. Their success was his legacy. By the outbreak of the Second World War, Arsenal had become the richest, most famous club in Europe.

But how can we test the greatness of Chapman's Gunners? The European Cup was still a pipe dream. So was the concept of floodlit football. Arsenal never had the chance to dominate a continent, as Real Madrid would dominate in the late 1950s. In the early 1930s, though, Arsenal wore an aura of virtual invincibility: witness the shock and amazement throughout England when they were beaten by Third Division Walsall in the FA Cup third round of 1933.

Would Chapman's side have maintained that aura if they had competed against the likes of Juventus (who supplied the nucleus of Italy's 1934 World Cup-winning side) or the top clubs from Vienna or Prague; the Spanish kingpins, Atletico Bilbao and Real Madrid; or the rising force of German football, Schalke?

European club football was virtually unknown in England at the time. The English still considered themselves masters of the game. Not until Dynamo Moscow's historic tour in 1945 would English fans begin to recognise the quality of foreign club sides. Those fans recognised the quality of Arsenal, though often through gritted teeth.

There had been dominant powers in English football before. Preston's 'Old Invincibles' had won the first two Football League championships, achieving the first league and FA Cup double in 1888–89. Aston Villa did the double in 1897 and won the championship five times in seven years. Between 1905 and 1911, Newcastle won the title three times and the FA Cup once. But those teams had achieved their glories in less competitive days, when the Football League consisted of just two divisions.

Between 1930 and 1935, Arsenal won the championship four times, the FA Cup once and supplied seven players to the England team which beat World Cup holders Italy 3–2 in 1934. In the only season (1931–32) when they did not win a trophy, they finished runners-up in both league and FA Cup.

Chapman was born in January 1878 in the small Yorkshire mining village of Kiveton Park. He was a bright boy in a time when the working classes had few opportunities to better themselves. He qualified at Sheffield Technical College as a mining engineer and combined his job with his football career up until he became Huddersfield manager in 1920.

Chapman had been a journeyman inside-forward for ten different clubs before he started his managerial career with Northampton (then in the old Southern League) in 1907. He took charge after they had finished bottom of the table. Two years later, he guided them to the championship. He moved onto Second Division Leeds City and turned them into promotion challengers.

After the First World War broke out, Chapman became the manager of a munitions factory. Leeds City were closed down by the Football

League in 1919 for making illegal payments to players. Chapman had been on war work at the time (1916–1918) but he was suspended by the Football League along with all the club's other ex-officials. It would be two years before the league cancelled his ban, thus enabling him to take charge at Huddersfield. He had been out of football for four years.

Chapman built shrewdly and Huddersfield prospered on principles he would refine at Arsenal. He organised them around a solid defence; a midfield general, Clem Stephenson, who could swiftly turn defence into attack; and two flying wingers, G.E. Richardson and W.H. Smith. They won the FA Cup in 1922, beating Preston 1–0 in the final with a Smith penalty. Two years later, they won their first championship, pipping Cardiff on goal average. The following season, they finished two points ahead of West Bromwich.

In 1926, Chapman's old club made it three in a row. They finished five points ahead of his new club, Arsenal, who were runners-up – then their highest-ever placing.

Chapman had long realised the potential for a successful club in London. Ivan Sharpe, the leading football writer of the inter-war years, remembered, 'More than once, Chapman said to me, "What a chance there is in London. I would like to build a Newcastle United there." The triumphant Newcastle of 1905–11, he meant.'

At the end of the 1924–25 season, Arsenal sacked Leslie Knighton and advertised for a new manager. Sharpe said, 'What Chapman wanted was an approach from the London end.' It came from the Arsenal chairman, Henry Norris, who offered to make him the highest-paid manager in England – at £2,000 per season. Chapman told his new club that it would take him five years to build a successful team. He would need to make several major signings along the way. Five years and several big money deals later, Arsenal won their first major honour, when they beat Huddersfield 2–0 in the 1930 FA Cup final.

Which modern club would have allowed their manager to spend pots of cash without winning a trophy for five years? But the Arsenal chairmen, first Norris, then Sir Samuel Hill-Wood, kept faith as Chapman assembled his team. The former Arsenal centre-half and *Evening Standard* football writer Bernard Joy said of him, 'His vision was of creating the greatest football team in the world. His genius was in creating something close to that.' Arsenal's brilliant left-winger Cliff Bastin said, 'There was an aura of greatness about him. His power of inspiration and gift of foresight were his greatest attributes.'

Chapman's first major signing showed his football judgement – and his flair for publicity. Arsenal signed the former England inside-forward Charlie Buchan from Sunderland. Buchan was 33, and Sunderland were prepared to let him go. But they wanted £4,000. Arsenal offered much less. The Sunderland manager Bob Kyle said that Buchan would score 20 goals in his first season with the Gunners. Norris worked out a deal that Arsenal would pay Sunderland £2,000 plus £100 for each goal that Buchan netted. It was a huge publicity coup, ensuring that Buchan and Arsenal were always in the news.

Buchan scored 19 league goals and one in the FA Cup but his impact was greater than his goal tally. His presence seemed to lift the players around him. Chapman made a clever change, too: switching Jimmy Brain from inside-forward to centre-forward. Brain set a club record of 34 league goals and Arsenal achieved their highest points total – 52.

That had seemed an unlikely outcome after they were thrashed 7–0 at Newcastle in October. Such a defeat led to a crucial team meeting. The recent change in the offside law had altered the balance in favour of forwards. Previously they needed to have three defenders between them and the goal to be onside. This had been reduced to two, effectively the goalkeeper plus one defender.

Buchan argued that this meant rethinking the role of the centre-half. Centre-halves – like Chapman's old number five at Huddersfield, Tom Wilson – had previously roved in support of the attack. But teams such as Newcastle were already experimenting with using the centre-half as an out and out defender. Buchan suggested Arsenal's centre-half Jack Butler should become a defender, with one of the inside-forwards dropping deeper behind the attack. Andy Neil took on the role for the game at West Ham. Arsenal won 4–0. Chapman stuck with the system and developed it.

Over the coming years, he devised revolutionary tactics. He moved his full-backs to mark the opposing wingers – a job previously done by the half-backs, who now moved into midfield. He used one inside-forward as his playmaker, with the other attacking from behind the centre-forward. They were flanked by two wingers, who could cut inside and shoot rather than hug the touchline like traditional wingers.

Chapman had changed his formation from the old 2–3–5 to 3–2–2–3, often known as the 'WM' formation. Sharpe wrote: 'Arsenal's formation was really this: a goalkeeper, three full-backs, two half-backs, one and often two forward half-backs and only three forwards – centre-forward and wing men.'

Such moves outraged traditionalists, who accused Chapman of being a negative influence in the game. But Italy's great coach Vittorio Pozzo (see Chapter 4) would use similar tactics to win the 1938 World Cup.

Chapman had to find the right pieces to fit his tactical jigsaw. In February 1926, he signed right-winger Joe Hulme from Blackburn. Hulme was reputed to be the fastest winger in England. He would score 124 goals in a 12-year Highbury career and set new fashions in wing play.

Chapman's next major signing was right-back Tom Parker from Southampton. He was 'Mr Consistency' – ever-present in each of his first three seasons. He would also be the first Arsenal captain to lift the FA Cup and the league championship trophy. Centre-forward Jack Lambert arrived from Doncaster for £2,500 that summer.

In 1927, Arsenal reached the FA Cup final for the first time. They lost 1–0 to Cardiff when goalkeeper Dan Lewis fumbled the winning shot. The Gunners' league form was disappointing, perhaps because Chapman was forever tinkering with his personnel and formation. They finished eleventh in 1927, tenth the following year and ninth in 1929. But Chapman kept building. When Buchan retired after the FA Cup final, Chapman targeted his successor, the Bolton and England inside-forward David Jack.

Bolton did not want to sell. When Chapman told them to name a price, they asked for £13,000, nearly double the previous record fee. Bolton thought the price tag would frighten Chapman off. Instead, the Arsenal manager, supported by director George Allison, haggled with Bolton officials for hours. Bolton eventually accepted an offer of around £11,000. Jack spoke to his father (who was manager of Plymouth) and agreed to move to north London. The Bolton party travelled by train to Euston, then joined Chapman and his assistant Bob Wall at a nearby hotel.

Wall, who later became club secretary, remembered in *Arsenal from the Heart* how Chapman wrapped up the deal. He wrote: 'We arrived half an hour early. Chapman immediately went to the lounge bar. He called the waiter and placed two pound notes in his hand. He said, "George, this is Mr Wall, my assistant. He will drink whisky and dry ginger. I will drink gin and tonic. We will be joined by guests. They will drink what they like. See that they are given double of everything – but

Mr Wall's whisky and dry ginger will contain no whisky and my gin and tonic will contain no gin.'"

Wall recalled that the Bolton officials were quickly in a cheerful mood and the deal was completed with no last-minute hitches.

Jack was a brilliant dribbler and prolific goalscorer. He would net 123 goals in 206 games for the Gunners. But he was not a leader on the pitch like Buchan. Chapman needed one more player to complete his team-building – a midfield general who could do for Arsenal what Stephenson had done for Huddersfield. In the summer of 1929, he got his man – Preston's Scotland inside-forward Alex James.

Arsenal beat off competition from Aston Villa and Liverpool. The Gunners paid £8,750 to Preston and helped James find a part-time job in the London department store Selfridges to supplement his wages. (Those were the days of the maximum wage.)

James had been an attacking inside-forward and regular scorer for Preston. But Chapman realised that his penetrating passes and eye for an opening made him the ideal hub of his new-look team. It took James most of the 1929–30 season to settle into his new role. Once he did, Chapman's Arsenal won trophy after trophy. James played much deeper than most inside-forwards of the time. He was probably the first of the footballing 'quarterbacks' – collecting the ball from his defence then unleashing the Arsenal attack with swift passes. His trademark was the long ball inside the full-back for Hulme or Bastin.

Parker may have skippered the team but James, a diminutive figure in his baggy shorts, became Arsenal's organiser. Chapman later said of him, 'He has justified all our hopes and expectations.' Allison added, 'He had wonderful, almost uncanny ball control, allied to a split-second thinking apparatus.'

Chapman was often accused of buying success. Yet he also plucked bargain buys seemingly from nowhere. The first was Herbert Roberts, the best of the early 'stopper' centre-halves, signed from Oswestry for £200. Three more of the Gunners' greats of the 1930s – Eddie Hapgood, Bastin and George Male – showed Chapman's rare ability for spotting talent.

Left-back Hapgood was a slight, spindly milkman from Bristol who had played a handful of games for non-league Kettering. Chapman signed the 19 year old for £750 and instructed trainer Tom Whittaker to build up his strength. Hapgood became one of Arsenal and England's best-ever full-backs.

Chapman spotted Bastin, then just 16, playing for Exeter in a Third Division South game. He went to Bastin's Devon home. Bastin wanted to go out and play tennis. Chapman persisted and persisted until he agreed to join the Gunners. Bastin said, 'I had visions of spending my life sitting there listening to him.' Bastin became another Arsenal and England legend. He won every major honour in English football while still a teenager. He set a club scoring record of 176 goals, only surpassed by Ian Wright in 1997.

In the early months of 1930, Chapman had successfully converted former Nottingham Forest left-winger Charlie Jones into a dependable wing-half. In 1932, he switched Male, signed from the amateur club Clapton as a wing-half, to right-back to succeed Parker. Male said, 'After he [Chapman] had finished talking to me, I was convinced not only that I was a right-back but also the best right-back in England.' Male and Hapgood became a legendary pairing for club and country.

Chapman would later pluck future England goalkeeper Frank Moss from the obscurity of Oldham's reserves, too.

Yet in January 1930, Arsenal's forthcoming hegemony seemed hugely unlikely. They lacked consistency in the league and would finish 14th. Tyler and Soar pose an interesting question: how would history have judged Chapman had he died in January 1930 rather than four years later?

On 22 March, Arsenal's dreams seemed as far away as ever. They trailed Second Division strugglers Hull City 2–0 with 20 minutes left of the FA Cup semi-final at Leeds. One was an own goal by Hapgood.

Then Jack fired in Hulme's cross to set up a frantic finish. With eight minutes left, Bastin controlled James's pass, beat two defenders and cracked the equaliser. Jack scored the only goal of the replay after Hull centre-half Arthur Childs was sent off for kicking Lambert.

Yet perhaps the crucial game in Arsenal's run to Wembley had been the 1–0 fourth-round replay win over Birmingham. James had missed the first match, a 2–2 draw, with ankle trouble. The next morning, Chapman went to his house and persuaded him to train at Highbury. Chapman predicted, 'You're going to win the match for us.'

Chapman had correctly foreseen that James would enjoy the responsibility. Joy believes it was one of the most important decisions that the manager ever made. The Gunners won a physical game 1–0 with a penalty. It was a turning point for James, whose confidence grew and grew.

He would demonstrate his influence in the final against Huddersfield. In the 17th minute, he took a quick free kick to Bastin while the Huddersfield defence dawdled. Bastin burst down the left, then slipped the ball back to James who scored with a low shot. It was one of only twenty-seven goals he netted for the Gunners and undoubtedly the most important.

Huddersfield pressed for an equaliser – and James cut them open on the break. His long pass found Lambert, who ran on to score from the edge of the box. That FA Cup final win was the catalyst for Arsenal's first championship the following year.

The Gunners set a new First Division points record, 66, finished seven clear of runners-up Aston Villa and scored a club record 127 goals. Lambert netted 38, another club record. Jack scored 33 and Bastin 28 from the left wing.

Chapman had assembled a wealth of attacking talent. Yet the Gunners' critics called them a defensive side and the taunt of 'Lucky Arsenal' began to be heard in the land.

Sharpe wrote: 'Arsenal's system was a packed defence to draw the opposition out, followed by a deadly breakaway. This led to the shouts of "Lucky Arsenal". It arose because the full-backs developed a splendid covering system to guard the line alongside the goalkeeper. Regularly they prevented a score while the crowd was yelling "Goal!" Come a sudden breakaway goal at the other end and the chagrin of the crowd created the "Lucky Arsenal" cry.'

Chapman certainly believed in a solid defence as the foundation of success. He said, 'The team that scores the most goals wins. To accomplish this, you must ensure that the defence is sound. It is elementary but it is also the rock bottom of football.'

Arsenal were ideally suited to strike on the break, too, because of James's deadly passing and the pace of Hulme and Bastin. The wing men were crucial to Chapman's tactics. Wingers of the time – and later greats such as Stanley Matthews – stayed wide to create chances for players in the middle. Arsenal used Hulme and Bastin in a completely different way, as part of a three-pronged spearhead. Arsenal's critics failed to understand Chapman's central concept: the team that scores most goals wins – not the team which attacks for longest.

Arsenal chased the elusive league and FA Cup double in 1932 – and failed narrowly in both. They finished two points behind Everton and lost the Cup final 2-1 to Newcastle after a controversial decision. The key to their failure was James's knee ligament injury in the 1–1 draw at West Ham in March after a collision with the Hammers' centre-half Jim Barrett. James did not play again that season and the Gunners won only one of their five games before the Cup final.

Whittaker worked day and night to get James fit to face Newcastle. Hulme was also doubtful. He gave them both fitness tests in front of a horde of photographers. Both were passed fit. But one photographer arrived late because his car had broken down. He asked Whittaker to tackle James for his camera. James slumped in pain, clutching his knee. He would not play at Wembley.

Chapman moved left-half Bob John forward and brought in Male. John headed Arsenal in front. Then, as the first half ebbed away, Newcastle's Jimmy Richardson centred. The ball looked well out of play before he crossed. Newsreel film confirmed that. The Arsenal defenders relaxed. Jack Allen put the ball in the net. The referee awarded a goal. That equaliser inspired Newcastle and Allen scored a second to win the game. The newspapers praised the Gunners for their good grace in accepting the referee's decision but Chapman's team had finished the season without a trophy.

James was back for the 1932–33 season. Chapman signed a new centre-forward, Ernie Coleman from Grimsby. He netted 24 goals. Bastin finished top scorer with 33, a record for a winger in English football. Hulme added 20. The Gunners totalled 118 goals and finished four points ahead of Aston Villa.

That summer, Chapman acted as team manager on England's summer tour to Italy and Switzerland. It seemed an obvious move with several Arsenal players in the squad. Pozzo's Italy would win the World Cup the following year. Chapman's England drew with them 1–1 in Rome and beat the Swiss 4–0.

In 1938, Italy won the World Cup with a team that bore many similarities to Chapman's Gunners. Pozzo fielded a 'stopper' centre-half, Michele Andreolo; a midfield general, Giovanni Ferrari; an inside-forward, Giuseppe Meazza, attacking from behind a prolific centre-forward, Silvio Piola; and a goalscoring left-winger, 'Gino' Colaussi.

Chapman had run the side despite objections from some of the selection committee who had traditionally picked England teams. Not until Alf Ramsey in 1963 would an England coach have unfettered control, free from interference by a selection panel.

In that, as in so much else, Chapman was decades ahead of his time. He advocated floodlit football more than 20 years before floodlights began to be installed at British grounds. He first put numbers on his players' shirts in 1928. The Football Association told him to stop. Players' numbers (1 to 11) were finally introduced five years after his death. He had a 45-minute clock put up on the Highbury terracing. The FA told him to take it down. (Chapman simply turned it into a standard clock, sited at the south end of the ground, known ever since as 'the Clock End'.)

Chapman persuaded the London transport authority to rename Gillespie Road tube station (at the north end of the ground) as 'Arsenal'. On the day the change was made, in November 1932, the Gunners won 7–1 at Wolves.

Chapman ensured that Arsenal invested in the finest medical and physiotherapy facilities in Europe – at a time when many clubs' treatment rooms were barely basic.

Whittaker, who would later became an outstanding Arsenal manager, was the leading trainer of his time. Chapman promoted him in February 1926. He told Whittaker, 'I'm going to make this the greatest club ground in the world and I'm going to make you the greatest trainer in the game.'

After an injury finished his career in 1925, Whittaker had attended a course in physiology, massage and the treatment of injuries, a rarity in days when the trainer was usually an unqualified ex-player with a so-called 'magic sponge'. Injured players who would have been sidelined for months at other clubs recovered speedily under Whittaker's care. Bastin said, 'I can never thank him enough for the expert treatment that he lavished on us.'

At Huddersfield, Chapman had overseen modest ground improvements. At Highbury, he oversaw the rebuilding of the stadium. The North Bank (then known as the Laundry End) was enlarged in 1931. The new West Stand was opened by the Prince of Wales in December 1932. Chapman was also the instigator of the East Stand re-development, though work did not begin until two years after his death. The famous bust of Chapman, by the sculptor Jacob Epstein, would feature prominently in its marble entrance hall.

Chapman insisted that every Arsenal side, from the first team to the juniors, should play in the same style – so that any player moving to a higher team could immediately fit into their pattern of play. He also instituted regular team talks and the players were urged to contribute and share ideas. He had a map of the pitch set up in his office, so he could discuss individual moves with his stars.

Chapman's Arsenal played many friendlies against non-English opposition, too. The Scottish champions Rangers – who included such luminaries as wing-half David Meiklejohn, inside-forward Bob McPhail and winger Alan Morton – became regular opponents. In December 1933, the Gunners played host to a 'Vienna XI' based on the Austrian Wunderteam (see Chapter 4) and beat them 4–2.

Arsenal played annual matches against the leading French side Racing Club de Paris and, at the end of their first championship season, enjoyed a successful tour to Denmark and Sweden. On that evidence – and everything else we know about Chapman – he would have loved the chance to pit his Gunners against the best in Europe. Gabriel Hanot's formula for the European Cup came more than 20 years too late for him.

Europe had been catching up. While Arsenal were dominating English football, some fine sides had emerged on the Continent.

Austria's Wunderteam – organised by Hugo Meisl and coached by Jimmy Hogan, from Bolton – were the most attractive international side in Europe in the early 1930s. That was reflected in the strength of their club football, dominated by the Viennese teams.

Rapid, led by Josef Bican, won the title in 1930. First Vienna, formed by English expatriates in 1894, succeeded them and won the Mitropa Cup (a competition for clubs from Austria, Czechoslovakia, Hungary, Italy and Switzerland) in the same season. Vienna contributed defenders Josef Blum and Karl Rainer, midfielder Leopold Hoffmann and forward Fritz Geschweidl to the Wunderteam. They won the title again in 1933.

Admira were champions in 1932 and 1934. Their stars were Austria goalkeeper Peter Platzer, defender Josef Urbanek and forwards Toni Schall and Adolf Vogl. Schall scored four goals in Austria's 8–2 win over Hungary in 1932. Admira won two more Austrian titles during the 1930s and reached the 1939 all-Germany final.

The greatest Austrian player of the time, centre-forward Mathias Sindelar, was the inspiration behind the 1933 Mitropa Cup winners,

FK Austria, who were cleverly prompted from inside-forward by Walter Nausch. Nausch, whose wife was Jewish, would leave Austria after the country was incorporated into Nazi Germany by the 1938 *Anschluss*.

Juventus, backed by the Agnelli family, the owners of Fiat, dominated Italian club football, winning five consecutive titles between 1931 and 1935. Eduardo Agnelli, son of Fiat's founder, was the club president. Five of Juventus's stars – goalkeeper Giampiero Combi, centre-half Luisito Monti, wing-half Luigi Bertolini, inside-forward Ferrari and forward Raimundo Orsi – played in Italy's 1934 World Cup final victory over Czechoslovakia (see Chapter 4). Two more Juve players, Felice Borel and Virgilio Rossetta, were also included in the squad.

Juve's biggest rivals were Ambrosiana-Inter, led by attacking inside-forward Meazza, and Bologna, whose centre-forward Angelo Schiavio would score the extra-time winner against the Czechs.

Czech football was the province of the two big Prague clubs, Sparta and Slavia. They supplied the whole Czech team for the 1934 World Cup final side, including two legends of Czech football, Slavia goalkeeper Frantisek Planicka and Sparta centre-forward Oldrich Nejedly. Six other Slavia players – Stefan Cambal, Frantisek Svoboda, Ladislav Zenisek, Jiri Sobotka, Antonin Puc and Rudolf Krcil – lined up against the Italians.

Germany were already one of the strongest football nations in Europe, although they would not establish a national league until the Bundesliga began in 1963. Hertha Berlin, who had lost four successive championship finals, finally won in 1930, beating Holstein Kiel 5–4. Their star player was Johannes 'Hanne' Sobek, an inside-forward in the Buchan mould. They retained the crown in 1931 with a 3–2 win over Munich 1860. That season, Hertha became the first German team to line up in Chapman's WM formation.

Bayern Munich won in 1932, beating Eintracht Frankfurt 2–0. Bayern were to suffer when the Nazis came to power on 30 January the following year. Their Jewish president Kurt Landauer was forced to step down and was later sent to a concentration camp, though he escaped to Switzerland in 1939.

Politics – and vicious anti-Semitism – began to overshadow football. The leading club of the 1920s, Nurnberg, expelled all their Jewish members. Frankfurt sacked their Jewish treasurer Hugo Reiss. The former Karlsruhe and Germany forward Julius Hirsch, another Jew, was forced out of the club and later killed at Auschwitz.

On the field, Germany's leading team of the 1930s were Schalke. Their coach was an Austrian, Gustav Wieser, and they played a style known as the 'spinning top' – a quick, short-passing game reminiscent of Hogan's Wunderteam. Schalke came from Gelsenkirchen, in the grimy western industrial heartland of the Ruhr.

Most of their players had been born and bred in the town. Most had worked in the mines or the steelworks. Many had known each other since boyhood. Their great inside-forward Fritz Szepan described the team as 'like playing with your mates'.

The 1930s had started badly for Schalke when 14 of their players, including future stars Szepan and Ernst Kuzorra, were banned by the German federation (DFB) after allegations of professionalism. They were reinstated a year later, though not before the club treasurer, Wilhelm Niet, had committed suicide by drowning himself.

Inside-left Szepan was the creative force. Kuzorra and Ernst Kalwitzki scored the goals.

Schalke lost the 1933 final, 3–0, to Fortuna Dusseldorf. In 1934, they trailed 1–0 to Nurnberg with two minutes left. Then Szepan prodded in a corner to level and a minute later, Kuzorra sped past two tackles to shoot the winner. Schalke would win five more championships between 1935 and 1942.

Szepan was no admirer of Chapman's Arsenal, as Uli Hesse-Lichtenberger reveals in *Tor! The Story of German Football*. When the national coach Otto Nerz told him that Germany would adopt the Gunners' formation for the 1934 World Cup finals, Szepan replied, 'If that means the whole team defends, with only three forwards, that's not my idea of football.' His words echoed Arsenal's domestic critics but Germany used the WM system and took third place.

In Spain, a pattern was quickly set: a struggle between Real Madrid and the Basques and Catalans. Barcelona took the first championship to Catalonia in 1929. Bilbao carried the title to the Basque country in 1930 and 1931. They beat Barcelona 12–1 that season. They also won the cup four years in a row between 1930 and 1933. Their coach was a bowler-hatted Englishman, Fred Pentland. Pentland had coached the Spain side that became the first foreign team to beat England, 3–2, in May 1929.

He changed Bilbao's tactics from the long ball to a swift-passing game, like Hogan. A club member of the time said, 'He was one of the best and most important coaches in Bilbao's history. We remember him very affectionately. There was the bowler hat and the big Cuban cigars that he used to smoke. He was also a connoisseur of wine.'

Bilbao's stars were the goalkeeper Blasco and their forward line of Lafuente, Iraragorri, Bata, Chirri and Gorostiza (league top scorer in 1930 and 1932). The Basque club would win further titles in 1934 and 1936, before the outbreak of the Spanish Civil War ended league competition.

Their domination was interrupted by Real Madrid in 1932 and 1933. Madrid had bought well. They had signed Barcelona's great goalkeeper Ricardo Zamora, two defenders from Alaves – Jacinto Quincoces and Errasti Cirriaco – and Luis Regueiro, a forward from Irun. They completed their jigsaw by snatching inside-forward Pepe Samitier from Barcelona, where his goals and creative skills had made him the idol of the Catalan fans.

These were the teams already shaping football on the Continent, many playing a different game from Chapman's Arsenal. What a contest a European Cup of the early 1930s might have been . . .

But the British associations seemed little concerned about football outside their shores. They had left FIFA in 1928 in a row over broken-time payments for amateurs. The British nations did not compete in the World Cups of 1934 and 1938, so it was impossible to tell if the English were still the masters they thought they were.

England had suffered further defeats by European opponents since that historic reverse against Spain. They had lost 5–2 to France in Paris in 1931. Then, shortly before the start of the 1934 World Cup finals, they were beaten twice in the space of six days: 2–1 by Hungary in Budapest and 2–1 by the Czechs in Prague. Yet England, under Chapman's guidance, had drawn in Italy and, including seven Arsenal players, would beat the World Cup holders 3–2 in November 1934.

Arsenal finished three points ahead of Huddersfield to win the championship in 1934. Chapman never lived to see it. In January 1934, he went to watch a third-team game despite suffering from a heavy cold. His condition worsened and he died of pneumonia on 6 January.

He had already realised that the team, and perhaps their tactics, needed an overhaul. The Gunners only scored 75 goals in 1933–34. He had told

Allison earlier that season, 'The team is played out, Mr Allison. We must rebuild.' He had already started the process by signing the Plymouth inside-forward Ray Bowden to replace Jack. Had he lived longer, would he have built a third great side and devised more innovative tactics?

Allison succeeded Chapman as manager, though real power rested in the dressing-room, with Whittaker and Chapman's assistant Joe Shaw. New signings arrived – wing-halves Jack Crayston and Wilf Copping and centre-forward Ted Drake – as the Gunners won a third successive title in 1935. Jack retired. Hulme slowed down. Arsenal won the FA Cup in 1936, James's last great triumph with the club. They added another league title in 1938. But they could never quite recapture Chapman's glory days.

They had set trends in the game, much to the distaste of their critics, like Sharpe and Szepan. Chapman's influence had spread far and wide. Germany had finished third in the 1934 World Cup by using Arsenal's formation. Italy would employ similar tactics to win in 1938.

Sharpe wrote: 'Arsenal set the fashion between the wars – a regrettable fashion of safety first, I shall always hold. Their style was good for them because they had the stars or specialists to make it pay. It was bad for the game at large because so few of the other clubs could exploit these methods attractively.'

Tyler and Soar reach a different conclusion, 'Chapman was the first real professional in a world of semi-amateurs. With the possible exceptions of Wolves' Frank Buckley and Charlton's Jimmy Seed, who can now name any other English manager of the inter-war era?'

POSTSCRIPT

The Russian side Dynamo Moscow made English football begin to question itself with a successful tour in 1945, shortly after the end of the war in Europe. Dynamo were clearly a propaganda weapon for Stalin's Soviet state (they were made Heroes of the Soviet Union on their return) and the teams they met were thrown together from whichever players were available. Clubs would regularly field several guest players to make up their numbers.

Even so, Dynamo surprised their British hosts with their imaginative passing and movement. They drew 3–3 with Chelsea, thrashed Cardiff 10–1, beat Arsenal 4–3 in the fog and drew 2–2 in a bruising clash with Rangers.

Sharpe wrote: 'Dynamo were first class footballers. They reached the highest standard of scientific and attractive play in attack. I wish we possessed their positional play.'

He added perceptively, 'Why did Dynamo cause such a surprise? Because the public has been slow to realise how the game has developed abroad and how brilliantly some foreign teams play.'

If only Chapman's Arsenal could have met some of them in the 1930s . . .

CHAPTER 4

POZZO, MUSSOLINI AND THE WORLD CUP

Vittorio Pozzo was the most successful national coach in Europe between the wars. He steered Italy to victory in the 1934 World Cup finals on home soil, the 1936 Olympics in Berlin and the 1938 World Cup finals in France.

Pozzo had almost completely rebuilt the side after Italy's 1934 success and their World Cup final victory over Hungary was his finest hour. But Italy's most successful coach died a lonely figure in December 1968. He had led the *Azzurri* to their greatest triumphs during Benito Mussolini's rule and he was tainted by his association with the Fascist regime.

Before Italy staged the 1990 World Cup finals, for instance, Pozzo's home city of Turin refused to name its new stadium in his honour, preferring to call it the Stadio delle Alpi.

The leading British football writer Brian Glanville wrote of Pozzo: 'His approach to football was somewhat militaristic. He was certainly an honest, decent man but he shamelessly made use of the bombastic nationalism of the time to enforce discipline and play on patriotism. Sometimes he could be comically hoist with his own petard, as he was over the case of the *oriundi* – the name given to players of South American birth and upbringing who held double passports as Italian citizens and thus became eligible to play for Italy – not least in World Cups.'

Pozzo was a strong disciplinarian and a clever tactician whose changes often foxed opponents. One such switch paved the way to victory in extra time of the 1934 World Cup final. He was a shrewd psychologist, too. He would sometimes order players competing for the same position to share a room – hoping that it would make them see the sense of working together. He knew when to shout at his players and when to protect them.

And Pozzo's association with the national team pre-dated Mussolini by many years. He first coached the side as far back as 1912, for the Olympic Games in Stockholm.

Pozzo was born in Turin in 1886. His parents wanted him to become a doctor or lawyer but his school grades were never quite good enough and he was naturally drawn towards sport: first athletics and then the new game of football which had swept across Europe at the start of the twentieth century.

Pozzo played for the Swiss club Grasshoppers in 1905, while he was studying German in Zurich. He returned home a year later and became a founder member of Torino. He ended his playing career in 1911 when he came to London to study English. He became a lifelong Anglophile and a fan of English football. His favourite player was the Manchester United centre-half Charlie Roberts. One of Pozzo's 'lucky charms' throughout his coaching career was the return ticket to England that his family bought for him following his first visit but which he never used.

When he returned to Italy, he was appointed coach of Torino, a post he held until 1924. Three months before the 1912 Olympics, he succeeded Umberto Meazza as national coach. Italy lost 3–2 to Finland in the first round, after extra time. They went into the 'consolation' competition, beating Sweden 1–0 before losing 5–1 to Austria. Pozzo resigned after the tournament but returned again briefly in 1921 as part of the 'technical commission' that prepared the Italian team for 2–1 wins over France and Switzerland.

Pozzo had another stint in charge of the Azzurri at the 1924 Olympics in Paris. This time, Italy beat Spain and Luxembourg before losing to eventual silver medallists Switzerland. Again, he quit after the tournament.

After the death of his first wife through illness, Pozzo worked in the public relations office of the Pirelli tyre company in Milan. He later returned to Turin and became a journalist with *La Stampa*. In 1929, Leandro Arpinati, the president of the Italian football federation (FIGC) persuaded him to fill the vacant post of national coach. This time Pozzo stayed – for 19 years. Italy celebrated his appointment with a bang – a 6–1 win over Portugal in the first match of his new reign, on 1 December.

On 11 May 1930, Pozzo's Italy won their first trophy – the Coppa Internazionale, as it was known in Italian. Italy played both home and away against Austria, Czechoslovakia, Hungary and Switzerland. They had to win their final game, in Budapest, to take the trophy. Italy's stars were Giuseppe Meazza and midfield general Giovanni Ferrari – both of whom would serve Pozzo for almost a decade.

Meazza scored a hat trick as Italy won 5–0. When the squad had crossed the Italian border, the trophy, made of Bohemian crystal, was paraded at every railway station. At Montfalcone, the trophy fell and a piece of glass broke off. That piece of glass became Pozzo's second lucky charm.

In February 1931, Pozzo's team achieved another first, Italy's first win over Austria, 2–1 in Milan, after ten attempts in eighteen years. That Austrian side – known as the Wunderteam – were one of the best in Europe. They were guided by Hugo Meisl and coached by Jimmy Hogan. Meisl was a Viennese bank manager who lived for football. The bank told him to choose between his job and his passion. So he became the driving force behind the Austrian football association and the national team. Ivan Sharpe, the leading British football writer of the inter-war years, wrote: 'Meisl was a gracious man and a football pioneer. He "made" Continental football and died before the sorrows and humiliations of the Second World War descended upon his country.'

Hogan, from Bolton, advocated quick passing and movement and 'keeping the ball on the carpet'. He was a major influence on the development of football in Austria and later in Hungary. Yet he was a prophet without honour in his own country. Sharpe later wrote: 'It was sad that some British players did not take kindly to Hogan's methods when he returned home as an instructor after a triumphant career abroad.'

The significance of Italy's win was demonstrated by Austria's form afterwards. They went on an unbeaten run of 14 matches and inflicted Scotland's first defeat by a foreign team, 5–0 in Vienna. (The Scots had not fielded any Celtic or Rangers players.) Inspired by their brilliant centre-forward, the 'paper dancer' Matthias Sindelar, they also beat Germany 6–0 in Berlin and 5–0 in Vienna and thrashed Hungary 8–2. Sindelar scored a hat trick against the Magyars.

The Austrians gave England a scare, too. They lost 4–3 at Stamford Bridge in December 1932, fighting back from two goals down before losing to a free kick deflected past goalkeeper Rudi Hiden.

But there was a political dimension to Italy's emergence as a footballing power. The dictator Mussolini wanted to use football as a propaganda weapon. Internazionale, for instance, were forced to rename themselves Ambrosiana-Inter, after the patron saint of Milan. The Fascist regime objected to their original title because it carried overtones of the communist 'Internationale'.

Mussolini's government promoted Pozzo's team as role models for young Italians. *Il Duce* told Sharpe, 'I want sport to become part of the life of young Italy. The Fascist state is giving every aid it can. The stars of football receive honour and praise. That is right, because they show the youth of the country what could be achieved by clean living.'

Sharpe noted: 'Sport and state came to be too much intermingled. Victory became a "victory for Fascism". The "state" was too much at stake.'

Mussolini's regime was the first to exploit football as a propaganda tool. It would not be the last. Nazi Germany followed Italy's lead. Franco's regime in Spain would later play on Real Madrid's European Cup successes, while the post-war communist governments of eastern Europe would proclaim the alleged superiority of 'socialist football' (see Chapters 5 and 7).

Italy's motivation for the 1934 World Cup finals was almost manic. Their preparation, at Roveta, near Florence, was painstaking. Pozzo could not understand the English custom of assembling the team two or three days before an international. He said, 'We assemble our squad three weeks before: for a week of relaxation in the mountains, a week of practice and teamwork and a week of quieter preparation to develop fitness and team spirit.'

Pozzo could call on some fine players, too. Goalkeeper Giampiero Combi is still ranked among Italy's greats. He won five championship medals with Juventus. Combi, the Czech keeper Frantisek Planicka and Spain's Ricardo Zamora were regarded as Europe's top three in the early 1930s. Combi promised to retire after the 1934 World Cup final – and did.

The inside-forwards, Ferrari and 'Peppino' Meazza were the only players to play in both World Cup finals. They would really come into their own in 1938, when Pozzo's team played a less direct, more technical game. Ferrari, another Juventus star, was the playmaker of the team. He won 44 caps.

Meazza was originally a centre-forward with Inter and made his early appearances for Italy as a striker. Pozzo switched him to inside-right for the 3–1 win over Germany in 1933 and that became his position. Meazza was a clever dribbler, strong in the air and had an eye for goal. He scored 33 goals in 53 appearances for his country – a record only beaten by Luigi Riva in the 1970s. Meazza's positional switch allowed Pozzo to field Bologna's Angelo Schiavio in the centre. He would net the winner in the final, the most important of the 15 goals he scored for the Azzurri.

Italy also included three oriundi. Skipper and centre-half Luisito Monti had played for Argentina in the 1930 World Cup final. Pozzo picked him ahead of the native centre-half and popular choice Fulvio Bernardini. Monti was more robust, more direct in his passing, rather in the style of Charlie Roberts. Pozzo said, 'Everybody praises clever Bernardini but he holds up the play.'

Monti was joined by the Argentine attackers Raimundo Orsi and Enrico Guaita. Pozzo, pointing out that the oriundi were liable for military service, said theatrically, 'If they can die for Italy, then they can play for Italy.' He was, therefore, hugely embarrassed when Italy invaded Ethiopia to begin the Abyssinian War in 1935 and Guaita was caught trying to sneak across the border into Switzerland to avoid a call-up.

Italy entered the 1934 World Cup finals as one of the favourites, along with Austria and Czechoslovakia. England, Scotland, Northern Ireland and Wales did not enter. They had withdrawn from FIFA in a row about broken-time payments to amateurs. The holders, Uruguay, boycotted the competition in protest at the small number of European teams who had travelled to the first-ever World Cup, in their country, four years earlier.

The competition featured 16 teams and it was a straight knockout. The only two South American entrants went out in the first round. Sweden beat Argentina's weakened side 3–2. Spain beat Brazil 3–1.

Meanwhile, expectations were at fever pitch throughout Italy. Posters all over the country featured Hercules with a foot on the ball and his right arm outstretched in the Fascist salute. That was how Pozzo's players greeted Mussolini as he took his seat before all of Italy's matches.

Mussolini's presence hung over the tournament. UEFA's archive notes, 'The Italian dictator's passion for football may have had something to do with a number of questionable refereeing decisions which seemed to go in the home side's favour.'

Italy opened with a then World Cup record 7–1 win over the United States in Rome. Schiavio scored a hat trick. Orsi netted twice.

That earned Pozzo's team a quarter-final meeting with Spain. Italy played a very physical game, largely unchecked by the Belgian referee Louis Baert. Yet Regueiro's cross-cum-shot deceived Combi to put Spain ahead, before Ferrari levelled in first-half stoppage time. Extra time could not separate the teams.

They played off the next day. Pozzo had torn into his team. He knew that only the World Cup would satisfy Mussolini. He made three changes. Spain were ravaged by injuries. They were without seven starters from the first match, including keeper Zamora, who had been hit in the throat by Schiavio at a corner. Meazza scored the only goal after 11 minutes. Spain had two goals disallowed by the Swiss referee Rene Mercet – one for offside, the other, strangely, for them to be awarded a free kick.

In the semi-finals, Guaita's 10th-minute goal beat the Wunderteam in Milan. Heavy rain turned the pitch into a quagmire, negating the more subtle skills of Sindelar and the Austrians. Monti, who had punched Sindelar in a previous Italy–Austria clash, marked him out of the game. Sindelar was injured and missed Austria's 3–2 defeat by Germany in the third-place play-off.

It had been a disappointing tournament for the ageing Austrians. Their championship had finished late and they were noticeably tired as they approached the finals. By the next World Cup finals, their country would not exist, swallowed up by Hitler's Germany in the 1938 Anschluss.

Planicka's heroics had enabled the Czechs to beat Switzerland in the quarter-finals. He was in top form again as they clinched a final place with a 3–1 win over Germany. Rudolf Krcil and Oldrich Nejedly scored in the closing minutes after Rudi Noack cancelled out Nejedly's early goal.

Fortune favoured Italy again in the final. The Czechs dominated for long spells with their quick-passing game. Antonin Puc fired them into a 76th-minute lead. They could have killed the game – and probably ended Pozzo's career as Italy's coach – in the next three minutes. Jiri Sobotka missed an open goal and Frantisek Svoboda hit a post.

Orsi curled in a brilliant equaliser to take the final into extra time. Pozzo switched Guaita and Schiavio, which seemed to confuse the Czech defence. After five minutes, Meazza found Guaita, who crossed for Schiavio to prod home the winner.

The players carried Pozzo from the field in triumph. The coach was both joyous and relieved. He knew just how close he had come to incurring Mussolini's wrath.

The dictator awarded him the title of *Commendatore* (great in his profession). But Pozzo knew he had to rebuild if Italy were to retain the trophy in 1938.

The Azzurri had one more match to win to prove their dominance – against England, still regarded as masters of the game. England had drawn 1–1 in Rome in 1933, when Mussolini invited the visitors to a post-match reception.

Masters v. World Cup holders: England won 3–2. But the game on 14 November 1934 has gone down as the 'Battle of Highbury'. England included seven players from champions Arsenal, on their home ground. Monti broke a bone in his foot after 90 seconds in a challenge with the England centre-forward Ted Drake. He claimed Drake had kicked him deliberately, something Drake always denied.

Italy retaliated with some tough tackling. Keeper Carlo Ceresoli saved Eric Brook's penalty but two goals by Brook and another from Drake gave England a 3–0 lead after 15 minutes.

Sharpe wrote: 'The Italians couldn't take it. The prize was too high. The second half became a dog fight with a furious finale when Meazza scored twice. At the banquet, Eddie Hapgood appeared with a plastered nose – bone broken. Brook's arm had been X-rayed. Drake's eyes were discoloured. Ray Bowden had a badly damaged ankle.'

Orsi played his last game for Italy in their 2–0 win over Austria in Vienna on 24 March 1935. He returned to Argentina a fortnight later. A debut-making striker from Lazio, Silvio Piola, scored both goals. He would make a crucial impact in 1938.

Now Pozzo set out to build a new team. Italy's new-look squad retained the Coppa Internazionale, winning five of their eight matches. The Olympic football tournament of 1936 was an important staging post, too.

Italy, whose players were officially registered as 'students', won the gold medal. They opened with a 1–0 win over the United States, during which Achille Piccini was sent off but refused to go. In the words of FIFA's magazine, 'Several Italian teammates surrounded the referee and covered his mouth with their hands. Piccini remained in the game.'

Italy beat Japan 8–0, then pipped Norway 2–1 in extra time to reach the final. Their victims were Austria, 2–1, after extra time again. Ambrosiana-Inter's Annibale Frossi scored the winner against Norway and netted both goals in the final. He finished tournament top scorer with seven. Pozzo's players celebrated victory by giving the Fascist salute.

Pozzo had gained more than Olympic gold. He had unearthed three players good enough to play for the 1938 World Cup winners – Juventus full-backs Alfredo Foni and Pietro Rava and the Ambrosiana-Inter wing-half Ugo Locatelli.

The Azzurri coach had also introduced a host of other new players. The prolific Triestina left-winger Luigi 'Gino' Colaussi made his debut in a 2–1 defeat away to the Czechs in October 1935. Bologna centre-half Michele Andreolo won his first cap in a 2–2 home draw against Austria seven months later. Uruguay-born Andreolo was another of the oriundi. But he played in a different style to Monti. He was a 'stopper' centre-back, not a roving attacker.

Pozzo introduced the Lucchese goalkeeper Aldo Olivieri for the 2–2 draw against Germany in November 1936 and recalled the Roma right-half Pietro Serantoni after an absence of 23 months. Italy's World Cup-winning squad was taking shape. There would be one more change during the tournament, when the Bologna right-winger Amedeo Biavati replaced Triestina's Piero Pasinati after the first match.

Pozzo's new team was more naturally gifted than the 1934 squad and they played in a different style, echoing Herbert Chapman's WM formation. Four years earlier, Monti had started attacks with sweeping passes. Now Andreolo was an out and out defender, so there was more emphasis on inside-forwards Meazza and Ferrari to create chances. FIFA's archive said, 'More refined and technical, the side now completely revolved around the inside-forwards.'

Piola and Colaussi supplied the cutting edge. Piola was known as '*Silvio gol*'. He was described by the leading Italian football writer Gianni Brera as, 'a splendid athlete: both agile and powerful, with excellent balance, remarkable speed over distance and a powerful shot with both feet.' He netted 30 goals in 34 appearances for the Azzurri.

Colaussi scored 15 in 26 games. Italy would also be handed a colossal slice of good fortune in the semi-finals . . .

The 1938 World Cup finals were held in France. Italy were strongly fancied to win again. The British nations remained on the sidelines. Austria had been incorporated into greater Germany. Spain was in the throes of a bloody civil war. Argentina snubbed the tournament because FIFA had not chosen them as hosts. Uruguay stayed at home, too.

Italy's chief rivals were Hungary, inspired by the great Ferencvaros forward Gyorgy Sarosi, and Brazil, who featured another brilliant attacker, Leonidas. Czechoslovakia and Germany were fancied outsiders. The Germans had included four Austrians in their squad. Sindelar was not among them. He refused to play and became a national hero for his courage as well as his football skill.

Sindelar died in mysterious circumstances in January 1939. His body was found next to that of an Italian girl he had met a few days earlier. The death certificate said he had died from carbon monoxide poisoning caused by a leaking gas tap. Other theories involve suicide or murder by the Nazis. The police reports on the case were lost during the Second World War.

The 1938 tournament was a straight knockout once again. Norway gave the Azzurri a first-round fright. Pietro Ferraris put Italy ahead in the second minute. Norway hit the woodwork three times and had a goal disallowed before Arne Brustad levelled seven minutes from time. Piola popped up with the winner five minutes into extra time.

Leonidas, the 'black diamond', scored four goals in Brazil's thrilling 6–5 win over Poland, even playing part of the game barefoot. Ernst Wilimowski netted four for the Poles. Hungary crushed the Dutch East Indies 6–0. Germany lost 4–2 to Switzerland in a replay, the most popular result of the first round.

In the quarter-finals, Colaussi, who had missed the game against the Norwegians, made a swift impact against France in Paris. He gave Italy the lead after nine minutes. Oscar Heisserer levelled within a minute. Two second-half Piola strikes clinched a 3–1 win to carry Pozzo's team into the semi-finals. Italy had played in provocative change colours – black shirts, a symbol of Fascism – which clashed with referee Baert's outfit. He controlled the game wearing a white vest.

Meanwhile, two Brazilians and one Czech were sent off by referee Paul von Hertzka in a bruising 1–1 draw. Five were taken off injured. Planicka played with a broken arm. FIFA appointed a different official,

George Capdeville, for the replay. Planicka and the Czechs' top scorer Nejedly were both sidelined. Leonidas scored twice to earn Brazil a 2–1 win after the Czechs led at half-time.

Sarosi and Gyula Zsengeller scored Hungary's goals in their 2–0 win over Switzerland. Sweden, who had a first-round bye because of Austria's withdrawal, thrashed Cuba 8–0.

Pozzo sat down to plan for the semi-final against Brazil. How would his side contain Leonidas? Would Andreolo tight mark him, as Monti had done to Sindelar in 1934? The Brazilian coach, Ademar Pimenta, solved Pozzo's problem for him. He left Leonidas out of the team, along with his striking partner Tim. He said, 'I'm resting him for the final.'

Perhaps Leonidas was tired after two gruelling games against the Czechs. Yet Pimenta's decision to leave out his star player against the world champions remains one of the most bizarre moves in World Cup finals history.

Pozzo could barely believe his side's good fortune. Italy settled the game in the space of four second-half minutes. Colaussi gave them a 56th-minute lead. Meazza added the second from a penalty. His finish was extra cool in the circumstances, not just because of the importance of the kick but also because the elastic in his shorts had broken. Meazza took the penalty while holding up his shorts with his left hand. Romeu scored Brazil's only goal three minutes from time.

Sarosi pulled the strings as Hungary thrashed Sweden 5–1 despite falling behind in the first minute. Zsengeller scored a hat trick. Pozzo's tactics for the final were simple: feed Piola and Colaussi, and stop Sarosi, by fair means or foul. They worked to perfection.

The Italians needed two attempts before they reached Stade Colombes in Paris. When their team bus was blocked by the crowds, Pozzo told the driver to return to their hotel. He did not want his players sitting stuck in traffic – fretting with possible negative thoughts – before a World Cup final. When the Italians set off again, the crowds had cleared and they reached the stadium without delay.

They soon made their presence felt. Colaussi finished off a sweeping left-side move to give Italy a fifth-minute lead. Pal Titkos levelled two minutes later with a powerful shot from a tight angle.

Piola restored Italy's lead from Meazza's pass after an intricate move inside the Hungarian box. Meazza found Colaussi who added a third in the 35th minute.

The Azzurri sat back after the interval. Sarosi stung them into action again with a 70th-minute goal. Piola killed the game with Italy's fourth, eight minutes from time, a left-foot shot from Biavati's back-heel.

Italy were not popular winners. The French had cheered for Hungary. Many of the Italian expatriates in France had fled Mussolini's regime. They did not warm to Pozzo's team either. But Meazza lifted the World Cup. Pozzo became the only man ever to coach two World Cup-winning sides. He had built two triumphant teams with vastly different personnel. And there were more Fascist salutes, because Pozzo and his team had delivered Italy's greatest sporting 'victory for Fascism'.

On the eve of the final, Mussolini had sent a telegram which simply read, 'Win or die'.

Now Pozzo's Azzurri had become the first team to win the World Cup outside their own country and Mussolini would proclaim the superiority of Fascist football.

There was time for Italy to draw 2–2 with England in Milan before the outbreak of the Second World War. England claimed that Piola punched in Italy's second goal. The German referee and Swiss linesman insisted it was fair.

Players such as Meazza (28 in 1938), Piola (25) and Colaussi (26) were at the peak of their careers. But the outbreak of the Second World War meant they never had the chance to defend the World Cup. Mussolini's Italy fought on the German side. The Western Allies invaded in 1943 and eventually defeated the German forces which had taken over the country. Mussolini was taken prisoner and killed by partisans.

After the war, Pozzo tried to create another great side but life had changed dramatically since the Mussolini era. He wanted to build the team around his beloved Torino and their star Valentino Mazzola. Mazzola (father of the Inter great Sandro) had made his name with Venezia in wartime football. There, he struck up a winning partnership with Ezio Loik, who would become his colleague at Torino.

Mazzola skippered the team to four successive championships between 1946 and 1949. His colleague, Mario Rigamonti, said, 'He alone is half the squad. The rest of it is made up by the rest of us together.' Torino finished 13 points ahead of Internazionale in 1946, ten points clear of city rivals Juventus in 1947 and 16 points clear of Milan the following year.

On 11 May 1947, Pozzo fielded all ten Torino outfield players for Italy's 3–2 win over Hungary. But Pozzo never built another World

Cup-winning team. A 5–1 defeat by Austria and a 4–0 defeat by England in May 1948 seriously damaged his prestige. He was in his 60s and those losses made him think about handing over to a younger coach.

He was also accused of being a Fascist collaborator because of his links with the old regime. It was time for him to go.

He stepped down in August 1948 after Italy's 5–3 defeat by Denmark in the London Olympics. No Italian coach has matched his record: 95 games in charge, 63 wins and 17 draws, two World Cups and an Olympic gold. Only Enzo Bearzot, in 1982, has emulated Pozzo's feat of coaching Italy to World Cup victory.

On 4 May 1949, nine months after Pozzo's departure, the great Torino squad died in the Superga air disaster. The team were coming home from a match in Lisbon when their plane crashed into the Superga Basilica, a monastery outside Turin. All 31 passengers were killed, including Mazzola, Loik, Rigamonti and 15 other players. Sauro Toma, who missed the trip through injury, was the only first-team player left alive. Pozzo, who still lived in Turin, was one of the first on the scene. He was asked to identify the bodies of his former players.

Torino's achievements had restored Italian pride after their wartime defeat. More than 500,000 turned out on the streets to pay their respects at the funeral service. The Superga disaster ripped the heart from Torino and from the national team for a decade.

Meanwhile, Pozzo increasingly became a recluse in his home in the centre of Turin. He turned his study into a museum of international football, full of memorabilia from his long career. His one regular excursion was a Wednesday visit to the Alpine Club, where he would drink in memory of his service with the Alpine regiment during the First World War.

When he died, at the end of a year in which Italy won the European Championship for the only time, the obituaries inevitably talked about his links with Fascist sport. Those links were undeniable. As Glanville said, Pozzo certainly tapped into the nationalistic spirit of the time.

Yet he came into football long before Mussolini's regime and remained in football after Mussolini's death. Was he really a Fascist ideologue, a Fascist stooge? Or, more likely, a blinkered football man who reached accommodation with the regime so he could do what mattered most to him – build a successful team?

CHAPTER 5

THE MAGNIFICENT MAGYARS

The radio commentator Herbert Zimmermann's words have passed into German folklore. '*Aus dem Hintergrund musste Rahn schiessen. Rahn schiesst. Tor!*' (Rahn must shoot from outside the box. Rahn shoots. Goal!)

Helmut Rahn's shot was the goal that won the 1954 World Cup final for West Germany. The triumph of Sepp Herberger's team has gone down as *Das Wunder von Bern* (the Miracle of Berne). It was made into a 2003 film of the same name. It gave much-needed ballast to the Federal Republic of Germany, created from the debris of wartime defeat by the victorious Western Allies.

And the Germans' unlikely 3–2 victory wrecked the image of the greatest team of the immediate post-war era: Hungary.

Hungarians called their side *aranycsapat* (the golden team). In the English-speaking world, they were known as 'the magnificent Magyars'. They were the team that won the 1952 Olympic title at a canter, then slaughtered England 6–3 at Wembley and 7–1 in Budapest.

Twenty years later, West Germany would beat a better side in the World Cup final again. Then it was Johann Cruyff's Holland. On 4 July 1954, it was Ferenc Puskas's Hungary.

Puskas was their skipper and leader. He was called the 'galloping major' because of the rank he held in the Hungarian army. The mere thought of Puskas as a military man was cause for laughter. But that was the way 'socialist' football worked. (See Chapter 18 for more on this.)

Puskas hardly looked athletic. He was short, squat and prone in later years to being overweight. He used his right foot to stand on. He rarely outjumped defenders. But he had a brilliant left foot, a stinging shot and a predator's eye for goal.

He established himself in his father's club, Kispest of Budapest, as a 16 year old. He made his international debut at 18, against Austria, in Hungary's first post-war international. He played 84 times for his country and became the team's talisman, scoring 83 goals.

Perhaps, on one day at least, they came to depend on him too much. He declared himself fit to face the West Germans in the final despite a lingering ankle injury. Brian Glanville in *The Story of the World Cup* judged, 'Puskas, clearly hampered by his ankle, was unwontedly heavy and slow.' There were no substitutes then.

Puskas played for a new team, Honved, the Hungarian army club. The communist government ran down the most popular pre-war team, Ferencvaros. Their leading players joined the best from Kispest to form the nucleus of the side.

Male military service was compulsory. So, like other army sides in the old east, Honved swept up the best players in the country and gave them army ranks to keep them at the club. The players, technically, were amateurs. In reality, they were state-subsidised professionals.

Honved won four national championships in five seasons. Puskas scored 50 goals in their first title season. They were one of the strongest teams in Europe in the days before the European Cup. Their only serious domestic rivals were Voros Lobogo (Red Banner), formed from the old MTK club.

The national side was built from the two teams. Honved supplied Puskas, Sandor Kocsis, Jozsef Boszik, Gyula Grosics, Zoltan Czibor and Gyula Lorant. Nandor Hidegkuti, Peter Palotas, Jozsef Zakarias and Mihaly Lantos came from Voros Lobogo. Puskas was the biggest star – but hardly the only one. Grosics was a brilliant goalkeeper. Boszik was the midfield orchestrator. Hidegkuti threaded slide rule passes through to the forwards. Czibor was a flying left-winger.

Kocsis, who had made his name with Ferencvaros, was Puskas's striking partner, for club and country. He was known as the 'man with the golden head' because of his aerial power. His goal ratio even bettered Puskas's – 75 in 68 internationals, including seven hat tricks. He finished league top scorer three times too.

Hungary used revolutionary tactics. Grosics often rushed outside the penalty area to clear attacks. They played with virtually a back four.

Centre-back Lorant was the deepest defender. Zakarias was the defensive wing-half who supported him. Jeno Buzansky on the right and Lantos on the left were probably the earliest of the overlapping full-backs. Boszik and deep-lying centre-forward Hidegkuti formed the midfield partnership. Puskas and Kocsis were the central strikers with Jozsef Toth or Palotas and Czibor the wingers.

It was a prototype of the 4–2–4 system that Brazil would refine to win the 1958 World Cup in Sweden. Puskas said, 'We were the forerunners for "Total Football". When we attacked, we all attacked and when we defended it was the same.'

The coach, Gusztav Sebes, preferred to describe it as 'socialist football'. He held the rank of deputy minister of sport in the communist government. Sebes had been a player with MTK and Vasas in the 1920s. The son of a cobbler, he had also been a trade union organiser, both in Paris and Budapest.

Grosics, an opponent of the regime, said, 'Sebes was very committed to socialist ideology. You could sense that in everything he said. He made a political issue out of every big match or competition. He often talked about how the struggle between capitalism and socialism takes place on the football pitch just like everywhere else.'

Sebes may have been a committed ideologue but when it came to football he was a free thinker. MTK club coach Marton Bukovi had first experimented with variants of 4–2–4 in domestic football. Sebes adapted the concept to his squad.

He was also heavily influenced by two Englishmen. Jimmy Hogan had coached in Austria and Hungary between the wars. He advocated a style based on passing and movement. After Hungary had won at Wembley, Sebes said, 'Hogan taught us everything we know about football.' Another of his heroes was Arthur Rowe, the architect of Tottenham's 1951 'push and run' championship team who had reinforced Hogan's principles during his coaching lectures in Hungary.

Sebes was given total control of the squad and all the resources he needed. Football was a matter of political prestige in ideologically conscious Hungary. The national team was one of the few officially sanctioned outlets for patriotism under Matyas Rakosi's Stalinist regime. It was also a propaganda weapon on the international stage, used to demonstrate the alleged superiority of socialism over its western capitalist rivals.

While Sebes preached 'socialist' football, his assistant, Gyula

Mandi, studied the very latest training methods and jollied the players along when the coach's political lectures became too strident.

The Hungarians rose to international prominence in the 1952 Olympics. They beat Romania 2–1 in the preliminaries, then crushed Italy 3–0 and Turkey 7–1 to reach the semi-finals. They thumped Sweden 6–0, and met Yugoslavia for the gold medal. On the eve of the final, Sebes received a phone call from Prime Minister Rakosi who warned that 'failure would not be tolerated'.

Hungary did not fail. Puskas gave them a 25th-minute lead. Czibor added the second, two minutes from time. That was just one of 31 games – including 27 wins – in which Hungary went unbeaten from 1951 to the 1954 World Cup final.

They achieved their most famous victory at Wembley on 25 November 1953. England were on the way down from their lofty perch. They had returned early from their first-ever World Cup finals entry in 1950 hugely embarrassed after losing 1–0 to the United States. Yet England had never lost to a Continental team on home soil – though they had needed a last-minute penalty to draw 4–4 against a FIFA XI in the Football Association's 90th anniversary match five weeks before.

The contrast between the teams was stark. Hungary concentrated on technique and tactics. England's fortes were strength and power. The Hungarians, hand-picked and nurtured by Sebes, had spent long periods training and working together. The England team, picked by a selection committee, assembled only for internationals. They usually practised together for only two days before a game.

Interest was intense throughout Europe. More than 100 foreign reporters turned up at Wembley. *L'Equipe's* famous football writer Jacques Ferran had presciently warned England, 'This is the match that matters.'

Sebes had given a typical motivational talk to his players, pointing out that they were upstarts from eastern Europe playing in the home of the British Empire, against the inventors of the game. He concluded, 'If we beat the English at Wembley, our names will be legendary.'

An unnamed England player is alleged to have looked at Puskas during the warm-up and said, 'Look at that little fat chap. We'll murder this lot.'

It was England who were 'murdered'. They could not fathom Hungary's fluid tactics. When Hidegkuti dropped deep, centre-half Harry Johnston did not know whether to follow or pick up one of the

Hungarian strikers. His colleagues dithered over who should mark Puskas and Kocsis. England's defenders were pulled all over the pitch.

Hidegkuti scored a hat trick. The 'little fat chap' Puskas netted twice. His party piece was the third goal, rolling the ball back with the sole of his boot, then turning to crash a shot past goalkeeper Gil Merrick. Boszik scored with another long shot.

It was a wake-up call for English football. England's coach, Walter Winterbottom, later wrote in his autobiography, 'We were so insular that we wouldn't believe that other ways of playing the game could be better than ours. That had to change.'

The great England forward Tom Finney, who missed the match through injury, said, 'This was the first time that it was brought home to the English people that we were no longer the so-called best side in the world and hadn't been for some time. That was the start of English football looking at itself and asking: where have we gone wrong? I came away wondering what we'd been doing all these years.'

Dave Sexton, later to become one of English football's finest coaches, added, 'We saw that their game was about passing and movement, while our game was static.'

England's right-back that day was Alf Ramsey. Twelve and a half years later, in another World Cup final, he would become the most successful coach in England's international history, though not by emulating the style of the Hungarians.

Hungary heaped even greater embarrassment on England in Budapest less than a month before the 1954 World Cup finals. Around one million Hungarians applied for the 100,000 tickets. The lucky ones who got in saw the Magyars inflict England's worst-ever defeat, 7–1.

England knew what they were up against. They changed their personnel but found it hard to change their tactics. Puskas and Kocsis scored twice. Lantos, Hidegkuti and Toth completed the rout.

Grosics said, 'For me, the biggest characteristic of the English is their huge respect for tradition, and why should football be an exception?'

Syd Owen was England's centre-half that day. He said, 'It was like playing people from outer space.'

No wonder Hungary arrived in Switzerland as short-priced favourites to lift the World Cup. They had lost the last pre-war final, 4–2, to Italy in Paris, after their great forward Gyorgy Sarosi was kicked repeatedly. The Hungarian people expected victory to lift the gloom of repression and austerity. The Hungarian government expected a propaganda victory for socialism.

Holders Uruguay and runners-up Brazil were expected to provide the toughest opposition. Austria, whose star was attacking defender Ernst Ocwirk, led the European challenge. Canny coach Sepp Herberger had turned West Germany into dangerous outsiders – and they were in the same group as Hungary.

The Germans began with a 4–1 win over Turkey, while Hungary demolished South Korea 9–0. Kocsis scored three, Puskas and Palotas two each.

Hungary then thrashed West Germany 8–3 in Basle. Herberger rested eight players. Kocsis added four more goals. Hidegkuti netted twice. But 20 minutes from time, with Hungary leading 5–1, Puskas went down after a tackle by the German defender Werner Liebrich.

Puskas lamented, 'He caught me from behind.' The German captain, Fritz Walter, felt that Puskas had twisted his ankle on landing. The Hungarian skipper and talisman missed the quarter-final against Brazil and the semi-final against Uruguay, and would be clearly below his best in the final.

Glanville called Liebrich's challenge 'the foul that won the World Cup'. But there were many other factors. The Hungarians clearly underestimated Herberger's much-changed side in the final. The rain and the mud did not suit their passing game either. They had been drained by their exertions against the South Americans. Luck (and a linesman) turned against them too. The Germans played the game of their lives.

Did Herberger deliberately field a weakened team to lull the Hungarians into a false sense of security? Did he have a cunning plan to avoid Brazil and Uruguay in the last eight? Or did he simply rest his stars ahead of the anticipated play-off with Turkey for a quarter-final place? Herberger smiled and replied that if people wanted to call him clairvoyant, he would not object. Max Morlock's hat trick propelled the Germans to a 7–2 win over the Turks and a quarter-final against Yugoslavia.

Right-winger Rahn had scored against the Hungarians in Basle. Now he had established himself in the side, ahead of Bernhard Klodt. He settled the quarter-final with an 85th-minute strike after West Germany had taken an early lead through Ivan Horvat's own goal. Meanwhile, Hungary emerged victorious from one of the most brutal games in World Cup history – the 'Battle of Berne' against Brazil.

Mihaly Toth replaced the injured Puskas and the Hungarians played fluent football in the driving rain. They led 2–0 by the seventh minute through Hidegkuti and Kocsis. Djalma Santos replied with a penalty. Lantos added Hungary's third with a spot kick on the hour. Julinho netted Brazil's second. Kocsis made it 4–2 in the 88th minute. That was the goal count.

The contest grew increasingly violent after Djalma Santos's goal. The English referee Arthur Ellis awarded more than 40 free kicks. Hungary finished with ten men, Brazil with nine. Brazil claimed that a Hungarian started the trouble with a sly foul. Whatever the provocation, the Brazilians responded by tackling ferociously and spitting at their opponents.

Hidegkuti was injured and police had to clear South American photographers off the pitch as he lay hurt. In the 71st minute, Ellis sent off Boszik and Nilton Santos for fighting. Humberto followed them to the dressing-room eight minutes later for kicking Lorant. Angry Brazil coach Alfredo Moreira claimed, 'We lost because of bad luck and bad decisions by the referee.'

The battle continued after the final whistle. The Brazilians invaded the Hungarian dressing-room. They accused Puskas, who had been sitting on the bench, of wounding their centre-half Pinheiro. Players and officials fought. Sebes suffered a cut cheek. Bottles and boots were thrown. Police had to restore order. FIFA reprimanded both sides but took no further action.

West Germany cruised through their semi-final, 6–1, against Austria, who had come from 3–0 down to beat Switzerland 7–5 in the quarter-finals. The Austrian keeper Walter Zeman had one of his poorest games. The Germans netted four goals from dead-ball moves. Morlock scored another hat trick.

Hungary had reached the final after another gruelling contest, running out 4–2 extra-time winners over Uruguay. This time, Laszlo Budai replaced Puskas.

Hungary made their usual flying start. Czibor scored after 13 minutes. Hidegkuti added a second. Juan Alberto Schiaffino inspired a Uruguayan comeback. Juan Holberg replied, then took the tie to extra time with an 85th-minute equaliser.

Kocsis, top scorer in the tournament, netted the goals that carried Hungary to the finals. But they had travelled by far the harder route through the last eight. The Germans were fresher and more relaxed.

They had nothing to lose. Reaching the final was an achievement in itself. All the pressure was on the Hungarians to fulfil their destiny.

West Germany had an advantage on the wet pitch in Berne, too. The Hungarians wore old-fashioned boots with fixed-length studs. Grosics, in those old-fashioned boots, would make a fatal slip.

Adi Dassler, boss of the recently formed adidas company, had equipped the Germans with lighter boots with screw-in studs. So they simply screwed in long studs which gave them a better grip on the surface. As the rain fell, Herberger turned to Fritz Walter. 'Your sort of weather, Fritz.' Walter smiled, 'I have nothing against it, boss.'

The wins over Brazil and Uruguay had taken their toll on the Hungarians, physically and mentally. Sebes admitted before the final, 'Our greatest enemy is nervous tension. I never realised that the World Cup could be such a test of nerves.' Grosics was physically sick before the game.

Perhaps Hungary were over-confident. Puskas insisted on playing – a dangerous gamble when Sebes could not substitute him. Their preparation, usually so thorough, was lacking too. They failed to note the threat of Rahn, who loved to wander from the right flank and unleash his fierce left-foot shot.

Before the finals, Herberger had shown his squad the film of Hungary's win at Wembley. Uli Hesse-Lichtenberger tells the story in *Tor! The Story of German Football*, 'When the pictures flickered across the screen for the first time, the players were in awe. The second time around, however, they began to see the flaws in the Hungarian game – and there were flaws. No team is unbeatable, says the gospel according to Herberger.'

Five of Herberger's side came from Kaiserslautern – centre-back Liebrich, left-back Werner Kohlmeyer, right-half Horst Eckel, midfield general Fritz Walter and his centre-forward brother Ottmar. They were the heart of the team.

Fritz Walter was Herberger's mouthpiece on the pitch, the leader and the inspiration. He scored 33 goals in 61 games for West Germany, besides more than 300 for his club.

But it was Morlock, from Nurnberg, who would claw the Germans back into the match. Then Rahn, the winger from Essen who only went to the finals as a reserve, would settle the final and cause one of the biggest shocks in World Cup history.

Even so, Hungary should have won. They made their usual

whirlwind start and led 2–0 after eight minutes. Puskas shot home after Czibor's shot rebounded off Eckel. Then keeper Toni Turek failed to grasp Kohlmeyer's weak back pass and Czibor scored.

The Germans fought back within two minutes. Hungarian over-confidence, or sheer nervous tension? Whatever the explanation, Buzansky lost the ball trying to skip past winger Hans Schafer. Fritz Walter found Rahn, who had popped up on the left. Rahn's cross deflected off Boszik. Morlock toe-poked the ball past Grosics. The Germans won three corners in a row. The third reached Rahn, who stabbed in at the far post while Grosics appealed for a foul by Schafer.

Now Hungary attacked furiously, even if Puskas was feeling his ankle. Hidegkuti hit the inside of a post. Kocsis hit the bar. Turek, considered a weak link by German critics, made a succession of flying saves. Kohlmeyer cleared off the line.

With six minutes left, the Germans broke away. Schafer crossed. Lantos headed out. Rahn shaped to shoot with his right foot, then hit it with his left. Grosics slipped.

As FIFA's archive soberly records, 'Rahn scored the winner when Grosics slid on the wet grass as he was about to go for the ball.' *Tor!*

Puskas had the ball in the German net again from Kocsis's cross. Welsh linesman Mervyn Griffiths flagged for offside. English referee Bill Ling disallowed the goal, though film footage suggests it was a good one. (Grosics said years later, 'It was a fair goal. New pictures shown by the media have proved it.') Turek saved point blank from Czibor in Hungary's last attack.

So Fritz Walter lifted the World Cup. West Germany had pulled off their 'miracle'. Soon their country would work an economic miracle too. But there was a symbolism in their victory. Germans could feel proud about something after their country's recent, horrific Nazi past. The players, Rahn most of all, had become role models for a new country. Herberger's biographer Mikos Nutt was one of many writers who suggested that the 'Miracle of Berne' was the *real* founding day of the West German state.

The Hungarians were shattered. They had won every game except the one that mattered most. Grosics admitted, 'I could never put the failure behind me.' FIFA's archive noted: 'The coach, the team and the entire country were crushed.'

Sebes blamed bad luck and listed the misfortunes that had befallen his team on the day. He received a host of death threats all the same.

Puskas was vilified. Grosics, in a bizarre development, was arrested on a charge of treason, though he was eventually released.

Puskas, in a later interview with *France Football*, claimed that the Germans had been doped. He pointed out that Rahn, the Walter brothers, Morlock and defender Karl Mai had all been treated for jaundice a few months after the final. He thought that was the result of artificial stimulants.

The German team doctor admitted injecting vitamins and glucose, nothing more. Rahn suggested that a dirty syringe had caused the problem. He wondered if he might have brought the disease back from South America after Essen's tour there earlier in 1954. The Essen goalkeeper Fritz Herkenrath, who did not play in the World Cup, had also gone down with jaundice. Puskas eventually withdrew his allegations.

Fifty years later, Walter Bonnimann, one of the ground staff at the Berne stadium, told a German TV crew that he had found several syringes after the final, along with several ampoules which *might* have been amphetamines. But the evidence was tenuous – and had long been destroyed.

The Hungarians continued to dominate every team they met. They were unbeaten after the World Cup final until 1956. Then the team's world was shattered by an event far beyond football – the Budapest uprising. The Hungarian people rebelled against their Stalinist regime. The revolt was crushed by Russian tanks. Hungary returned to the Soviet fold.

Honved were in Spain at the time, for a European Cup first-round tie against Atletico Bilbao. Their stars declined to return home. They decided to defect to the west. They were suspended by FIFA at the request of the Hungarian football association.

Puskas spent 18 months in Austria, under a FIFA ban, piling on weight and hoping for a move to Italy. He was rescued by his old Honved general manager Emil Oesterreicher. Oesterreicher had also defected and had joined European champions Real Madrid. They wanted a goal poacher to play alongside the great Argentine centre-forward Alfredo Di Stefano. So, at the age of 30, Puskas started a new career in Spain.

Kocsis and Czibor eventually joined Madrid's bitter rivals Barcelona – and tasted defeat again in Berne in the 1961 European Cup final.

Sebes, the socialist ideologue, remained in Hungary. So did Boszik.

After the new-look Hungary's defeat in Belgium, Sebes was replaced by a selection committee, headed by Bukovi. The 'golden team' was scattered. Hungary did not defend their title at the 1956 Olympics. They were eliminated at the group stage in the 1958 World Cup finals.

A new group of players emerged in the early '60s – centre-back Kalman Meszoly, graceful centre-forward Florian Albert, strikers Janos Farkas and Ferenc Bene. Hungary finished third in the 1964 European Championship. Two years later, that side reached the World Cup quarter-finals after beating Brazil 3–1 in their group. They lost 2–1 to the Soviet Union.

They lost to the Soviets once more, 1–0, in the 1972 European Championship semi-finals.

They have never been major players in international football since. There have been no more golden generations. Modern Hungarian clubs are struggling financially and they are resigned to losing their best players to western Europe. Hungary's great days of the early 1950s are but distant memories.

West Germany – now the greater part of a unified Germany – have gone from strength to strength since Rahn settled the argument in Berne. They won the World Cup again in 1974 and 1990, and the European Championship in 1972, 1980 and 1996.

Kocsis died before his 50th birthday. Sebes passed away in 1986. Puskas guided Panathinaikos to become the first, and only, Greek side to reach the European Cup final in 1971.

In 1993, he returned for a brief spell as Hungary's coach. But he could not inspire them to a place in the World Cup finals in the United States. He has spent the last five years fighting aginst Alzheimer's disease.

Fritz Walter, the grand old man of the Kaiserslautern club, died in June 2002. Grosics and Buzansky attended his memorial service. Rahn died, aged 74, in August 2003. He never lived to see the film of which he was the hero. But Franz Beckenbauer, who captained the World Cup-winning side of 1974 and coached the 1990 winners, recognised the Essen winger's place in German football history. He said, 'Rahn was one of the last legends. He shaped an entire generation.'

CHAPTER 6

THE GENESIS OF THE EUROPEAN CUP

The European Cup was born from two forces: French vision and English triumphalism.

The vision came from Gabriel Hanot, the editor of the influential French sports paper *L'Equipe*. The old French international was a man of ideas, usually proposed through the paper's columns. The former Football Association and FIFA president Sir Stanley Rous once remarked, with tongue in cheek, that he wished Hanot would not publish so many! One of them was his long-held dream of an annual competition for Europe's top clubs.

The triumphalism came from the English newspapers such as the *Daily Mail*, which hailed Wolverhampton Wanderers as 'champions of the world' after they beat Spartak Moscow 4–0 and the Hungarian army side Honved 3–2 in friendlies at Molineux.

English football was desperate for good news to lift the gloom surrounding the national team, which had been thrashed 6–3 and 7–1 by Hungary, and eliminated by Uruguay in the 1954 World Cup quarter-finals.

Wolves, a team which relied on the long ball, had overpowered their eastern European opponents under the Molineux lights. But these were not competitive games, nor did Wolves play return matches against their visitors.

Hanot said, 'We had better wait until Wolves travel to Moscow and Budapest before proclaiming their invincibility. But if the English are so sure about their hegemony in football, then this is the time to create a European tournament.' Hanot's tournament brainchild would soon go ahead – but without the English.

He unveiled his draft proposals on 16 December 1954, three days after Wolves had beaten Honved. His plan was a round-robin, league competition involving 16 of Europe's leading clubs. Games would be played in midweek, under floodlights, which had been installed throughout Europe's major stadia in the early 1950s.

There had been pan-European contests before. The Mitropa Cup, for instance, had featured teams from Austria, Czechoslovakia, Hungary, Italy, Switzerland and Yugoslavia. But never before had there been a competition on this grand scale.

Hanot's scheme ran into an immediate problem: fixture congestion. Clubs and national associations were sceptical about fitting in another league competition besides their domestic league. Most of the clubs consulted by *L'Equipe* favoured a knockout format, to reduce the number of games. Hanot redrafted his proposal. Now there would be home and away legs in all the rounds up until the final. That suited the clubs and their associations far better. It also tilted the balance in favour of the bigger clubs and against upsets on the FA Cup model. The big boys would have a second chance if they suffered a surprise defeat by unfancied opposition. As Brian Glanville wrote in *Champions of Europe*: 'David might connect with his first sling shot but he was still vulnerable to Goliath's great bludgeon.'

In April 1955, 18 of Europe's leading clubs – including Real Madrid and Milan – met in Paris and agreed that the competition should begin the following season. Several of the clubs were not current domestic champions. *L'Equipe* had invited them on the basis of their past achievements and spectator appeal. The rules would change for the 1956–57 competition, when only national champions, plus the holders, were allowed to enter.

FIFA gave the go-ahead for the European Cup, provided the competing clubs had the approval of their national associations. In May 1955, representatives of the clubs met officials of the fledgling European governing body, UEFA, in Paris. UEFA – founded only in June 1954 – agreed to take over the running of the competition. Its president, the Dane Ebbe Schwartz, became chairman of the organising committee.

Hanot's dream had been realised in six months. Sixteen teams took part in the inaugural competition. The first-ever European Cup tie took place in Lisbon on 4 September 1955: a 3–3 draw between Sporting and Partizan Belgrade.

There were absentees. There was no team from Czechoslovakia or the Soviet Union, for instance. Or England. Chelsea, the English champions, were the most notable absentees of all. One of the motivating forces behind Hanot's dream was to see just how good the English teams really were. He would have to wait another year to find out.

Chelsea had won the championship for the first time in 1955. Alan Hardaker, the secretary of the Football League, 'advised' them not to take part in the European Cup. The Chelsea chairman, Joe Mears, was also president of the Football League. He could have rejected Hardaker's advice. Instead, he gave in to the league secretary. So Chelsea remained on the sidelines: a source of great regret to Mears's son Brian, who followed him as chairman.

Brian Mears wrote in his autobiography: 'Chelsea could and should have been the first English team to play in the European Cup. Sadly, the offer was refused. I'm not sure why it was turned down, but the club probably just chickened out of something few people knew enough about.'

Glanville re-examined the reasons for Chelsea's absence in *The Times*, in April 2005. He judged, 'It was Joe Mears who "chickened out" of the first European Cup, for reasons that were plain enough. He was bullied into it, or out of it, by the notoriously xenophobic Hardaker.

'Hardaker's attitude was supremely negative, probably influenced by the fear that his own competition would be overshadowed by the new one.'

Whatever Hardaker's attitude, the first European Cup was a huge success. It was prestigious and profitable for the clubs. It was popular with the fans. Nearly 1,000,000 attended the matches. And it ended with a thrilling final – Real Madrid's 4–3 win over Reims in Paris – which heightened enthusiasm for the new tournament.

There were 22 entrants for the 1956–57 competition, including holders Madrid and champions Atletico Bilbao from Spain. The champions of Bulgaria, Czechoslovakia, Luxembourg, Romania and Turkey took part for the first time. So did the champions of England. Manchester United manager Matt Busby saw the potential of the European Cup. He was determined that his 'Busby Babes' should play in it. His directors ignored Hardaker's advice and backed their manager.

United's 2–0 win over Anderlecht in Brussels was the first appearance by an English club in the competition. Busby's side reached the semi-finals in 1956–57 and 1957–58.

Hardaker would have his revenge. When UEFA invited United to compete in the 1958–59 competition as a gesture of sympathy after the Munich air crash, the league secretary effectively forced them to withdraw.

By then, though, the exploits of clubs such as Madrid, United, Milan, Reims and Red Star Belgrade had excited fans across the Continent – and the European Cup was firmly established as the most glamorous club tournament of all. Hanot's vision had been vindicated on the pitch.

The First Sixteen

The 16 teams which took part in the historic first competition were:

Aarhus: Aarhus succeeded Koge as Danish champions in 1955 to earn a European Cup place. The provincial team had broken the Copenhagen clubs' monopoly by winning the title in 1954. Aarhus won the Danish championship three years in a row between 1955 and 1957. The Danish league had begun in 1916 and was still an amateur competition.

Anderlecht: The Brussels side were by far the leading club in Belgium. They won seven championships in ten seasons between 1947 and 1956, including three in a row twice – 1949–51 and 1954–56.

Djurgarden: Small Stockholm club Djurgarden had won their first league title since 1920. They succeeded GAIS Gothenburg as champions. Post-war Swedish football had previously been dominated by Malmo and Norrkoping, who had shared eight titles. Like Denmark, Sweden was then an amateur footballing country.

Gwardia Warsaw: Gwardia had won the Polish Cup in 1954, their biggest post-war achievement. They entered the European Cup ahead of Legia Warsaw, who won the Polish league and cup double in 1955.

Hibernian: Hibs, with their 'famous five' forward line, had emerged as serious challengers to Rangers and Celtic in the early 1950s, winning the Scottish League on three occasions. They only finished sixth in 1955, but took part ahead of champions Aberdeen. Their inclusion was probably helped by the fact their chairman, Harry Swain, was also chairman of the Scottish Football Association.

Milan: In the six years since the Superga tragedy, Milan, Juventus and Inter had each claimed the championship twice. Milan's attack had been bolstered by the arrival of Sweden forward Gunnar Nordahl in 1949. Nordahl was to become their all-time top scorer with 210 league goals. He was later joined by Swedish teammates Gunnar Gren and Nils Liedholm to form the feared strike force known as 'Gre-No-Li'. Gren had left by the time of the first European Cup but Milan had replaced him with Uruguay forward Juan Alberto Schiaffino, signed after the 1954 World Cup finals.

Partizan Belgrade: Partizan were formed in 1945 as the army club in the newly communist Yugoslavia. They were invited into the European Cup although they had last won their championship in 1949. Partizan, arch rivals Red Star and the Croatian sides Dinamo Zagreb and Hajduk Split were the leading Yugoslav clubs of the time.

PSV Eindhoven: PSV were not champions either. They had won the title just once since the war, in 1951. The club was formed in 1913 by electronics giant Philips. The Dutch league had remained amateur since 1898. Professionalism was only introduced in the season after the inaugural European Cup.

Rapid Vienna: Austrian football had been dominated by the Viennese clubs since the league began in 1911. Rapid had won five titles since the war, two more than their arch rivals FK Austria. Austrian internationals Ernst Happel and Gerhard Hanappi were their stars.

Reims: France's national professional league was formed in 1932. Champions Reims, Lille and Nice were the top post-war clubs. Reims won the title three times between 1949 and 1955. Their stars were three French internationals – elegant defender Robert Jonquet, winger Michel Hidalgo and the brilliant forward Raymond Kopa.

Rot-Weiss Essen: West Germany had no national league at the time. The Bundesliga was not formed until 1963. Rot-Weiss had beaten Kaiserslautern 4–3 in the 1955 championship final. Their most famous player was Helmut Rahn, hero of West Germany's 1954 World Cup final win over Hungary.

Saarbrucken: Saarbrucken were also invited from West Germany because, technically, the Saar was not yet part of the Federal Republic.

Servette: Servette, from Geneva, were coached by the Austrian Karl Rappan and had won the first Swiss national league championship in 1934. Rappan was the inventor of the *verrou* (bolt), a defensive system which was the forerunner of *catenaccio*. Servette had last won the Swiss title in 1950.

Sporting Lisbon: Sporting were the top team in Portugal. They won seven titles in eight seasons between 1947 and 1954, including four in succession from 1951. But they did not finish champions in 1955. Lisbon rivals Benfica had claimed that honour and would soon take over as Portugal's leading force.

Voros Lobogo: Voros Lobogo had beaten Budapest rivals Honved to the top spot in Hungary. They were also holders of the Mitropa Cup. Their star was Nandor Hidegkuti, the deep-lying centre-forward of the national side.

The other team in the tournament, **Real Madrid** (see Chapter 7), were to become one of the greatest club sides in the history of football.

CHAPTER 7

BERNABEU, DI STEFANO AND MADRID

Santiago Bernabeu built the modern Real Madrid. Alfredo Di Stefano inspired them to become the greatest team in Europe. The side that won the first five European Cup finals. The side that demolished Eintracht Frankfurt 7–3 in the 1960 final, one of the most memorable games ever played.

Bernabeu, the son of a lawyer from Albacete, became a wealthy and successful lawyer. But he will always be best remembered for his huge contribution to Madrid. The name of their giant stadium, Estadio Santiago Bernabeu, pays tribute to the most influential president in the club's history.

Bernabeu, a promising centre-forward, arrived at Madrid in 1909, aged 14, to play for their youth team. He broke into the first team at 17. His death, from cancer, in 1978, ended a 69-year association with the club.

He was elected president in September 1943. He later recalled, 'We were in a rut.' Madrid's Chamartin Stadium held only 16,000. Bernabeu's plan was to build a super stadium, in the hope that his ambition would catapult the club into a successful new era. He had made several notable banking contacts through his legal work. They would aid his project with loans on favourable terms.

The Madrid members and fans would play their part, too. Bernabeu appealed directly to them to back the scheme by buying club bonds (a scheme later used by many English clubs to allow them to comply with the Taylor Report). The response astonished even

Bernabeu. Money poured in. Madrid's membership shot up to 35,000.

Building work began in October 1944 and took just over three years. The new Chamartin Stadium – holding 75,000 – was inaugurated with a friendly against the Portuguese side Belenenses on 14 December 1947. After more successful fundraising, another tier was added, raising the capacity to 125,000. In January 1955, the stadium was renamed after Bernabeu.

There was another, darker, side to Bernabeu's vision – his links with the fascist regime of Generalissimo Francisco Franco who had emerged as Spain's strong man after his forces defeated the Republican government in a bitter civil war. Before the civil war, Madrid had strong links with the Republicans. The club's senior figures paid for it. Pre-war president Rafael Sanchez Guerra was forced into exile. Vice-president Gonzalo Aguirre and treasurer Valero Rivera were both murdered.

But Bernabeu had fought on Franco's side. One of his first acts as president was to send a telegram of greetings to General Moscardo, one of Franco's commanders now promoted to minister for sport. Phil Ball in *White Storm: 100 Years of Real Madrid* notes that Bernabeu, significantly, addressed him as 'heroic soldier of the fatherland'.

Bernabeu had made no secret of his politics and he clearly decided that Madrid would benefit from close links with the regime. Franco wanted to centralise power in Madrid and subjugate troublesome regions such as Catalonia and the Basque country. Bernabeu wanted to centralise footballing power in Madrid, too.

Madrid's success in the European Cup would burnish Spain's image abroad. People who knew nothing about Spanish politics came to admire Di Stefano and his colleagues, who won with flair and imagination. Holidays in Spain suddenly became fashionable. It had excellent beaches, it was cheap, it was safe – and it was the country of Real Madrid.

As Franco's foreign minister, Fernando Maria de Castiella, said, 'Real Madrid represent a style of sportsmanship. They're the best ambassadors we've ever had.'

By Christmas 1947, Bernabeu had his super stadium. He had hugely enlarged Madrid's fan base. What he needed now was a team. Madrid won the Spanish Cup (called the Copa del Generalissimo) in 1946 and 1947. But they made little headway in the league.

Their bitter rivals Barcelona dominated post-war football in Spain. They won the title in 1948 and 1949, followed by the league and cup double in 1952 and 1953. Madrid were not even the best team in their home city. Atletico finished champions in 1950 and 1951. They were coached by Helenio Herrera, who would become a frequent thorn in Madrid's side – first with Barcelona, then with Internazionale.

Madrid had not won the title since 1933. Indeed, in 1949, only a 2–0 win over Oviedo in their final game had saved Bernabeu's club from relegation.

Barcelona's side of the early '50s was inspired by the Hungarian forward Ladislav Kubala. Bernabeu had tried to sign him for Madrid. Kubala agreed to come, provided his father-in-law, Ferdinand Daucik, replaced Madrid's English coach, Mike Keeping. The Madrid president refused. Kubala joined Barca and both prospered. Bernabeu – with a little help from influential friends – would have better luck with another star import: Di Stefano.

Di Stefano had joined the wealthy Colombian club, Millonarios of Bogota, after the Argentine players' strike – demanding better pay and conditions – of 1948. Bernabeu met him on a radio show when Millonarios came to play in Madrid's 50th anniversary tournament in March 1952. Di Stefano scored twice in a 2–2 draw against Norrkoping, then twice again as Millonarios beat Madrid 4–2.

Bernabeu resolved to sign him. But which club owned Di Stefano's contract? His Argentine club, River Plate, or Millonarios? Colombia had only just rejoined FIFA after a spell outside the fold and there were possible legal complications.

Bernabeu sent his young treasurer Raimundo Saporta to negotiate with Millonarios. Barcelona were on the trail, too. Barcelona reached agreement with River Plate. Saporta cut a deal with Millonarios. But FIFA approved Di Stefano's transfer to Barcelona. Cue General Moscardo, who suddenly introduced a statute banning the further importation of foreign players. That seemed to end Di Stefano's chances of playing for Barcelona.

The Spanish football federation, probably after a hint from the sports ministry, then issued a bizarre ruling. Di Stefano would be exempt from the ban, provided Madrid and Barcelona agreed that he should play alternate seasons for each club, beginning at Chamartin.

Di Stefano made a sluggish start for Madrid at the start of the 1953–54 season. Barcelona decided to cut their losses. It was apparent after just three friendly appearances that they would find it hard to accommodate such commanding egos as Kubala and Di Stefano in the same team. Perhaps they also feared that the sports minister would never allow Di Stefano to play for them anyway. Madrid compensated them for their payment to River Plate and became sole owners of Di Stefano's contract.

As Ball notes, 'Moscardo's previous legislation was suddenly inapplicable to Di Stefano, because the small print of the law stated that any negotiations that had begun before the passing of the legislation were to remain exempt. Funny old coincidence.'

Di Stefano was *the* most important signing in Madrid's history. Before him, the club had underachieved. Now Bernabeu had brought in the catalyst for the greatest achievements in their history.

Brian Glanville, in *Champions of Europe*, wrote: 'Di Stefano was a remarkable mixture of arrogance and selflessness. To his strength, stamina and electric change of pace, he allied superb ball control. He was an absolute perfectionist. He scored goals in abundance – with his head or his feet – yet made so many for others.'

Di Stefano said, 'I'm always on the move so that the defenders can't pin me down. Or I may be moving quickly to help the next man on the ball. Because forwards should accept that helping the defence is part of their job. If the defence fails, the forward's job becomes much harder because he has to score more goals. So the obvious thing is to get back and help the defence. It eases your own job over the game.'

As Glanville concluded, Di Stefano was a 'total footballer' years ahead of his time. He was not an out and out striker. He would often drop deep to set up attacks. But he was a lethal finisher. He said, 'My greatest pleasure is in scoring goals.'

He soon made Barcelona suffer, scoring two in Madrid's 5–0 win over Barca at Chamartin. He scored 29 that season as Madrid won only their third championship and their first for 21 years. Di Stefano was league top scorer that season – and again for four successive years between 1956 and 1959.

In December 1954, Gabriel Hanot, the editor of French sports paper *L'Equipe*, unveiled his draft plans for the European Cup. Madrid were invited to represent Spain. Bernabeu, aided by Saporta, was among the most enthusiastic supporters of the new competition. He became a senior member of its executive committee until the fledgling European governing body, UEFA, took charge of organising the contest.

What if? What if Di Stefano had not joined Madrid? What if Barcelona had won another championship? Would the Catalans have been invited to take part in the European Cup instead? After all, their past record bettered whatever Madrid could muster and they had beaten Bernabeu's team in the Spanish Cup semi-finals.

But Di Stefano had joined Madrid, had inspired them to a title. Now the man nicknamed 'the blond arrow' would inspire their domination of the European Cup.

Di Stefano used his star status to influence Bernabeu's signings, too. It was Di Stefano who insisted that a flying young left-winger from Racing Santander, Paco Gento, should play for Madrid rather than going out on loan. Gento offered much more than pace. He could pinpoint crosses on the run, picking out Di Stefano or Luis Molowny, or he could cut in to strike at goal. Gento would play for Madrid until 1971, gaining six European Cup winner's medals.

In the summer of 1954, Di Stefano recommended another player, his old friend from Argentina, Hector Rial. Rial became the prompter who made the bullets for the forwards to fire. He would stay for seven years. Madrid won the title again, with a record points total. They finished five points ahead of Barcelona and again beat them 5–0.

Bernabeu's dream was taking shape. He had the stadium. Di Stefano had galvanised the club. The team was taking shape. Miguel Munoz, an all-action attacking right-half, was an ideal foil for Rial. The centre-half, Marquitos, was outstanding in the air and ruthless on the ground. Defensive wing-half Jose Maria Zarraga supplied extra cover. The fans were flocking in. And soon Madrid would have the European Cup.

Atletico Bilbao finished champions of Spain in 1956. Madrid came third, ten points behind the Basques. But Madrid finished champions of Europe. They played their first-ever European Cup tie against Servette in Geneva on 8 September 1955. Munoz broke the deadlock against a physical Swiss side. Rial added the second in the 89th minute. Madrid won 5–0 at the Bernabeu. Di Stefano scored twice.

Only 16 teams entered the first competition. Now Madrid were in the quarter-finals against Partizan Belgrade from communist Yugoslavia. Franco had spent the last 20 years trying to eradicate communist influences. Would politics wreck the fixture?

Saporta, rapidly emerging as Bernabeu's fixer-in-chief, made sure that never happened. He persuaded Franco that it would be good for

Spain's international image to welcome a football team from the other side of the ideological divide.

Partizan had two goals disallowed at the Bernabeu before reserve right-winger Castanos scored twice for Madrid. Gento netted a third. Di Stefano made it 4–0. The return was played on a snowy pitch in sub-zero temperatures. Ball quotes Madrid's keeper Juanito Alonso, 'It was freezing. They were used to it. They were all over us. I can't believe we only lost 3–0. We should have been stuffed.'

Milan, featuring the gifted Uruguayan Juan Alberto Schiaffino and the veteran Swedes Nils Liedholm and Gunnar Nordahl, came next. Nordahl and Schiaffino twice levelled after Rial and Joseito gave Madrid the lead. Gento caught out Milan's defence four minutes before half-time. Di Stefano, inevitably, added a fourth goal. Joseito scored first at San Siro. Madrid lost to two penalties on the night but reached the final on a 5–4 aggregate.

Their opponents in the final in Paris (home of *L'Equipe*) were Reims, the 1955 French champions. Reims' star player was centre-forward Raymond Kopa (see Chapter 17) and they were coached by Albert Batteux, one of the great figures of French football.

Reims made a flying start. They led 2–0 after ten minutes through Michel Leblond and Jean Templin. Di Stefano rallied Madrid with a brilliant goal, running on to Munoz's pass, leaving a string of defenders in his wake to shoot home. Di Stefano had started the move, inside his own half. Rial levelled.

Gento had a goal disallowed before Michel Hidalgo headed in Kopa's free kick to put Reims ahead again. Marquitos charged forward to equalise with a shot that ricocheted off a French shin. Gento set up the winner for Rial, 11 minutes from time. Templin hit the bar but Madrid survived. Gento reckoned this was the most hard-fought of all their European Cup final wins.

Franco showed his appreciation by awarding Bernabeu the equivalent of the freedom of the city of Madrid. To the Catalans and the Basques, this proved that Madrid were the regime's team.

Yet Franco had been furious with Bernabeu at the start of the European Cup campaign, after the Madrid players were pictured in Geneva with Queen Victoria Eugenia, the exiled Spanish monarch. Her son Juan Carlos, the modern Spanish constitutional monarch, even went into the Madrid dressing-room at half-time. Saporta, typically, had made the arrangements.

The incidents beg many questions. Was Bernabeu really a fascist? Or was he a royalist who had fought on Franco's side to try and eventually restore the monarchy? Or was he a shrewd politician who wanted to cover all his options?

Madrid signed Kopa that summer. Coach Jose Villalonga felt that Madrid's attack was too biased towards the left side. He used Kopa on the right wing to add balance. The move surprised Kopa himself, who wondered why Madrid needed him. Kopa spent three seasons at Madrid, collected three European Cup winner's medals – but was always in the shadow of Di Stefano. At Reims, he was the fulcrum of the team. At Madrid he was merely an aide to the great man. He returned to Reims after the 1959 European Cup final.

Di Stefano was the unchallenged king of the Madrid dressing-room. He outlasted not only Kopa but also the great Brazilian midfielder Didi, who spent just a season at the club, and the player signed to be his long-term replacement, the Swedish forward Agne Simonsson. He did not like sharing centre stage, even with Ferenc Puskas.

Madrid regained the league title, finishing five points ahead of Sevilla. But retaining the European Cup, now open only to national champions and the holders, was the real test.

Madrid went straight into the second round to meet Rapid Vienna. Di Stefano scored twice in a 4–2 home victory. At half-time in Vienna, they were tottering. Rapid led 3–0. Ernst Happel had scored a hat trick, one a penalty.

An angry Bernabeu entered the dressing-room to deliver a pep talk. He demanded more effort, called on the players to show pride in their shirts and ended by imploring the team not to let down the thousands of expatriate Spanish workers who supported Madrid on their travels.

Di Stefano scored the goal that took the tie to a third game – the away goals rule had yet to be invented. Saporta then offered Rapid half the gate receipts to play in Madrid rather than on a neutral ground. Rapid took the bait. Joseito and Kopa scored and Madrid won 2–0.

They beat Nice 6–2 on aggregate in the quarter-finals, then met the English champions Manchester United for a place in the final. By now, Enrique Mateos had broken into the team to partner Di Stefano. He scored a crucial third goal at the Bernabeu after Tommy Taylor had replied to second-half strikes by Rial and Di Stefano. The young Bobby Charlton watched and noted: 'These people are just not human. It's not the game that I've been taught.'

But Matt Busby had built a fine young side. Roger Byrne was England's left-back. Small, skilful Eddie Colman and England powerhouse Duncan Edwards were outstanding wing-halves. Centre-forward Tommy Taylor was another England regular. He combined brilliantly with the stealthy Dennis Viollet. Charlton was a rising star.

United tried to water the pitch heavily. The Madrid party protested. United turned the sprinklers off.

United had beaten Bilbao 3–0 at Old Trafford to win the quarter-final. Busby forecast another United victory. But the tie was over before half-time. Kopa scored after 27 minutes. Rial added a second, five minutes later, after Gento's shot was blocked. Taylor and Charlton earned a 2–2 draw on the night for United. Charlton's goal came three minutes from the end, too late for a glorious finale. Busby said, 'A great, experienced team will always beat a great inexperienced team.' But the Madrid players had marked out United as dangerous future rivals.

The final, against Fiorentina, was played at the Bernabeu. Fiorentina defended in depth for 70 minutes until Mateos was brought down. Fiorentina protested that he was offside. Referee Leo Horn waved away their protests and Di Stefano netted the penalty. Gento made it 2–0 with a clever lob. Madrid were champions of Europe again. Franco himself presented the trophy to skipper Munoz.

The club hierarchy's links with the government were obvious. The team were subjected to anti-Franco demonstrations on several European away trips for that reason. But the players preferred to stay away from politics. Di Stefano told Jimmy Burns (author of *Barca: A People's Passion*), 'I'm a footballer. I'm not interested in talking about politics, particularly when people ask me about the games we played against Barcelona.'

Madrid had suffered one painful defeat in 1956–57: 6–1 by Barcelona in the Spanish Cup. Bernabeu responded by importing the Uruguay centre-half Jose Santamaria. Saporta did the deal with Nacional of Montevideo. Santamaria was tough, mobile and constructive. He said, 'In my opinion, football begins from the back.'

Bernabeu was building off the field, too. Madrid built new training facilities at Ciudad Deportiva (Sports City) and the president began to institute the policy of continuity – keeping on famous players in coaching or administrative roles – that has continued to the present day.

Munoz, for instance, would soon become Madrid's coach. Bernabeu moved decisively in that area, too, sacking Villalonga, after the coach and his assistant, Juan Antonio Ipina, had one row too many. The former Nice coach Luis Carniglia replaced him. Ipina remained as his assistant.

Carniglia tightened up in defence. Santamaria replaced Marquitos, who eventually became a right-back. Zarraga dropped deeper to support the centre-half. Like the Hungarians before them – and Brazil's 1958 World Cup winners, Madrid were now playing a version of 4–2–4.

They won the league yet again, conceding nine goals less than the previous season. Bilbao denied Madrid a domestic double, beating them 2–0 in the Cup final, at the Bernabeu.

But Madrid finished champions of Europe for the third year in a row. The threat posed by Manchester United died in the horror of the Munich air disaster. The plane carrying the United party home from their quarter-final success over Red Star Belgrade crashed in the snow as it tried to take off after a refuelling stop. Byrne, Colman, Mark Jones, Liam Whelan, Taylor, David Pegg and Geoff Bent died instantly. Edwards died 15 days later. Busby had a punctured lung and spent three months fighting for his life. Johnny Berry and Jackie Blanchflower were so badly hurt that they never played again.

United's patched-up squad somehow beat Milan 2–1 in the semi-final first leg at Old Trafford. Schiaffino scored twice as Milan won the return 4–0.

Madrid had been imperious on their way to the final. They began by putting eight past the Belgian champions Antwerp, winning both legs. Di Stefano became the first player to score four goals in a European Cup tie as Madrid saw off a physical Sevilla side 8–0 at the Bernabeu. Di Stefano netted another hat trick to clinch a 4–0 win over Vasas Budapest in the semi-final first leg and set up a meeting with Milan in Brussels.

Milan had scored 26 goals on their way to the final. The veteran Liedholm was still creating goals. Schiaffino was in top form and he had been joined by the gifted Argentine forward Ernesto Grillo.

Madrid were twice behind before winning in extra time. Schiaffino finished off Liedholm's pass to give Milan a 59th-minute lead. Di Stefano levelled. Grillo netted for Milan. Rial equalised within a minute. Tito Cucchiaroni rattled the Madrid bar in extra time before Gento settled the game in the 111th minute, shooting past unsighted keeper Soldan after his first effort was blocked.

Fortune favoured Madrid but that night they had shown character as well as skill.

Two crucial developments impacted on Spanish football in the summer of 1958. Puskas arrived at Madrid and Helenio Herrera took over as coach of Barcelona.

Puskas, the skipper of Hungary's great team, had been with the Honved squad for the European Cup tie at Bilbao when the Budapest uprising of 1956 broke out. He defected to the west, along with Sandor Kocsis, Zoltan Czibor and the general manager Emil Oesterreicher, who was now on the staff at Madrid. All the players had been suspended from football for at least a year at the request of the Hungarian association. Kocsis and Czibor would eventually join Barcelona.

Puskas had been out of the game for 18 months and was considerably overweight. That did not deter Bernabeu, who remembered Puskas as a great goalscorer from the days of the 'Magnificent Magyars'. Oesterreicher persuaded Puskas to come to Madrid, while Saporta lobbied UEFA to ensure that the Hungarian's ban was lifted.

Carniglia seemed surprised at Puskas's poor physical condition but Bernabeu told him to get Puskas fit again. Puskas smiled, 'I was accused of being too slow after my early matches in Spain. I think that was an illusion.' The 'Little Cannon' – as he became known in Spain – would score more than 200 goals for Madrid, including four in the 1960 European Cup final.

Di Stefano supplied so many of those goals. But Puskas knew who was king of the dressing-room. Glanville tells the tale, that, on the last day of the season, he was level on goals with Di Stefano. But he passed up a chance and rolled the ball to Di Stefano so he could finish league top scorer.

Madrid's aura was immense and it had been polished by a new medium: television. TV – strictly controlled by the Francoist state – was a 1950s phenomenon in Spain. Madrid were the team screened most often, usually accompanied by admiring commentary. The Basques and the Catalans had their own loyalties but TV made Madrid the natural focus of support throughout the rest of the country.

As the Barcelona legend Charly Rexach told Burns, 'In those days, you supported the team from the town where you lived or you supported Madrid. That's because people identify with the team they can see and Madrid were the most visible team in Franco's Spain. They were promoted as Spain's club.'

Herrera felt that Madrid's successes had psychologically intimidated their rivals. His answer was to develop his own 'mind games'.

Herrera was born in Argentina, brought up in French North Africa and spent his playing career in France. After his success with Atletico, he had coached at Malaga, Deportivo, Sevilla and the Portuguese club Belenenses.

His aim was to establish psychological supremacy over his opponents before the game even started. He called it 'winning without getting off the bus'. He was one of the first coaches to use bonding rituals to build team spirit and confidence.

In the dressing-room before the game, Herrera would throw a ball at each player while shouting such questions as 'What do you think of the match? Why are we going to win? How are we going to play?' Goalkeeper Antonio Ramallets would reply, 'We're one of the best teams in the world. That's why we'll win.' The Brazilian forward Evaristo would say, 'We'll win because we want to win.' Then the players would link arms in a huddle and shout, 'We're going to play for each other. We're going to win together!'

Herrera soon fell out with Kubala, who cast a sceptical eye on the coach's methods. Herrera admired Kubala's talent, hated his liking for strong drink and finally dropped him for missing training sessions. Herrera and the Barca president, Francesc Miro-Sans, publicly accused Kubala of 'lacking commitment' and being a bad influence in the dressing-room. Seven Barcelona directors resigned in protest at Herrera's treatment of Kubala. The coach's critics claim that Herrera sidelined Kubala because he did not want any rivals as Barcelona's leading figure. But Herrera was the boss and Kubala was not restored to the team until the coach moved on to Internazionale.

Even without Kubala, Barcelona boasted a squad full of quality. Herrera thought it was an 'extraordinary' group of players. Ramallets was Spain's top keeper. He was protected by tough defenders Gracia, Segarra and Gensana – 'my big Catalans' as Herrera called them. In attack were the coach's 'tricky foreigners' – Kocsis, Czibor, Evaristo and the Paraguayan Vilaverde. Former Deportivo inside-left Luis Suarez was the midfield general who supplied them.

Herrera prided himself on knowing how to get the best out of them. In retirement, he told the writer Simon Kuper, 'You have 25 players and you don't say the same things to everyone. I told the Catalans to think about playing for the colours of Catalonia, playing for their people. To the foreigners, I talked money. I talked about their wives and kids.'

Barcelona won the domestic double, finishing ahead of Madrid, setting a points record and scoring 96 goals – a far cry from the defensive tactics that Herrera would employ at Internazionale. They beat Madrid 4–0 at the Nou Camp. They thrashed Granada 4–1 in the Spanish Cup final, at the Bernabeu.

Yet Madrid trumped them by winning the European Cup for the fourth year running. They opened with a 3–1 aggregate win over Besiktas, then thrashed Wiener SK 7–1 at the Bernabeu, after a bruising 0–0 draw in Vienna when Puskas was sent off for retaliation. Wiener SK had done Madrid one good turn, though, eliminating one of the pre-tournament favourites, Juventus, in the first round.

The semi-final was a Madrid derby. Atletico's strength was in attack. Vava, the Brazilian World Cup-winner, was at centre-forward, supported by the Spain midfielder Joaquim Peiro and the Portuguese inside-forward Mendonca. Madrid offered Atletico the chance to make money by playing both legs at the Bernabeu. They refused. They had seen what happened to Rapid.

Madrid's Argentine keeper Rogelio Dominguez was their first leg hero, saving Vava's penalty to preserve a 2–1 lead. Chuzo netted first for Atletico. Rial equalised and Puskas blasted a penalty to give Madrid the lead.

Puskas was injured for the second leg. Winger Enrique Collar scored the only goal as Atletico won 1–0 to take the tie to a play-off in Zaragoza. (There was no 'away goals' rule then.)

Puskas, fit again, decided the match with a low shot after Collar had equalised Di Stefano's opener. Atletico would gain some measure of revenge by beating Madrid in the 1960 and 1961 Spanish Cup finals.

Puskas was injured again for the final, against Reims in Stuttgart. This was Kopa's last match for Madrid. Reims singled him out for some tough treatment. Jean Vincent felled him with one particularly nasty challenge. Kopa waved away his apologies. Mateos, who stood in for Puskas, scored after two minutes and later missed a penalty. Di Stefano, almost inevitably, made it 2–0. Zarraga lifted the European Cup to overshadow Barcelona's achievements.

Barca won the title again in 1960, and the Fairs Cup. The race with Madrid went right to the tape. The teams finished level on points. Barcelona won because they had the better record in their two head-to-head clashes with Madrid. The key result was Barca's 3–1 win over

Madrid four weeks from the end of the season. That scoreline cost the Paraguayan coach Fleitas Solich his job. Solich had succeeded Carniglia but had never gained the full confidence of the dressing-room. Gento said, 'He failed with us on one major issue – he didn't understand the team.'

Bernabeu went for continuity and stability. Munoz became coach. His reign lasted 14 years. One particular highlight was probably the greatest night in Madrid's history: the 7–3 win over Eintracht Frankfurt in the 1960 European Cup final. But Madrid had to knock out Barcelona in the semi-finals first.

Herrera's side were majestic in the early rounds, sweeping aside CDNA Sofia, overpowering Milan at San Siro and at the Nou Camp, then thrashing the English champions Wolves 4–0 and 5–2. Madrid advanced past Jeunesse d'Esch of Luxembourg and Nice.

The showdown was seen as payback time in Catalonia. The rivalry between Barcelona and Madrid dated as far back as the 1916 Spanish Cup semi-final, when the Barcelona team, 4–2 down, walked off in protest at allegedly biased refereeing by the ex-Madrid player Jose Angel Berraondo. Madrid lost the final to Atletico Bilbao, on Espanol's ground in Barcelona. Thousands of Barcelona fans crossed the city to watch – and pelted the Madrid players after their 4–0 defeat.

The Catalans, like the Basques, had traditionally resisted central authority imposed from Madrid. Since the 1920s, there had been a political dimension to the rivalry, too. The right-wing government of Primo de Rivera had tried to crush Catalan culture. Franco's government did the same after the Civil War, banning overt symbols of Catalan identity and removing Catalan as an official language of the province.

Barcelona fans saw Madrid as Franco's team, a symbol of the dictator. Fascist troops loyal to Franco had murdered the Barca president, the left-wing Catalan member of parliament Josep Sunyol in August 1936. The Fascists had shelled Barca's old Les Corts Stadium.

Barcelona fans also believed that referees, under pressure from the sports ministry, routinely helped Madrid and hindered Barca. They pointed to Madrid's 2–1 win in November 1955 as an example, claiming that Marquitos was allowed to score a stoppage-time winner despite being offside and fouling the Barca keeper.

On the eve of the first leg at the Bernabeu, two days after the end of the league season, the Barcelona players were in dispute with the directors over bonuses. They wanted the same bonus for winning as their Madrid counterparts. It was hardly the best preparation for such an important match. Bernabeu treated the Madrid players to another pep talk, urging them to play for the prestige of the club and the supporters. The symbolism was obvious, 'Spain's team' versus the Catalan separatists.

Madrid won 3–1. Di Stefano scored twice, Puskas once. Herrera made the mistake of saying that Barcelona would settle the tie at the Nou Camp. Puskas, Gento and Puskas again gave Madrid a 3–0 lead by the 74th minute. Kocsis's last-minute header was scant consolation for Barcelona. Herrera was summarily sacked.

So to the final at Hampden Park, Glasgow. Madrid showed several changes from the 1959 final. The Brazilian winger Canario had succeeded Kopa. The youngster Jose Vidal was at right-half. Full-back Enrique Pachin had arrived from Osasuna. Inside-forward Luis del Sol had come from Betis of Seville.

Madrid's opponents were Eintracht Frankfurt who had hammered the Scottish champions Rangers 6–1 and 6–3 in the semi-finals.

Richard Kress scored first for Eintracht. That just roused Madrid, Di Stefano most of all. He levelled from Canario's centre then hit a second after keeper Egon Loy failed to hold Canario's shot. Puskas smashed the third from a tight angle.

The Hungarian romped through the second half, netting a penalty, scoring that rarity, a Puskas header, and adding a fourth with a blistering shot. When Erwin Stein pulled one back for Frankfurt, Di Stefano replied within three minutes. As Ball wrote: 'The game immortalised Real Madrid and turned them into a concept as much as a club. It stands as the embodiment of everything good in the aesthetics of the game.'

Munoz became the first man to win the European Cup as a player and a coach. Madrid seemed invincible. Yet this would be their last European Cup triumph for six years. Other clubs were about to stake their claims to dominance – the Portuguese champions Benfica, Milan and Internazionale, coached by Herrera.

Barcelona beat Madrid in the 1960–61 first round to end their dominance of the European Cup. Santamaria was injured and Suarez scored twice in a 2–2 draw at the Bernabeu. Barca won the second leg 2–1, after the English referee, Reg Leafe, disallowed three Madrid goals. The Madrid players surrounded Leafe after the post-match banquet. He was rescued by a Scottish journalist who pushed him into a taxi.

Victory brought no lasting joy to Barcelona. They reached the final for the first time and surprisingly lost to Benfica in Berne. Then the club imploded, in the dressing-room and the boardroom. Meanwhile, Munoz's side won eight championships in nine seasons between 1961 and 1969. They reached three more European finals, losing in 1962 and 1964 and winning in 1966.

The 1964 defeat by Internazionale was Di Stefano's last appearance for Madrid. He was 38 that July. Herrera's tactics had neutralised him in the final. He was less prolific than before and Munoz feared that Di Stefano's continued presence as king of the dressing-room might inhibit his new generation of players. He decided not to offer Di Stefano another contract. Di Stefano thought he could play on for another two years. Bernabeu backed Munoz.

It had been a traumatic year for Di Stefano. He had been kidnapped by anti-government guerrillas in August 1963 during Madrid's trip to Venezuela. It was a stunt designed to gain maximum publicity for their cause, in Europe and in Latin America, and it worked. Di Stefano's abduction was front-page news the next morning. He was later released and sought safety in the Spanish embassy. He admitted there were times when he wondered if his captors might kill him.

All that and now this. Di Stefano angrily accused the club of maliciously ending his stay at Madrid. Bernabeu retaliated by banishing Di Stefano from the club. It was a sad end to the partnership between the two men who had turned Madrid from an underachieving side with potential into the most famous club in Europe.

Di Stefano finished his career with Espanol. His first competitive game in their colours was against Madrid at the Bernabeu. Madrid won 2–1. Di Stefano did not score.

The relationship between Di Stefano and Bernabeu was patched up. Celtic, the European Cup holders, came to Madrid for Di Stefano's testimonial match in 1967. Di Stefano would return to Madrid as coach in the mid-1980s.

Meanwhile, Madrid had won the European Cup for a sixth time. Munoz's new generation beat Partizan Belgrade 2–1 in Brussels in the 1966 final. Of the players, only Gento remained from the team that had won the first European Cup ten years earlier.

There was one other constant: Bernabeu. Whatever his links with Franco's regime, he had presided over the building of a stadium, the building of a team and the building of a legend that still endures.

CHAPTER 8

INTER AND THE DARK DAYS OF *CATENACCIO*

Internazionale were the unloved masters of European football in the mid-1960s. They won the European Cup in 1964 and 1965 and reached the final in 1967. They won the Italian title in 1963, 1965 and 1966. These were the greatest days in their history, eclipsing even the championship victories of 1930 and 1938, inspired by their great forward Giuseppe Meazza.

But their achievements were clouded by controversy. Inter were the antithesis of free-flowing attacking teams, like Alfredo Di Stefano's Real Madrid or Madrid's successors as European champions, Benfica. Inter's *catenaccio* defensive tactics, honed by coach Helenio Herrera, were derided throughout Europe and some of their most important victories were achieved in questionable circumstances, with the help of refereeing decisions.

As Brian Glanville wrote in *Champions of Europe*: 'Would Inter have won without the cheating and finagling, the suborning of referees which went on in the background? Such a question must forever tarnish their achievements. Nor was their style an endearing one. Yet their team bristled with fine players.'

In 1960, when club president Angelo Moratti brought Herrera to Inter from Barcelona, a new force was rising fast: Benfica. Benfica had appointed a new coach, Bela Guttmann, the year before, after his Porto side had beaten them to the Portuguese championship. Guttmann was a Hungarian Jew who had played for the pre-war Viennese Jewish club Hakoah. He somehow survived the Holocaust (he said, 'God helped me.') and made his name as coach of Brazilian club Sao Paulo.

Benfica drew their players only from Portugal and its African colonies. Guttmann could call on probably their best-ever crop. He made shrewd signings in centre-half Figureido Germano, plucked from Lisbon minnows Atletico of the second division, and speedy right-winger Jose Augusto from Barreirense. He already had a top-class goalkeeper in Mozambique-born Costa Pereira, one of several fine players from Africa. Jose Aguas, the centre-forward from Angola, was a quick-thinking target man as well as a lethal finisher who netted 290 goals in his Benfica career. He was well supported by another Angolan, inside-right Joaquim Santana.

Mario Coluna from Mozambique was the skipper and midfield general. Coluna, once a teenage high-jump champion, dictated the tempo with penetrating left-footed passes and broke forward to strike fierce shots.

Guttmann's favoured formation was 4–2–4 and his instinct was to attack. His Portuguese champions announced their intentions in the 1960–61 European Cup by beating Scottish title holders Hearts 2–1 in Edinburgh and 3–0 at the Estadio da Luz (Stadium of Light). Hearts' hugely experienced winger Gordon Smith said, 'We were simply outclassed.'

Benfica then destroyed Ujpest Dozsa 6–2 in Lisbon and coasted through the second leg despite losing 2–1. In the quarter-finals, they beat Aarhus 3–1 in Lisbon and 4–1 in Denmark.

Coluna, Aguas and left-winger Domiciano Cavem scored to build a 3–0 lead over Rapid Vienna in the semi-final first leg.

Aguas put Benfica ahead midway through the second half in Vienna. Rapid scored a consolation equaliser. Then, with two minutes left, the first serious crowd trouble in European Cup history erupted. The English referee, Reg Leafe, refused a Rapid penalty appeal. The Rapid players attacked their opponents. Fans ran on to join the fighting. Police intervened and escorted the Benfica team – and Leafe – to safety. UEFA awarded the game to Benfica and banned Rapid from playing European home games at the Prater Stadion for three years.

Benfica met Barcelona in the final in Berne. Barcelona had overcome the West German (not yet Bundesliga) champions Hamburg 1–0 in a semi-final play-off in Brussels. The Brazilian striker Evaristo netted the winner after Sandor Kocsis's header had saved them from elimination in Hamburg.

Barcelona had ended Real Madrid's five-year domination of the competition in the first round. Madrid were without injured centre-back Jose Santamaria for the first leg at the Bernabeu. They led twice but two goals by playmaker Luis Suarez – the second a controversial penalty after Kocsis went down – earned Barcelona a 2–2 draw. Suarez would soon rejoin his old mentor Herrera at Inter.

It was the first time that Madrid had failed to win a European home game. They had three goals disallowed by Mr Leafe in the return at the Nou Camp. An own goal by Pachin and an Evaristo header settled the tie 2–1 in Barcelona's favour.

Barcelona started the final firm favourites. Guttmann admitted that he was 'worried about their forwards'. The Catalan club featured the Hungarian trio of Kocsis, Kubala and Czibor, with Evaristo at centre-forward and Suarez pulling the strings.

They also had one of Europe's finest goalkeepers in Spanish international Antonio Ramallets. This was to be the worst day of his distinguished career.

Kocsis met Suarez's 19th-minute cross with a diving header to give Barcelona the lead. Benfica replied with two goals in two minutes. On the half-hour, Coluna's through pass split the Barcelona defence. Ramallets charged recklessly off his line. Cavem by-passed him and squared the ball for Aguas to tap in the equaliser. Then defender Gensana back-headed Neto's lob and wrongfooted Ramallets. The keeper could only palm the ball against the woodwork and watch it drop into the net. Coluna volleyed a third, after 55 minutes, with his right foot.

Barcelona surged forward and Czibor pulled one back. But luck favoured Benfica. Kocsis, Kubala and Czibor hit the woodwork. Costa Pereira was heroic. Benfica survived and Coluna lifted the European Cup. Kocsis and Czibor, stars of the Magnificent Magyars of 1954 tasted defeat yet again in a major final at Berne. Kubala said it was the saddest day of his life.

Benfica lost the Portuguese title to Sporting in 1961–62. But they came out even stronger to defend their European crown. Guttmann had unearthed a gem of a 19-year-old forward from Mozambique: Eusebio. The ex-Brazil wing-half Carlos Bauer, who played under Guttmann at Sao Paulo, had tipped off his old boss about this precocious talent. Worried that representatives from their arch rivals, Sporting, might try to snatch him from under their noses, Benfica 'hid' him in a fishing village on the Algarve while they completed his signing from Lourenco Marques.

Eusebio was to become the greatest Portuguese player of them all: a lethal combination of skill, pace and power with an explosive right-foot shot. He scored a record 319 goals for Benfica and 41 for Portugal. How much less effective would club – and country – have been without such stars from Portugal's colonies?

Guttmann called up Eusebio for the World Club Cup play-off against South American champions Penarol in Montevideo. Benfica lost 2–1 but Eusebio scored and became a fixture in the side thereafter.

Benfica had unearthed another teenage talent: 17-year-old left-winger Antonio Simoes also played against Penarol. Cavem moved back to midfield.

Benfica opened their European Cup campaign with a 1–1 draw against FK Austria in Vienna, then trounced them 5–1 in Lisbon. Eusebio was injured for the quarter-final first leg in Nurnberg. Benfica lost 3–1. He was fit for the return. Benfica won 6–0.

They met the English double winners Tottenham in the semi-finals. Spurs were strengthened by the signing of England's leading goal poacher Jimmy Greaves, home after an unhappy spell at Milan. Greaves made his European debut in the first leg in Lisbon. Tottenham's strength was in attack. That night they tried to defend and handed the initiative to Benfica. Simoes and Jose Augusto gave them a 2–0 lead inside 20 minutes. Bobby Smith pulled a goal back but Jose Augusto's header clinched a 3–1 win for the holders.

Aguas scored in a 16th-minute breakaway at Tottenham. Smith levelled on the night and skipper Danny Blanchflower tucked away a penalty. Pereira and Germano held Benfica together under a second-half battering. Once more luck – and the woodwork – favoured Guttmann's team. Tottenham hit the post twice, then Dave Mackay's shot cannoned off the bar.

Benfica's opponents in the final in Amsterdam were Real Madrid's ageing superstars who had thrashed Standard Liege 4–0 in Madrid and 2–0 in Belgium. They had demolished Hungarian champions Vasas 5–1 on aggregate and routed Odense of Denmark 3–0 and 9–0 in the early rounds. But they needed a play-off to eliminate Juventus in the quarter-finals after losing their first-ever home tie. Di Stefano's goal had settled the first leg in Turin. Omar Sivori's strike at the Bernabeu forced a third game in Paris. Second-half goals by Luis del Sol and Justo Tejada earned Madrid a 3–1 win.

Benfica twice came from behind to win 5–3 in a gloriously open contest. Puskas, now 36, fired Madrid into a 2–0 lead by the 23rd minute. Aguas and Cavem replied. Puskas completed his hat trick and Madrid led 3–2 at the interval. The second half belonged to Benfica and Eusebio

At half-time, Guttmann ordered Cavem to tight mark Di Stefano and cut off the supply to Puskas. Benfica pressed forward and Madrid tired under the assault. Coluna equalised with a 25-yard strike after a mistake by Puskas. Eusebio shot Benfica ahead from the penalty spot after Pachin brought him down. He sealed Benfica's triumph with a deflected shot from Coluna's rolled free kick. At the end, he swapped shirts with Puskas.

The game was a watershed. It was the last of the finals in which attacking sides tried to outscore each other: a carefree finale before the cynical defensive play that lay ahead.

It was also the end of Guttmann's time at Benfica. His contract did not include bonuses for winning the European Cup. The Benfica directors held Guttmann to the contract. Guttmann decided to quit while he was ahead. He took over at Penarol, while the Chilean coach Fernando Riera replaced him at Benfica.

Riera was less flamboyant than Guttmann but Benfica continued to thrive. A new striker broke through: Jose Torres, a towering centre-forward, exceptional in the air. He replaced Aguas, who moved to Austria Vienna. Benfica's new front four – Jose Augusto, Eusebio, Torres and Simoes, prompted by Coluna – would form the strike force for Portugal's finest-ever team, which finished third in the 1966 World Cup finals.

Benfica regained their Portuguese title from Sporting and reached the European Cup final again. Eusebio scored four times in their 6–2 second-round aggregate win over Norrkoping. Sporting were eliminated by Dundee at the same stage.

Coluna struck both goals in Benfica's 2–1 quarter-final first-leg win over Dukla Prague and they drew 0–0 in Czechoslovakia, despite the continued absence of the injured Germano. Another goalless draw, against Feyenoord in Rotterdam, paved the way for a 3–1 second leg semi-final victory. Eusebio opened the score in the 20th minute. Jose Augusto and Santana finished the job.

Their opponents at Wembley were Milan, who had won the Italian title by five points from Inter. Their stars were the Brazilian centre-forward Jose Altafini, who had finished Serie A top scorer with 22 goals, and the new golden boy of Italian football Gianni Rivera, a cultured playmaker who had joined Milan from Alessandria at 16 for a record £65,000 fee.

Giovanni Trapattoni was a powerful defensive wing-half, while the Brazilian attacking right-half Dino Sani was a fine foil for Rivera. In between them was the rock-solid stopper Cesare Maldini, father of modern Milan idol Paolo.

Milan finished third in Serie A in 1962–63, winning only seven of their 17 home games. They saved their best performances for the European Cup. They annihilated US Luxembourg 14–0 on aggregate. Left-winger Paolo Barison scored twice as they beat the English champions, Alf Ramsey's Ipswich, 3–0 at San Siro.

Milan mixed a cutting edge with a hard edge. After Ipswich won the return 2–1, their players complained about Milan's off-the-ball fouls. The Ipswich centre-half Andy Nelson said, 'They were up to all the cynical stuff, pulling your hair, treading on your toes . . .'

Milan settled their quarter-final against Galatasaray by winning the first leg 3–1 in Istanbul. Altafini netted a hat trick in their 5–0 victory at San Siro. A 5–1 home win over Dundee saw them through the semi-final. Barison scored twice again. The Dundee striker Alan Gilzean headed the only goal of the second leg, then was sent off for retaliation after he was fouled.

Milan showed their hard edge again at Wembley. Barison was dropped despite his goals. The Milan coach Nereo Rocco brought in reserve midfielder Gino Pivatelli to mark Coluna. Germano was still injured, leaving a gap that Altafini would exploit.

Eusebio fired Benfica into an 18th-minute lead, outpacing Trapattoni to shoot home off the inside of a post. Altafini levelled 13 minutes after half-time, spinning on a clever pass by Rivera to hit a low drive beyond Costa Pereira. A minute later, Pivatelli brought down Coluna so badly that the Benfica skipper was a passenger for the rest of the game. (There were no substitutes in European Cup games then.)

It was a pivotal moment. Benfica's supply line was cut. Rivera dominated midfield and Milan pressed for the winner. Altafini scored it in the 70th minute. Rivera prodded the ball forward after a Benfica mix-up. Altafini ran from just inside his opponents' half. Costa Pereira saved his first effort but Altafini tucked away the rebound. Glanville summed up, 'The determining factor was the foul by Pivatelli on Coluna. Cynicism ruled.'

Meanwhile, Herrera's Inter won the *scudetto* for the first time since 1954. Herrera had made good use of oil magnate Moratti's resources. He had signed playmaker Suarez for £215,000 from his old club Barcelona, brought in Mario Corso, the first of the wide left midfield players, from Verona and snapped up the pacy Brazilian winger Jair. In defence, skipper Armando Picchi arrived from Livorno in the summer of 1960. Tarcisio Burgnich came from Juventus two years later. Goalkeeper Giuliano Sarti followed from Fiorentina in the summer of 1963. But Inter's two biggest stars – Giacinto Facchetti and Sandro Mazzola – joined them without a fee.

The teenage Facchetti, from Treviglio near Bergamo, was on the brink of joining local club Atalanta when wealthy Inter moved in. He made his debut, against Roma, as an 18 year old in 1961 and played 476 Serie A games for Inter. Facchetti accumulated 94 caps, won a European Championship medal in 1968, played in the 1970 World Cup final and later became Inter's president.

He only scored three goals for his country. He netted more than 50 for Inter in Serie A at a time when Italian football was riddled with caution. Once a youthful centre-forward, he used those attacking skills to great effect. Facchetti was a new kind of full-back, the forerunner of the modern wing-back. Ironically, the solidity of Inter's defence allowed him that freedom to venture forward, especially at free kicks.

Mazzola was the son of a famous father – the great Valentino Mazzola. Valentino, captain of Italy, inspired Torino to four successive championships and scored more than 100 Serie A goals, before he was killed in the Superga air crash that destroyed the Torino side.

Valentino played his last game for Torino in Lisbon, where Sandro's Inter would lose the 1967 European Cup final to Celtic. Sandro was seven at the time of the crash. He said, 'Every time I think of that day, it hurts. Whenever the anniversary comes round, the bad memories come flooding back.'

Inter had stepped in ahead of Torino to sign Sandro and his brother Feruccio as juniors. They moved the boys and their mother from Turin to Milan. Sandro was the one who became the star. He was a subtle attacker who operated just behind a central striker. He had close control, vision and could turn instantly in the tightest areas. He made his debut as an 18 year old, too, when Inter fielded their youth team against Juventus and suffered their record defeat, 9–1.

Mazzola scored 116 goals in more than 400 Serie A appearances. He won 70 caps, a European Championship medal and also played in the 1970 World Cup final, although he often competed with Rivera for the same position.

Herrera was a strict disciplinarian. The English centre-forward Gerry Hitchens, sold to Torino during the 1962–63 winter break, likened leaving Inter to 'coming out of the army'. Glanville, for instance, tells the story of how Hitchens, Suarez and Corso lagged on a pre-season cross-country run and Herrera ordered the team bus to leave the training ground without them.

Herrera had a flair for publicity and revelled in the nickname of *Il Mago* (the Magician). He also recognised the value of the Inter fans. He persuaded Moratti to set up an 'Inter Club' for the supporters, who became part of Herrera's project. When Inter won the European Cup in 1964, more than 30,000 fans travelled to the final in Vienna. A year earlier, only a few thousand had followed Milan to Wembley.

There was another side to the supporters, though. The Everton players complained bitterly about being kept awake for most of the night by carloads of fans driving around their hotel honking their horns and making a noise before their 1963–64 European Cup game at San Siro. It became a familiar complaint from Inter's opponents.

The statistics of Inter's 1963 title victory were an ominous hint of things to come. They finished four points ahead of Juventus, conceded just 20 goals in 34 games and scored 56. Their top scorers were Jair and Mazzola with ten goals each. Herrera had given an indication of his intentions early in his reign when he sold the Argentine centre-forward Antonio Valentin Angelillo, who had scored 33 Serie A goals in 1958–59.

Herrera had won two Spanish championships at Barcelona with an array of attacking stars. At Inter he became the high priest of catenaccio. It was as if he had suddenly swallowed whole the ethos of Italian football with its emphasis on stopping opponents.

Catenaccio had been adapted from the defensive tactics devised by Switzerland's Austrian coach Karl Rappan in the late 1930s. Rappan withdrew one of his wing-halves to operate behind the centre-half, providing additional cover at the back. Italian clubs had adopted the system in the 1950s, initially to combat the attacking stars imported by the leading sides. The Milan coach Rocco had been a famous exponent when he was in charge at Padova. Now all the Serie A teams played that way.

The long-serving Aristide Guarneri was the centre-half in Inter's formation. The mobile Picchi swept behind him. He was a defender pure and simple. Not until Franz Beckenbauer, a decade later, would sweepers join the attack. They were flanked by Burgnich on the right and Facchetti on the left.

The system was known as the 'bolt'. Herrera added an extra lock. He withdrew a midfield player – Carlo Tagnin or Gianfranco Bedin – to play as a man-to-man marker or an extra defender. Inter's system was based on frustrating opponents, then hitting them on the counter-attack. Suarez, a master of the long pass, sprung the trap. Jair and Mazzola converted his passes.

Inter had succeeded Milan as champions of Italy. Now they had to succeed them as champions of Europe. As journalist Giancarlo Rinaldi later wrote: 'It was the only response the supporters would accept, having had to watch Milan become the first Italian team to win the European Cup.'

Inter began by eliminating Everton. They shut the door on the English champions in a 0–0 draw at Goodison Park. Jair hit the only goal of the tie at San Siro. Benfica went out in the second round. They beat Borussia Dortmund 2–1 in Lisbon, but without Costa Pereira, Germano and Eusebio they crashed 5–0 in West Germany.

Inter took a 1–0 home lead against Monaco, then won the return, at Marseilles, 3–1. Mazzola, in imperious form, scored twice. Jair and Mazzola again sank Partizan 2–0 in Belgrade in the quarter-final first leg. Inter then cruised to a 2–1 win at home.

Dortmund were their semi-final opponents. Now, for the first time, allegations surfaced about Inter and referees. They drew the first leg 2–2 in Dortmund. Corso scored the equaliser after two goals by Franz Brungs cancelled out Mazzola's fourth-minute strike.

Mazzola gave Inter the lead at San Siro and Jair's goal settled the tie. Dortmund played much of the game with ten men. Suarez had kicked the Dortmund right-half Hoppy Kurrat and put him out of the match. The Yugoslav referee, Tesanic, took no action.

A Yugoslav tourist, who met Tesanic on holiday that summer, claimed the referee admitted that Inter had paid for his vacation. The West German press tried to follow up the allegation but there was no reaction from the rest of Europe. UEFA declined to investigate further.

(This was the first of several allegations that Italian clubs had bribed referees in Europe. Glanville and Keith Botsford investigated for the

Sunday Times in the early 1970s and published their findings in April 1974, detailing what they called 'The Years of the Golden Fix'.)

Inter's final opponents, Real Madrid, had injected fresh blood in the form of defender Zoco from Osasuna and flying winger Amancio from Deportivo La Coruna. He scored the opening goal as Madrid beat holders Milan 4–1 in the quarter-final first leg and went through 4–3 on aggregate. Madrid, still including Di Stefano and Puskas, crushed Zurich 8–1 on aggregate in the semi-finals.

Herrera had a score to settle with Madrid. He was coach of the Barcelona side eliminated by Real in the 1960 semi-finals. It was a clash of opposites. Madrid had reached the final by scoring 27 goals in eight games. Inter had conceded just four. In Vienna, Madrid attacked but catenaccio prevailed. As Inter's archives say, 'Tagnin cancelled out Di Stefano and Guarneri stopped Puskas.'

Mazzola's 25-yarder gave Inter the lead at half-time. Luck favoured them when Puskas's shot beat Sarti but cannoned off the bar, and Madrid keeper Vicente's mistake soon presented Aurelio Milani with Inter's second. Felo headed in a corner in reply but Suarez ran the game as Madrid's old legs tired. Mazzola pounced on Santamaria's weak clearance to net Inter's third.

It was Di Stefano's last game for Madrid and his last in the European Cup. He had scored a record 49 goals in the competition.

Inter were unpopular winners. Early in the competition, the Monaco forward Yvon Douis had criticised their dour tactics. Madrid wing-half Lucien Muller echoed him after the final. Herrera just pointed to the result.

Inter now had the chance to complete the domestic and European double. They had finished level with Bologna at the top of Serie A. The title was settled by a play-off in Rome. Now fortune turned against them. Facchetti put through his own goal after 75 minutes and Serie A top scorer Harald Nielsen sealed the title for Bologna. With hindsight, Inter's 2–0 defeat by Milan on 19 January – their only home defeat – had been crucial.

In 1964–65, though, Inter triumphed in Serie A and in Europe. They trailed Milan by three points (two points for a win then) with nine games to go. Inter then thrashed Milan 5–2 in the derby to cut their lead to one point. The key date was 16 May, when Suarez scored the first goal and inspired Inter to a 2–0 win at Juventus, while Milan lost 2–0 at home to Roma. Inter then beat Atalanta 3–1 and Catania 5–1 and a

2–2 draw with Torino on the final day clinched the title by three points as Milan lost 2–1 at Cagliari.

Inter led the Serie A scoring charts with 68 goals – proof of their attacking potential, had Herrera loosened the shackles. Mazzola finished joint top league scorer with 17 goals. Jair netted ten. Right-winger Angelo Domenghini, a shrewd signing from Atalanta, added nine.

But the latter stages of the European Cup showed Inter at their worst. They began their defence by crushing Dynamo Bucharest 6–0; Mazzola and Jair scored two each. Three goals in four minutes – one by Suarez, two by Joaquin Peiro – beat Rangers 3–1 in the quarter-final first leg. Jim Forrest scored after seven minutes at Ibrox but Rangers were without their inspirational midfielder Jim Baxter, who had broken a leg in the second round, and Inter's catenaccio stonewalled the Scottish champions for the rest of the game.

Their semi-final victory over Liverpool brought more whispers about refereeing decisions. Liverpool had won the FA Cup the weekend before the first leg at Anfield. Roger Hunt gave the English champions a third-minute lead but Peiro squared Facchetti's pass for Mazzola to level. Liverpool regained the lead with a clever free-kick routine, when Ian Callaghan drove Hunt's pass past Sarti. Ian St John made it 3–1 after Sarti parried Hunt's shot.

Liverpool had high hopes of becoming the first English club to reach the European Cup final. But their manager Bill Shankly later claimed he was told by an Italian journalist, 'You'll never be allowed to win.'

Ortiz de Mendibil, the Spanish referee for the second leg, made two decisions that cost Liverpool dear. After eight minutes, he signalled an indirect free kick on the edge of the box. Corso drilled a shot past Liverpool keeper Tommy Lawrence and the referee gave a goal. Two minutes later, he allowed Peiro to kick the ball out of Lawrence's hands and roll it into the net. Facchetti hit a spectacular third after a lengthy run but the referee had already settled the issue.

Benfica, in high-scoring form again, were Inter's opponents in the final at San Siro. They demanded a change of venue, threatening to boycott the game or send their youth team. UEFA insisted. The arrangements had already been made. Switching venues at short notice would be commercially impossible. It was San Siro or nowhere. Benfica, under protest, agreed to play.

Jair scored the only goal in the 42nd minute, on a soaking night and a sodden pitch, when his shot slipped through Costa Pereira's grasp. Costa Pereira later went off injured. Germano took over in goal and Benfica played the last 30 minutes with ten men.

Inter did not try to take advantage. They shut the game up and wasted time. It was a far cry from Benfica v. Madrid in Amsterdam three years earlier. It was also Inter's last European Cup success.

They won the Italian title for the third time in four years in 1965–66 finishing four points ahead of Bologna and totalling 70 goals in 34 games. Mazzola scored 19, Domenghini 12 and Facchetti ten from left-back. Their victories included a 5–2 win over Varese, 4–0 against Torino, 5–0 over Foggia and Sampdoria and 7–0 against Brescia: evidence surely that they could have profited with a more adventurous style.

In the European Cup, Inter eased past Dynamo Bucharest and Ferencvaros. Then Madrid took revenge in the semi-finals. Pirri scored the only goal of the first leg at the Bernabeu. The Hungarian official, Gyorgy Vadas, refereed without favour. Paco Gento laid on a 20th-minute goal for Amancio. Facchetti replied for Inter, 11 minutes from time. Madrid advanced, 2–1 on aggregate, to a final against Partizan Belgrade.

(Madrid won 2–1, with goals by Amancio and Serena, after falling behind to Velibor Vasovic's header.)

Vadas later blew the whistle on Inter. He claimed that Dezso Solti – another Hungarian, and a 'fixer' sometimes employed by the club – had offered him 'enough money, in dollars, to buy five, maybe six Mercedes cars'. He said, 'Basically, I was to referee the game so that Real did not go forward.'

Vadas refused. Years later, he told the Hungarian investigative journalist Peter Borenich, 'I told my linesmen straightaway and we went on the pitch determined to control the game honestly.'

By the spring of 1967, Inter were on course to win both Serie A and the European Cup again. They led the title race and had beaten Real Madrid home and away in the European Cup quarter-finals. They had discovered a new forward talent in Renato Cappellini, who had returned from a loan spell with Genoa. He scored the only goal against Madrid at San Siro and the first when Inter won 2–0 at the Bernabeu.

Mazzola was in top form. He had scored two brilliant goals against the Hungarian champions Vasas in the second round and he would end the Serie A season with 17.

Then Inter collapsed. On 16 April, after their 3–2 win at Venezia, they led Serie A by four points from Juventus. Perhaps the first chink had shown a few days earlier, when CSKA Sofia left San Siro with a 1–1 draw in the European Cup semi-final first leg. The Bulgarians had played the last hour with ten men after Raikov was sent off for fighting. Facchetti scored in first-half stoppage time. Chanev levelled midway through the second half.

Facchetti fired Inter ahead in Sofia, too. Radlev equalised with 12 minutes left. The tie went to a play-off, at Bologna. It was almost a home match for Inter but the financial guarantees were too enticing for CSKA to turn down. Cappellini settled the issue with a 12th-minute goal.

In Serie A, Inter ground to a halt. They were held 0–0 at home by Lazio, then drew 1–1 at Cagliari. They went down 1–0 at Juventus in the top of the table clash. That left them with a two-point lead over Juve. But Mazzola was carrying a knock and tiredness was taking its toll. Inter drew again, 1–1 against Napoli. Juve were held 1–1 at Mantova. Burgnich conceded an own goal in a 1–1 home draw with Fiorentina while Juventus won 1–0 at Lanerossi Vicenza.

Inter still led Juve by a point. Their season remained in their hands. It hinged on two matches – the European Cup final against Celtic in Lisbon and the last game of the Serie A campaign at Mantova.

Suarez was injured and missed the European Cup final. Facchetti said, 'I can't stress enough that his absence was a major blow to us . He was our playmaker and the most vital member of our team.'

The game was seen again as a clash of opposites – Inter's catenaccio against the Scots' rapid attacks. Inter, vastly experienced, started favourites. Mazzola's penalty gave them a sixth-minute lead after Jim Craig fouled Cappellini. This was the time for Inter to retreat and kill the game. But Celtic kept coming. Corso dropped deeper and deeper to reinforce the defence. Left-back Tommy Gemmell's explosive 20-yard shot broke down Inter's resistance. The momentum was with Celtic. Inter, without Suarez, could not respond. Steve Chalmers scored the winner seven minutes from time, diverting Bobby Murdoch's shot past Sarti.

Herrera blamed his central defenders for Celtic's victory. Picchi was sold to promoted Varese in the summer. He said bitterly, 'When things go right, it's always because of Herrera's brilliant planning. When things go wrong, it's always the players who are to blame.' Guarneri went to Bologna.

Another disaster awaited Inter on the last day of the Serie A season. Sarti's blunder at Mantova presented the home side with a 1–0 win. The keeper let a hopeful effort by ex-Inter midfielder Beniamino Di Giacomo slip past him. Inter's archive calls it a 'tragi-comic moment'.

Juventus beat Lazio 2–1 in Turin and pipped Inter to the title by a point. The sports media turned on Herrera, whose ego had made him many enemies.

Inter's bolt was shot. Their confidence was drained and they finished fifth the following season, 13 points behind champions Milan. Herrera left at the end of the campaign. The clothing manufacturer Ivanoe Fraizzoli succeeded Moratti as president. Sarti moved to Juventus. Domenghini went to Cagliari and helped them win the scudetto in 1970. Suarez joined Sampdoria that same year.

Six of Herrera's stars remained when Inter won the title again in 1971 – Burgnich, now a centre-back, Facchetti, Bedin, Corso, Jair and Mazzola. Inter reached the European Cup final the following season, only to be overwhelmed 2–0 by Ajax in Rotterdam. They had lost 7–1 at Monchengladbach in the second round, a result overturned in a committee room (see Chapter 11) after a protest that seemed to typify Inter's campaigns in Europe. They have never played in a European Cup final since.

Inter had great players who could light up the game. They did not need to be negative. Nor did they need to cheat behind the scenes. But their successes will always be tarnished by complaints about their style and suspicion about their circumstances.

CHAPTER 9

RAMSEY'S WINGLESS WONDERS

The afternoon of 30 July 1966 was the pinnacle of England's football history. Skipper Bobby Moore lifted the World Cup after his side had beaten West Germany 4–2 in extra time at Wembley. Midfield hard man Nobby Stiles performed a jig of joy. Manager Alf (later, Sir Alf) Ramsey, who had plotted the victory, allowed himself a smile as he remained seated calmly on the bench.

Ramsey would later be criticised for negative tactics, blamed for two morale-sapping defeats by West Germany and sacked in 1974 after his side failed to reach the World Cup finals. But this was his finest hour. His 4–4–2 system – using Alan Ball and Martin Peters as wide midfield players instead of conventional wingers – had been much questioned. He had been vindicated by the result.

World Cup victory had seemed an unlikely outcome when former England full-back Ramsey succeeded Walter Winterbottom in 1963. Ramsey had made his name with unfashionable Ipswich, guiding a team of journeymen players from the old Third Division South to the League Championship in 1962. Ramsey had built his success on sound defence, shrewd tactics, a relentless work ethic and a pair of dangerous strikers, Ray Crawford and Ted Phillips. Ramsey's Ipswich were more than the sum of their parts. He would bring the same virtues to the national team.

Football was Ramsey's obsession. On away trips, his Ipswich players would take bets on how long they could speak to him before he mentioned football. The record, apparently, was four minutes.

He was a meticulous organiser and a strict disciplinarian. Years later

Ball would speak of the players regarding him with 'a little awe, a little fear'. Geoff Hurst scored a hat trick in the 5–0 win over France in March 1969. 'See you next game,' he said to Ramsey as he left the dressing-room. The England manager replied, 'Perhaps.' Hurst remembered, 'Alf rarely raised his voice but he had a powerful manner.'

Ramsey took the job on one crucial condition: he would be in sole charge of the team. The Football Association reluctantly agreed, sweeping away the selection committee that had picked previous England teams. Then Ramsey made the worst possible start. His experimental line-up was thrashed 5–2 by France in the preliminary round of the 1963–64 European Championship and eliminated 6–3 on aggregate.

Ramsey was naturally cautious. Yet when the former England full-back took over, he forecast, 'We will win the World Cup.' After the defeat in Paris, it sounded a hollow boast. Many in the media were thankful that England gained automatic entry as hosts of the 1966 World Cup finals, so Ramsey's team were spared the rigours of the qualifying competition.

But Ramsey had inherited some fine players from the Winterbottom regime. The skipper, West Ham centre-back Moore, was already one of the most assured defenders in Europe. Ray Wilson, then of Huddersfield, was a solid, composed left-back. Manchester United's Bobby Charlton, later to be deployed so successfully in midfield, was an exciting left-winger. In attack, Tottenham's Jimmy Greaves was a world-class poacher. He scored 44 goals in 57 appearances for England but he would miss out on the greatest day of all.

Ramsey made an important change after the defeat in Paris. He dropped goalkeeper Ron Springett and brought in Leicester's Gordon Banks. Banks would become probably the greatest of all England keepers and make the most famous save in World Cup history.

By the spring of 1965, Ramsey had built solid foundations. When England drew 2–2 with Scotland on 10 April, a soon-to-be-familiar unit made its debut. Banks was in goal. Fulham's George Cohen, one of the first overlapping full-backs, played right-back. Wilson was on the left. Beanpole centre-half Jack Charlton – Bobby's older brother – was outstanding in the Leeds side that finished runners-up in league and FA Cup. He replaced Maurice Norman as Moore's defensive partner.

Jack Charlton won his first cap that day. So did Manchester United's Stiles. United used him as a defender. Ramsey picked him as a defensive midfield player. Stiles was barely 5 ft 6 in. tall. He sported both contact lenses and dentures. But he terrified opponents with his ruthless tackling. A journalist once asked Ramsey, 'How much does Nobby weigh?' The England boss replied, 'About ten tons, I should think.'

England finished their home season with a 1–0 win over Hungary, then raised hopes with three impressive performances on their summer tour – a 1–1 draw in Yugoslavia, a 1–0 win over West Germany and a 2–1 victory against Sweden. Another important figure made his England debut against the Yugoslavs, the young Blackpool midfielder Ball.

Ramsey now had a rock-solid defence. Finding the right balance in attack was another matter. But observers sensed a growing spirit in the squad. The much-respected sportswriter Hugh McIlvanney noted, 'Tactical organisation, especially in defence, has been a huge element in the encouragement provided by these performances. Ramsey has not yet found a final World Cup team but he and his players are rapidly evolving a World Cup ethic.'

Ramsey continued to experiment. He first used Bobby Charlton as midfield playmaker in England's 0–0 draw with Wales in October: a role that Charlton would fill with distinction for the rest of his international career. Liverpool striker Roger Hunt, who had won just six previous caps in more than three years, returned and scored in England's 2–0 win over Spain in December.

Two more members of the World Cup-winning side made their debuts the following spring: Hurst and Peters, the West Ham pair who would score the goals against West Germany.

England went into the World Cup finals buoyed by another impressive summer tour. They beat Finland 3–0, Norway 6–1 (Greaves scored four) Denmark 2–0 and Poland 1–0.

Ramsey had used wingers for much of his time in charge – Southampton's Terry Paine, John Connelly of Burnley, then Manchester United, and, less often, the mercurial Liverpool dribbler Peter Thompson. He began the World Cup campaign, against Uruguay, with Connelly on the left. England stuttered to a 0–0 draw. Uruguay's formidable defence dealt comfortably with England's succession of crosses to the far post.

Paine played in the 2–0 win over Mexico, when Bobby Charlton kick-started England's challenge with a brilliant 35th-minute goal. He picked up the ball on the halfway line, ran 30 yards, then unleashed a stinging shot. He said, 'I started quite deep and at first I had no intention of shooting. I didn't really expect Mexico to let me keep going. So I just banged it at goal.' Hunt scored the second.

Liverpool right-winger Ian Callaghan played in the 2–0 win over France that clinched England's place in the quarter-finals. His Liverpool clubmate Hunt netted both goals. Ramsey was satisfied with none of the wingers. He ditched them entirely for the quarter-final against Argentina. Two midfield players would now start from wide positions – Ball and Peters. Ball had energy to burn while Peters had a knack of popping up unmarked to score crucial goals. Ramsey described him as 'ten years ahead of his time'.

Ramsey made two other important decisions for that game against Argentina. Greaves had suffered a badly gashed leg against the French. Hurst replaced him. Ramsey also successfully resisted pressure from the FA secretary Denis Follows to drop Stiles for his brutal challenge on France's Jacky Simon. Ramsey threatened to resign if he were forced to leave out Stiles. Follows relented. Stiles played.

Stiles said, 'Alf was very loyal to the players and that loyalty was returned. It worked both ways. Because he was loyal to you, you'd go through brick walls for him. Everyone concerned with England was doing it for Alf.'

It was a tough World Cup, a world away from FIFA's crackdown of 2002. The great Pele was hacked mercilessly by the Bulgarians and the Portuguese. He said, 'My legs ached with the constant kicking and tripping.' Brazil were eliminated at the group stage as a result. Uruguay had two players sent off in their 4–0 quarter-final defeat by West Germany.

Argentina said they were worried by the vigour of England's play. They decided to get their retaliation in first. The West German referee, Rudi Kreitlein, whistled for a succession of fouls, each hotly contested by the Argentine captain, Antonio Rattin. In the 36th minute, Rattin contested one decision too many. Kreitlein sent him off.

England struggled to break down Argentina's ten men, until the 77th minute, when Hurst glanced a header past keeper Antonio Roma. A furious Ramsey refused to let the England players swap shirts with their opponents. He described the Argentine team as 'animals'.

England had reached the semi-finals by scoring five goals and conceding none. Eusebio ended that defensive record with an 82nd-minute penalty after Jack Charlton punched a shot from under the bar. But England already led Portugal 2–0 by then. Bobby Charlton gave them the lead when he sidefooted in after Costa Pereira lost the ball under Hunt's challenge. Hurst set up the second with a cross that Charlton crashed home. Eusebio, the top scorer of the tournament, left the pitch in tears.

For the final against West Germany, Ramsey stuck with the team that had beaten Argentina and Portugal, even though Greaves was fit. Greaves was distraught. He was never quite the same player again, though he led the English scorers' list in 1969. He retired in 1971, at the age of 31, and became an alcoholic. He later recovered to become a popular TV pundit. Cohen said, 'We knew that Jimmy had a nasty injury. He could never have played in the match after France. When we changed to 4–4–2, with Roger and Geoff up front, it worked so well that Alf didn't really have a choice. He chose to keep it and we just accepted the fact that Jimmy wasn't there.'

The final minute of the contest, accompanied by the commentary of BBC TV's Kenneth Wolstenholme, has passed into English folklore. England lead 3–2. Moore wins the ball and plays a long pass to Hurst. Wolstenholme exclaims, 'Some people are on the pitch. They think it's all over.' Hurst shoots. The German net bulges. Wolstenholme cries, 'It is now!'

The West German coach, Helmut Schoen, overruled his assistant, Dettmar Cramer, and detailed midfielder Franz Beckenbauer, one of the finds of the tournament, to tight mark Bobby Charlton. Beckenbauer said later, 'England beat us because Bobby Charlton was just a little bit better than me.'

Helmut Haller fired the Germans into a 12th-minute lead after Wilson failed to clear Siggi Held's cross. England levelled six minutes later. Wolfgang Overath tripped Moore, who flighted a perfect free kick for Hurst to head the equaliser. Banks made a double save from Overath and Lothar Emmerich. Peters then shot across goal after keeper Hans Tilkowski collided with Beckenbauer.

England went ahead in the 78th minute. Hurst's shot looped up off Horst Hottges and Peters slammed home the loose ball. Bobby Charlton, Hurst and Peters all shot wide as England tried to finish the job.

The Wembley crowd were already starting their victory roar when referee Gottfried Dienst penalised Jack Charlton for an 89th-minute foul on the edge of the box. Emmerich blasted the free kick at the wall. The ball ricocheted through. The bobble eluded Banks and Wolfgang Weber fired the loose ball into the roof of the net. England claimed Karl-Heinz Schnellinger had handled Emmerich's shot. But the goal stood.

Ramsey raised his deflated players as the teams prepared for extra time. Moore said, 'Alf told us, "You've won it once, now go and do it again."' The England manager pointed to the Germans who were struggling with cramp. He said, 'Look at them. They're flat out. Down on the grass having massages. They can't live with you in extra time.'

England carried the game to the Germans. Bobby Charlton's shot on the turn hit an upright. Peters flashed another effort wide.

The game turned on a linesman's decision in the 101st minute. Ball found Hurst, who swivelled and shot. The ball hit the underside of the bar and bounced down. The England players wheeled away in celebration. Dienst was unsure if the ball had crossed the line. He consulted his Soviet linesman, Tofik Bakhramov. Bakhramov said 'goal'. The England players were jubilant. The Germans surrounded the referee, to no avail.

The goal has been analysed in frequent replays ever since. The suspicion remains that the whole of the ball did not cross the line. But Hurst said, 'Roger Hunt was closest to the ball and he put his hands up immediately. There's never been any doubt in my mind that it was a goal.'

(Bakhramov was from the Soviet republic of Azerbaijan. After Azerbaijan became independent, the national stadium in Baku was named in Bakhramov's honour. A statue of him, outside the stadium, was unveiled before Azerbaijan's World Cup qualifier against England in October 2004. Hurst was one of the guests at the ceremony.)

The Germans were finished and Hurst became the first player to score a hat trick in a World Cup final. He said, 'My father-in-law told my wife that I was going to score three in the final. I just thought that was highly amusing. It was quite quirky really that I managed to do it. It changed my life.' Hurst had become England's leading striker. He had seized his chance and Greaves was out in the cold.

Nowadays, the celebrations would have gone on for days, with trophy parades up and down the land amid a media circus. In 1966, England's victorious squad travelled to a hotel in Kensington for a celebratory meal. Greaves remembered, 'The celebration really was quite low-key. Everyone cheered but only a couple of thousand people went to the hotel.' Three days later, the World Cup was safely stored in the Football Association's keeping and attention turned to the start of the new Football League season. England's greatest achievement had been greeted with a whimper rather than a bang.

Nor was there the furore that might have been expected in West Germany, whose players were greeted as returning heroes. Weber said later, 'Too much has been made of England's third goal. They were worthy champions.' Skipper Uwe Seeler said the tournament had been 'a fantastic experience' for the team, who were simply delighted to have reached the final. Overath agreed that England deserved to win.

Not everyone admired Ramsey's England, though. The *New Statesman* music critic and football fan Hans Keller wrote: 'Next week I'll tell you how England won the World Cup – and what we can do about it.'

Ramsey's critics saw England's success as a victory for solid defence and relentless effort rather than artistry. They had played all their games at Wembley and they had benefitted from crucial refereeing decisions against Argentina and West Germany.

The cult of the hard man, *à la Stiles*, began to take root. Soon, almost every First Division team had one. Leeds fielded several, led by the formidable Norman 'bites-yer-legs' Hunter. Chelsea had Ron 'Chopper' Harris and John Boyle. Liverpool boasted Tommy Smith. Peter Storey played an important part in Arsenal's 1971 double victory. Old-fashioned wingers began to disappear from English football as more and more coaches imitated Sir Alf's 4–4–2 formation.

Yet wingers were a vital ingredient of the teams who won the European Cup in 1967 and 1968: Celtic and Manchester United. And it was a winger, Yugoslavia's Dragan Dzajic, who sank England in the 1968 European Championship semi-finals.

Celtic and Manchester United both used wingers to unlock defences. Celtic's attacking ace was the tiny, flame-haired right-winger Jimmy 'Jinky' Johnstone, a bewildering dribbler who laid on a host of chances for Joe McBride, Willie Wallace and Steve Chalmers. Midfielders Bobby Murdoch and Bertie Auld repeatedly fed Johnstone who would torment the best left-backs in Europe. The high points of Johnstone's effectiveness were his inspirational displays when Celtic beat Leeds home and away in the 1970 European Cup semi-finals. On the left, in a 4–2–4 formation, manager Jock Stein used Bobby Lennox or John Hughes. Both loved to cut inside with an eye for goal.

Celtic famously beat Internazionale 2–1 in the 1967 final to become the first British team to win the European Cup. They reached the 1970 final and the semi-finals in 1972 and 1974 – when Johnstone was cynically kicked out of the first leg by Atletico Madrid, on a night when three Atletico players were red-carded. They also won nine successive Scottish titles.

Another winger, George Best, spearheaded United's effort to become the first English team to win the European Cup. He had announced his arrival at the highest level with two goals in the first 12 minutes when United beat Benfica 5–1 in Lisbon in the 1965–66 quarter-finals. Best was carrying a cartilage injury in the semi-final first leg against Partizan Belgrade and missed the second leg. United were eliminated 2–1 on aggregate.

Best was the outstanding figure in United's 1966–67 championship team, which also featured Bobby Charlton and Denis Law. A year later, he was named European and England's Footballer of the Year when he top-scored for United with 28 goals.

The most important was the match-turning extra-time goal in the European Cup final against Benfica. That gave United a 2–1 lead and demoralised the Portuguese champions. Best waltzed past two defenders, dribbled round keeper Jose Henrique and slid the ball into the empty net. It was the sort of solo goal that England rarely scored.

Belfast-born Best was the first player to 'cross over' from footballer to pop icon and superstar. He found it increasingly hard to shoulder the burden at United after Charlton and Law passed their peak. He effectively retired from senior football when just 26 and his later life was dogged by a battle against alcohol abuse. He died, aged 59, from multiple organ failure in November 2005. But he was the most gifted British player of his generation.

United boss Matt Busby employed another winger, too: John Aston on the left. He gave one of his finest displays in that 4–1 European Cup final rout of Benfica.

Another winger, the veteran Swede Kurt Hamrin, scored both goals in Milan's 2–0 win over Hamburg in the Cup-Winners' Cup final that same season – and played in the European Cup victory over Ajax in 1969. Ajax themselves would dominate European football using two wide players, Sjaak Swart and Piet Keizer. But Sir Alf had set his face against wingers.

England had been fortunate to reach the 1968 European Championship quarter-finals. The British Home Championships of 1966–67 and 1967–68 served as a qualifying group. Scotland became the first team to beat the world champions when they won 3–2 at Wembley in April 1967: a victory orchestrated by Law and the midfield combination of Billy Bremner and Jim Baxter. But Best tore Scotland apart in Belfast and Northern Ireland won 1–0. Scotland had to beat England at Hampden Park to win the group. The biggest crowd in European Championship history – 130,711 – watched England hold out for a 1–1 draw, after Hughes missed a glorious chance from two yards for the Scots.

Bobby Charlton scored the only goal of the quarter-final first leg against Spain at Wembley. In Madrid, Sir Alf played only one striker and brought in Hunter as an extra defensive midfield player. Hunter scored the second goal in England's 2–1 win.

Sir Alf used the same tactics for the semi-final, against Yugoslavia in Florence. Alan Mullery, who had succeeded Stiles, and Hunter both played as midfield ball-winners. Yugoslavia began with a sweeper and had a hard man of their own, Dobrivoje Trivic. He kicked Charlton and Ball in the opening minutes. Hunter kicked Yugoslavia playmaker Ivica Osim in the fifth minute, leaving him a passenger for the rest of the game. Mullery kicked Trivic.

Ball shot over from England's best chance but England had no one to match Dzajic, who took on two or three players at a time. With time running out, Dzajic nipped behind Moore to collect a centre from the left and shot past Banks. Mullery became the first England player ever to be sent off after another kick on Trivic.

Hosts Italy beat Yugoslavia 2–0 in a replayed final. England, now with two strikers, beat the Soviet Union 2–0 in the third-place play-off. UEFA's archive noted: 'England might have crushed Yugolsavia's ten fit men if they had had the firepower.' It concluded, 'Ramsey has only himself to blame. The choice of Hunter was a tactical mistake.'

England automatically qualified for the 1970 World Cup finals in Mexico as holders. The games would be staged in baking heat and many were to be played at high altitude, especially in Mexico City, the venue for the final. The effects on the players – dehydration and breathing difficulties – were obvious when England drew 0–0 there in June 1969. Sir Alf responded by appointing England's first-ever full-time team doctor, Neil Phillips. His job was to discover everything he could to combat the effects of playing in such conditions.

Ramsey oversaw travel arrangements and dietary planning with typical thoroughness. Stiles remembered, 'Alf's preparations for Mexico were incredible. They'd be reckoned obsolete by today's standards, but in those days, they were revolutionary. No stone was left unturned. He even took HP sauce to Mexico. I'll always remember that . . . HP sauce on the tables!'

Many English critics believed the squad was stronger than in 1966. Everton's Keith Newton and Leeds' exciting overlapper Terry Cooper had succeeded Cohen and Wilson. Cultured Everton centre-half Brian Labone had taken over from Jack Charlton. Hunt was gone, but Manchester City's Francis Lee added weight to the attack. His colleague Colin Bell was a prolific scorer from midfield.

Banks was at his peak. So was Moore. He had been England's youngest-ever skipper. He played 108 times for England and captained them on 90 occasions. Sir Alf called him 'my leader and right-hand man, the supreme professional'. Moore offered almost telepathic anticipation – which more than compensated for lack of explosive pace – majestic timing in the tackle and massive composure. He was the organiser of the team.

But England's preparations were thrown into chaos when Moore was arrested after their 4–0 warm-up win over Colombia in Bogota. He was accused of stealing a bracelet from a hotel jewellery shop. (Cynics at home suspected a South American 'plot' to wreck England's World Cup defence.)

Moore was held under house arrest in Bogota while England won their final friendly, 2–0 in Ecuador. He was detained for four days and arraigned at a four-hour court hearing. After the intervention of FA secretary Follows, the England skipper was released to join the squad in Mexico. He was finally cleared weeks after the tournament ended. It was a tribute to Moore that he played so well in England's four matches, never better than when he faced Pele against Brazil.

The snapshot of Moore and Pele swapping shirts at the end remains an enduring image of the tournament. Moore died of cancer, aged just 51, in 1993. Pele said, 'He was the greatest defender I ever played against. His shirt is one of my most prized possessions.'

(Supporters voted Moore the best England player of the past 50 years in an FA poll in 2003.)

Hurst scored the only goal of England's opening win against Romania. Then they faced Brazil at Guadalajara. The Brazilians boasted flamboyant creative attacking talent – Carlos Alberto powering forward from right-back, the livewire Clodoaldo, playmaker Gerson and dead-ball expert Rivelino, behind a front three of Pele, tournament top scorer Jairzinho and Tostao. Jairzinho scored the only goal, on the hour, after Tostao drew the England cover. Ball hit the bar and sub Jeff Astle scuffed a glorious chance wide. But the game will be best remembered for the finest save in World Cup history – Banks's incredible jack-knife to keep out Pele's downward header. Banks said, 'Jairzinho whipped in a cross from the right. I ran from my near post to the centre of the goal as Pele was about to head the ball. He caught it perfectly and headed it down about three yards in front of my goal line. I had to push across goal to get my hand on it and guess how high it would bounce from the ground. When I got there, I lifted it up and it went over the bar.'

Brazil went on to crush Italy 4–1 in the final. Banks said, 'For me, they were the greatest international team ever.' But a bug would sideline Banks and cost England dear.

Allan Clarke scored a decisive penalty in England's 1–0 win over Czechoslovakia, to set up a quarter-final rematch with . . . West Germany.

Two years before, Beckenbauer had scored the only goal of a friendly in Hanover, when the Germans beat England for the first time. That had given them confidence. England had also suffered a bout of food poisoning on their way from Guadalajara to the game in Leon. Bobby Charlton recovered from the bug. Banks did not. So Sir Alf had to call up the reserve keeper, Chelsea's Peter Bonetti.

Yet England played their best football of the tournament and took a deserved 2–0 lead through Mullery and Peters. Beckenbauer was once again detailed to mark Charlton. With 22 minutes left, he gambled on venturing forward and shot. It was a soft effort but it squirmed under Bonetti.

England still looked in control when Sir Alf sent on Bell for Charlton. Now though, Beckenbauer roamed forward, directing the German attacks. Seeler levelled with a back header over the stranded Bonetti 12 minutes from time. The momentum was with the Germans. Sir Alf introduced a defender, Hunter, for Peters, as extra time approached.

Hurst had a goal disallowed but Gerd Muller volleyed home Hannes Lohr's 108th-minute knock down to settle the tie. Banks's absence had been bad luck. The English press pointed fingers at Bonetti, who was playing the biggest match of his career. They also pointed fingers at Ramsey for his substitutions, especially the replacement of Charlton, which freed Beckenbauer from his marking role and handed the initiative to the Germans. Charlton retired from international football after the match.

Beckenbauer felt England had only themselves to blame. He said, 'England dominated the first hour. They could have been more than 2–0 ahead. But they allowed us back into the game. When we pulled one back, the whole team stepped up a gear.' The Germans had used wingers – Reinhard Libuda, later replaced by Jurgen Grabowski – to stretch England's defence.

The West Germans were England's nemesis again in the 1972 European Championship quarter-finals.

England reached the last eight without losing a game, topping a group that also included Switzerland, Greece and Malta. By now, though, critics such as McIlvanney and Brian Glanville were bemoaning the lack of flair in Sir Alf's side. The England boss was reluctant to encourage skilful youngsters like the Chelsea playmaker Alan Hudson. And his mind remained closed to wingers, despite the huge influence of the effervescent George Armstrong in Arsenal's 1971 double season.

An experimental West German side, including Grabowski and Held on the flanks, came to Wembley and ripped England apart 3–1 in the first leg. Late goals by Gunter Netzer (a penalty) and Muller sealed the Germans' victory. They had played adventurous football – led by attacking sweeper Beckenbauer and midfield general Netzer, and capped by Muller's lethal finishing. It was the last of Hurst's 49 England appearances.

Sir Alf picked both Storey and Hunter for the return in West Berlin, a brutal 0–0 draw which gave his critics more ammunition.

McIlvanney, a Scot, had become increasingly vocal in his opposition to Ramsey. He had come to loathe both the England coach's preference for industry over flair and the dour efficiency that had become the team's trademark. He wrote: 'Cautious, joyless football was scarcely bearable when it was bringing victories. When it brings defeat, there can only be one reaction.'

Now the writing was on the wall for Sir Alf. In June 1973, England lost a World Cup qualifier 2–0 to Olympic champions Poland in Chorzow. Robert Gadocha scored after seven minutes. Wlodzimierz

Lubanski robbed Moore to score the second. It was Moore's last competitive appearance for England. Ball became the second player in England history to be sent off, after a skirmish with home midfielder Leslaw Cmikiewicz.

Poland's 2–0 victory over Wales set up a grand finale at Wembley. Sir Alf's team had to beat the Poles to reach the 1974 finals in West Germany. They warmed up with a 7–0 rout of Austria. Sir Alf picked the same line-up. England flung everything at the Poles but their goalkeeper, Jan Tomaszewski, played the game of his life. The Polish defence was heroic. England did everything but score. Then in the 55th minute, Grzegorz Lato slipped Hunter in a breakaway and crossed for Jan Domarski to shoot under the diving Peter Shilton. (Banks was forced to retire after losing an eye in a car crash in 1972.)

Clarke levelled from a penalty eight minutes later. Substitute Kevin Hector came within inches of snatching a last-gasp winner but the Poles survived and advanced. Sir Alf did not. He was officially sacked on 1 May 1974.

Ramsey said, 'It was the most devastating half-hour of my life. I stood in a room full of staring committee men. It was like I was on trial. I thought I was going to be hanged.'

His teams had won 69 and lost only 17 of 113 matches. He had brought England glory by employing those same virtues of organisation and discipline that delivered success for Ipswich. But his teams rarely stirred the pulse, unlike the 1970 Brazilians or the 1972 West Germans. If Beckenbauer's legacy was to define the role of attacking sweeper, then Sir Alf's was a reinforced midfield and 4–4–2: the system that became the staple English club formation.

Sir Alf's instincts erred on the side of caution. Like Helenio Herrera at Inter, his success had come through emphasising defence and solidity. Hard work mattered to him more than inspiration. As a popular phrase of the early '70s suggested, 'He distrusted skill unless it came dripping in sweat.' When that sweat failed to bring results, it was time for him to go. His greatest day had come nearly eight years earlier.

CHAPTER 10

CRUYFF, AJAX AND HOLLAND

It was approaching midnight in Belgrade on 30 May 1973. Ajax's empire had reached the height of its power after a third successive European Cup final win. Its king, Johan Cruyff, ruled supreme. Yet, like all empires, the Ajax imperium was at its most vulnerable when it seemed impregnable. Within a few months, Ajax had lost their European crown, their king had been deposed and their heroes prepared to scatter all over Europe. It was the end of a story that had begun in January 1965, when Ajax were at their lowest point.

The club from the east side of Amsterdam were a power in decline in Holland, then regarded among Europe's weaker footballing nations. They were facing relegation and they had just fired their English coach Vic Buckingham.

Ajax had built secure foundations though. In the 1920s, another Englishman, Jack Reynolds, had started the youth system that would produce so many fine players. Reynolds emphasised technique, quick accurate passing and attacking with width: qualities that would define the great Ajax side of the early 1970s.

Buckingham had been hugely impressed by Ajax's youth set-up. He remembered the 20 pitches around the stadium, with 14 or 15 youth matches going on every week. He remembered how good some of those 'kids' were.

One of those kids was extra special: Cruyff. The club had given his widowed mother a cleaning job to help the family survive. His uncle Henk was the groundsman at Ajax's De Meer home. Cruyff recalled, 'When I made my first-team debut, I already had a whole football life behind me at De Meer. I'd been running around there for ten years. I arrived when I was six and became a member of Ajax at ten.'

The young Cruyff was a skilful, fast right-footed attacker. Ajax youth coach Jany van der Veen saw his potential – and his weaknesses. He lacked body strength and he needed to develop his left foot.

Cruyff practised and practised on his left, so he was comfortable passing or shooting with either foot. Van der Veen devised weight exercises to strengthen his lower body muscles, making him lie on his back and lift his feet with weights around the ankles. Buckingham said, 'Cruyff showed us how to play. He was so skinny but he had immense stamina. He could do everything, right foot, left foot, anything – and such speed. He was God's gift to mankind in the football sense.'

The adult Cruyff went on to win the European Cup three times with Ajax, score 33 goals in 48 appearances for Holland and captain his country in 33 games. He was three times voted European Footballer of the Year. He was the catalyst for Ajax's rise and the man who galvanised the Holland team after years of underachievement. As the Dutch writers Frits Barend and Henk van Dorp stress in *Ajax, Barcelona, Cruyff: The ABC of an Obstinate Maestro*, 'Cruyff woke Holland up and took us to a world-class level. Holland was at the level of an amateur football nation when Cruyff began his career. This thin, fragile-looking Cruyff dragged Dutch football along in his wake.'

Cruyff is the world's best-known living Dutchman and his significance as a cultural icon has been endlessly debated in his homeland. He has even been characterised as the leading symbol of social change, from the staid, conservative Holland of the 1950s to the liberal, hippyish nation of the late 1960s and early 1970s.

He had little formal education, yet he became fluent in several languages and rose to reach almost prophet-like status in Holland and in his 'second home' Barcelona.

He has exercised a massive influence on the game throughout Europe: first as a player, then as a coach. At Ajax, he developed two of the greats of Holland's 1988 European Championship side – Marco van Basten and Frank Rijkaard, both of whom went on to star for Milan. He also encouraged a promising youngster called Dennis Bergkamp. Then he built Barcelona's dream team, which won four consecutive championships, and led them to the only European Cup success in their history.

He was a man of strong convictions, who often fell out with club presidents – Ton Harmsen at Ajax and Josep Lluis Nunez at Barcelona. Some considered him arrogant. He was never one for false modesty. He said things like, 'I don't think there'll come a day when you say "Cruyff" and people won't know what you're talking about.' And, 'Before I make a mistake, I don't make that mistake.'

He certainly knew the value of his own ability, and his representative – his father-in-law Cor Coster – negotiated vigorously on his behalf. Yet Cruyff also believed in football with style and imagination. He said, 'The game should be played beautifully. It should be a spectacle. I had my reward because I played in a thrilling team.'

Buckingham gave Cruyff his senior debut at 17. Buckingham's successor, Rinus Michels, picked Cruyff for his first match in charge. Ajax beat MVV Maastricht 9–3 and collected enough points in their next 11 games to avoid relegation.

Michels, who died in March 2005, was another key figure in Ajax's rise to greatness. He had played for Ajax in the closing days of Reynolds' regime in the late 1940s. He was regarded as one of the easygoing members of the team. He was the opposite as coach. A tough disciplinarian with an obsessive eye for detail, his nickname was 'the General'.

Michels' assistant was his old Ajax colleague Bobby Haarms. He said, 'I remember thinking that he [Michels] had changed. The main thing with him now was discipline.'

In his book *Brilliant Orange*, David Winner quotes centre-back Barry Hulshoff: 'Michels was tough. He used to say, "When you come to the ground, you're a footballer with a number. When you leave, you're a person and I can talk to you. When you're in the ground, I'll judge you only by your football ability."

'It was a learning process. Later we learned to criticise each other, too. Later on, we talked very openly. For instance, everyone knew that Cruyff couldn't defend and I was weak in other areas. And we could say these things to each other.'

Not all the players were comfortable with Michels' approach. Soccernet's Holland correspondent Ernst Bouwes recalled, 'Piet Keizer could not cope with this coldness and hardly talked to his coach for several years. It's said that he danced on the table at the news of Michels' departure to Barcelona in 1971.'

Michels' approach to training was also revolutionary. At a time when many coaches prepared their teams with cross-country runs, the Ajax squad built stamina with a week-long pre-season slog, then their coach concentrated on technical ability, working always with the ball. Michels also ensured that physiotherapist Salo Muller was given modern facilities and his own room where he could talk to the players in private. The coach regularly consulted the physio about the players' fitness and mental state.

Most important, Michels made Ajax a full-time professional club. Until the mid-1960s, even top Dutch players had day jobs. Michels saw that Ajax could never compete with Europe's best while they were part-timers. He persuaded the board to guarantee the players' wages, so they became full-time pros. He realised the motivational advantages too. Once players saw they could make a good living from football, they would work extra hard to ensure they never returned to their humdrum jobs.

Michels brought in new players, tightened the defence and gave Cruyff his head. The 19 year old inspired Ajax to the championship in 1966, supported by experienced right-winger Sjaak Swart and gifted left-winger Keizer.

Cruyff made his Holland debut against Hungary – who had beaten Brazil in the 1966 World Cup finals – on 7 September 1966. Holland fielded the Ajax front four – Swart, Cruyff, Klaas Nuninga and Keizer. Cruyff scored in a 2–2 draw. In his next international, against Czechoslovakia in Amsterdam, Cruyff was sent off by East German referee Rudi Glockner for retaliating after a bad tackle. Angry fans invaded the pitch, which led to the installation of barbed wire fencing around the Olympic Stadium.

Glockner made things even worse when he said that Cruyff had been dismissed for attempting to strike him. TV replays showed that Cruyff was standing nowhere near Glockner but the Dutch federation (KNVB) suspended him from internationals for a year. Two days after his ban, he responded by masterminding a 5–0 demolition of Ajax's arch rivals Feyenoord.

Cruyff and Ajax made Europe sit up and take notice a few weeks later. On a foggy night in the Olympic Stadium, they thrashed the English champions Liverpool 5–1 in the European Cup second round. The Liverpool manager, Bill Shankly, then accused Ajax of being a 'defensive side' and promised that his team would overwhelm them in the second leg at Anfield.

Instead, Cruyff netted twice in a 2–2 draw. Keizer played a part in both goals. Ajax led 2–1 until the 85th minute when Roger Hunt scored Liverpool's equaliser. Michels believed Ajax had announced their arrival in European football. He said, 'It was a moment for us to be recognised internationally. The result in the first game could have been an accident. But drawing at Liverpool was proof that we could compete at international level.'

Ajax went out in the quarter-finals. They drew 1–1 at home to the Czech army side Dukla, then lost 2–1 in Prague after leading through Swart. Centre-back Frits Soetekouw conceded an own goal for Dukla's winner. Michels would later ruthlessly cast Soetekouw aside, along with other '60s stars such as Nuninga and Ruud Suurendonk.

Ajax won three successive Dutch titles between 1966 and 1968, but Michels knew he had to strengthen if they were to beat the best in Europe. He made a vital signing when he brought in Yugoslav centre-back Velibor Vasovic, the Partizan Belgrade skipper in the 1966 European Cup final. Vasovic became the team's defensive strongman and the voice of experience in the dressing-room. Wim Suurbier, another graduate from the Ajax youth ranks, established himself at right-back.

In 1967–68, Ajax went out to Real Madrid in the first round, 3–2 on aggregate, after losing 2–1 at the Bernabeu. The following season, they reached the final for the first time – and discovered how much further they had to travel.

They knocked out Nurnberg and Fenerbahce, then crashed 3–1 at home to Benfica. Dutch TV did not bother to screen the second leg in Lisbon. They missed a great comeback. Ajax won 3–1 and forced a play-off in Paris. They won 3–0. In the semi-finals, they took a 3–0 home advantage over Czechoslovak champions Spartak Trnava and edged through on a 3–2 aggregate.

The final, against Milan in Madrid, was built up as a clash between Ajax's youthful attacking flair and the Italian side's canny experience. Cruyff, the talisman, played though not fully fit. He said later, 'I always played in important games, even though I was sometimes injured. I had too many pain-killing injections in my career.'

Milan caught the Dutch side cold with a sixth-minute goal by Pierino Prati, who added a second just before half-time. Vasovic replied with a penalty before Angelo Sormani restored Milan's two-goal margin and Prati completed his hat trick.

The 4–1 scoreline did not flatter Milan. Hulshoff said, 'They say that sometimes you have to lose a final to win a final and it's true. Milan overwhelmed us. They were better than us in every way.'

Ajax had lost their Dutch title to Feyenoord, too. It was time for Michels to overhaul the squad. The next 18 months saw change after change. Out went Nuninga, to be replaced by left-side midfielder Gerrie Muhren from Volendam. Another youth-team graduate, Ruud Krol, displaced left-back Theo van Duivenbode, who joined Feyenoord. Michels rebuilt the midfield with, first, Nico Rijnders partnering Muhren. Then Arie Haan came through the ranks. Heinz Stuy took over from Gert Bals in goal.

Michels made probably his best-ever signing, when he plucked a teenage midfielder, Johan Neeskens, from struggling RCH Heemstede. Neeskens would be Cruyff's lieutenant for club and country.

Michels tinkered with Ajax's formation, too. They had usually played 4–2–4. A 3–3 draw against Feyenoord, who had overloaded the Ajax midfield, prompted him to experiment with 4–3–3. There was one constant, though: Cruyff was always the focal point of the side.

Ajax won back their Dutch crown in 1970. But they lost to Arsenal in the Fairs (now UEFA) Cup semi-finals. And Feyenoord, with van Duivenbode at left-back, became the first Dutch team to win the European Cup.

Feyenoord's 2–1 victory over Celtic in Milan was the high point of their history. They were coached by the charismatic and tactically shrewd Austrian, Ernst Happel, who later led Holland to the 1978 World Cup final. Rinus Israel was a formidable sweeper. Left-footed Wim van Hanegem was their midfield general, supported by the tireless Wim Jansen and the Austrian, Franz Hasil. Swedish striker Ove Kindvall supplied their cutting edge.

They knocked out KR Reykjavik, Milan, Vorwarts of East Germany and Legia Warsaw to reach the final.

Celtic, who had beaten English champions Leeds in the semi-finals, started favourites. They took a 29th-minute lead through Tommy Gemmell. Israel headed in Hasil's free kick three minutes later to level.

Feyenoord dominated the rest of the game. Celtic's star winger Jimmy Johnstone was off form and manager Jock Stein had gambled on a 4–2–4 formation. Happel outfoxed him by playing an extra man in midfield and using Israel in support when Feyenoord had possession.

Hasil hit the woodwork twice before Kindvall scored the winner four minutes from the end of extra time.

Feyenoord had achieved the greatest feat yet in the annals of Dutch football. But they would soon be eclipsed by Ajax. Vasovic said, 'When we got Krol, Muhren and Neeskens in the team and Stuy in goal, we improved our quality. Cruyff was the best player but he couldn't do it all himself. Now he had support from both the defence and the attack.'

A few months later, Feyenoord were eliminated on away goals by the unfancied Romanians, UT Arad, while Ajax began their European Cup campaign with a 4–2 aggregate win over Nendori Tirana. Suurbier scored both goals in the 2–2 first leg draw in Albania when Cruyff was out with a groin injury.

Suurbier's strikes emphasised the effectiveness of the game Ajax had started to play: the fluid, position-switching style that came to be known as Total Football, attacking opponents from all angles.

In the second round, they beat Basle 3–0 in Amsterdam, when Keizer was outstanding. Cruyff returned with a flourish for their 2–1 win in Switzerland. He scored six goals in a league match against Alkmaar a few weeks later.

In the quarter-finals, Cruyff destroyed Celtic at the Olympic Stadium. He opened the score from Neeskens' flick and escaped his marker, Scotland midfielder David Hay, to set up a series of chances. Hulshoff netted the second from a free kick. Keizer made it 3–0 after a mazy dribble by Cruyff.

Another of Michels' clever signings made his European debut in that tie: Horst Blankenburg, the long-term replacement for Vasovic, signed from Munich 1860, then in Germany's Regionalliga Sud.

Ajax lost 1–0 at Celtic Park and advanced to meet Atletico Madrid in the semi-finals. They trailed 1–0 from the first leg. Keizer wiped out the deficit but Ajax had to wait until the 76th minute before Suurbier shot them ahead on aggregate. Neeskens burst forward to hit the third and take Ajax to the final at Wembley.

Their opponents were Panathinaikos, coached by Ferenc Puskas. They had knocked out English champions Everton on away goals, then, in the semi-final, beat Red Star Belgrade 3–0 in Athens after losing 4–1 in Yugoslavia.

Ajax coasted to victory. They scored in the fifth minute when Dick van Dijk headed in Keizer's cross. The Panathinaikos keeper, Economopoulos, denied Cruyff a hat trick. The Dutch side eased up in the second half. Substitute Haan collected Cruyff's pass to score their second with a deflected shot.

Vasovic lifted the European Cup. Cruyff was later named European Footballer of the Year. Michels, the man who built the team, left to make his fortune at Barcelona.

Total Football had proved a resounding success. Yet, even now the Ajax players cannot agree on who invented it – or whether it simply happened because of the players' familiarity with each other. It is a topic that Winner debates at length in *Brilliant Orange*.

Michels was obviously the prompter, urging his players to attack from all angles to break down the massed defences they faced most weeks. He said, 'I tried to introduce some ideas that would surprise our opponents.' Vasovic said, 'Michels was the architect.' Krol agreed, 'Michels invented the system. He refined it year after year until he had the perfect team and the perfect style.'

Cruyff was obviously an influence, too. He always advocated that defenders, midfielders and attackers should play close together. Haarms said, 'Cruyff was a big influence, especially as he grew older and talked more about tactics with the other players. But Michels was the man who pulled the system together.'

Hulshoff took another view: 'Sometimes we just did things automatically. It came from playing together for a while. Then a lot of other people made theories about it.' Swart supports him. He said, 'When I saw Suurbier going forward, I knew I had to step back. And after two years together, everyone knew what to do.'

Michels' successor, the Romanian coach Stefan Kovacs, loosened the reins. Michels had given orders; Kovacs consulted the players, especially Cruyff and Keizer. At the end of the 1971–72 season, Ajax were crowned champions of Europe and champions of Holland. Cruyff said, 'The results show that Kovacs has not been wrong. Our team was ready to take part in making decisions.'

Blankenburg succeeded Vasovic as sweeper. Young forward Johnny Rep challenged Swart for a place on the right. Ajax played 4–3–3 now, with Haan, Neeskens and Muhren in midfield. They opened their European Cup defence with a 2–0 aggregate win over Dynamo Dresden, followed by a 2–1 win in Marseilles and a 4–1 triumph in Amsterdam. Cruyff scored in both legs.

They met English double holders Arsenal in the quarter-finals. The Gunners even went ahead in Amsterdam when Ray Kennedy seized on a weak Keizer back pass. Ajax levelled when Muhren's deflected shot beat keeper Bob Wilson and won with a debatable penalty, tucked away by Muhren after van Dijk went down.

The tie was settled in the first few minutes at Highbury. Blankenburg's mistake let in Peter Marinello but Stuy made a fine save. Then George Graham looped an attempted back header over Wilson to give Ajax a 3–1 aggregate lead.

Swart headed the only goal of the semi-final first leg against Benfica in Amsterdam. Benfica had knocked out Dutch champions Feyenoord after beating them 5–1 in Lisbon. Ajax mounted a successful rearguard action to draw 0–0 and reach the final again.

They met Internazionale at the Feyenoord Stadium in Rotterdam. Inter were fortunate to be in the competition, let alone the final. Their 7–1 defeat at Monchengladbach (see Chapter 11) had been annulled because of a can thrown from the crowd and they had edged through the semi-final only on penalties after two 0–0 draws against Celtic.

Krol hit an upright early on. Cruyff scored the first goal, knocking in the loose ball after Inter keeper Bordon and defender Oriali collided. He also netted the second with a jackknife header. Three saves by Bordon kept the margin down. Ajax's Total Football had overwhelmed Inter's defensive tactics.

Kovacs, it seemed, had led Ajax to even greater heights than Michels. But Muhren believes that Kovacs's relaxed approach sowed the seeds for the team's break-up.

He told Winner, 'Kovacs was a good coach but he was too nice. Michels was more professional. He was very strict, with everyone on the same level. In the first year with Kovacs, we played even better because we were good players who had been given freedom. But after that, the discipline went and it was all over. We didn't have the same spirit. We could have been champions of Europe for years if we'd stayed together.'

Even so, Ajax eased into the 1973 quarter-finals with two wins over CSKA Sofia, then gave one of their finest European displays, against Bayern Munich. Cruyff was inspirational, totally overshadowing Bayern's Franz Beckenbauer. Haan scored twice, Muhren added a third and Cruyff made it 4–0. Cruyff missed the return with an injured knee but Keizer's early goal put the tie beyond Bayern's reach.

Two defenders, Hulshoff and Krol, scored as Ajax beat Real Madrid 2–1 in the semi-final first leg. Muhren struck for Ajax's winner at the Bernabeu.

Rep headed the only goal of another disappointing final, against Juventus in Athens, after four minutes. The Dutch fans could not understand why Juventus stuck to their negative tactics after they fell behind. Cruyff pulled the strings again. It was his last great night for Ajax.

Cruyff had been linked several times with a move to Barcelona, to rejoin Michels. Other Spanish and Portuguese clubs were interested, too. In December 1970, a Dutch paper claimed that Cruyff had agreed to join Benfica. He remained with Ajax only after lengthy contract negotiations in the summer of 1971, when he signed a seven-year contract. Instead, in August 1973, he left Ajax for Barcelona.

The catalyst was the election of a team captain. Keizer had been skipper when Ajax won the European Cup in 1972. Cruyff took over the following season. Georg Knobel, who succeeded Kovacs after the third European Cup final victory, decided to hold a pre-season election. He thought he was simply continuing a club tradition. Muhren disagreed. He claimed that the players had only ever held one election in his nine years with Ajax. He said, 'It was a decision for the coach to make.' The candidates were Keizer, Hulshoff and Cruyff. Keizer won.

Jan Mulder, who had joined Ajax from Anderlecht that summer, said, 'I saw the look on Cruyff's face. He didn't know it was coming. It was like a coup. His confidence in the other players was shattered. He was furious. It was over for him in that moment.'

Both Knobel and Muhren believed other players were jealous of Cruyff's fame and influence. Knobel felt that the other players resented him – and some thought they were as good as him.

Hulshoff said that Cruyff was still the undoubted star and leader of the team on the pitch. But he added, 'Off the field, in dealing with the board, Keizer thought more about the team.'

Cruyff played his last match for Ajax against FC Amsterdam on 19 August, then joined Barcelona two weeks later.

CSKA Sofia eliminated Ajax in the second round of the European Cup. Knobel was sacked at the end of the season after publicly falling out with the players.

Neeskens followed Cruyff to the Nou Camp that summer. Keizer summarily quit the game a few months later after a row with Knobel's successor Hans Kraay. Haan went to Anderlecht, Blankenburg returned to Germany, Rep joined Valencia, Muhren signed for Sevilla, Hulshoff and Suurbier left in 1977. Only Krol stayed.

Ajax had to wait until the emergence of a team of young Dutch stars in the early 1990s – under another disciplinarian coach, Louis van Gaal – before they became a force in the European Cup again.

Mulder believes the great Ajax team would have broken up anyway. Ajax were not a rich club, despite their European triumphs. They played many league games at De Meer in front of 15–20,000 spectators. Their stars welcomed the prospect of bigger contracts abroad. He said, 'The team fell apart. It was just natural. Some of them wanted to earn as much as Cruyff did.'

Barend and van Dorp asked Cruyff why it all went wrong at Ajax. He replied, 'There's so much behind that. I'd have to open a whole world. Losing the captaincy was the last straw. The other players said that they didn't like it that I was changing my lifestyle and isolating myself. But it wasn't like that. They started to live differently, too.'

Less than a year later, Cruyff would inspire his old Ajax colleagues and their rivals from Feyenoord to propel Holland to the 1974 World Cup final. He said, 'When I left, there were problems that, looking back, could have been solved. The World Cup proved that. But at that moment, I just couldn't stay.'

Holland had not played in the World Cup finals since 1938. They had lost out to Bulgaria for a place in the 1970 finals in Mexico, despite all the talent available at Ajax and Feyenoord.

In 1974, they were fortunate to qualify. They had been reprieved by Russian referee Pavel Kazakov's whistle in the dying minutes of their final qualifier, against Belgium. The Dutch finished ahead of Belgium on goal difference after beating Norway 9–0 in Rotterdam and trouncing Iceland 5–0 and 8–1. They also won 2–1 in Oslo thanks to an 87th-minute goal from Hulshoff.

They had drawn 0–0 with Belgium in Antwerp and needed only a draw in Amsterdam to go through. The game was goalless when Belgium skipper Paul van Himst deceived Dutch keeper Piet Schrijvers with a free kick. Jan Verheyen tapped the ball in. Kazakov blew for offside, though TV replays showed Verheyen had been onside when van Himst took the kick.

Michels took over from Frantisek Fadrhonc, who had coached the team in the qualifiers. Fadrhonc became his assistant. Hulshoff and the Den Haag stopper Aad Mansveld missed the finals through injury. They would be important losses. Regular keeper Jan van Beveren was also injured. Michels' surprise first choice was FC Amsterdam's Jan

Jongbloed, who had expected to be the third goalkeeper. Jongbloed became famous for his dashes outside the penalty area to 'sweep up' behind his makeshift centre-backs.

The squad included Suurbier, Krol, Neeskens, Haan, Rep and Keizer, plus Israel, van Hanegem, Jansen, Theo de Jong, and Wim Rijsbergen from Feyenoord, who had won the Dutch championship and the UEFA Cup. Muhren did not join the squad because of a family illness. Feyenoord sweeper Israel missed the opening game against Uruguay because of his father's death.

Michels switched Haan from midfield to sweeper and brought in 22-year-old Rijsbergen to form the centre-back pairing against Uruguay. He stuck with them through the tournament, even when Israel was available. He also snubbed 34-year-old Keizer in favour of Anderlecht left-winger Rob Rensenbrink.

The Holland players had begun the tournament in dispute with the KNVB over payments, a forerunner of the rows within the camp that have become a staple drama at major finals. Van Hanegem said later, 'We've come to think there's a problem if we don't have a problem.'

The row hardly affected the team on the pitch. Cruyff ran the show and Rep scored both goals in a 2–0 opening win over the ruthless Uruguayans who had Montero-Castillo sent off. Sweden held the Dutch to a 0–0 draw in a game always remembered for Cruyff's famous turn past defender Jan Olsson. Cruyff seemed to twist his body back to front, almost defying his own bone structure, to glide away from the Swede before crossing with the outside of his right foot. Olsson said, 'I thought I had him for sure but he tricked me. But it was still the proudest memory of my 18-year career. I was not humiliated. I had no chance. Cruyff was a genius.'

Cruyff was at his peak. The *Sunday Times*' commentator Brian Glanville wrote: 'He was a greyhound. How quickly he sized up and exploited situations. He could drop deep, beat opponents with ease and serve his teammates with delectable passes.' The Groningen defender Piet Fransen spoke for opponents down the years when he said, 'Cruyff beats you every time though he doesn't seem to mean to do it. Before you can see what he's going to do, he's gone past you.'

Holland went up a gear to beat Bulgaria 4–1. Neeskens scored two first-half penalties. Rep and De Jong netted in the second half. Even Bulgaria's reply was an own goal by Krol.

The Dutch exploded in the first game of the second phase, thrashing

Argentina 4–0. Cruyff, who scored twice, pulled the Argentine defence apart. Krol scored the second goal and Rep flung himself to head the third. Neeskens rampaged from box to box and Rensenbrink scored the goals that beat East Germany.

Their last game, against Brazil, was effectively a semi-final. The Brazilians, now without Pele, Tostao and Gerson, were a shadow of their great World Cup-winning side of 1970. They were also very tough. So were the Dutch. Holland needed only a draw to reach the final on goal difference. They won 2–0 anyway. Neeskens volleyed a brilliant first goal from Cruyff's measured chip. Cruyff finished off Krol's cross for the second and Luis Pereira was sent off for chopping down Neeskens.

Krol said, 'That game had everything. It was football played at its very limits.' The world enthused about Holland's quality. Michels, the instigator of Total Football at Ajax, had transferred the concept to the national team.

The Dutch started favourites against West Germany, who had only come alive in the closing stages of the tournament. The chauffeur to Holland's Prince Bernhard summed up the result, 'The best team didn't win.'

The day before the final, the German tabloid *Bild* claimed that four Dutch players and four German girls had taken part in a 'naked party' in the swimming pool at the team's hotel before the win over Brazil. A furious Michels accused the German media of trying to stir up trouble in the Dutch camp. Danny Cruyff allegedly called her husband and kept him up for much of the night before the final to discuss the story.

The Dutch never found the skill or the fire they had shown against Brazil – despite taking the lead without a German touching the ball. Cruyff burst into the box after a move of 14 passes. Uli Hoeness tripped him. Neeskens dispatched the penalty. Beckenbauer, the German skipper, said to English referee Jack Taylor, 'You are an Englishman.' (A reference to two world wars and the 1966 World Cup final, and, perhaps, a hint to the referee in case a German went down in the box.)

The Germans feared the Dutch would hammer them. Full-back Paul Breitner wondered why they did not press home their advantage. He said, 'They could have dominated us.'

Rep said, 'We wanted to make fun of the Germans. We didn't consciously think about it but we did it. We kept passing the ball around and passing the ball around. We forgot to score the second goal.'

Cruyff, voted the Player of the Tournament, played deeper than usual. He rarely escaped the attention of 'Guard Dog' Berti Vogts. He lamented, 'Vogts is the type you think you beat on either side and make him do what you want. But when you go past him and turn around to see what to do next, there he is again.'

Rensenbrink, who had passed a fitness test on the morning of the final, was struggling. He was replaced by Rene van der Kerkhof at half-time. Haan was not fully fit. Rijsbergen had to limp off in the second half.

The Germans made the Dutch pay for not exploiting their advantage. In the 25th minute, Bernd Holzenbein went down under Jansen's challenge. Taylor pointed to the penalty spot. Breitner levelled. Two minutes before the break, Rainer Bonhof centred. Somehow Gerd Muller met the ball, spun back and rolled a low shot past Jongbloed.

Holland were fired up for the second half. Cruyff moved forward. Breitner cleared after Maier fumbled a corner. The keeper held van Hanegem's header. Neeskens shot into the side netting. Van der Kerkhof screwed wide from Cruyff's pass. Rep hit a post. Neeskens shot wide in Holland's last attack. The Germans should have had a third goal, though. TV replays proved that Muller's offside goal was good.

The two Germans who had done most to ensure victory had no place in Total Football, where defenders became attackers and attackers covered for them seamlessly. Vogts was a man marker of massive intensity. Muller hardly played outside the box, yet he scored 68 goals in 62 games for West Germany.

For the Dutch, it was a case of: what if? What if they had pressed for another goal while the Germans were rocking? What if Hulshoff had been fit for the competition? What if Israel had played at the back instead of Haan?

The Dutch public greeted the result as a huge anticlimax. Once more, as in 1954, the West Germans had beaten a technically superior side in a World Cup final.

'What if?' has become a mantra for Holland sides ever since. What if the dressing-room had not been so divided for the 1976 European Championship semi-final against Czechoslovakia, when the Dutch lost 3–1 in extra time? What if Rensenbrink's shot had been a few inches more accurate with the score 1–1 in the 1978 World Cup final against Argentina? What if Cruyff had played in that competition?

'What if?' has become combined with a sense of wasted opportunity.

Losing unexpectedly to Denmark on penalties in the 1992 European Championship semi-finals; losing the penalty lottery to Brazil for a place in the 1998 World Cup final; losing the shootout again to ten-man Italy in the semi-finals of Euro 2000. What about the racial tension in the dressing-room that caused Holland's downfall at Euro 96? Or their failure to qualify for the 2002 World Cup finals after losing 1–0 to the ten-man Republic of Ireland? Or the dissent in the camp at Euro 2004?

Only in 1988, when they won the European Championships in West Germany – with Michels imposing discipline as coach – have Holland fulfilled their potential. Yet such complaints are complaints about a team that is always expected to beat the best: recognition of how high Johan Cruyff raised the expectations of Dutch football.

POSTSCRIPT

Cruyff never achieved European Cup glory as a Barcelona player. Their best run with Cruyff in the team came in 1975, when they lost to Leeds in the semi-finals.

He played on for Holland in the 1976 European Championship finals and the World Cup qualifying competition. He retired from international football in 1977 and refused to go to Argentina for the 1978 World Cup. He cited injuries, stress and a reluctance to be away from his young family.

Neeskens, Haan and Krol were stars of the Holland side which lost the World Cup final in extra time to Argentina. Haan scored a memorable long-range goal against Italy which took them to the final.

In 1988, Holland, with Michels as coach, won their only major international trophy, the European Championship. A team including Ruud Gullit, van Basten, Rijkaard and Ronald Koeman beat hosts West Germany 2–1 in the semi-finals and the Soviet Union 2–0 in the final.

CHAPTER 11

BAYERN, GLADBACH AND WEST GERMANY

German fans of a certain vintage regard the years between 1970 and 1976 as a golden age. It was shaped by a mighty force: Bayern Munich. Bayern filled the vacuum left by Ajax's decline after the departure of Johan Cruyff. They were the first West German club to win the European Cup when they beat Atletico Madrid in the 1974 final replay. They emulated the Dutch side by winning the trophy three years in a row. At home, their rivalry with Borussia Monchengladbach split West German society – and the fusion of the two clubs' stars was the cornerstone of West Germany's European Championship and World Cup victories.

Three of those Bayern greats have become legends of German football. Franz Beckenbauer was the imperious midfielder who dropped back to create the role of attacking sweeper, while skippering club and country to glory. Sepp Maier, the goalkeeper with the outsize gloves, was a brilliant shot stopper and cross catcher who dominated his box for more than a decade until a car accident ended his career in 1979. Gerd Muller was simply the most lethal European finisher of the modern era. A supporting cast of quality and strength backed them – winger Uli Hoeness, raiding left-back Paul Breitner, towering centre-back Georg Schwarzenbeck and midfielder Franz Roth, who scored so often in major finals.

Bayern were reaching their peak when Cruyff's move to Barcelona in 1973 signalled the break-up of Ajax's great side. They were the Dutch club's natural successors.

Ajax had beaten their German challengers in the European Cup quarter-finals earlier that year. Cruyff bestrode the first leg in Amsterdam and Ajax won 4–0. Maier reckoned it was his worst game for Bayern. Muller was not fully fit.

The following season, CSKA Sofia eliminated a Cruyff-less Ajax in the second round. The European road was open for Bayern, though they stumbled on the way.

They needed penalties to knock out the Swedish champions Atvidaberg. Hoeness's goal forced extra time after the Swedes led 3–0 at home and 4–3 on aggregate. Connie Torstensson scored twice for Atvidaberg and Bayern snapped him up soon after. They took a 4–3 first-leg lead against East German champions Dynamo Dresden, led 2–0 in Dresden, then conceded three goals before Muller netted to see them through. Torstensson scored twice in the 4–1 win over CSKA Sofia which clinched Bayern's semi-final place. He netted in both games as they beat Ujpest 3–1 in Munich after a 1–1 draw in Budapest. Muller, inevitably, scored twice.

Bayern met Atletico Madrid in the final in Brussels. Atletico had disgraced themselves in the semi-final against Celtic. They had three men sent off at Parkhead but kept the score goalless and won the second leg 2–0. Atletico almost ruined Bayern's script. They contained them for 90 minutes, plus 23 more in extra time. Then midfield veteran Luis Aragones shot the Spanish team ahead from a free kick. Time was ticking away when deliverance came from an unlikely source. Schwarzenbeck's hopeful drive skidded past unsighted keeper Reina and Bayern were reprieved.

Beckenbauer dictated the pace in the replay two days later and Bayern ran the legs off Atletico, 4–0. Hoeness and Muller scored twice. Beckenbauer strolled up to collect the European Cup. Little more than seven weeks later, he would raise the World Cup, too.

Muller netted twice in each leg as Bayern began their 1974–75 trophy defence by knocking out the new East German champions Magdeburg. Coach Dettmar Cramer gambled on the patched-up Hoeness as a substitute in the quarter-final against Ararat Erevan. Hoeness broke the deadlock, Torstensson added a second and Bayern survived a 1–0 defeat in the Soviet Union to face Saint-Etienne in the semi-finals.

They defended deep for a 0–0 draw, then Beckenbauer slid home a second-minute corner in Munich and Bernd Durnberger's goal clinched their place in the final. They beat Leeds 2–0 in Paris, with goals from Roth and Muller. The game was marred by questionable decisions in Bayern's favour and a riot by Leeds fans who ripped up seats and threw them onto the pitch.

Bayern made it three in succession at Hampden Park in 1976. They beat Saint-Etienne again, 1–0. Roth scored their winner. They had produced some of their best-ever European performances to reach the final.

Bayern, now including a young winger called Karl-Heinz Rummenigge, eased past Jeunesse d'Esch and Malmo, then met Benfica in the quarter-finals. Maier was outstanding in a goalless draw in Lisbon before they swept Benfica aside 5–1 in Munich. Durnberger and Muller scored twice. Rummenigge netted the third goal.

In the semi-finals, Bayern faced Real Madrid – and Breitner, now a Madrid midfielder. Breitner, who had moved to escape a tense relationship with Beckenbauer, was injured for the first leg at the Bernabeu. Muller brushed off some harsh treatment to earn Bayern a 1–1 draw. He was felled after the final whistle as home fans attacked him and the Austrian referee Linnemayr. Muller gave his answer in Munich. His two goals settled the tie. The jubilant Bayern crowd booed Breitner.

Those three triumphant campaigns established Bayern among Europe's greatest clubs.

Now they are a pillar of the Champions League elite: Germany's richest and most successful club. It was not always so. Bayern were not even original members of the Bundesliga in 1963. They were one of 13 clubs who filed protests with the German federation (DFB) against their exclusion. The DFB refused to listen.

Bayern only reached the Bundesliga by winning promotion in 1965. Their old rivals 1860 held sway then. 1860, the Blues, were Munich's traditional club. They were one of the 16 clubs who competed in the first-ever Bundesliga. They beat Eintracht Frankfurt 2–0 to win the West German Cup in 1964 and reached the Cup-Winners' Cup final – losing 2–0 to West Ham at Wembley – the following season.

In 1966, under the guidance of Austrian coach Max Merkel, 1860 won the Bundesliga. It was their one and only championship. Their stars were Yugoslav goalkeeper Petar Radenkovic, who loved to charge out from his goal area, the ex-Dortmund forward Timo Konietzka and the hugely gifted Rudi Brunnenmeier.

Brunnenmeier scored 58 goals in the Bundesliga's first three seasons and spent his money on cars, women, drink and gambling. He once famously scored twice in a B international against the Soviet Union while trying to shake off a hangover. Brunnenmeier lost virtually all he owned in a divorce settlement, and spent the rest of his life living with his mother and doing manual work.

As Brunnenmeier fell from the heights, so did 1860. They spent the 2004–05 season in the Bundesliga second division, living in the shadow of their illustrious neighbours.

Bayern have built a reputation for being lucky. '*Bayern Dusel*' is the German phrase.

Their greatest player joined them through a stroke of fortune. Beckenbauer grew up in the working-class suburb of Giesing: 1860 territory. He said years later, 'I supported them even when they were relegated and it was always my dream to play for them.' That was until a fateful slap in a youth tournament at Neubiberg in 1958. Beckenbauer, a young centre-forward, was playing for a team called SC 1906. They met 1860 in the final. Beckenbauer had scored, against Bayern, in the semi-final. He had already decided to join 1860 because SC 1906 lacked the cash to maintain their schoolboy squads.

As Uli Hesse-Lichtenberger explains in *Tor! The Story of German Football*, 'There are two versions about how it came to pass that the 1860 centre-half hit Beckenbauer in the face.' The first says that Beckenbauer fouled the defender, who retaliated with a smack. The second says that the 1860 player called Beckenbauer an idiot. When Beckenbauer scored a few minutes later, he taunted the centre-half, who then lashed out. Beckenbauer decided that he would never join a club whose players behaved like that. Instead, he applied to join Bayern's youth section.

Bayern president Willi Neudecker was ambitious. His club had unearthed a seam of youthful talent: Beckenbauer, now a midfield player; Maier and Schwarzenbeck. Neudecker used that promise to persuade Tschik Cajkovski, coach of 1962 champions Cologne, to take a step down and shape the new Bayern. Two more young hopefuls emerged under Cajkovski's direction, strong-running Roth and the shy, chunky Muller.

Bayern scored 164 goals in the Regionalliga and play-off matches when they won promotion in 1965. The team that went up with them were . . . Gladbach. Bayern were a young side. Gladbach even younger.

Bayern finished third in their first Bundesliga campaign. They beat Duisburg 4–2 in the West German Cup final. Beckenbauer was outstanding in the West Germany side that reached the 1966 World Cup final.

A year later, Bayern beat Hamburg 4–0 to retain the cup. Roth scored the only goal in extra time as they beat Rangers 1–0 at Nurnberg in the Cup-Winners' Cup final. Then coach Branko Zebec, who replaced Cajkovski in 1968, made a decisive tactical change. He switched Beckenbauer from midfield to defence, and ordered him to dictate play from deep. Helmut Schoen would make the same switch for the national side three years later.

Beckenbauer was no conventional sweeper, tidying up behind a big centre-half and covering the back three. He strode forward at every opportunity, the focal point of the patient possession that became Bayern's hallmark.

In 1969, Bayern won their first Bundesliga title and their first championship since 1932. They finished eight points ahead of nearest rivals Alemannia Aachen.

Gladbach, under Hennes Weisweiler, had built strong foundations, too. He nurtured young talent – playmaker Gunter Netzer, forwards Jupp Heynckes, Herbert Laumen and the speedy Bernd Rupp. He brought in two crucial additions: limpet-like defender Berti Vogts and tireless midfield workhorse Herbert Wimmer.

Gladbach won the Bundesliga in 1970, then became the first team to retain the crown, thanks to Bayern's surprise defeat at Duisburg on the last day of the league season. Bayern had stayed in the race thanks to the DFB. The federation had awarded both points to Werder Bremen after their game at Gladbach was abandoned because of a broken goal post. (The score was 1–1 at the time, but the federation blamed Gladbach for not having a replacement post.)

Duisburg had nothing to play for. Instead, they fought as if their lives depended on the result, driven on by a packed 34,000 crowd determined to see Bayern deprived of the title. Beckenbauer felt that 'hate' was in the air. Muller was suspended. Rainer Budde scored twice in the second half and Duisburg won 2–0. The delighted Duisburg fans jeered Bayern off.

Gladbach won 4–1 at Frankfurt and finished two points ahead of Bayern. It was not the first time that Bayern had felt the wrath of opposing fans that season. Maier remembered a win at Oberhausen when the players had to run the gauntlet of hundreds of home supporters to reach their team bus. He said, 'It was like lynch law in the wild west.'

Bayern oozed class, but they remained unloved outside Bavaria. Their contest with Gladbach symbolically divided West Germany. The country was in turmoil as students took to the streets to protest against both the Vietnam War and the governing 'grand coalition' of Christian Democrats and Social Democrats.

Bayern were somehow cast as the forces of conservatism, while Gladbach stood for change and modernity. Bayern represented the old Catholic south, Gladbach the liberal Protestant north. The debate would rage throughout the 1970s, as first Bayern won three successive titles from 1972 to 1974, then Gladbach emulated the feat. They accomplished it with a 2–2 draw on the last day of the 1976–77 season, at Bayern.

Bayern were supposedly pragmatic and boring. Gladbach, nicknamed 'the Foals', played with freedom, discounting risk. Those were the stereotypes. Academics and sociologists queued to pontificate. Lichtenberger quotes the writer Holger Jenrich: 'All the reformers and progressives sided with Borussia instead of Bayern. They considered Gladbach's risk-taking football a continuation of political change by footballing means.'

The labels hardly fitted the facts. For instance, between Bayern's first Bundesliga title in 1969 and Gladbach's last in 1977, Bayern scored more goals than Borussia (715 to 676) – and conceded more (402 to 374). When Gladbach won their first title, they owed much to a defence that kept 13 clean sheets. It was Gladbach who relied on the ruthless efficiency of 'Guard Dog' Vogts.

Both teams were built on young talent and shrewd signings. They played in different styles. Beckenbauer steered Bayern from the back. Schwarzenbeck was often their only out and out defender. Bayern were masters at keeping possession, pressing and squeezing, changing angles, then quickening the pace for a telling pass. Muller finished so many of them. Squat and powerful, he was a phenomenon. He scored 365 goals in 427 Bundesliga appearances and 68 in 62 games for West Germany, including the winner in the 1974 World Cup final.

The West German athlete Heidi Rosendahl, pipped to a 'Sports Personality of the Year' award by Muller, complained that 'all he ever did was hang around the penalty area and score goals'. Exactly: at a time when defences were tighter than ever before, Muller could score with his head, his feet, his shin or his knee. He described himself as a scorer of 'little' goals, close-range efforts in confined spaces. His ability to manufacture shots or headers under pressure was unrivalled and he had the happy knack of scoring in big games. Some said Muller's low centre of gravity enabled him to turn quicker than his markers. Others pointed to the speed of his reactions. Some even said he was blessed by *Fingersputzengefuhl*, a sixth sense in the box. Whatever his gift, Muller worked overtime on the training ground to perfect it: hours of spinning off markers, hours of playing one-twos with Beckenbauer, hours of target practice.

Beckenbauer recognised Muller's genius at the striker's 50th birthday party. Muller had been picked up by the club again after a broken marriage and a descent into alcoholism.

Beckenbauer said, 'Without Gerd Muller we'd probably still be in the wooden hut that was once our clubhouse.'

Gladbach's style was swifter. Weisweiler urged his team to go forward. Netzer argued, saying there was a time to take the heat out of a game. He realised that Bayern were better at conserving energy, running down the clock. Yet Gladbach were at their most dangerous on the counter-attack, when Netzer could split defences with measured long passes, often for the bustling Heynckes. Gladbach spread their goals around, too. They had three prolific strikers rather than one phenomenon.

The teams' great stars contrasted. Beckenbauer was portrayed as being aloof and conservative. Netzer was the rebel, the artistic maverick with the flowing hair. Lichtenberger quotes Jenrich again: 'At best Beckenbauer became a star, while Netzer turned into a myth.'

Netzer cultivated the image. He was frequently photographed at the wheel of a sports car. He owned a pub disco called Lovers' Lane and his girlfriend was a goldsmith who usually dressed in black. He even called his autobiography *Rebel on the Ball*. Yet the apparently conservative Beckenbauer had made his girlfriend pregnant at the age of 18, then refused to marry her. He was temporarily banned from the West German youth team as a result. The biggest rebel in either squad however was Breitner, who sported an Afro haircut, adopted a Vietnamese orphan, flirted with Maoist politics and refused to sing the national anthem.

There were reasons for Bayern's unpopularity. Attitude for a start. Beckenbauer glided around, disdaining physical contact. He made the game look so simple. That made others jealous. As he said when he returned to West Germany after three years at New York Cosmos, 'As soon as I heard the catcalls, I knew I was home.'

Bayern rarely seemed to enjoy their victories. Breitner was reprimanded by the club for dancing naked by a swimming pool after their 1973 title victory. He moaned, 'This is a *Scheissverein*. We can't even celebrate properly.' The following year, Bayern's championship celebrations were so low-key that less than 2,000 fans turned up.

Finance was another reason. Bayern were the first Bundesliga club to appoint a business manager, Robert Schwan, who doubled as Beckenbauer's agent. They had moved into the new 80,000-capacity Olympic Stadium and could generate far more cash than Gladbach, stuck at the cramped Bokelberg which could only hold 28,000.

Then there was Bayern Dusel. Attacking full-back Breitner and winger Hoeness injected fresh urgency into Bayern – and West Germany – in the early '70s. Both had decided to join 1860. They changed their minds when Udo Lattek took over at Bayern in 1970. Lattek, engaged on Beckenbauer's recommendation, had coached them both in the West German youth squad.

Bayern rode their luck in all three of their European Cup final wins. Schwarzenbeck's lifesaver against Atletico Madrid was one of only 21 goals he scored in 14 years with them. A year later, French referee Marcel Kitabdjian turned down two penalty appeals against Beckenbauer and disallowed a Peter Lorimer goal for a technical offside before Roth put Bayern ahead. In 1976, Saint-Etienne's Dominique Bathenay and Jacques Santini had hit the Bayern woodwork before Roth struck again.

Contrast Bayern's good fortune with the jinx that seemed to haunt Gladbach. Take the night of 20 October 1971, the most bittersweet in their history. It was the European Cup second-round first leg against Internazionale. Roberto Boninsegna cancelled out Heynckes's early goal. Then Netzer was inspirational, scoring with a free kick and a delicate chip, as Gladbach took the Italians apart 7–1. Gladbach scored five times in half an hour. Klaus-Dieter Sieloff added the seventh in the 82nd minute.

Former Manchester United boss Matt Busby watched the game for UEFA. He enthused, 'What a team – such pace, power and invention.' Except that victory was wiped out in a committee room. Gladbach were 2–1 up when a hail of cans was thrown onto the pitch. Boninsegna was struck by a Coca Cola tin and fell. He was carried off and substituted. Inter appealed against the result on the grounds of Boninsegna's injury.

UEFA upheld their protest. The result was annulled. Gladbach were ordered to replay their home leg in Berlin. The game finished 0–0. Inter reached the quarter-finals thanks to their 4–2 win at San Siro.

It was a curious case. The medical attendants said Boninsegna was unmarked. The fans close to the incident thought Boninsegna was acting. Hesse-Lichtenberger quotes the watching Max Merkel: 'Boninsegna was talking to his mates as he was lying down, telling them to complain to the referee.'

Who threw the can, a German, or Italian? Why should a home fan hurl a can, when Gladbach were ahead? Was the can full or empty? Brian Glanville, in *Champions of Europe*, claimed that Inter's Sandro Mazzola admitted the can which hit Boninsegna was empty. But the can that Mazzola handed to the referee was full. That was typical of Gladbach's luck in Europe.

Three years later, they needed to beat Milan by three goals to reach the Cup-Winners' Cup final. They scored early, then had two blatant penalty appeals turned down. Milan's German defender Karl-Heinz Schnellinger stayed on the pitch despite breaking Christian Kulik's ankle with a wild tackle.

Then came the European Cup quarter-final second leg against Real Madrid at the Bernabeu in 1976. The first leg finished 2–2. The return ended 1–1. Madrid advanced on away goals. Netzer was playing for them now. He said his colleagues were amazed that Dutch referee Leo van der Kroft disallowed two Gladbach goals in the second half.

Glanville wrote: 'Van der Kroft's refereeing provoked an angry protest by Monchengladbach, with some justification.' The referee was suspended by UEFA, but Gladbach were still eliminated.

No wonder many Gladbach fans believed that their team had triumphed over fate to win the UEFA Cup in 1975 (and again in 1979) and reach the 1977 European Cup final.

Yet there were times when Bayern, Gladbach, and the rest of West Germany, called a truce to their conflict: when the national team needed their stars. Between 1972 and 1974, Bayern and Gladbach underpinned West Germany's best-ever teams.

Maier, Beckenbauer and Muller had been the stars of West Germany's run to the World Cup semi-finals in 1970. Beckenbauer scored the goal that kick-started the Germans' revival after England led

2–0 in the quarter-final. He said, 'After that goal, our whole side stepped up a gear.' Muller, almost inevitably netted the extra-time winner after Uwe Seeler equalised.

Helmut Schoen's side were beaten 4–3 by Italy in a dramatic semi-final. Muller struck twice more in extra time, only for Gianni Rivera to stroke home Italy's late winner.

Now the Bayern trio would be reinforced, by rising stars from their own ranks – Hoeness and Breitner – and the Gladbach contingent.

West Germany's great team came together on 29 April 1972 at Wembley, in the first leg of the European Championship quarter-finals. The omens were inauspicious. The Bundesliga was gripped by a bribery scandal which led to the suspension of internationals Bernd Patzke, Reinhard Libuda and Klaus Fichtel. The experienced Cologne duo of Wolfgang Weber and Wolfgang Overath were injured.

Schoen gambled on the inexperienced Breitner at left-back with Hoeness on the right of midfield. He entrusted Netzer to dictate the play. Wimmer would be his ball winner, as he was at Gladbach. Beckenbauer played sweeper as he had for years with Bayern. There were five Bayern players in the line-up and two from Gladbach. (Vogts was injured, otherwise he would have played at right-back.)

Beckenbauer was impeccable, Netzer magnificent. The image of Netzer striding forward, long hair glinting in the floodlights, became a classic of German football. Hoeness put the Germans ahead. Francis Lee levelled in the 77th minute. Then Siggi Held fell under Bobby Moore's challenge and Netzer fired the penalty past Gordon Banks. Muller administered the *coup de grâce*. Two goals for Bayern, one for Gladbach.

The English media, so full of pre-match confidence, acknowledged the Germans' calibre. *The Times* praised their 'elegance and invention'. Glanville wrote in the *Sunday Times* that Beckenbauer had set new standards of aspiration for German players and fans.

The second leg, in West Berlin was a goalless anticlimax, notable for England's physical approach. Netzer said, 'I think the English team all autographed my leg.'

Vogts was still missing but a third Gladbacher, striker Heynckes, came into the side for the finals in Belgium. In the semi-finals, Netzer conjured a magical long pass to Muller, who shot the Germans ahead against the host nation in Antwerp. Belgium lacked invention in the absence of injured playmaker Wilfried van Moer, out with a broken leg.

Muller finished the job 18 minutes from time. Odilon Polleunis's reply was only a consolation.

The final, against the Soviet Union, was a 3–0 stroll. Netzer wrote the script and directed. Muller scored twice more. Wimmer even added a rare goal, from a pass by Heynckes.

Hosts West Germany, holders Brazil and Cruyff's Holland led the fancied sides for the World Cup finals two years later.

The Germans' preparations almost collapsed in farce. The players had heard what the Holland and Italy squads had been offered for winning the tournament. They wanted the same. They were still arguing with the DFB about bonuses a week before the competition. Schoen could not understand why players wanted such cash incentives to play for their country. He threatened to send the whole squad home. Breitner considered walking out anyway and had to be dissuaded by his teammates.

Beckenbauer resolved the issue in telephone negotiations with DFB vice-president Hermann Neuberger. The squad split 11–11 on Neuberger's offer. Beckenbauer recommended that they should accept it. The skipper's authority prevailed.

Schoen feared the fallout from the bickering would affect the team's form. He was right. They stuttered to a 1–0 victory against Chile in their opening group match, laboured to a 3–0 win over Australia, then lost 1–0 to East Germany in the first-ever meeting between the two sides. Jurgen Sparwasser lobbed the only goal after Muller had hit a post.

After the Second World War, Schoen had fled from Dresden in the east to resume his football career. He had been desperate to win the game, for personal reasons as well as to restore morale. The media began to question their former heroes. Schoen's side had reached the second phase. But the strain was taking its toll on the coach.

Enter Beckenbauer again. He joined Schoen at a delayed press conference. Now, it seemed coach and captain were sharing command. Young Gladbach midfielder Rainer Bonhof and Frankfurt winger Bernd Holzenbein came in against Yugoslavia. Hoeness was dropped to sting more effort from him.

Netzer, the mercurial genius of Wembley and Belgium, was cast aside. He had been struggling with a knock before the competition. Beckenbauer wanted the more hard-working Overath in midfield. Netzer played just 20 minutes in the tournament, as a substitute against East Germany.

Breitner and Muller scored in a 2–0 win over the Yugoslavs. Then West Germany clicked, at last, against Sweden. Schoen's team showed character as well as skill. They came from a goal down at half-time to win 4–2: one each by Overath, Bonhof and Grabowski and an 89th-minute penalty by the rejuvenated Hoeness.

The Germans' last second-phase game was effectively a semi-final. They and Poland both had maximum points from two games. The Poles, the Olympic champions, had beaten Argentina, Haiti, Italy, Sweden and Yugoslavia, despite missing injured striker Wlodzimierz Lubanski for the whole tournament. Their stars were the big centre-back Jerzy Gorgon, midfield general Kazimierz Deyna and flying wingers, Grzegorz Lato and Robert Gadocha.

The kick-off in Frankfurt was delayed for half an hour while the ground staff pumped water off the pitch. One commentator compared the surface to a swimming pool, with a 'deep' end and a 'shallow' end.

The game was a lottery. Maier, at his sharpest, saved twice from Lato in the first half. Hoeness wasted a penalty, shooting too close to keeper Jan Tomaszewski. Muller settled the contest in the 75th minute, firing home the loose ball as Bonhof was tackled. Muller said, 'We were terrible in our first three matches. Then we pulled ourselves together after that.'

The final against Holland was played at Bayern's home ground in Munich. West Germany's starting 11 included six Bayern players – Maier, Beckenbauer, Schwarzenbeck, Breitner, Hoeness and Muller – plus Vogts and Bonhof from Gladbach.

Cruyff and Johan Neeskens had inspired some magical Dutch performances, a 4–1 win over Bulgaria, 4–0 against Argentina and a 2–0 victory against Brazil to reach the final. They were the masters of Total Football, switching positions at will in a fluid system first devised by Holland coach Rinus Michels at Ajax. But it was the specialists that Holland lacked who made the difference – Gladbach 'Guard Dog' Vogts and the Bayern phenomenon Muller.

When Hoeness brought down Cruyff and Neeskens despatched the first-minute penalty, the Germans trembled. Holland failed to press home their advantage. Breitner said, 'The Dutch failed to grasp that they could have dominated us on the day. They failed to add to their lead and they couldn't come back later. And they were punished for carelessness.'

When Holzenbein went down under Wim Jansen's challenge,

143

Breitner took responsibility. He said, 'I was nearest to the ball and Uli [Hoeness] had missed against Poland. Without thinking, I grabbed the ball because I was sure I'd find the back of the net. [Holland goalkeeper] Jongbloed moved to his left, so I put the ball the other side for our equaliser.'

Cruyff had been the magician of the tournament. This time his influence was curbed. Vogts saw to that. He harried, chased, pushed and kicked to subdue Holland's talisman. The English media had nicknamed him 'Dirty Berti'. Cruyff felt the same, judging by some of his gestures to English referee Jack Taylor as they walked off for half-time.

By then, Muller had scored the Germans' 43rd-minute winner. He said, 'Bonhof and Grabowski did the work on the right. The ball bounced off my foot but I reached the loose ball first, spun, hit it and it went in.'

Perhaps Holland's defence would have coped better with Muller had the Ajax centre-back Barry Hulshoff been fit for the tournament or if Michels had picked the Feyenoord sweeper Rinus Israel. Instead, he had switched Ajax midfielder Arie Haan to centre-back.

But then, that's what Muller did, wasn't it? Hang around the penalty area and score goals?

The Germans lost the 1976 European Championship final to Czechoslovakia in Belgrade after a penalty shootout. Hoeness missed again and Antonin Panenka's spot kick won the game. But it was a different German team. Muller retired from international football after the World Cup. So did Breitner. Netzer was gone. Beckenbauer left Bayern for New York Cosmos in the spring of 1977 and dropped out of international reckoning. The squad that Schoen took to Argentina in 1978 was shorn of the flair of his earlier teams.

Time caught up with Bayern and Gladbach, too. Bayern were eliminated by Dynamo Kiev in the 1977 European Cup quarter-finals. Rummenigge was their crown jewel. Otherwise their seam of talent had been mined dry.

Bonhof, Uli Stielike and the Danes Henning Jensen and Alan Simonsen kept Gladbach's dream flickering a little longer but they could no longer find the talent to replace Weisweiler's young Foals.

Hoeness played his last game for Bayern in 1978. The ageing Muller joined Fort Lauderdale Strikers in the North American Soccer League. Neudecker resigned as president early in 1979, as the club slipped down the table. He was later found guilty of tax evasion. Bayern were fined 2.5 million Deutschmarks. Neudecker and Schwan were fined too. It was the end of an era. Bayern would rise again to win the European Cup a generation later, with Beckenbauer as president, Hoeness as chief executive and Ottmar Hitzfeld as coach. Gladbach are still trying to recapture their former glories.

CHAPTER 12

THE ENGLISH ARE COMING

The decline of Bayern Munich left a power vacuum in Europe: a vacuum that would be filled by three English clubs – Liverpool, Nottingham Forest and Aston Villa.

Liverpool won the European Cup four times between 1977 and 1984. Forest won it in 1979 and 1980. Villa won in 1982. Only Hamburg, in 1983, broke the English domination. Liverpool and Forest were managed by hugely contrasting characters – Bob Paisley and Brian Clough – each a genius in his own distinctive way. Meanwhile, Villa blazed like a comet for two seasons – first in the Football League, then in Europe – before they tailed off and fell to earth.

Those teams were very different from modern Premiership squads. For one thing, they were composed almost entirely of British (and some Irish) players. For another, they usually played more than 50 domestic matches a season – including the League Cup, treated by today's Champions League contenders as at best an inconvenience. The game was much more physical then – modern referees would have run out of cards by half-time in some matches – and played on much heavier pitches than the lush Premiership grounds.

Not everyone welcomed the English teams' dominance. Brian Glanville spoke for many when he wrote in the *Sunday Times* (in the spring of 1983) that the success of English clubs in the European Cup reflected a decline in standards. He argued: 'English clubs have surely prevailed through organisation, stamina, pace and morale in a way they never could when Real Madrid, Ajax or Bayern Munich were at their peak.' That was probably unfair on Liverpool, especially the impressive unit that Paisley left to his assistant and successor Joe Fagan in 1983. Alan Hansen and Mark Lawrenson were classy constructive footballers as well as solid defenders. Graeme Souness mixed stern tackling with vast technical quality in midfield. Kenny Dalglish and Ian Rush formed a mercurial strike force.

The ban imposed on Liverpool after the Heysel stadium tragedy of 1985 denied that side the chance to dominate Europe. Paisley, a quiet, shy Geordie, stepped from the Anfield 'boot room' to succeed his old boss Bill Shankly in 1974. Shankly had taken over when Liverpool were at their lowest ebb, stuck in the old Second Division. He turned them into English champions three times and a formidable force in Europe.

Shankly was an abrasive Scot with a line in memorable quotes, such as the famous 'Football is not a matter of life or death – it's more important than that.' He quit sudddenly after Liverpool's 3–0 win over Newcastle in the 1974 FA Cup final, saying he was 'tired'.

Shankly built the modern Liverpool. Paisley turned them into champions of Europe. He was the temperamental opposite of the ebullient Shankly. Paisley, who had played wing-half in Liverpool's successful post-war team, had the air of a genial uncle. He never seemed comfortable in the spotlight, never courted headlines, unlike Shankly, or Clough at Forest. He was, though, a brilliant judge of players, a clever organiser and a master of team building.

Liverpool centre-back Phil Thompson said, 'He bought players and moulded them together to create great teams. People talked about him as "Uncle Bob" but he could be ruthless when he needed to be. He had a genius for creating teams.' Liverpool goalkeeper Ray Clemence remembered, 'I think when he first succeeded Shanks, he was a bit overawed. He told us that the board had given him the job even though he didn't really want it. He saw it as his duty to take it. Yet he set an incredible record that will probably never be beaten. He was a coach rather than a motivator, a shrewd judge of a player and very strong tactically.'

Paisley also had an uncanny eye for detail, based on a phenomenal footballing memory. Liverpool's former youth officer Tom Saunders said, 'I watched many matches with him and nothing escaped him. When a goal was scored, he'd have the whole move analysed in a flash. Every scrap of information was stored in his memory.'

Liverpool had pipped Queens Park Rangers to the English

championship in 1976. They had also won the UEFA Cup, beating Brugge 3–2 at Anfield and drawing 1–1 in Belgium. That was a more measured, less frantic Liverpool side than the team which had won the trophy three years earlier against Borussia Monchengladbach. The catalyst had been elimination from the European Cup by Red Star Belgrade in 1973–74. Red Star's incisive passing had pulled Liverpool apart 2–1 at Anfield in the second leg. Shankly, Paisley and the boot room knew they had to change their approach, shelve the long-ball game and emphasise the importance of patience and possession.

Paisley took over a high-class squad and refined it. Liverpool had an excellent goalkeeper in Clemence. Thompson and skipper Emlyn Hughes were quality centre-backs. Right-back Phil Neal loved to support the attack.

Glanville criticised their 'unimaginative, one-paced midfield – perm any three from Ian Callaghan, Jimmy Case, Terry McDermott and Ray Kennedy'. But McDermott and Kennedy, converted from a striker by Paisley, could both chip in with crucial goals.

Liverpool's forwards were anything but one-paced. The tireless Kevin Keegan was an army of one. Steve Heighway was a wonderful dribbler. Then there was Paisley's secret weapon, flame-haired 'Super Sub' David Fairclough. Liverpool cruised through to the 1977 quarter-finals by eliminating the Northern Ireland champions Crusaders, then crushing Trabzonspor 3–0 at Anfield with goals from Heighway, David Johnson and Keegan.

They met the previous season's unlucky runners-up, Saint-Etienne, in two titanic quarter-finals. Keegan was injured for the first leg in France. Heighway shot against an upright but Dominque Bathenay scored the only goal of the game for the French champions.

Keegan squeezed a shot past keeper Ivan Curkovic inside three minutes of the return at Anfield. But another Bathenay piledriver gave Saint-Etienne a 2–1 aggregate lead. Kennedy restored Liverpool's advantage on the night – but Saint-Etienne had a potentially decisive away goal. Enter Fairclough, 13 minutes from time. Five minutes later, he chested down Kennedy's pass, left two defenders trailing and smashed the winner past Curkovic. Liverpool scored three at home and away to beat Zurich in the semi-finals.

Their opponents in the final in Rome were Monchengladbach. West German internationals Berti Vogts, Rainer Bonhof, Herbert Wimmer and Jupp Heynckes remained from the great days of the early '70s.

They had been joined by the hard-tackling midfielder Uli Stielike and the small but brilliant Danish striker Allan Simonsen.

'Last time I was in Rome, I was on a tank,' said Paisley, who served with the British forces that liberated the city during the Second World War.

Keegan had decided to join Hamburg in the summer. This was his last game for Liverpool. His contest with the 'Guard Dog' Vogts was crucial. Vogts had famously subdued Dutch great Johan Cruyff in the 1974 World Cup final. Keegan dragged him all over the pitch.

McDermott fired Liverpool ahead from Heighway's pinpoint through ball. Keegan's sprint had taken Vogts away to create the gap for McDermott's run. Simonsen levelled after a weak back pass by midfielder Case, and Clemence saved from Stielike. Then Keegan attracted two defenders to him at Heighway's corner and veteran Tommy Smith – deputising for the injured Thompson – headed Liverpool in front again. Vogts brought down Keegan and full-back Phil Neal stroked home the penalty for Liverpool's third.

Liverpool had comprehensively outplayed one of Europe's most experienced teams. Cruyff, among others, had argued that English teams' natural attacking instincts worked against them at the highest level in Europe. Liverpool had proved that English sides could play with tactical intelligence as well as verve.

Liverpool were only the second English club to win the European Cup. They were the first to retain it. Paisley had moved swiftly to replace Keegan with the Celtic and Scotland striker Dalglish, a prolific scorer who could spin off his marker to create chances for others too. Paisley also signed Hansen, a dominant, ball-playing centre-back from Partick Thistle. Later that season he added another key component to the Liverpool machine, Souness, a £325,000 buy from Middlesbrough.

Liverpool cruised into the quarter-finals with a 5–1 home win over Dynamo Dresden, then beat Benfica in Lisbon and at Anfield. Their semi-final opponents were Gladbach. Stielike had joined Real Madrid now. Simonsen was injured for both legs. Bonhof's deflected free kick gave Gladbach a 2–1 first leg win. Souness was outstanding in the return and Liverpool won 3–0 with goals from Kennedy, Dalglish and Case. Vogts admitted that Gladbach had been intimidated by the Anfield atmosphere.

In the final at Wembley, Liverpool's opponents were the Belgian champions Brugge, surprise semi-final conquerors of Juventus. Rene van der Eycken had scored their winner four minutes from the end of extra time after Juve defender Claudio Gentile was sent off.

Brugge's top scorer Raoul Lambert and midfielder Paul Courant were both injured. Coach Ernst Happel sent his team out to pack in defence. It made for a dismal spectacle. Brugge's Danish keeper Birger Jensen denied Liverpool until the 66th minute. Heighway found Souness who split the Brugge defence and Dalglish coolly lobbed the winner.

Liverpool remained champions of Europe. But they had lost their English crown to Nottingham Forest, who had also beaten them in the League Cup final. Soon, Forest would knock the holders out of the European Cup.

It would be unthinkable now that an unfashionable club of modest means, such as Forest, could even finish in the top four of the Premiership, let alone win the European Cup two years running. Yet Clough – aided by Peter Taylor – achieved remarkable feats with them.

Clough – 'Old Big Head' as he styled himself – was egotistical, opinionated and rarely out of the news. He was not burdened by false modesty. He said, 'I wouldn't say that I was the best manager in the business but I was in the top one.'

Forest midfielder Martin O'Neill, later a successful manager with Leicester and Celtic, said, 'Brian was absolutely sensational and I don't think he would disagree! He had fantastic charisma. He had this massive self-belief and self-confidence.'

Yet Clough's combative reputation cost him the chance of becoming England manager after Sir Alf Ramsey's departure, and again when Don Revie quit in 1976. He had been a prolific centre-forward with Middlesbrough and Sunderland before a serious leg injury cut short his career. He had made his name, in partnership with Taylor, at Hartlepool, one of the least promising outposts of the Fourth Division. Clough steered them to promotion before taking over at Derby, a once-proud east midlands club marooned deep in Division Two.

Clough led them back to Division One in 1969. Three years later, they won the championship for the first time. The following season, they reached the European Cup semi-finals. They lost 3–1 to Juventus in Turin in the first leg, lost two key players, Roy McFarland and Archie Gemmill, suspended, for the return and drew 0–0 after missing a penalty.

Clough left that summer after a row with the Derby chairman Sam

Longson over the locking and unlocking of a drinks cabinet. He and Taylor took charge at Brighton, before Clough spent an abortive 44-day spell as Revie's successor at Leeds. The Forest chairman, Brian Appleby, brought him to the struggling Second Division club early in 1975 to 'stave off disaster'. It took Clough nearly 18 months to persuade Taylor to leave Brighton and rejoin him. Clough was the motivator and organiser; Taylor was the man who sized up players. The pair would fall out bitterly in the early '80s, a rift that was never healed. Between them though, they had a gift for spotting stars in unlikely settings and extracting the very best from them.

John Robertson was an overweight, underachieving winger. Clough and Taylor turned him into the fulcrum of Forest's attack. Robertson said, 'There have been some brilliant managers but Clough was at the top of the list for what he achieved. He achieved success at two provincial clubs which were not very big and not very fashionable, yet he went on to win the European Cup twice.'

Full-back Frank Clark, released by Newcastle, revived his career at Forest. He said, 'Clough's greatest strength was man-management. He hadn't learned it from books or going on courses. He was just a natural. He had the gift of getting 100 per cent from everyone who played for him.'

Ex-Liverpool defender Larry Lloyd, a centre-back with a weight problem, regained his best form at the City Ground, too. Clough and Taylor signed Kenny Burns, a talented but wayward centre-back-cum-striker from Birmingham and made him the organiser of the Forest back line. Taylor prevailed on Clough to sign a young striker called Gary Birtles from local non-league side Long Eaton. He became an England forward.

Clough carried other players around with him. Young midfielder John McGovern played for him at Hartlepool, then followed him to Derby, Leeds and Forest. Striker John O'Hare played for him at Derby, Leeds and Forest. Clough signed Scotland midfielder Gemmill for Derby, then Forest.

Forest also had young talent in the form of right-back Viv Anderson, the first black player to win an England cap, sparky forward Tony Woodcock, Northern Ireland midfielder O'Neill and versatile Ian Bowyer.

As Forest took on the elite, Clough was given the cash to sign England stars such as goalkeeper Peter Shilton and striker Trevor

Francis. Clough's teams were built on solid defence, accurate short passing and quick counter-attacks, sprung by midfielders like Gemmill who could run with the ball or pass it. He loved a tricky winger in his line-up, too: Alan Hinton at Derby, then Robertson at Forest. Like Paisley, he eschewed the long-ball game. He said, 'If God had meant us to play football in the clouds, he'd have put grass up there.'

And his players were among the best-behaved in England. Any player who argued with a referee would quickly feel Clough's wrath. O'Neill insists that Clough was a brilliant coach as well as a motivator. He said, 'One of the great myths of all time is that he was seldom seen on the training ground. When he came for a 20–25 minute spell, you'd pick up enough to last you a lifetime.'

Robertson denied that Clough 'ruled by fear'. But all the players knew who was in charge.

When Clough signed Shilton from Stoke, he ordered the England goalkeeper to make tea for the waiting press corps. After signing Birmingham forward Trevor Francis, the Football League's first £1 million player, he sent him off to make his Forest debut in the reserves. Clough said, 'If a player disagrees with me, I talk to him for 20 minutes, then we agree that I was right.'

Clough was the manager who invented the mid-season club break. The players 'bonded' in the sun while he thought up ideas for the campaign ahead. He often re-created the atmosphere of the mid-season winter break to relax his players before big matches, sometimes with enough drink to make modern coaches' hair turn white.

Forest claimed the mighty scalp of Liverpool in the 1978–79 European Cup first round. They won the first leg 2–0 in Nottingham. Birtles scored from Woodcock's pass. Full-back Colin Barrett hit the second from Woodcock's header.

Liverpool felt they had treated the game too much like a league match instead of a European Cup tie. Hughes said, 'We attacked too much, which suited them.'

At Anfield, McGovern sat tight on Souness, and Bowyer tight-marked McDermott. Forest frustrated Liverpool 0–0. The watching Shankly observed, 'There was too much frenzy. Liverpool were doing things in too much of a hurry.' It was as if, faced by English opposition, Liverpool temporarily reverted to their pre-Red Star persona.

Forest beat AEK Athens home and away. A 4–1 home win over Swiss champions Grasshoppers saw them through to the semi-finals – against

Cologne, coached by Hennes Weisweiler, the architect of Gladbach's great side. Anderson was injured and Burns suspended for the first leg at Nottingham. Cologne took a 2–0 lead within 20 minutes. Birtles replied. Bowyer equalised. Robertson headed Forest in front. Cologne's Japanese substitute Yasuhiko Okudera made it 3–3 nine minutes from time with a shot that deceived Shilton on the muddy surface.

Forest saved their best for the second leg in Cologne. Anderson and Burns returned and Forest kept the game tight. After 65 minutes, Lloyd flicked on Robertson's corner and Bowyer headed the only goal of the game. Shilton, in top form, made sure that they reached the final.

Their opponents were Swedish champions Malmo, coached by Londoner Bobby Houghton. Taylor watched them beat FK Austria 1–0 in the semi-finals and told Clough that Forest should beat them comfortably in Munich. Francis, making his European Cup debut, headed home Robertson's cross for the winner, in first-half stoppage time. It was another poor spectacle. Malmo's defensive tactics saw to that. The following season, Forest would be equally culpable.

Clough sold Gemmill to Birmingham a few weeks later, signed Asa Hartford from Manchester City to replace him, then sold him to Everton within months. Forest's next midfield signing, Stan Bowles from QPR, walked out on them as the season reached its climax. Woodock left six months after the triumph in Munich: for Cologne.

Forest still retained the European Cup, though their prospects looked bleak after they lost 1–0 at home to Dynamo Dresden in the quarter-final first leg. Shades of the second leg in Cologne: they won 3–1 at Dresden. The hesitant East Germans were unsure whether to attack or sit on their lead.

Francis punished them with two goals and Robertson netted the third from a penalty. Francis scored again and Robertson tucked away another penalty as Forest won the semi-final first leg 2–0 against Ajax. Shilton pulled off save after save to restrict Ajax to a 1–0 margin in Amsterdam.

Forest's final opponents were the West German champions Hamburg. Their general manager was the great Gunter Netzer, their coach the old Bayern Munich supremo Branko Zebec. Their stars were Keegan and the giant Horst Hrubesch, who had torn through the Bundesliga the previous season, scoring 30 goals between them. Manny Kaltz was a brilliant attacking full-back. Felix Magath pulled the strings in midfield.

Hamburg had hammered Real Madrid 5–1 in the semi-final second leg at the Volkspark. Kaltz and Hrubesch scored twice. Vicente del Bosque was sent off for hitting Keegan.

Hrubesch did not start the final because of an ankle knock, though he played the second half as a clearly unfit substitute.

Forest were without Francis who had torn an Achilles tendon. Bowles had left in a fit of pique after he was dropped for Robertson's testimonial match. Shilton, who had another inspirational game, played after pain-killing injections for a calf injury. Teenager Gary Mills started in a five-man midfield, with Birtles the lone attacker.

Forest aimed to soak up pressure and strike on the break. After 20 minutes, Robertson burst past Kaltz and scored with a shot off a post. They defended for the rest of the match. Burns tight-marked Keegan superbly and Hamburg could not break down their well-organised resistance. Clough said, 'It was one of the best 90 minutes we've ever had.' Others disagreed. This time, an English side's negative tactics had killed the final as a spectacle. Glanville, in the *Sunday Times*, complained, 'Forest's second half strategy was a craven one, worthy of Juventus at their worst.'

Clough and Taylor could not work a third successive miracle. Forest went out to CSKA Sofia 1–0 in both legs in the 1980–81 first round. They never played in the European Cup again, nor challenged for the championship.

Paisley had been rebuilding at Liverpool. They had been eliminated in the first round the previous season, after a 3–0 defeat at Dynamo Tbilisi. Now they would pick up England's banner again – and suffer more criticism after winning another dismal final.

Paisley had promoted the young Scouser, Sammy Lee, on the right of midfield, and made another clever signing in left-back Alan Kennedy from Newcastle. Liverpool struggled to fifth place in the league. Paisley blamed a series of long-term injuries, most notably to Hansen and Thompson. They saved their best for Europe, cruising past Olu Palloseura of Finland and Alex Ferguson's Scottish champions Aberdeen. Souness scored a hat trick of spectacular shots as they crushed CSKA Sofia 5–1 in the quarter-final at Anfield.

Bayern Munich's Paul Breitner then slammed Liverpool – and their English counterparts – after a 0–0 draw in the semi-final first leg. Breitner said, 'English football is stupid. There's no subtlety to it. They just rely on pressure to break down opposing teams.'

Liverpool replied by eliminating Bayern in Munich. Souness, who had missed the first leg, returned to add guile in a harsh contest. Ray Kennedy gave Liverpool the lead. Karl-Heinz Rummenigge levelled. But Liverpool reached the final, against Real Madrid, on away goals.

It was hardly a vintage Madrid side that faced them in Paris. Their English winger, Laurie Cunningham, played his first game for six months after injury and looked rusty. Their other winger, Juanito, faded after a bright start. Stielike, their playmaker, was hustled relentlessly by the Liverpool midfield. Their top scorer, Carlos Santillana, could make no headway against Hansen and Thompson.

Alan Kennedy hit the winner eight minutes from time, chesting down Ray Kennedy's throw, to brush off Garcia Cortes's challenge and shoot past reserve keeper Agustin.

A French commentator described the game as 'chloroform football'. Alfredo Di Stefano and Ferenc Puskas, greats of Madrid's past, were not impressed either. Madrid coach Vujadin Boskov called Liverpool 'programmed, like a machine'. Paisley admitted, 'We've given better performances to win the trophy.'

Glanville again spoke for many when he called it 'the fourth rotten European Cup final in a row'. How fair, though, was it to lay all the blame on the English teams? Football throughout Europe had become more defensive, more physical – witness the muscular West German side which had won the 1980 European Championship. And no Continental team had arisen to mount a consistent challenge to the English.

Forest had been negative against Hamburg. Liverpool had been surprisingly cautious against Madrid. Yet both Brugge (against Liverpool) and Malmo (against Forest) had come solely to defend. (Steaua Bucharest and Red Star Belgrade would later win the European Cup on penalties with such tactics.) Liverpool's clash with Gladbach had been the last classic final – because both teams came out to attack.

By now, winning the Football League seemed a passport to European Cup glory. Yet Aston Villa were the least likely of the English winners. They had pipped Ipswich to the 1981 league championship after Bobby Robson's team wilted under a pile-up of fixtures. They used only 14 players all season, as many as modern Premiership teams use in one match!

Villa's manager Ron Saunders had instilled a ferocious work ethic, though his side lacked the star quality of Liverpool, Forest or Ipswich, who were inspired by the Dutch duo of Arnold Muhren and Frans Thijssen. Villa were robust, organised and full of energy. They may have fallen short of the highest levels of technique but they worked their socks off. As full back Kenny Swain said, 'We buzz.'

Jimmy Rimmer, formerly of Manchester United and Arsenal, was an experienced keeper. The Scottish stopper Allan Evans held the back four together. Gordon Cowans, the son of the Villa kit man, was the fulcrum of the side. Gary Shaw, whose career would be cut short by injury, was a young striker of great potential. Peter Withe, once of Forest, was a powerful target man and Tony Morley a speedy winger.

Villa struggled in their championship defence. But in Europe, they went from strength to strength while their fancied rivals fell by the wayside. Juventus were knocked out by Belgian champions Anderlecht in the second round. Liverpool went out 2–1 on aggregate to the Bulgarian champions CSKA after losing 2–0 in extra time in Sofia. Bruce Grobbelaar, signed after Clemence joined Tottenham, gave an erratic display in goal. Lawrenson, who had taken over from Thompson, was sent off. Bulgaria winger Mladenov scored twice for CSKA.

Villa eased past the Icelandic champions Valur, then beat Dynamo Berlin on away goals after a 2–1 victory in East Germany, when Morley ran nearly 80 yards to score a solo winner. By the quarter-finals, Tony Barton had taken charge after the unexpected departure of Saunders.

Villa finished only 11th in the First Division that season. Like Liverpool the year before, they saved their best for Europe. They held Dynamo 0–0 in Kiev, then beat them 2–0 in Birmingham. Morley scored the only goal of the semi-final against Anderlecht at Villa Park.

Villa met Bayern Munich in the final in Rotterdam. This was hardly the dominant Bayern of Beckenbauer, Maier and Muller. Karl-Heinz Rummenigge and an ageing Paul Breitner remained from the great days. As Uli Hesse-Lichtenberger says in *Tor!*, 'There were also nine others – men like Manfred Muller, Hans Weiner, Wolfgang Krauss, Gunter Guttler and Kurt Niedermayer. Even German fans recall these players only hazily, which is probably just as well. With such limited but determined men, the Bayern teams of the 1980s delivered technocratic, boring football.'

Villa showed their resilience after Rimmer was injured in the ninth minute and replaced by Nigel Spink, who had made just one first-team appearance. He pulled off wonderful saves from Rummenigge and

Bernd Durnberger. Swain blocked a Klaus Augenthaler shot on the line. Morley set up Villa's 67th-minute winner, turning his marker to find Withe with a low cross. The big striker toe-poked it in off an upright.

Villa never touched such heights again. In the next four seasons, they finished 6th, 10th, 10th and 16th in the First Division before they were relegated in 1987.

Hamburg broke the English stranglehold in 1983, beating favourites Juventus 1–0 in the final in Athens. Holders Villa and champions Liverpool both fell in the quarter-finals.

Yet Hamburg possessed many of the virtues of their English counterparts: strength, stamina and resilience. Their star striker, the towering Hrubesch, could have been a traditional English centre-forward.

Keegan had returned to England, to be replaced by the Danish forward Lars Bastrup. Kaltz and Magath remained the creative forces. Netzer was still general manager but Zebec, who had an alcohol problem, was fired in December 1980 for being drunk on the bench. His successor was the man Netzer wanted to appoint in the summer of 1978, Ernst Happel.

Eight years before his exploits with Brugge, Happel had steered Feyenoord to European Cup victory. He was famous for his downbeat manner but he was much respected by his players. He guided Hamburg to the Bundesliga title in 1982 and 1983. And his side upset the favourites again in the European Cup final, just as Feyenoord had against Celtic.

Liverpool and Juventus entered the last eight contesting the 'favourites' tag. Juventus had spent a fortune on French great Michel Platini and the quicksilver Polish attacker Zbigniew Boniek. They also fielded six of Italy's 1982 World Cup winners – Dino Zoff, Claudio Gentile, Gaetano Scirea, Antonio Cabrini, Marco Tardelli and Paolo Rossi.

Boniek's old club, Widzew Lodz, eliminated Liverpool, after a mistake by Grobbelaar in Poland. The keeper lost a left wing cross and Tlokinski put Widzew ahead. Wraga scored again in an 80th-minute breakaway. Liverpool had to pile forward at Anfield. Phil Neal gave them a 14th-minute lead. Tlokinski and Smolarek replied to put Widzew 4–1 ahead on aggregate. Goals by Rush and David Hodgson came too late for Liverpool.

Juventus knocked out Villa. Rossi set them on the way to a 2–1 win at Villa Park, heading in Cabrini's cross in the first minute, without a Villa player touching the ball. Boniek scored the winner after Gordon Cowans levelled. Platini netted twice as Juventus won the second leg 3–1. Bastrup, meanwhile, grabbed a hat trick as Hamburg settled their quarter-final with a 3–0 win in the first leg at Dynamo Kiev.

Goals by Tardelli and veteran Roberto Bettega sank Widzew in the semi-final first leg and Juve drew 2–2 in Poland. Hamburg drew 1–1 at Spanish champions Real Sociedad. Young striker Thomas van Heesen scored the goal that clinched their 2–1 win in the return.

Perhaps Juventus underestimated Hamburg in the final. The outstanding Magath curled an eighth-minute shot beyond Zoff for the only goal of the game. Happel's clever tactics crowded out Platini. The disappointing Rossi was substituted after 54 minutes and Roberto Bettega, playing his final game for Juve, was off form, too. Boniek posed their biggest threat but keeper Uli Stein made two fine saves to thwart him.

Hrubesch left the next season and Hamburg never replaced him. They lost the 1984 Bundesliga title to Stuttgart on goal difference, then slipped down the table, fifth in 1985, seventh the following season – when Netzer left the club. Happel, now suffering from cancer, returned to his native Austria at the end of the campaign.

Juventus would win the European Cup at last in 1985, beating Liverpool in the final. But their 1–0 victory would pale into insignificance against the background of the most horrific stadium tragedy in European Cup history: Heysel.

The aftermath of the 1984 final, between Liverpool and Roma in Rome, would play its part, too. By now, Joe Fagan had taken over from Paisley after another championship success. When Liverpool won the League Cup final, in March 1983, Souness stepped aside to let Paisley collect the trophy. It was a fitting tribute to one of the club's greatest figures.

Lee, the lively Australian winger Craig Johnston and the clever Republic of Ireland inside-forward Ronnie Whelan now featured alongside Souness in a vibrant midfield.

Rush and Dalglish formed a formidable partnership. Dalglish scored three times in Liverpool's 6–0 aggregate demolition of Danish side Odense in the first round. Rush hit the winner at San Mames after Atletico Bilbao had held Liverpool 0–0 at Anfield and scored the only goal again as they beat Benfica 1–0 in the quarter-final first leg. They won 4–1 in Lisbon with two goals from Whelan and one each from Johnston and Rush.

Dynamo Bucharest were brutal semi-final opponents. Four Romanians were booked in the first leg at Anfield but Liverpool won 1–0, with a header by 5 ft 4 in. Lee. Fagan said, 'I thought that at this stage, the European Cup was supposed to be about skill.' Rush bagged both goals as Liverpool won the return 2–1 in Romania.

Roma had eliminated IFK Gothenburg, CSKA Sofia, Dynamo Berlin and Dundee United to reach the final, in their own Olympic Stadium – the site of Liverpool's first triumph seven years before. Their coach, the veteran Swede Nils Liedholm, encouraged attacking football. In midfield, the Brazilian stars Cerezo and Falcao were complemented by Agostino di Bartolomei, the master of the long pass, a man who would commit suicide ten years later by shooting himself. Winger Bruno Conti had been one of the heroes of Italy's 1982 World Cup win. Roberto Pruzzo was a prolific striker.

Neal gave Liverpool a 13th-minute lead, though Roma protested that Whelan had fouled goalkeeper Franco Tancredi first. Pruzzo headed Roma level from Conti's cross three minutes before half-time. There were no more goals, despite extra time. The game was settled on penalties. Grobbelaar, bobbing up and down on his line had forced a dramatic miss from Conti. So Liverpool led 3–2 on spot kicks when Francesco Graziani stepped up for Roma's fourth attempt. Graziani's shot hit the top of bar and sailed over. Kennedy planted the last Liverpool penalty past Tancredi.

It was Liverpool's fourth European Cup victory. Only Real Madrid had lifted the trophy more often. Liverpool had done it at their opponents' home against a hostile crowd. Some of those Roma fans attacked Liverpool supporters in the streets after the match. The innocent fans of another Italian club, Juventus, would suffer in retaliation at Heysel.

Liedholm said, 'They knew how to keep the ball, which is usually our game.' Cerezo added, 'When they passed the ball to each other, I felt like going mad. I couldn't do anything to block their style of play.'

Fagan's men were playing the most fluent football any Liverpool team had played in Europe. How diligently Liverpool had absorbed the lessons learned from defeat by Red Star in 1973. Yet their triumph in Rome was the last by an English club until Manchester United's victory over Bayern Munich 15 years later.

Fields of Glory, Paths of Gold

In 1984–85 – with John Wark in place of Souness, who had joined Sampdoria – Liverpool strode imperiously past Lech Poznan, Benfica, FK Austria and Panathinaikos to meet star-studded Juventus in the final in Brussels. It should have been one of the great nights of European football. Instead it was the most awful.

CHAPTER 13

HEYSEL, HILLSBOROUGH AND BASTIA

Three major stadium tragedies blighted European football between 1985 and 1992. Thirty-nine people, most of them Juventus supporters, died after they were attacked by Liverpool fans on the terraces of the Heysel Stadium in Brussels before the 1985 European Cup final. Four years later, 96 Liverpool supporters were crushed to death before the FA Cup semi-final against Nottingham Forest at Hillsborough. In May 1992, 15 fans were killed and nearly 2,000 injured when a temporary stand collapsed before Bastia's home French Cup semi-final against Marseilles. All had far-reaching effect.

The Heysel tragedy was a disaster waiting to happen. A combination of hooliganism and inadequate security at an antiquated stadium turned a showpiece of the European game into a graveyard. Hooliganism at football matches was a phenomenon which had grown at pace since the mid-1960s. English supporters had taken the lead. Imitators quickly arose throughout Europe. In England throughout the 1970s and most of the 1980s, major football matches were ringed by hundreds of police who escorted visiting fans from their trains or buses to the ground and back as if they were passing through a war zone. Groups of fans fought each other, or the police and stewards, and whole districts were caught up in the turmoil.

Gerald McKinley, a Liverpool fan and spectator at Heysel, spoke for many, when he told the BBC: 'An incident like Heysel was almost certainly going to happen, because no one, anywhere, seemed capable of stopping the violence.' Brian Glanville in *Champions of Europe* contrasted Liverpool's achievements with the behaviour of their supporters. He claimed that Liverpool fans were the first of the 1960s hooligans, attacking rival supporters at home and committing robberies on trips abroad.

Liverpool and Manchester United fans had clashed at the FA Cup semi-final a few weeks before Heysel, when Liverpool supporters launched flares into the United section of the crowd.

Yet football hooliganism was not just an English disease. It had taken hold throughout western Europe. West Germany was a case in point. In 1982, a 16-year-old Bremen skinhead was kicked to death by a gang of Hamburg hooligans. Hertha Berlin supporters set fire to a train. Far-right groups openly tried to recruit at grounds such as Dortmund. Attendances began to plummet.

In Holland, fan groups usually known as 'Vak . . .' (after their area number in their home ground) caused mayhem every weekend. The major Italian and Spanish clubs were followed by groups of hooligans known as '*ultras*' for whom fighting was almost a rite of passage. That fashion spread to France, where the ultras of Paris Saint-Germain and Marseilles became notorious.

The difference was that the English fans exported their violence. Tottenham supporters had fought with Dutch police at the UEFA Cup final second leg in Rotterdam in 1974. Leeds fans had rioted at the European Cup final in Paris the following year. Drunken England fans had caused trouble at the 1980 European Championship finals in Italy.

The presence of English hooligans acted as a challenge to the local thugs, too. A key date in the development of football-related violence in France was 29 February 1984, when Parisian skinheads ambushed visiting England fans at the Parc des Princes before the 'friendly' match.

There were also scores to be settled between Liverpool supporters and Italian fans, dating back to the 1984 European Cup final in Rome. Liverpool had beaten Roma on penalties. Roma ultras then attacked Liverpool supporters with knives and iron bars as they left the Olympic Stadium. Liverpool's Kenny Dalglish said, 'The horror of Heysel arose partly from events that happened in Rome. Our supporters were attacked in alleys. People for whom I'd left tickets at the stadium said they'd been hammered with stones. Coaches were ambushed by Roma fans tossing bricks at them.'

The Liverpool secretary, Peter Robinson, had already warned UEFA about likely ticketing problems at Heysel. A year earlier, Robinson had held on to tickets for the final that Liverpool could not sell – rather than send them back to Rome and risk Roma fans obtaining tickets for Liverpool areas. Robinson was concerned about the antiquated state of the stadium, a concern later borne out by Alain Gilbert, the local fire brigade commander. Gilbert was not even asked to inspect the ground. He said, 20 years later, 'I feared there would be an incident. If I'd been asked to inspect the stadium, I'd have pointed to the weak fence that was erected to divide the fans. I'd have said that they needed wider and more numerous escape routes from the standing areas.'

Robinson was even more concerned that tickets for the Z sector of the ground – next to the Liverpool fans – were on sale in Belgium. He wanted the whole ticket allocation to be split solely between Liverpool and Juventus. Instead, those Z sector tickets were snapped up by the large Italian immigrant community in Belgium. So a group of Italian fans stood right next to the Liverpool supporters, far away from the main body of Juventus support at the other end of the stadium.

Dalglish said, 'Liverpool did all the warning. Liverpool had tried to keep fans out of that unsegregated area. Liverpool had made every effort to prevent trouble – and when the worst happened, Liverpool received all the blame.'

Scores of Liverpool fans were drunk by the time they entered the stadium. The Belgian police failed to search fans of either side for weapons. Many fans got in without even having their tickets checked. The Liverpool supporters were tightly packed in the X and Y terraces – separated from the Z sector only by a string of chicken wire.

Some Juventus fans began lobbing stones into the Liverpool support. Liverpool fans retaliated. Glanville quotes an Italian eyewitness, Marco Fornelli. He said, 'The first attack by the Liverpool fans consisted of rocks and rockets. The Juventus supporters were terrified and withdrew. About half an hour later, the second assault started. The English began to break down the fence and pelt the Italians with all sorts of missiles. The Italians moved back quite a way.'

The police were still standing by when the third, decisive, charge began 15 minutes later. Glanville says he counted only eight policemen inside the stadium. Fornelli said, 'The English came over the broken fence and charged the Italians with bottles, rocks, cans and fists.'

The Juventus fans panicked and tried to escape. But they could not scale the walls of the terraces, which were topped with barbed wire. Their exit was also blocked by a brick containing wall. Many tried to scale the wall, which collapsed under the pressure. Thirty-nine people – mainly Italian and some Belgian – were crushed or trampled to death in the stampede. Hundreds more were injured.

Alessio Degrandi, then 14, was one of the Juve fans who survived, thanks to mouth-to-mouth resuscitation. He said, 'I remember thinking that I was losing a shoe, so I bent down to fix it. The next thing I recall was people scrambling all over my body. I couldn't breathe. Then this arm reached down and a hand grabbed me. The next thing I knew was when I woke up in hospital.'

Degrandi's rescuer was a policeman. But the inaction of the police before the fatal stampede led to calls for the resignation of Belgium's interior minister, Count Nothomb. His refusal to quit sparked a storm of indignation which eventually brought down the Belgian government.

UEFA insisted that the game went ahead, even though bodies had been piled up under one of the stands. Dalglish said, 'We were all changed and ready to go when a UEFA representative came in and said, "You can't go out. There's been some trouble." We didn't know for sure that anyone had died. If UEFA had told the players that people had died, I don't think we'd have wanted to go on.

'We knew something serious had happened because the game was delayed for 90 minutes. The players saw the huge gaps at one end. Some people thought that not playing the match would have been a mark of respect to the dead. But UEFA decided that it had to be played for fear of even greater trouble. The decision taken at the time was understandable.'

Liverpool skipper Phil Neal said, 20 years later, 'I wish I'd been strong enough as the captain to say, "We're not playing." I wish we'd been stronger as a team and refused to play.'

Juventus, who included Michel Platini, the brilliant Polish attacker Zbigniew Boniek and a host of Italian internationals, won 1–0 and lifted the European Cup for the first time. The result hardly mattered. Platini, who scored the winning penalty, has been haunted by the memories ever since.

He said, 'I've never returned to Heysel. It's something I'd prefer not to talk about. I'm physically and mentally incapable of going back there. It's a deep wound that can't be healed. People think and talk about it but they don't know what we players knew or didn't know.'

UEFA blamed Liverpool and their fans for the tragedy. It banned all English clubs from European competitions indefinitely as a result. The ban was later reduced to five years – with an extra three-year suspension for Liverpool. Neither UEFA, nor the Belgian authorities, ever launched an enquiry into the causes of the tragedy. The Liverpool police examined video evidence with their Belgian counterparts. Several Liverpool fans were brought to trial in Brussels.

The British prime minister, Margaret Thatcher, summoned leading football figures to Downing Street. She said, 'It is an appalling thing that one set of supporters could not stand beside another set of supporters without being attacked.' The government's answer was more intensive police measures and identity cards for football fans.

Heysel was, too late, deemed an inappropriate venue for major matches. It was torn down, rebuilt and renamed the King Baudouin Stadium to stage games at Euro 2000.

Britain's minister of sport, Colin Moynihan, was pressing ahead with ID cards for fans when English football was shattered by another tragedy: Hillsborough. The English game had mourned 56 victims of the Bradford fire disaster a few weeks before Heysel – when the wooden stand at Bradford's Valley Parade ground went up in flames. Hillsborough would dwarf that.

The problem was massive overcrowding at the Leppings Lane end of the ground. The authorities had an early warning at the 1981 FA Cup semi-final between Tottenham and Wolves. Spurs' supporters complained of overcrowding in the central areas of the stand. Some, literally, watched the game with their faces pressed against the perimeter fencing.

Liverpool had been allocated the smaller Leppings Lane end despite having a much bigger following than Forest. By 2.30 p.m. (30 minutes before kick-off), most of the Forest supporters had taken their places. There was still a big queue of Liverpool fans – many delayed by motorway hold-ups – trying to enter the Leppings Lane turnstiles.

By 2.45 p.m., around 5,000 Liverpool supporters were still trying to get in. It was clear that many of them would miss the kick-off. There was also a risk that some might be injured in a crush. At 2.52 p.m., the police opened gate C in the perimeter wall to let fans through and relieve the pressure.

The fans at the front tumbled through. Those at the back pushed to move forward. Around 2,000 fans passed through the gate in a few minutes. But there was no one inside to direct them to terrace bays which still had empty spaces. The entrances to the already-filled bays were not sealed off.

Most of the fans continued down gangway 2 and into bays 3 and 4. These were already uncomfortably full. The result was that fans at the front were crushed against the fencing. Many fans lost their footing and were swept along by the crowd. Some fell and were trampled.

Some fans tried to escape on to the pitchside track but were pushed back by the police. Others were passed overhead to supporters in the seats above the terrace.

Six minutes into the match, the police at the Leppings Lane end realised what was happening. The referee stopped the game and the scale of the disaster became apparent. Bodies were lifted forward and laid out on the pitch. The dead were taken to the Hillsborough gymnasium, which served as a makeshift mortuary. Many were teenagers and children: one was Jon-Paul Gilhooley, just ten years old. Advertising boards were torn out and used as makeshift stretchers.

Some families lost two people – Gary and Stephen Harrison, Carl and Nick Hewitt, Thomas and Tommy Howard, Chris and Martin Traynor and the Hicks sisters, Sarah and Victoria.

John Traynor will never forget identifying his dead brothers in the gym at 3 a.m. the next morning. He said, 'It was like I was in some sort of trance.'

The Hillsborough head groundsman, Dave Barber, has had nightmares and panic attacks ever since. He remembers 'five young men turning as blue as the colour of my sweatshirt'.

The Guardian's chief football correspondent David Lacey wrote: 'English football grounds are many times safer than they were in the rickety days immediately after the second world war but the capacity for human error and faulty judgement in a crisis is undiminished. Hillsborough proved that.'

Liverpool defender Alan Hansen said, 'It's incongruous to draw a parallel between the two disasters, given that the cause of Heysel was hooliganism. However, if there was one common denominator, it concerned the inadequate crowd arrangements.'

Chief superintendent David Duckinfield, in charge of police operations that day, and his number two, Bernard Murray, were later charged with 'manslaughter by gross negligence' in a case brought by the Hillsborough Family Support Group, which represented the families of the victims. Murray was found not guilty. The jury failed to reach a verdict in Duckinfield's case.

Murray said, 'I'm haunted by the memories that if I had cordoned off the tunnel [gangway 2] it might have saved lives. That's the way I have felt ever since. I feel great sympathy for the people I saw in court every day. I know a lot of them blame me.'

Dalglish, by now Liverpool manager, earned great credit for the way that he handled the tragedy. He represented the club at all the funerals and came to embody Anfield's response to the disaster. He admitted later, 'There were times when I felt that my head was going to burst.'

The government set up an inquiry into the tragedy, chaired by Lord Justice Peter Taylor. His findings were to change the course of English football. He produced two reports. The first set out the causes of the Hillsborough tragedy. His second recommended a series of measures to prevent another disaster.

Taylor was one of the first judges to talk openly with the media about his findings. A leading law journal said, 'He broke new ground with his regular press conferences and interviews.'

Taylor was not afraid to disagree with the government either. He concluded that the ID card scheme would not have prevented the Hillsborough tragedy. (He believed that the time needed to check ID cards would have created even bigger queues.) Nor was it the solution to the hooligan problem. Taylor's judgement effectively killed the scheme. Many political pundits thought he had been brave – or foolhardy – to destroy a scheme approved by the prime minister. She had the power to block Taylor's rise to become Lord Chief Justice. But Mrs Thatcher held back and Taylor was appointed the head of Britain's judiciary in 1992.

Taylor produced an even more far-reaching recommendation: the introduction of all-seat stadia at all major (i.e. Football League) clubs and at Wembley, the Cup final venue and home of the England team. First and Second Division clubs had to comply by the start of the 1994–95 season. Third and Fourth Divisions were given an extra five years to meet the requirements.

Taylor's judgement was years ahead of its time. FIFA and UEFA would not make all-seat stadia compulsory for major matches until well into the 1990s. And the government legislated. After the Bradford stadium fire, Lord Justice Popplewell had recommended a voluntary code of conduct for club grounds. Now, all-seat stadia become mandatory for senior clubs. The cost implications were huge.

Chris Lightbown, then a senior *Sunday Times* football writer, became an expert on the Taylor Report and its consequences. He said, 'The clubs were trapped. They could hardly complain at whatever Taylor recommended because the tide of public opinion was so powerful. But they didn't have the money and they were terrified of the cost.' They had no choice but to accept. A *Sunday Times* survey a year after Taylor's recommendations revealed that all but one of the 92 clubs were implementing the proposals. Only one club, Barnsley, wavered, and they gave in soon after.

Meanwhile, an unlikely ally rode to football's rescue – the Conservative government. In 1990, the chancellor, John Major, a keen Chelsea fan, announced a 2.5 per cent reduction in the football pools betting levy. The money saved was earmarked for the redevelopment of football grounds. The cash amounted to £100 million, handed out as grants over five years and channelled through an organisation called the Football Trust. The clubs had devised ways to raise money for redevelopment too – usually by bond schemes which gave supporters the right to buy tickets for a set period, in return for a lump sum payment.

The Arsenal bond scheme, designed to raise £16.5 million towards the £22.5 million needed to make Highbury an all-seat arena, was typical. The club issued 12,120 bonds, priced at £1,500 or £1,100 each. According to the prospectus, fans who bought bonds were then entitled to 'the exclusive right to purchase an attractive and competitively-priced season ticket in the new North Bank Stand for up to 150 years'. The North Bank Stand, a state-of-the-art building, replaced the old North Bank terrace, where the hardcore supporters stood.

The government was encouraged by the clubs' reaction and extended the Football Trust grant scheme for five more years. The government contributed £200 million over ten years to help the clubs rebuild. Most rebuilt existing stadia. Some used the opportunity to move to state-of-the-art, all-seater grounds. Bolton Wanderers, Middlesbrough, Derby County, Sunderland and Stoke City, for instance, all built new stadia in the mid and late '90s. Southampton followed in 2001.

The brighter club directors saw the potential of all-seat grounds: increased ticket prices, a better-off, more middle-class audience and a consequent reduction in hooliganism.

The Premier League began in August 1992, buoyed by its ground-breaking TV deal with Sky Sports, worth £191 million over five seasons.

168

The cost of rebuilding England's grounds is usually estimated at around £800 million. Sky's millions undoubtedly gave the major clubs' finances a huge boost. Yet Lightbown believes the clubs would have implemented Taylor's recommendations even without the Sky deal. He said, 'I spoke to government and football people at the time and there was no doubt that the government was virtually winking at football, saying, "Go on, make an effort, show the public that you're trying to make this work – and when the pips start to squeak, we'll step in and save the day", as they did with the betting levy reduction.

'I have no doubt that if the betting levy money had proved insufficient, the government would have found other ways of putting in money – in return, one would assume, for the game rationalising its structure.

'Taylor was politically very astute. He knew the government would cough up the money if the game was seen to be doing its best to put its house in order.'

Many fans opposed the abolition of the terraces. Supporters' groups opposed bond schemes and all-seater grounds at most of the major clubs. Several of English football's leading fanzines grew out of supporter opposition to bond schemes. There were sitdown protests at Arsenal and pitch invasions at West Ham. Even sections of the media opposed the death of the terraces. Lightbown said, 'Many of the media didn't read the overall situation well at all.'

By 1995, though, all England's major club grounds were seats-only. English football's reward was to be chosen as hosts for the 1996 European Championship finals, Euro 96. UEFA president Lennart Johansson emphasised that without the revolution wrought by Taylor's second report, England could never have been a candidate.

Yet, as late as 2000, the British sports minister Kate Hoey considered demands to bring back standing areas, similar to those at Bundesliga clubs such as Borussia Dortmund which retain terraces for domestic games but convert them to seating for European matches. The government rejected the calls.

Terraces in England had become an anachronism. UEFA had made all-seater grounds mandatory for all matches in its senior competitions. Europe's top clubs converted their stadia. Real Madrid, for instance, reduced the capacity of their Bernabeu home from 125,000 to 75,000.

And English football has acquired a wealthier audience as admission prices have risen. Chelsea, once home to The Shed, some of London's most notorious football hooligans, charged between £480 and £845 for a season ticket in 2004–05. Manchester United's match-day prices ranged from £21 to £34.

Trouble inside the grounds decreased as the audience changed. Old-style fans began to complain about 'lack of atmosphere'. Corporate hospitality became big business. The then Manchester United skipper Roy Keane famously complained about lack of vocal support from 'the prawn sandwich brigade'. Smaller ground capacities meant fewer fans travelled to away games, lessening the potential for conflict.

Long experience had made the police experts in crowd containment. They heightened security in the grounds, aided by the introduction of closed-circuit TV. The National Criminal Intelligence Service (NCIS) collected important intelligence about the hooligans and their activities. The courts were given powers via the Football (Disorder) Act of 1999 to serve banning orders on known troublemakers.

Yet England came close to being thrown out of Euro 2000 because of the drunken violence of their fans in Brussels and Charleroi. The Football (Disorder) Act was extended as a result, to stop known hooligans travelling to matches abroad. It was as if those who could no longer cause trouble at club games attached themselves to the England side. Others argued that the problem had never really gone away – and mobile phones and the Internet offered the hooligans new methods of arranging their 'rucks'.

An NCIS spokesman admitted that: 'Most of the trouble usually happens outside the stadium.' Dougie Brimson, the ex-hooligan turned writer, said, 'It only takes a few blokes who want a fight. That kind of thing goes on all the time. You'll never get rid of it.'

So perhaps Euro 2004 was a false dawn. English police cooperated with the Portuguese hosts to devise an anti-hooligan strategy and helped train Portuguese anti-hooligan squads. Police forces across Europe worked together to spot and turn back known troublemakers. English courts used banning orders to keep convicted hooligans at home. (Other countries, particularly Germany and Holland, used similar methods to restrain troublemakers.)

More than 50,000 England fans travelled to Portugal. Paul Hayward wrote in the *Daily Telegraph*: 'The shires had all sent their delegations. Every town seemed to have its flag.' They did not come seeking trouble, even after England's stoppage-time defeat by France, or elimination by Portugal. There was only one incident, when 33 people were arrested after a skirmish with riot police in the Algarve town of Albufeira. Paulo Gomes, deputy head of the committee that took charge of tournament security, said, 'I thought that the number of arrests for public disorder would be much higher. Perhaps there is a new fan culture, where supporters concentrate on the football, on living the moment, on enjoying themselves.'

The jury is still out. But maybe, just maybe, a change in 'fan culture' is another long-term consequence of Lord Justice Taylor's report.

The Furiani Stadium in Bastia was the scene of Europe's last great football ground disaster. On 5 May 1992, Bastia, then in the second division, were to play champions Marseille in the French Cup semi-final. The winners would meet Monaco in the final. The island of Corsica was buzzing. This was Bastia's biggest night since they won the cup in 1982.

The Furiani's capacity had been doubled by the erection of a temporary stand. A short while before kick-off, that temporary stand collapsed, bringing more than 3,000 people down with it. Fifteen died. Nearly 2,000 were treated for injuries. The match was called off and the cup competition abandoned for the season.

Monaco played Werder Bremen in the European Cup-Winners' Cup final in Lisbon the next day. Arsene Wenger had intended to lead his players on a stroll around the city. Instead, they were besieged by reporters at their team hotel, seeking their reaction to the tragedy. Their director of football, Henri Biancheri, remembered, 'Our spirit had gone. We deserved to lose and we did.'

The Marseille midfielder Franck Sauzee recalled, 'Football should be about joy and happiness. But that night was not football. It was horrific.'

A journalist whom Sauzee knew well was among the dead. Another friend was left wheelchair-bound by his injuries.

Sauzee said, 'When we went out for the warm-up, there didn't appear to be any problems. We'd been back to the dressing-room and we were ready to go onto the pitch when we were told there had been a problem with the stand. At first, we had no idea of how serious it was, but it soon became clear. There were injured people lying all over the pitch and the players ran out to help the paramedics, trying to give first aid. I remember helping to load people into the helicopters that arrived to airlift them to hospital.

'I didn't manage a single night's sleep for a week because of the

171

things that I'd witnessed. It had a deep psychological effect on everyone involved. It remains my worst moment in football.' He added, 'I remember going back to the Furiani Stadium during my time with Strasbourg a few years later and all those terrible emotions came rushing back.'

Doctor Daniel Digiambattista, in charge of the emergency medical services, reflected, 'A week before the match, the extra stand was erected in haste. The match also coincided with the Tour de Corse car rally, so all emergency medical services were on standby. Access was hampered by a railway line, a narrow two-lane road and a pond. Around 700 patients had to be evacuated, 250 by helicopter, and the rescue operation went on until the next morning.'

The French government set up an inquiry which pointed to criminal negligence, shoddy work and lack of safety checks. Prosecutions followed. The inquiry opened up other issues, too, such as possible financial links between the club and the island's separatist movement, and the involvement of local criminals in the construction process.

Bastia's separatist club president, Jean-Francois Filippi, was found shot dead, nine days before he was due to stand trial for criminal negligence. More than £12 million was awarded to the victims of the disaster and their families.

The writer Daniel Singer summed up, 'Corsica was promised a fiesta. Instead, it got a massacre. The inquiry has shown beyond doubt that the dead and injured were the victims of greed.'

Bastia was a wake-up call as France prepared to host the 1998 World Cup finals. The French government exerted major influence on the organising committee, led by co-presidents Michel Platini and Fernand Sastre. Platini was the fundraiser, the public face of the operation. Sastre, who died at the start of the finals, was the administrator. As Geoff Hare notes in *Football in France*, 'Decisions about the World Cup, from the highest level of the state down, followed the tradition of the way sport in France has been seen as a matter of public interest and as a legitimate concern of the public authorities. The government (Fifth Republic) continued that tradition.'

Or to put it bluntly: no more Bastias. The World Cup finals were an international showcase for French organisation and style. Nothing was left to chance, or the whim of host clubs. Platini explained the organisation: 'Virtually everything was done three months before the finals began. Only a few details remained to be sorted out. All the major decisions had been made, everyone knew what they had to do, the tickets had been sold and the marketing completed.'

FIFA president Sepp Blatter said, 'Hillsborough led to changes in stadium design and ultimately to a trouble-free Euro 96 in England. The Bastia tragedy prompted tighter restrictions on temporary grandstands and a safe France 98. But there is disturbing evidence that these lessons have not been learned everywhere.'

Disaster has continued to strike outside Europe. In 1996, more than 80 people died and many more were injured when hundreds tumbled down stairs at the Guatemala v. Costa Rica World Cup qualifier in Guatemala City. In April 2001, 43 fans were killed and hundreds injured after a crush at Ellis Park, Johannesburg, before the meeting of South Africa's best-supported clubs, Kaiser Chiefs and Orlando Pirates. A month later, more than 100 died in a stampede at the game between Ashanti Kotoko and Hearts of Oak at the Accra Stadium.

FIFA's 'Working Group for the Prototype Football Stadium' has issued guidelines for stadium building and management. It insists, 'It should be clearly understood by everyone involved that human safety is the first and foremost consideration – a consideration that should not be put aside under any circumstances.'

That is why the preparations for the 2006 World Cup finals in Germany have been the most rigorous yet. More than 1.4 billion euros were spent on upgrading the 12 venues to the highest safety standards. Germany's Interior minister Otto Schily monitored the building programme in conjunction with the World Cup Organising Committee (WCOC). All the venues were subjected to a stringent *Stiftung Warentest* (Testing Foundation) inspection in January 2006 and each stadium was required to provide the WCOC with a safety certificate as a condition of staging matches. The testing process also focused on measures for dealing with scenes of crowd panic.

As Blatter added, 'Building safe and modern stadia is one thing. Managing them properly is another. We want fans to go to matches in safety and comfort. So the level of responsibility can never be set too high.'

CHAPTER 14

ITALY, BEARZOT AND THE UGLY GERMANS

This is a tale of the two teams which contested the 1982 World Cup final in Madrid. Italy, guided by Enzo Bearzot, broke free of their negative shackles to score eight goals in their last three matches and become world champions. It was Italy's most prestigious moment since Vittorio Pozzo's team won the tournament in 1938.

Meanwhile, West Germany trampled over the traditions laid down by their great side a decade earlier. They played a charade of a match to reach the second phase, then their goalkeeper committed one of the worst fouls ever seen in a World Cup semi-final. The West German team's reputation was at its lowest ebb when they returned from Spain.

Italy entered the 1982 World Cup finals as serial underachievers. They had won the trophy in 1934 and 1938. Their post-war record was scratchy. They did not even qualify for the finals in 1958. Eight years later, in England, they crept home early, hugely embarrassed by defeat against North Korea. In 1974, they were eliminated at the group stage again, after losing 2–1 to Poland in Stuttgart.

Only in 1970 had the Italians mounted a serious challenge. They pipped West Germany 4–3 in a dramatic extra-time finish to reach the final. Then they crumbled 4–1 against a Brazil team including Pele, Gerson, Jairzinho, Rivelino, Tostao and Carlos Alberto.

Yet Bearzot's new-look side, based around champions Juventus, had exceeded expectations in the 1978 finals in Argentina. Italy had completed their preparations with a dismal 0–0 draw against

Yugoslavia. The fans were pessimistic. The media wanted the coach sacked.

Italy's plight grew even worse 30 seconds into their first group game when Bernard Lacombe put France ahead with one of the fastest goals in World Cup history. Italy fought back. Paolo Rossi levelled. Renato Zaccarelli scored the winner. Italy's confidence soared. They beat Hungary 3–1, then edged hosts Argentina 1–0 with a brilliant finish by Roberto Bettega after a one-two with Rossi.

In the second phase, Bearzot's team drew 0–0 with West Germany and beat Austria 1–0. Their last second-phase game against Holland was effectively a semi-final. Ernie Brandts' own goal gave Italy an early lead. But two spectacular long-range goals – from Brandts and Arie Haan – took Holland to face Argentina in the final. Haan struck his swerving, dipping winner from more than 35 yards. Goalkeeper Dino Zoff has grimaced through frequent TV replays. He said, 'I'd had a very good game against Germany but I wasn't on top form against Holland.'

Two years later, in the European Championships, Italy lost a third-place play-off to Czechoslovakia on penalties on home soil. They scored only twice in four matches. Perhaps they had reverted to type in familiar surroundings. Or, perhaps, they lacked the cutting edge of the suspended Rossi.

Bearzot became even more determined to wean the national side away from the defensive, counter-attacking football that was the norm in Serie A and threatened to become the hallmark of the national team again. He said, 'For me, football should be played with two wingers, a centre-forward and a playmaker. That's the way I see the game. I select my players and then I let them play.' He believed Italy had the sparkle to beat the world's best. He said, 'We have attackers who can make the difference.' The Azzurri would prove him right in the closing stages of the 1982 finals, when Rossi finished top scorer.

The Italian journalist Gian Paolo Ormezzano said, 'Bearzot wanted to change the mentality of Italian football. He was a man of courage and ideas and he was strong enough to go against accepted wisdom.' *Sunday Times* writer and Italian football expert Brian Glanville said, 'One of Bearzot's great qualities was his ability to "de-intoxicate" his players, as he put it, after the trials and tribulations of Serie A football.'

Yet Italy began the tournament firing blanks. They barely scraped through their group after three draws. They pipped Cameroon for second place behind Poland only on goals scored.

They began with a tentative 0–0 draw against the Poles. Bruno Conti gave them an 18th-minute lead against Peru. Toribio Diaz levelled seven minutes from time. Poland beat Peru 5–1 to clinch their place in the second phase. The Azzurri had to draw against Cameroon at least. Francesco Graziani scored after an hour. Gregoire M'Bido equalised within a minute. Italy survived the closing stages to go through with the Poles. The Italian media was withering. Bearzot, fiercely protective of his players, bore the brunt of the criticism. The players responded with a media boycott. Zoff, the squad's elder statesman, was the only one who would speak to reporters.

Twenty years later, he reflected on the psychology of those early games, 'Italy always have problems in the first round of major tournaments. As a leading football nation, we're always under massive pressure on these occasions. Everyone wants to knock us off our pedestal and yet our progress to the next stage is regarded as a formality.

'This responsibility weighs heavily on the players, who are afraid of failure and the consequences that would bring. Once we get past the first round, the team can express themselves freely. That's exactly what happened in 1982.'

The second phase comprised four groups of three. The section winners would go into the semi-finals. Italy were pitted against holders Argentina and favourites Brazil. They opened against Argentina and the emerging genius of Diego Maradona. Bearzot detailed Juventus defender Claudio Gentile to mark him. Maradona was not quite the force he would be in Mexico four years later. Gentile just about won the battle – after a bruising encounter. He said, 'Maradona was the best opponent I ever faced. He gave me an incredibly hard time. But I'm proud of the job that I did.'

It was a good day for Juventus. Marco Tardelli gave the Azzurri a 55th-minute lead. Antonio Cabrini added a second. Argentina replied only once, through Daniel Passarella. Italy were buoyant. Bearzot said, 'We found our form in an important game. The players showed what they can achieve. We believe in ourselves again.'

The Brazilians trumped Italy's 2–1 win with a 3–1 victory over the Argentinians. So Bearzot's side had to beat Brazil in Barcelona to reach the last four. A draw would be enough for the Brazilians. Their team featured such attacking stars as Zico, Socrates, Falcao and Eder. They had already scored 13 goals in four games. Caution was not in their nature. Rossi made them pay for it. His killer hat trick was another triumph for Bearzot. The striker was only in the squad because the coach believed in him so much. Small and mobile, he had been a revelation in the 1978 finals. But he had been suspended for two years after a match-fixing scandal. He had played for barely two months before the 1982 finals.

The ban was the result of a league inquiry into Perugia's 2–2 draw with Avellino in December 1978. Rossi and two Perugia colleagues were among those accused of fixing the game and found guilty. An Avellino player claimed that he asked Rossi, '2–2?' and the striker replied, 'If you want.' Rossi, then 22, insisted it was an innocent, flippant response. He was suspended for three years, reduced to two on appeal. (Avellino's Stefano Pellegrino received the longest ban – six years.)

Bearzot had taken another huge gamble by starting Rossi in all Italy's four previous games. The media called for Rossi to be dropped, claiming he lacked match sharpness. Bearzot refused. The coach said, 'I knew that if Rossi wasn't there, I wouldn't have an opportunist inside the box. That was where he was really sharp, really quick.'

Rossi showed that sharpness in the fifth minute. Gabriele Oriali found Cabrini and Rossi stole behind the Brazilian defence to bury a header.

Serginho and Leandro went close for Brazil before Socrates turned their pressure into an equaliser. Tackles flew thick and fast as the Brazilians camped in the Italian half. Gentile was booked. Oscar lashed out at Tardelli.

Rossi struck again in a classic 25th-minute counter-attack. Cerezo swept a careless crossfield ball into his path. Rossi ran on and dispatched it beyond keeper Valdir Peres.

Zoff was inspirational as Italy repelled attack after attack, sometimes with luck on their side. Zico looked stunned when Gentile's tug ripped his shirt and Israeli referee Abraham Klein waved away Brazil's penalty appeals.

Falcao, Zico and Serginho all went close. Cerezo's drive crashed off a post. Then Falcao made it 2–2. Cerezo's run distracted the Italian defence, allowing Falcao to cut inside into space and crash a rising shot beyond Zoff.

Other teams would have sat back and held on. Tele Santana's Brazilians went looking for a winner. Instead, Rossi completed his hat trick, 16 minutes from time. Tardelli's half-cleared corner was knocked back into the box. Rossi nipped ahead of Valdir Peres and stabbed home the loose ball.

Italy needed more heroics from 40-year-old Zoff to keep their lead. He said, 'It was the 90th minute and I blocked a shot from Oscar. It wasn't the most spectacular save of my career but it was the most crucial. I have fond memories of that match.'

Rossi said, 'I felt protected by Bearzot and that was a decisive factor.'

Italy had ridden their luck and beaten one of the most gifted Brazil sides ever. That was the night the Brazilian dream of *o jogo bonito* (the beautiful game) died. By the 1986 finals, they included at least one defensive midfielder, just like everyone else.

Two more Rossi goals settled a one-sided semi-final against Poland, 2–0. The Poles badly missed their star attacker Zbigniew Boniek, who was suspended after collecting two yellow cards.

Italy faced West Germany in the final, without playmaker Giancarlo Antognoni, who had broken a toe against the Poles. Bearzot had taken another gamble in the semi-final, replacing the suspended Gentile with 18-year-old defender Giuseppe Bergomi. He stayed in for the final. Gentile came back for Antognoni.

The Azzurri suffered an early blow when Graziani landed on his shoulder after a collision with Wolfgang Dremmler. Bearzot had to send on Alessandro Altobelli after only seven minutes. Cabrini then became the first player to miss a penalty in a World Cup final when he shot wide after Hans-Peter Briegel fouled Conti.

Bearzot was smoking heavily on the bench as usual. His nerves began to settle in the 57th minute. Tardelli took a quick free kick, Gentile crossed, Altobelli missed the ball – and Rossi stole behind him to head Italy in front.

Tardelli finished off Gaetano Scirea's pass with a low 20-yarder for the second. Screaming, head swaying, tears streaming down his face, Tardelli's emotions ran away with him. Zoff said, 'At that moment, I knew the World Cup was in our grasp.'

Altobelli turned in the third after a quick break by Conti. Bearzot sent on veteran Franco Causio, one of the stars of 1978, for the closing minutes. Paul Breitner scored a late goal for the Germans. They did not even bother to celebrate.

Zoff, the oldest player in the competition, lifted the World Cup. He said, 'This was the zenith of my career. I was so excited that I almost kissed the queen of Spain at the presentation!' He added, 'This was the best Italy side of modern times because we were so flexible and so fast.'

The much-criticised Bearzot, the team's former technical director, had guided Italy to their third World Cup victory. His players chaired him off the pitch. The TV commentator Nando Martinelli famously said, '*Campioni del Mondo; Campioni del Mondo; Campioni del Mondo.*' (World Champions – three times.)

It was Italy's last major tournament victory. The Azzurri failed to qualify for the 1984 European Championship finals, from a 'group of death', which included Romania, Sweden and Czechoslovakia. In Mexico, two years later, the World Cup holders lost to France in the last 16. It was Bearzot's last game in charge. He said, 'The coach's job requires that we reach the semi-finals at least. Otherwise the coach goes.'

Zoff said, 'When I think of the national team, I think of Enzo Bearzot. He was a man of great moral stature, the best that I've met in football. Gentile declared, 'Bearzot was a great – Italy's best-ever coach after Vittorio Pozzo.'

Zoff went on to coach the Azzurri. Rossi retired at the age of 31 to follow his passion for deep sea diving.

Yet the images of 1982 remain fresh in Italian minds: the goals, the celebrations, the photos on the plane home. Bearzot smoking his pipe, playing cards with Zoff, Causio and the president of Italy, Sandro Pertini. The World Cup stands beside them.

West Germany had won the European Championship in 1980. Yet so many of those players were a world removed from such stylish talents as Beckenbauer and Netzer, eight years earlier.

Helmut Schoen had stayed on at the German federation's request to guide the holders into the World Cup finals in Argentina. They were deprived of a spot in the third-place play-off by Austria, who beat them 3–2. Hans Krankl scored the winner two minutes from time. It was Austria's first win over their old rivals since 1931. Schoen went and was succeeded by his assistant Jupp Derwall. Schoen had questioned modern players' values in 1974. He worried about the game's increasingly commercial ethos – he called it 'football as show business'. He was concerned about the motivation of future international stars.

179

The Germans won a dire competition in 1980 beating Belgium 2–1 in the final. Giant Hamburg striker Horst Hrubesch scored both goals, one set up by the young Cologne midfielder Bernd Schuster. The 20 year old had a hand in each of Klaus Allofs' three goals against Holland. The Germans' 3–2 win virtually clinched their place in the final.

Schuster left for Barcelona a few months later. Michel Platini said of Schuster, 'I watched him play once at Barcelona and I was in awe of his talent.'

He seemed a natural heir to the traditions of Netzer. Instead, he played only 21 times for West Germany. He married a glamorous model, Gabi, who doubled as his agent, and preferred playing the piano at home to hanging out with his teammates. He was no diplomat, either. After a friendly against Brazil, he shunned a birthday party given by his national colleague Hansi Muller, saying, 'I don't like Hansi Muller.' Derwall wanted Schuster to socialise with the rest of the squad. Instead, he fell out with the coach, too – and turned his back on the national squad. He was coaxed into an occasional comeback but he was still only 24 when he made his last appearance for West Germany. His departure robbed the team of their most creative talent.

(Schuster clearly had a talent for falling out with people. He was furious with Barcelona coach Terry Venables, who substituted him during their European Cup final shootout defeat by Steaua in 1986. He walked out of the stadium and did not play for a year. He later took legal action against the club – alleging 'unfair dismissal' – before joining their arch rivals Real Madrid.)

Meanwhile, in the early 1980s, the Bundesliga's top teams were shorn of flair and what style there was was provided by foreigners, such as Kevin Keegan at Hamburg. Karl-Heinz Rummenigge at Bayern Munich was an exception, when he remained free of niggling injuries. But Bayern were in financial trouble until they sold him to Internazionale in 1984. Uli Hoeness, now their general manager, operated a 'value for money' policy – winning trophies with a minimum of big names or big signings.

So the new stars of the German team were muscular journeymen, such as Hans-Peter Briegel, their other young 'find' of 1980; the pragmatic midfielder Lothar Matthaus, or 'the monster' Hrubesch. In 1972, Beckenbauer and Netzer had led the team to glory as well as victory. The next generation ground out results, often by cynical means.

West Germany's new image came to haunt them in the 1982 finals.

They began their group games with a shock 2–1 defeat against Algeria in Gijon, then gave themselves a lifeline with a 4–1 win over Chile. Rummenigge scored three. Austria beat Chile 1–0 and Algeria 2–0 to book their place in the second phase. The Algerians then beat Chile 3–2. That meant West Germany had to beat Austria to edge out Algeria on goal difference.

Four years earlier, the teams had fought a battle royal in Argentina. The game in Gijon mocked the competitive spirit of football. Hrubesch gave the Germans a tenth-minute lead. Both sides knew they were through if the score stayed 1–0. They spent the remaining 80 minutes wasting time, passing back to the keeper (who could pick the ball up then) and avoiding any attempt to score again. The furious Algerians felt they had been cheated.

One paper said the teams had 'agreed a non-aggression pact'. The German TV commentator at the game said, 'The ends don't justify these means.' The nation's biggest-selling tabloid *Bild* called the spectacle 'shameful'.

Bild might have felt shame. The squad did not. Derwall said, 'We wanted to get through, not play well.' Matthaus said, 'We're through. That's all that matters.'

Uli Hesse-Lichtenberger, in *Tor!*, quotes more angry media reaction. 'Never before have German fans been told so bluntly that they shouldn't count on being offered matches worth watching.' And when a number of travelling fans tried to remonstrate with the squad, some of the players doused them with water.

In the second phase, West Germany drew 0–0 with England and beat hosts Spain 2–1 to reach the semi-finals. They met France in Seville. The score was 1–1 in the second half. The French were in full flow after equalising. Michel Platini split the German defence with a through ball and Patrick Battiston burst onto it. The German goalkeeper Harald Schumacher poleaxed him with a violent charge.

Battiston, unconscious, was surrounded by anxious colleagues. The Frenchman lost several teeth and suffered broken ribs. Schumacher stood in his penalty area as if nothing had happened. The Dutch referee Charles Corver did not even caution him – just restarted play with a goal kick.

The irony was that Schumacher's save decided the penalty shootout after the Germans, inspired by substitute Rummenigge, had fought back from 3–1 down in extra time. Schumacher had committed a potentially life-threatening foul – and got away with it. Even worse, he showed no remorse.

His attitude provoked fury in France, where an older generation recalled the wartime German occupation. Schumacher had become the symbol of a new German brutality.

Yet most Germans shared their neighbours' feelings. Hesse-Lichtenberger quotes the writer Dietrich Schulze-Marmeling, who said that Schumacher had resurrected the image of 'the ugly German'. No cheering crowds welcomed the squad when they returned home after the final.

Two years later, a continent smiled when Antonio Maceda's stoppage-time header knocked out West Germany and took Spain into the European Championship semi-finals instead. Derwall was sacked. His assistant Erich Ribbeck was discounted as a successor because of his association with Derwall. West Germany were about to follow a tried-and-tested route in crisis: turn to Franz Beckenbauer.

CHAPTER 15

BECKENBAUER TO THE RESCUE

There was one major problem about installing Franz Beckenbauer as West Germany's national coach. He was not interested. After the 1982 World Cup finals, he said that he would never make a successful coach. So the German federation considered approaching Helmut Benthaus, coach of Bundesliga champions Stuttgart.

Then, two days after the defeat by Spain, *Bild* ran a story headlined 'Franz: I'm ready'. Beckenbauer was baffled. He did not even hold a coaching licence. The story had been concocted by *Bild*'s sports desk together with Beckenbauer's agent Robert Schwan. The subsequent conversation between Beckenbauer and Schwan might have been interesting, to say the least. But the story put great pressure on Beckenbauer to ride to the ailing national team's rescue.

It also gave the DFB their chance. DFB president Hermann Neuberger met Beckenbauer and persuaded him to take over as caretaker, while Benthaus extricated himself from his contract at Stuttgart. Instead, Stuttgart plummeted in 1984–85. Benthaus moved on to a job in Switzerland. Suddenly, Beckenbauer, the 1974 World Cup-winning skipper, became a permanent appointment.

Beckenbauer said later that he felt a responsibility to take the job. He had gained fame and fortune through German football. He wanted to restore the national team's reputation in return. He said, 'I couldn't live on something that had lost its credibility.'

West Germany qualified for the 1986 World Cup finals in Mexico from a group including Portugal, Sweden, Czechoslovakia and Malta. It was not a smooth passage. Portugal even inflicted their first home defeat in a World Cup qualifier, 1–0 in Stuttgart. Beckenbauer feared an early return home from Mexico. He felt that too many of his players were 'reliable but unimaginative'.

Rummenigge carried a heavy creative burden. Yet West Germany had bags of determination, some tough defenders and an emerging striker, Rudi Voller. The squad would surprise their coach – and vindicate his decision to take charge.

Klaus Allofs scored an 84th-minute equaliser to earn a 1–1 opening draw against Uruguay. Voller and Allofs turned an early deficit into a 2–1 win over Scotland. That result saw the team into the last 16, although they lost their final Group E match 2–0 to a Denmark side inspired by Michael Laudrup.

Matthaus grabbed an 87th-minute winner against Morocco, then Beckenbauer's side held their nerve in the quarter-finals to eliminate hosts Mexico 4–1 in a penalty shootout. Their form was improving, their confidence growing.

The Germans gave their best performance in the semi-final. This time there was no controversy, no bad feeling, as they beat France 2–0. Andy Brehme fired in a ninth-minute free kick. Voller sealed victory in the last minute.

Beckenbauer had felt that the World Cup would at best be an exercise in building for the future. He admitted he was surprised that West Germany had reached the final.

His team did him proud in defeat against Argentina, galvanised by Diego Maradona at his peak. They looked finished when Jorge Valdano scored Argentina's second goal, ten minutes after half-time. For the next 25 minutes, the Germans were inspired. It was as if they were determined to confound their coach's expectations of them. Rummenigge pulled one back, then Voller levelled.

Maradona sliced the Germans open three minutes later. Jorge Burruchaga's finish won the World Cup for Argentina. The Germans won praise for their courage.

However, Beckenbauer's squad was not all sweetness and harmony. Goalkeeper Uli Stein was sent home after a public row with the coach. Beckenbauer had another slanging match with striker Dieter Hoeness. He wondered to Neuberger whether he would ever discover the knack of handling the media.

Yet Beckenbauer had succeeded in his self-imposed task. He had made the best use of West Germany's resilience and fighting spirit, without the sourness that scarred the 1982 finals. He had laid down sensible tactics and encouraged the side to go forward. He and his players had re-established the team's credibility and regained the nation's support.

Now Beckenbauer wanted to win a major trophy. He would accomplish that four years later, in Italy. He became the first man to captain and coach World Cup-winning teams. He claimed that it was the pinnacle of his career. He said, 'Italy 1990 was the most important for me. It doesn't get any better than coaching a team to win the World Cup.'

A rising generation of players fuelled Beckenbauer's optimism. Rummenigge was past his peak but Jurgen Klinsmann had joined Voller in attack. Andy Moller and Thomas Hassler added flair in midfield. Klaus Augenthaler and Jurgen Kohler were solid defenders. Matthaus was still there in midfield, almost an elder statesman.

Italia 90 was not a great World Cup. As FIFA's official archive notes, 'It was a disappointing competition with too much dull defensive football and too many matches won on penalties. The final, between West Germany and Argentina, was the least inspiring in the history of the competition. Argentina became the first team not to score in the final – and the first to have two players sent off.'

That was hardly West Germany's fault. Beckenbauer's side were one of the few prepared to take risks. They opened with a 4–1 win over Yugoslavia, then crushed the United Arab Emirates 5–1. Beckenbauer had freed Matthaus, a midfield marker in 1986, to roam. He scored three goals in those two games. The Germans eased through their final group game, a 1–1 draw against Colombia.

In the last 16, they met Holland. Beckenbauer predicted to Dutch coach Leo Beenhakker that the winners would go on to lift the trophy. He said, 'We're the two teams with the best players.' West Germany prevailed, 2–1, in an ill-tempered match: the sequel to a bitter clash two years earlier.

West Germany had staged the 1988 European Championship finals. They topped their group with two wins and a draw, including a 2–0 victory over Spain, who had eliminated them in 1984. They met Holland in the semi-finals, at the Volkspark in Hamburg. The Dutch still felt they had been robbed by the Germans in the 1974 World Cup final. Dutch striker Dick Naninga and West Germany's Bernd Holzenbein had stood toe to toe in the 1978 finals. The German players complained about the Dutch tackling after their Euro 1980 meeting.

From the Dutch viewpoint, the game at the Volkspark became a double payback: for 1974 and, two generations later, for Germany's wartime occupation of Holland.

The Dutch fans were allocated 6,000 tickets. On match day, a convoy of cars with Dutch number plates rolled through Germany. How all those Dutch supporters got tickets remains a mystery. At kick-off time, there were more than 30,000 of them in the Volkspark. It was almost a symbolic gesture, an occupation in reverse. As the German midfielder Frank Mill said wryly, 'It would have been better if we had played in Germany . . .'

The Dutch coach Rinus Michels said, 'It was more than a football match. It was about an old quarrel.' Goalkeeper Hans van Breukelen remembered watching Holland lose the 1974 final. He said, 'I was 17 then and I've not forgotten. It was one of my motivations not to lose again. I think the whole team had that kind of feeling. We had to beat them this time.'

The Dutch side included such greats as Ruud Gullit, Frank Rijkaard, Marco van Basten and Ronald Koeman. They dominated the first half but could not score. Beckenbauer's side broke up their rhythm with some harsh challenges, then Matthaus netted a debatable penalty after Klinsmann fell over Rijkaard.

The Romanian referee Ion Igna evened things up with another dubious spot kick, belted home by Koeman after van Basten collapsed under Kohler's challenge. Van Basten, top scorer in the tournament, struck the winner two minutes from time, running across Kohler to tuck away Jan Wouters' pass.

It was Holland's first win over West Germany since 1956 and the Dutch greeted it like a heroic resistance victory over the occupying power. As Simon Kuper (who grew up in Holland) wrote in *Football Against the Enemy*: 'Hamburg was not only the [wartime] resistance that we never quite offered but also the battle that we never quite won.'

The Germans failed to understand the Dutch attitude. Beckenbauer even boarded the Dutch team bus to congratulate them. He said, 'Matches against Holland have cost me years of my life. But I wouldn't have missed them for anything. Those matches always breathed class, emotion and fantastic tension.'

Kuper saw it differently. He wrote: 'For the Dutch, the rivalry wasn't just about football. It was about something darker.'

The game in Milan boiled over in the 22nd minute. Rijkaard fouled Voller and was booked. That yellow card ruled him out of the quarter-finals. He spat at Voller, then ran after him and spat again. Rijkaard was sent off. So, somewhat mysteriously, was Voller. Rijkaard later said he had not meant his action as an anti-German gesture; he had simply lost his head amid the tension of the occasion. He denied suggestions that Voller had shouted racist abuse at him. The Dutchman apologised to Voller when they met next, in a Serie A match between Milan and Roma.

The incident fired up the Germans, who turned their anger to seizing the game. Klinsmann pulled out one of his finest, bravest performances. He gave West Germany a 51st-minute lead. Brehme added a second eight minutes from time. Koeman's 89th-minute penalty came too late for Holland. It was a sweet victory for Beckenbauer's team. The German coach repeated his forecast to Beenhakker after the match: the victors would win the World Cup.

The quarter-final against Czechoslovakia was an anticlimax, settled by a Matthaus spot kick. England, sparked by Paul Gascoigne, were tougher opponents. Beckenbauer and his players said it was their toughest contest.

Brehme's swerving shot deceived Peter Shilton to give West Germany the lead. Gary Lineker poached an equaliser. There were no goals in extra time. Beckenbauer shook hands with England's Bobby Robson before the penalty shootout. Germany won the lottery 4–3 to reach the final. Stuart Pearce and Chris Waddle missed their kicks. They suffered their anguish frequently re-run on TV throughout the months ahead.

Beckenbauer had decided to quit after the 1990 finals. He had one match left: the final against Argentina. Maradona, carrying a knee injury, was not the force of old. Meanwhile, Argentina's cynical progress had produced a rash of cards and suspensions. Four of their regular starters were banned for the final. They massed in defence and kicked out. Pedro Monzon and Gustavo Dezotti were sent off in the second half. Brehme settled the game with a penalty five minutes from time after Voller went down.

Beckenbauer walked to the tunnel satisfied, while his celebrating players were engulfed by cameramen. For once, he was not the centre of attention. But he had restored West Germany's credibility with a vengeance.

Fields of Glory, Paths of Gold

The transformation of Matthaus demonstrated Beckenbauer's achievement. In 1982, Matthaus had been one of most distinctive of the ugly Germans. In 1990, he was voted European Footballer of the Year for his creative contribution to West Germany's success.

And there was a postscript a decade later when a reluctant coach was installed after Germany had been humiliated at Euro 2000 – and he led the team to the World Cup final two years later. His name? Rudi Voller.

CHAPTER 16

FORZA MILAN!

In the beginning, there was Franco Baresi: a promising young centre-back from Travagliato, near Brescia, who had joined Milan after he was turned down by Internazionale. The young Baresi had quickly learned about overcoming adversity. His mother died when he was 13. His father died four years later. It was hard enough for Franco, brother Giuseppe – later to play for Inter and Italy – and sister Lucia just to keep their family together.

Football was Baresi's escape route. He made his Serie A debut for the *rossoneri* as a 17 year old, in a 2–1 win at Verona on 23 April 1978. As Milan's official website says, 'From that day, the story of Franco Baresi was the story of Milan.'

Over the next 19 years, until his retirement in 1997, Baresi – *Il Capitano* – skippered Milan to three European Cup final wins and five Serie A championships. He was skipper for 16 seasons. He played 81 times for Italy and captained them in the 1994 World Cup final.

Baresi was quiet, taciturn, off the pitch. As one journalist wrote: 'Interviewing Baresi was like a kind of torment, minutes waiting for answers that never came.' On the field, he was a great defender, an organiser and a leader who had proved his commitment to Milan during their dark days in Serie B.

There were other major players, of course. Silvio Berlusconi, the entrepreneur later turned politician, whose fortune transformed the club in the late 1980s. The great Dutch trio of Ruud Gullit, Marco van Basten and Frank Rijkaard. Another great Italian defender, Paolo Maldini. The skilful winger Roberto Donadoni. The visionary coach

189

Arrigo Sacchi and his successor Fabio Capello. The midfield stars from the old Yugoslavia, the Serb, Dejan Savicevic, and the Croat Zvonimir Boban. But Baresi was there from start to finish, as Milan rose from their lowest point to celebrate their finest era.

The ban imposed on the English teams after Heysel had left a gap to be filled. Juventus, the 1985 winners of the European Cup, had failed to build on that victory. In 1986, their conquerors, Barcelona (coached by Terry Venables) started huge favourites in the final against Steaua Bucharest in Seville – and lost on penalties after a goalless draw.

A year later, Porto beat Bayern Munich 2–1 in Vienna. Real Madrid, who had knocked out Juventus, lost to Bayern in the semi-finals. Rabah Madjer and Juary scored twice in two minutes after Bayern led through Ludwig Kogl.

Liverpool, who still included several of their 1984 winners, would surely have remained leading contenders. As Brian Glanville wrote in *Champions of Europe*: 'With the departure of the English clubs, the European Cup was hugely devalued. No one wanted the English hooligans back but almost every country wanted the English clubs, with their robust commitment.'

In 1988, PSV Eindhoven beat Benfica on penalties in Stuttgart after another goalless draw. This was the breach into which Milan stepped.

The rossoneri had won the championship in 1979, when Baresi collected his first title medal. Then they spent the early 1980s alternating between Serie A and Serie B. They were eliminated 1–0 by Porto in the first round of the 1979–80 European Cup. Worse followed at the end of the season.

Goalkeeper Enrico Albertosi and club president Felice Colombo were implicated in a major betting scandal. Milan were punished with relegation to Serie B for the first time in their history. They won promotion the following season but went straight down again. Baresi remembered, 'After the final game, at Cesena, I cried in the dressing-room like several of my teammates.'

Milan bounced back in 1983, with Baresi now a vital member of the side. Then club president Giuseppe Farina fled the country after a financial scandal and took a lot of the club's money with him. He was tried in 1989 on charges of tax evasion and found guilty. He received a heavy fine and a suspended prison sentence. Midfielder Alberigo Evani remembered, 'I went through some tough times under the Farina presidency. We'd gone backwards as a club and the company was about to go bankrupt. There were some really tough moments. Then, fortunately, Berlusconi arrived and took the team to the top.'

The former Leeds, Manchester United and Scotland striker Joe Jordan played in that side of the early '80s. He said, 'We were a young team that was emerging and finally did emerge. Players like Baresi, Evani and Mauro Tassotti came through to become top class.'

Berlusconi took over in March 1986 after protracted negotiations. Milan-born Berlusconi was already a controversial figure in Italy. He had made his fortune through property development, then made an even bigger fortune as the proprietor of the down-market Channel Five TV station. In 1990, he tried to buy one of Italy's major publishing businesses but was halted by organised opposition in parliament. He later went into politics as founder and leader of the Forza Italia party and in 2001 was elected for a second term as Italy's prime minister.

Berlusconi's opponents claim that he became Milan president to raise his public profile in preparation for a political career. They claim, too, that he entered politics to promote and protect his business interests – and point to serious conflicts of interest between Berlusconi the politician and Berlusconi the media magnate. One major area of contention was legislation passed under Berlusconi's government which allowed him to retain control of his three national TV channels.

Berlusconi also had to fight allegations of corruption over the world record £13 million deal which took Gianluigi Lentini from Torino to Milan in 1992. The fee astonished most Italian observers. Charges of false book-keeping against Berlusconi were dropped only when a statute of limitations expired.

Berlusconi's government also passed a law granting him immunity from prosecution while he was in office, a move to halt a long-running corruption trial while the Italian prime minister held the rotating presidency of the European Union. Italy's constitutional court annulled the immunity law in January 2004, so the case continues. Berlusconi claims he is the victim of a 'vendetta' by left-wing investigating magistrates and judges.

What can never be denied is that his arrival galvanised Milan. He invested nearly £30 million in the club. His first moves were to reorganise Milan's business structure, improve the training complex at Milanello and develop the youth set-up.

But Berlusconi was not the only wealthy man in charge of a major club. The Agnelli family, for instance, the owners of Fiat, had long reigned at Juventus. However Berlusconi overshadowed his rivals by the shrewdness of his signings.

Defensive midfielder Carlo Ancelotti arrived from Roma and gave Milan years of outstanding service despite his knee problems. Donadoni, a tricky right-winger with an eye for an opening, joined from Atalanta. In the summer of 1987, Berlusconi recruited two crucial imports from Holland – Ruud Gullit and Marco van Basten.

Gullit, a dreadlocked giant of Surinamese ancestry, had been an outstanding attacking midfielder with PSV Eindhoven. He was a clever strategist, an accurate passer over long distances and he scored goals, with his head or powerful right foot. He netted 24 in 1985–86 and 22 the following season as PSV won the Dutch championship twice running. Gullit was voted Dutch Footballer of the Year in both campaigns. (He was voted World and European Player of the Year in 1987, when he dedicated his award to the then-jailed African National Congress leader Nelson Mandela.)

Milan brought him to Italy for a medical in early 1987 and made him a fantastic offer. PSV had Gullit under contract until 1990 and protested to UEFA. But Berlusconi was determined to sign him – and Gullit joined them that summer in a world record £6.5 million deal.

Van Basten had been nurtured by the great Johan Cruyff at Ajax. He had already won the Golden Ball as Europe's top scorer. Van Basten scored the winner for Ajax against Lokomotiv Leipzig 1–0 in the 1987 European Cup-Winners' Cup final. He had power, technique and, even more than Gullit, a lethal eye for goal.

Legend has it that Berlusconi had to choose between van Basten and the Liverpool striker Ian Rush. After watching van Basten on video, he picked the Dutchman. Van Basten, out of contract at Ajax, was a snip at $750,000. Rush, meanwhile, spent a brief, unhappy spell at Juventus before returning to Liverpool.

Berlusconi also made a crucial change as coach, replacing former Milan great Nils Liedholm in 1987 with a virtual unknown from Parma, a man with no playing pedigree: Sacchi. Sacchi's response was, 'Do you have to have been a horse before you can be a jockey?'

Sacchi had taken Parma to the brink of promotion to Serie A in 1986–87 and his team had given Milan a hard time in the Coppa Italia. He challenged the stars of the Milan dressing-room, 'What have you won in your careers?' They would soon deliver decisive answers.

Sacchi was a rarity among Italian coaches. He emphasised attack

Visionary manager Herbert Chapman built the Huddersfield side that won three successive championships, then used innovative tactics to make Arsenal the dominant force of the early 1930s. Chapman (centre, far left) is pictured with the Arsenal team that won the FA Cup in 1930. Back, from left: Alf Baker, Jack Lambert, Charlie Preedy, Bill Seddon, Eddie Hapgood, Bob John. Centre, from left: Chapman, David Jack, skipper Tom Parker, Alex James, trainer Tom Whittaker.
Front: Joe Hulme, Cliff Bastin.

The two outstanding figures of Real Madrid's early domination of the European Cup, Alfredo Di Stefano (left) and president Santiago Bernabeu (centre), welcome Raymond Kopa to the club in 1956.

Hat-trick hero Geoff Hurst holds the World Cup aloft after England's win over West Germany in the 1966 final. Nobby Stiles jigs for joy, while skipper Bobby Moore and Martin Peters look on.

Attacking genius Johan Cruyff (pictured during Ajax's 2–1 win over Real Madrid in the 1973 European Cup semi-final first leg) has been one of the biggest influences on modern European football – first as a player, then as a coach. Cruyff inspired Ajax to win the European Cup three seasons running between 1971 and 1973, before moving to Barcelona. In 1974, he was the fulcrum of the Holland side that reached the World Cup final and lost to West Germany. He later became a talismanic coach, steering Ajax to their first European trophy for 14 years, then building Barcelona's 'dream team', which won four consecutive Spanish titles and the European Cup in 1992.

West Germany captain Franz Beckenbauer lifts the World Cup after their 2–1 victory over Cruyff's Holland in the 1974 final. Beckenbauer has been another huge influence on the development of European football and is the only man to have captained and coached a World Cup-winning side. Beckenbauer later became president of Bayern Munich and was appointed president of Germany's 2006 World Cup organising committee.

Attacking midfielder Michel Platini (pictured scoring the first
goal in the final against Spain) towered over the 1984 European
Championship finals as France won on home soil. He was
deadly in open play and lethal from dead ball kicks – scoring
nine of France's thirteen goals, including two hat tricks. He was
by far the greatest French player of his generation. He also
conquered his grandfather's homeland, Italy, finishing Serie A
top scorer three years running with Juventus. Platini formed a
legendary midfield trio – with Alain Giresse and Jean Tigana –
which inspired France to two World Cup semi-finals as well as
their 1984 success. He went on to become co-president of the
organising committee for the 1998 World Cup finals in France
and has become a high-profile figure in both FIFA and UEFA.

The Heysel stadium tragedy was a watershed in European Cup history. Thirty-nine Juventus supporters were crushed to death when a retaining wall collapsed as they tried to escape an attack by Liverpool supporters before the 1985 final in Brussels. The photo shows the horrific scenes as police and medical crews try to remove the dead and treat the injured. English clubs were banned from European competition for five years as a result, thus ending an era of English dominance. Heysel was followed four years later by the Hillsborough disaster, when 96 Liverpool fans died in a crush. That disaster led to the Taylor Report and the introduction of all-seater stadia throughout England, a move later copied throughout Europe.

Pavel Nedved (right) – European Footballer of the Year in 2003,
the first time a Czech player had won the honour since Josef
Masopust in 1962.

Winning coach Jose Mourinho kisses the European Cup after his Porto side beat Monaco 3–0 in the 2004 final. Mourinho, once Bobby Robson's translator at Sporting Lisbon, also steered Porto to two Portuguese titles and UEFA Cup final victory over Celtic in 2003. He led Chelsea to their first championship for 50 years in 2005.

The Milan players troop off dejected and disbelieving after Liverpool's sensational comeback in the 2005 European Cup final, now known on Merseyside as 'the Miracle of Istanbul'. Milan led 3–0 at half-time but Liverpool replied with three goals in seven minutes to force extra time – then won the penalty shootout thanks to Jerzy Dudek's save from Andriy Shevchenko. From left: defender Jaap Stam tries to console right-back Cafu. Jon Dahl Tomasson looks incredulous while midfielder Kaka holds his head in his hands. Shevchenko, the 2004 European Player of the Year, stands distraught in the background.

rather than caution. As the journalist Paolo Menicucci wrote years later: 'He'd made it his life's mission to preach "*il bel calcio*" – attractive football – to a footballing nation used to grinding down opponents and winning 1–0.' In that, he resembled another deviation from the norm – Enzo Bearzot, who had urged the national team forward to win the 1982 World Cup.

Sacchi demanded a pressing game in midfield, trying to win the ball back as close to the opponents' goal as possible, before launching Milan's offensive power. He also believed in a flat back four, rather than catenaccio. Baresi and Sacchi did not always see eye to eye. But that tactical switch suited Baresi, who had at last established himself as sweeper in the national side.

Glanville said, 'Baresi had developed into a complete footballer: strong in the air, powerful, mobile and skilful on the ground and always ready to burst into attack. Such chances tended to be limited when playing for Italy. But when Milan went over to a back four, he found no trouble at all in becoming an adventurous centre-back.'

Ancelotti and Rijkaard, both later successful coaches, acknowledged Sacchi's influence. According to Ancelotti, 'The Milan of Berlusconi was born under Sacchi in 1987 with the mission of winning and entertaining. The objectives were always clear.'

Rijkaard further explained, 'I learned a lot under Sacchi, most of all that you have to play as a unit, with defenders helping attackers and attackers helping defend.'

Milan stuttered at first under the new regime but Berlusconi kept his nerve. He stuck by Sacchi as the critics hovered, after the rossoneri were knocked out of the UEFA Cup by unfashionable Spanish club Espanol.

Van Basten scored on his debut, in a 3–1 win at Pisa. Then he was sidelined by the ankle trouble that plagued his career and needed the first of his four operations. The 30-year-old Sardinian Pietro Virdis filled the gap as Sacchi's team gathered momentum. He finished with 11 league goals. Gullit netted eight from midfield.

Milan lost just twice in 30 Serie A matches and went the whole league season unbeaten away from home. They won both Milan derbies, won at Juventus, thrashed reigning champions Napoli 4–1 at San Siro, then effectively clinched the title with a 3–2 win in Naples, two weeks before the end of the season. Virdis scored twice. Van Basten, fit again, stepped off the bench to add the third.

The rossoneri defence, superbly marshalled by Baresi, conceded just 14 league goals.

The left-back was a teenager called Paolo Maldini, son of a Milan great, Cesare. He would break appearance records for Milan and Italy, ending his career as an elder statesman of a central defender.

Paolo had made his Serie A debut as a 16 year old. Naturally right-footed, he practised and practised on his left until it was hard to tell which was his stronger foot. Maldini smiled, 'It wasn't my choice. I always used to play on the right . . . until Milan needed a player on the left.'

Another young defender broke into the side during that championship campaign – tough centre-half Alessandro Costacurta, nicknamed 'Billy' after his favourite basketball player. He had emerged after spending a season on loan with Monza in Serie C. He said, 'I always had to work really hard, whereas Franco and Paolo had so much natural talent.' He would play alongside Baresi for almost a decade.

That summer, van Basten forced his way into Holland's European Championship side and became their star striker, destroying England with a hat trick, settling the semi-final against West Germany with a late winner, then netting a spectacular flying volley as the Dutch brushed aside the Soviet Union in the final. Gullit skippered the side and headed the opening goal against the Soviets. He was ably supported in midfield by Rijkaard, who had grown up with Ajax but left after a row with Cruyff.

Sacchi was determined to sign Rijkaard from Zaragoza, where his club career had languished. Berlusconi refused. He wanted instead to bring back the Argentine striker Claudio Borghi from a loan spell at Como. The coach kept insisting. The president finally gave way. Ancelotti said, 'Rijkaard was such a good all-rounder – one of the first midfield players who could do every job on the pitch.'

Thus was born Milan's great Dutch trio of Gullit, van Basten and Rijkaard, a force even more formidable than the legendary Swedish threesome of Gren–Nordahl–Liedholm.

The rossoneri lost the Serie A crown to Inter, who won the first Milan derby 1–0 and forced a 0–0 draw in the second. With hindsight, Milan's unexpected 1–0 defeat at Cesena proved decisive.

But they achieved their top priority – to become the third Milan side to win the European Cup. They eased through the first round 7–2 on aggregate against the Bulgarian side Vitosha – then came close to grief against Red Star Belgrade. Both legs finished 1–1. The second leg in Belgrade was marked by a vicious foul on Donadoni. The Milan winger lay senseless, gasping for oxygen. He was only saved by the prompt action of the Red Star physio.

Gullit, ravaged by knee trouble, had come on as a substitute, though he was clearly unfit. Milan's hero was keeper Giovanni Galli who saved twice in the penalty shootout to take the rossoneri to the quarter-finals. There, they met Werder Bremen in two abrasive contests. Both teams had a goal disallowed in a 0–0 draw in Bremen. Van Basten's 33rd-minute penalty, after a foul on Donadoni, decided the tie at San Siro.

Sacchi's team gave their finest display in the semi-final. Van Basten levelled at the Bernabeu after Hugo Sanchez fired Madrid ahead. Milan's flair and movement tore Madrid apart at San Siro. Ancelotti drove home a 25-yard shot. Rijkaard headed in Tassotti's cross. Gullit nodded in Donadoni's corner. Van Basten netted the fourth, created by Gullit and Rijkaard. Donadoni scored the fifth.

But Milan had paid a price. Gullit had torn a cartilage in his right knee. He needed surgery, returned too early, played majestically in the final, then missed most of the following season.

Steaua, so resilient against Barcelona in 1986, were their opponents in the final in Barcelona. They had been strengthened by the signing of Gheorghe Hagi, Romania's most creative midfielder.

Gullit, who had seemingly made an incredible recovery, gave Milan an 18th-minute lead after keeper Lung and defender Bumbescu failed to clear van Basten's shot. Then Steaua surrendered. Van Basten headed the second from Tassotti's centre. Gullit controlled Donadoni's pass to volley the third. Van Basten finished off Rijkaard's pass to make it 4–0 in the 46th minute. Milan cruised through the rest of the match. Baresi, who had known the despair of relegation from Serie A, lifted the European Cup.

Why had Steaua collapsed so easily? Were they unable to cope with the expectations placed on them by their patron Nicu Ceausescu, son of the Romanian dictator Nicolae Ceausescu? Or had the Ceausescu family been involved in other ways? Whatever the reasons, Milan had been magnificent, giving the best display in a European Cup final since Liverpool's win over Monchengladbach 12 years earlier.

They went on to beat the South American champions, Atletico Nacional of Colombia, 1–0 in the Intercontinental Cup in Tokyo. Evani scored the winner, two minutes from the end of stoppage time. Baresi said, 'The most beautiful, exciting, moments of my career were winning the first European Cup and winning the Intercontinental Cup for the first time. Knowing that you're the best team in the world is an exhilarating experience.'

Milan lost out in Serie A again in 1989–90. The long-term absence of Gullit was too much to bear, despite van Basten's 19 goals – which made him Serie A top scorer – and the emergence of the former Como striker Marco Simone.

Champions Napoli beat the rossoneri 3–0. Then, in one week in March, Milan lost 3–0 at Juventus and 3–1 at home to Inter. A surprise 2–1 defeat at Verona finally ended their title hopes.

The European Cup was a different matter. Sacchi's men would become the first Milan side to retain the trophy after a re-match with Benfica, the team the rossoneri beat to win their first final in 1963.

Milan eased past HJK Helsinki in the first round then knocked out Real Madrid again. They scored twice in the first 13 minutes to win 2–0 at San Siro. Rijkaard headed in van Basten's cross and van Basten scored the second from a penalty after keeper Buyo brought him down.

Van Basten was marked brutally in the second leg. He said, 'I expected all the kicks and I got them.' Baresi was superb at the back. Emilio Butragueno scored the only goal of a bad-tempered night and Milan advanced to a quarter-final meeting with the Belgian champions Mechelen.

Sacchi was grateful for Galli's heroics – and the aid of an upright – in a 0–0 draw in Brussels. Bruno Versavel hit an early shot against the post with Galli stranded. Sacchi admitted, 'That post saved us.'

Milan were still suffering the after-effects of those defeats by Juve and Inter when Mechelen came to San Siro. Donadoni and van Basten were targeted by the Belgian defenders. Clijsters was sent off in the 90th minute for a professional foul on Donadoni.

Donadoni himself was red-carded in extra time for retaliation, punching one of his markers. Van Basten broke the deadlock and Simone scored in the dying minutes.

Sacchi spoke of Milan's durability, of their physical and mental strength. They showed all those qualities in the semi-final against Bayern Munich. Van Basten, from the penalty spot, settled the semi-final first leg. Thomas Strunz's goal forced extra time in Munich. Reserve striker Stefano Borgonovo chipped Milan's crucial away goal. Alan McInally gave Bayern a 2–1 win on the night but the rossoneri were in the final again.

Benfica had reached the final by eliminating Derry City, Honved, Dnepr Dneprpetrovsk and Marseille. The French champions complained bitterly that Vata Garcia had scored Benfica's semi-final winner with his hand.

Gullit was back for the final in Vienna, though he had played only two Serie A matches since his latest knee surgery, his second operation of the season. He missed two chances that at full pelt he might have taken. Rijkaard hit the only goal of an unspectacular match, a 67th-minute shot with the outside of his right foot, from van Basten's pass. It was time for Baresi to lift the trophy again: time for Berlusconi to celebrate on the pitch, chaired by the Milan players, holding the European Cup on his head.

There was no repeat in 1990–91. The durability, the mental and physical strength, that Sacchi had praised, deserted Milan. Successive home defeats by champions-to-be Sampdoria and Inter heaped pressure on the coach. Gullit was still hampered by knee trouble. Van Basten, who scored 11 league goals, was unhappy at Sacchi's tactics, complaining about lack of support.

Berlusconi had backed Sacchi when the coach had been under pressure. Now their relationship deteriorated fast. The Italian federation (FIGC) wanted Sacchi to take over the national team. Berlusconi wanted the former Milan and Juventus midfielder Capello to take over the rossoneri.

A shameful night at Marseille marked the end of Milan's European dominance. The warning signs were obvious as they squeezed past Brugge 1–0 in the second round. Van Basten was sent off in the second leg and banned for four games for elbowing his marker Pascal Plovie.

Baresi was also out, injured, for the quarter-final first leg against Marseille. Gullit gave Milan a 16th-minute lead but Jean-Pierre Papin levelled. Chris Waddle scored the only goal at the Velodrome, 16 minutes from the end. In the dying minutes, the floodlights failed. Milan walked off and refused to return when power was restored, obviously hoping for the game to be replayed. The referee, Karlsson, insisted that Milan played out the remaining minutes. They refused: a far cry from their heroics against Mechelen and Bayern a year earlier. Milan were banned from Europe for a year by UEFA. General manager Adriano Galliani took the blame for their behaviour. Milan appealed but UEFA stood firm, despite Berlusconi's lobbying.

The 1991 European Cup final between Marseille and Red Star was one of the most negative ever. Red Star played for penalties and duly won the shootout 5–3. It was a triumph for cynicism.

Meanwhile, Capello had replaced Sacchi, who would steer Italy to the 1994 World Cup final. Capello had spent a brief spell as Milan's caretaker coach after Liedholm departed in 1987. He had also coached the juniors before taking a job as a TV football pundit with Berlusconi's company Mediaset. As the 'Hall of Fame' on Milan's club website says, 'Capello was greeted with scepticism but surprised everyone, turning Milan into four-time champions and European Cup winners again.'

Milan fans still debate whether Sacchi or Capello was the greater coach: witness the endless discussions on the host of rossoneri web forums. The fans view Sacchi as the innovator, the man who ushered Milan into an attacking game rarely seen in Italy. They admire Capello for the quality and expressiveness of his early teams. But they regard him as much more of a pragmatist than Sacchi, most of all during his later years as Milan struggled to find a successor to van Basten.

Sacchi's insistence on forcing the players to watch instructional videos – usually involving his 'old boys' at Parma – exasperated Baresi. *Il Capitano* had his run-ins with Sacchi when he was Italy coach, too. Yet perhaps Baresi has come to agree with the fans. He said, 'In the late 1980s and early 1990s, we combined spectacular football with very good results.' Or perhaps he means that was when van Basten was at his sharpest.

Maldini said, 'Sacchi just lived for football. He always demanded concentration and commitment. He instilled a winning attitude in us. Capello was the first coach I had with Milan's juniors. He was a sort of mentor to me. He taught me how to play, technically and tactically. I never doubted that he would also become a great coach.'

Berlusconi gave himself some credit too, 'I still feel close to both these Milan sides who were lucky enough to be led by two great coaches, whom I discovered and chose myself.'

In the absence of European competition, Milan focused on the league and turned the 1991–92 title race into a procession. They went through the 34-game season unbeaten, scored 74 goals and finished eight points clear of their closest challengers, Juventus. They hammered the outgoing champions – and European Cup finalists – Sampdoria 5–1 as if to prove a point. They beat Samp 2–0 in Genoa too. They thrashed Roma 4–1, Napoli 5–0 and ended the season with an 8–2 win at Foggia. The Juventus coach Giovanni Trapattoni said, 'Milan can change up into a gear beyond the rest of us.'

Van Basten was in his pomp. The Italian critic Gianni Brera wrote of 'the divine van Basten'. He scored 25 goals in 31 games, an incredible return for Serie A, including hat tricks against Foggia, Atalanta and Cagliari. The treble against Cagliari was the most dramatic. The Sardinian side led 1–0 at half-time. As Milan emerged from the visitors' dressing-room, Capello held up three fingers to van Basten. The Dutch striker responded with three goals in 18 minutes to propel the rossoneri to a 4–1 win.

Barcelona had won the European Cup in 1992 beating Sampdoria 1–0 in the final at Wembley. Milan were favourites to take their crown. They had brought in Lentini as a long-term replacement for Gullit. France striker Jean-Pierre Papin came from Marseille. Savicevic followed from Red Star. Boban, once of Dinamo Zagreb, joined from Bari. Demetrio Albertini had established himself as a defensive midfielder.

Van Basten and Milan started the Serie A season on fire. The rossoneri won 5–4 at Pescara, 7–3 at Fiorentina, beat Lazio 5–3, won 2–0 at Parma and 5–1 at Napoli. Van Basten scored a hat trick at Pescara, two at Fiorentina, two against Lazio and four more at Napoli. He also scored all four as Milan opened their Champions League campaign with a 4–0 win over Gothenburg after easing past Olimpia Ljubljana and Slovan Bratislava in the opening rounds.

Then van Basten's ankle trouble flared up again during the 2–0 win over Ancona in December 1992. He needed surgery but returned briefly at the end of the season and played in the European Cup final against Marseille. Van Basten never played for Milan again. After operations in June 1993 and July 1994, he was forced to quit. His loss was immeasurable. The rossoneri were never as prolific again, at least not until the arrival of Andriy Shevchenko nearly a decade later.

They won the title once more, finishing four points ahead of Inter. But the 4–0 wins over Pescara and Sampdoria were rarities. Parma ended Milan's amazing 58-game unbeaten Serie A run when they won 1–0 at San Siro on 21 March 1993. Juventus won there 3–1 a month later.

Gullit's relationship with Capello turned frosty as the coach preferred to start with Lentini. Savicevic may have been one of Berlusconi's favourites but he was also unhappy at his lack of starts. So was Boban.

Rijkaard, another whose place was under threat, shot Milan ahead in the Champions League at PSV Eindhoven. Simone added a second and the rossoneri won 2–1, despite Romario's brilliant strike. Papin scored the only goal at Porto and Eranio netted the winner against the Portuguese side at San Siro. Massaro was the matchwinner in Gothenburg to clinch Milan's place in the final.

Their opponents were Marseille, who had pipped Rangers by one point in Group A. Rijkaard announced on the morning of the match that he would leave in the summer. Lentini started. Gullit was not even on the bench. Basile Boli headed Marseille's winner from a 43rd-minute corner. Van Basten was clearly suffering. Capello sent on Papin but he could not save Milan.

Marseille's triumph would later be tarnished by a match-fixing scandal which saw them banned by UEFA and relegated by the French league. But they had become the first French club to win the European Cup, and at Milan's expense.

Rijkaard rejoined Ajax. Gullit was loaned to Sampdoria. Lentini suffered a fractured skull in a car crash. He never held a regular place again and returned to Torino in 1997.

In came Danish midfielder Brian Laudrup from Fiorentina, Romanian striker Florin Raducioiu from Brescia, defender Christian Panucci from Genoa and the most important signing, Marcel Desailly from Marseille as midfield enforcer.

Capello rotated the squad. Milan won a third successive title, finishing three points ahead of Juventus. They became the first team since the great Torino to win three consecutive championships. But they scored only 36 goals in Serie A. Massaro led their marksmen with 11, including the clincher in a decisive 2–1 win over Juve. Papin was next with five goals. He would leave for Bayern Munich in the summer.

Milan's strength was their defence, superbly organised as ever by Baresi. They conceded just 15 goals. But Gullit scored Samp's winner when they beat Milan 3–2 in Genoa. Berlusconi wailed, 'Giving away Gullit ranks as my biggest mistake in football.' Capello blamed referee Marcello Nicchi for two of Samp's goals.

Milan eased into the Champions League proper with a 1–0 aggregate win over Swiss champions Aarau, thanks to Papin, and a 7–0 demolition of FC Copenhagen, marked by a 6–0 win in Denmark when Simone and Papin scored twice and Laudrup netted on home soil. The rossoneri would save their most attractive displays for Europe, although their opening 0–0 Champions League draw at Anderlecht was not among them. At Berlusconi's insistence, Savicevic replaced Papin against Porto. Savicevic created all the goals in a 3–0 win, for Raducioiu, Panucci and Massaro.

Savicevic's strike clinched a 2–1 win over Werder Bremen and put them firmly in charge of the group. They drew their next three games, scoring only one goal, but still finished a point ahead of Porto.

This time, Milan had to play a one-off semi-final – with home advantage as group winners. Their opponents were Monaco, who had replaced the disgraced Marseille. Monaco, coached by Arsene Wenger, had finished runners-up to Barcelona in the other group. Their stars were midfielder Enzo Scifo and the German striker Jurgen Klinsmann.

Desailly headed Milan into a 14th-minute lead from Boban's cross. Costacurta was sent off for a foul on Klinsmann. But Albertini added a second with a 25-yard shot and Massaro volleyed in Panucci's pass to make it 3–0.

Baresi collected a yellow card that kept him out of the final against Barcelona in Athens. Costacurta was suspended, too. Maldini switched to centre-back.

Johan Cruyff's Barcelona were expected to attack, Milan to play on the break. Instead, the rossoneri revived memories of their attacking past. Massaro finished off Savicevic's low cross in the 22nd minute, then volleyed a second in first-half stoppage time. Savicevic lobbed the third. Desailly hit the fourth from Albertini's through ball.

Milan had won none of their last six Serie A games. Capello said, 'Our schedule was very tight in the last part of the season. We needed to save our strength for the important matches in the Champions League.'

Gullit returned briefly to San Siro before completing his move to Sampdoria. His swansong was a two-goal display in the 2–1 win over Lazio. Laudrup had gone to Rangers, Raducioiu to Espanol in Spain.

Italy's World Cup campaign had taken its physical – and mental – toll. Baresi recovered from a knee injury in the group game against Norway to skipper Italy in the final against Brazil. The Brazilians won the penalty shootout after Roberto Baggio missed the vital kick.

Baresi said, 'The World Cup final was one of my best games, especially since it came after an injury and not even I knew if I'd make it through the match. It was such a shame how the match finished. Losing on penalties in the World Cup final makes you feel powerless. At that moment, I felt as if my world had fallen in.'

Maldini, Albertini, Massaro and Donadoni also started against the

Brazilians. Evani came on as a sub. Costacurta had played most of the earlier matches.

Costacurta, Maldini and Savicevic were all injured at the start of the new season. Milan lost 1–0 at Cremonese, where Panucci was sent off, 2–0 at Padova and 1–0 at Juventus. They had also lost 2–0 to Ajax in the Champions League, which they had automatically entered as European Cup holders. As Capello stated, 'It's not a case of us losing confidence. It's just that several of our senior players are still not fit.' Berlusconi added, 'This is the result of a run of injuries coupled with the effect of fatigue on key players after the World Cup.'

Milan faced further problems in the Champions League. Casino Salzburg keeper Otto Konrad had been hit by a bottle after the first goal in Milan's 3–0 win at San Siro. He played on after treatment but was substituted after the second goal.

Capello accused Konrad of trying to 'con' UEFA. The Milan coach said, 'He walked off OK at half-time, so why did he end up asking for an ambulance? It's a joke.'

UEFA took a different view. Its disciplinary committee effectively wiped out the two goals by Marco Simone and the other by Giovanni Stroppa. Milan were deducted two points and ordered to play their remaining two group games at least 300 kilometres from San Siro.

They drew 1–1 against AEK in Athens, when Maldini suffered a broken nose. Panucci rescued the rossoneri with two goals in seven minutes against the Greek side at their temporary home in Trieste, after Tony Savevski had given AEK the lead. Milan then lost 2–0 at home to Ajax, when Baresi conceded an own goal after Jari Litmanen put the Dutch champions ahead.

Baresi's misfortune seemed to sum up Milan's season. They had to win their final group game, against Salzburg in Vienna, to reach the semi-finals. Massaro scored the only goal in the 26th minute. Capello breathed a sigh of relief and said, 'We have no chance of winning the championship, so we'll concentrate our efforts on retaining the European Cup.'

In Serie A, Milan's 3–1 win at Foggia in December was their first away victory for nine months. Their fans had been involved in more trouble when the match at Genoa on 29 January was abandoned after a Genoa supporter was stabbed to death and a Milan fan charged with murder. The rossoneri crashed 4–0 at Lazio and lost 2–0 at home to Juve in the aftermath of the tragedy.

Milan were still seeking a finisher to succeed van Basten, though Simone ended with 15 goals in Serie A after a spring flourish. Their new target was the Liberian forward George Weah, striking star of their European Cup semi-final opponents Paris Saint-Germain.

Simone had scored twice at San Siro to break the resistance of Benfica and their Belgian goalkeeper Michel Preud'homme. A Baresi-organised rearguard action kept the score goalless in Lisbon.

Savicevic, still admired more by Berlusconi than Capello, engineered Milan's 1–0 win in Paris after David Ginola had hit the bar for PSG. Simone and Maldini had squandered chances created by the Serb. The Croat, Boban, applied a cool sidefoot finish from Savicevic's pass to win the game in stoppage time. Savicevic turned the second leg too, first controlling Albertini's pass to beat PSG keeper Bernard Lama, then firing low past Lama again after Desailly dispossessed Daniel Bravo. Baresi had been imperious, Weah peripheral.

Milan had to win the final, against Ajax in Vienna, to play in the Champions League the following season. The tie was settled by the intervention of a Milan great – wearing an Ajax shirt again: Rijkaard. His pass unpicked the Milan defence five minutes from time and 18-year-old Patrick Kluivert scored the only goal.

The injured Savicevic's absence was crucial. The rossoneri dominated possession but lacked penetration. Desailly and Simone had tested keeper Edwin van der Sar. Massaro and Simone shot wide. Maybe Weah, the major summer signing, would provide the cutting edge. Maybe he and Baggio, signed from Juventus, would form a prolific partnership.

Milan won another championship in 1996, finishing eight points ahead of Juventus. Weah scored 11 goals: a far cry from the heady days of van Basten. Simone added eight. Baggio netted seven. The key victory was a 2–1 success over Juventus, when Simone and Weah scored in the first 12 minutes. Baresi made his 500th league appearance in a 2–1 win at Piacenza. The rossoneri clinched the title with a 3–1 home win over Fiorentina in which Baggio scored a penalty and Rossi saved Rui Costa's spot kick with the score at 2–1. Donadoni left after 10 years with Milan.

Capello's future was in doubt despite his success. He did not share Berlusconi's views about team selection, most of all about Savicevic. Berlusconi invited him for 'further discussions'. Capello decided to join Real Madrid instead. It was the end of an era for the rossoneri.

Coaches came and went (including brief encores for Sacchi and Capello) until ex-Milan great Ancelotti restored their fame and fortune.

Capello's successor, the Uruguayan Oscar Washington Tabarez resigned after a disastrous start culminated in a 3–2 defeat by Piacenza. Milan were knocked out of the Champions League at the group stage after losing 2–1 at home to Rosenborg Trondheim. Berlusconi said, 'This is the lowest point in the 11 years that I've been at Milan. I'm disappointed and I'm sad. We have to learn our lessons and rebuild.'

Baresi's fitness was suspect too, as age and injuries took their toll. He quit in June 1997. He said, 'Let's just say that I'm giving up because I'm not as young as I used to be.' Giancarlo Rinaldi summed up Baresi for the magazine *Football Italia*, 'He could time a tackle better than anyone in the game and combined that with a sharp professional brain. Add the invisible thread that seemed to link his arm to the linesman's flag and you have one of the most complete defenders the game has ever seen.' Galliani said simply, 'He was the symbol and flag carrier for Milan for 20 years.'

Maldini became Milan's new symbol and flag carrier. He said, 'Baresi was a model for me, on and off the field. I always admired his commitment and his honesty. He had such a long and successful career. You can only achieve that if you're as professional and determined as he proved to be.'

Baresi was named Milan's Player of the Century in a poll to mark the club's centenary in 1999 – ahead of Gullit, van Basten, Maldini, Rijkaard, and the greats of two previous European Cup-winning teams. It was a fitting tribute to the part he played in Milan's golden era.

CHAPTER 17

LES BLEUS, PLATINI AND ZIDANE

The national team, *Les Bleus*, has always been the focal point of French football.

There have been fine French club sides. Reims won six championships in 14 seasons and reached the European Cup final in 1956 and 1959. Saint-Etienne dominated the 1970s and got to the 1976 European Cup final. Marseille won the trophy in 1993 after losing on penalties to Red Star Belgrade two years earlier. Yet none had the aura of Les Bleus. Support for club football was never as popular, or passionate, as in England, Germany, Italy and Spain: countries with a historic network of club rivalries.

The French club game had to compete with rugby, cycling, athletics, motor racing – and foreign football – for media attention. French teams rarely threatened to lift European trophies. Even when Marseille won the European Cup, they were later thrown out of the competition because of a bribes scandal.

Many French stars played abroad. In the mid-1990s, French coaches such as Gerard Houllier and Arsene Wenger followed them.

As Geoff Hare wrote in *Football in France: A Cultural History*: 'Whereas the aura of club heroes has remained at a relatively local level, the French players who have become legends and national heroes are those who have made their names representing the national team.'

It is a recurring theme that many of those national heroes are of immigrant origin. Les Bleus has been the vehicle for their rise to status and acceptance in French society. Take the team which finished third in the 1958 World Cup finals. Striker Just Fontaine, who set a tournament record of 13 goals, was born in Marrakech, Morocco, to a Spanish mother. Inside-forward Roger Piantoni was of Italian extraction.

France's greatest player of the time, Raymond Kopa, came from a Polish immigrant family in the northern mining town of Noeux-les-Mines. He adopted French citizenship after he was ruled ineligible for the national youth team and changed his name from Kopaszewski to Kopa.

He moved from Reims to Real Madrid in 1956, when he was voted European Footballer of the Year. Kopa reflected, 'Without the mine, I'd have been a good player, nothing more. But there was the mine. My name was Kopaszewski – and to get out, all I had was football.'

Zinedine Zidane, the star of the 1998 World Cup victory, would echo those sentiments from a North African perspective, two generations later. Football was an escape route, a path to respect. Even now, the immigrant areas of French towns remain fertile ground for club scouts seeking raw talent to develop in their youth academies.

France went into a trough after that flourish in 1958. They reached the World Cup finals in England in 1966 and were knocked out at the group stage. They were eliminated at the same stage on their next appearance, in Argentina, 12 years later. That team included a young attacking midfielder called Michel Platini who would become an even greater player than Kopa.

Platini was another from an immigrant background. Unlike Kopa and Zidane, though, he was the grandson of an immigrant, Francesco Platini, who came to France from Novara in Italy. His family had laid down roots in France. They ran a café in the small Lorraine town of Joeuf. He had a more comfortable upbringing than Kopa or Zidane.

Platini rose through the ranks at Nancy, made his name with Saint-Etienne, then went off to conquer his grandfather's homeland with Juventus.

Nancy had considered dismissing young Michel from their youth academy, until the famous ex-Reims coach Albert Batteux persuaded them to think again. The young Platini, was quite thin – and his schoolwork had suffered because of his enthusiasm for football!

Platini was voted France's greatest-ever player in a *France Football* poll. He later served as co-president of the France 1998 World Cup organising committee and became a senior adviser to FIFA president Sepp Blatter.

Kopa played down his Polish roots and emphasised his Frenchness.

A generation later, Platini could feel at ease with his Italian ancestry, saying, 'It was my good fortune to have the opportunity to learn and embody two cultures at the same time.' But he left no doubt about his commitment to France, 'My heart is completely French.'

On the night that Les Bleus won the World Cup, Platini wore a France shirt under his business suit. He said, 'I became a fan again. I felt a bit nostalgic, remembering that French team which had twice missed victory at the World Cup by so little.'

Platini had scored the winner against Holland which took France to the 1982 World Cup finals in Spain. He reflected, 'It wasn't my best goal. But it was the most important one for a generation. If we hadn't qualified for the World Cup in Spain, perhaps that side would never have won the European Championship in 1984 or reached the World Cup semi-finals in 1986.'

In Spain, they fell victim to a mighty injustice.

France lacked a cutting edge. Dominique Rocheteau was their only attacker of genuine class. So coach Michel Hidalgo based his tactics around his midfield trio: Platini, the tireless Alain Giresse and the elegant, Mali-born Jean Tigana.

France lost their opening game 3–1 to England, for whom Bryan Robson scored twice. They recovered with a 4–1 win over Kuwait and needed a draw against Czechoslovakia to reach the second stage. Didier Six gave them a 66th-minute lead. Antonin Panenka's penalty equaliser came too late for the Czechs.

Bernard Genghini scored the only goal of the game against Austria. That set up a crunch match against Northern Ireland, who had drawn 2–2 with the Austrians. The winners would go into the semi-finals. Giresse and Rocheteau scored two each and France won 4–1.

Their semi-final opponents were West Germany, in Seville. FIFA's archive recalls a contest between 'French flair and German spirit'. It adds, 'With Platini pulling the strings in midfield, it was clear that the French would have the technical edge over a typically solid German outfit.'

The Germans took the lead when Pierre Littbarski fired home a 25-yard volley after France keeper Jean-Luc Ettori beat out Klaus Fischer's shot. The French responded with all-out attack. Rocheteau was hauled down in the box and Platini levelled from the penalty spot.

The injustice happened in the 57th minute. Platini's lofted pass sent substitute Patrick Battiston through, one-on-one with German goalkeeper Harald Schumacher. Schumacher rushed out to the edge of the box and flattened Battiston as the Frenchman slipped the ball past him. Battiston was caught high in the face. He crumpled, unconscious, surrounded by anxious colleagues. He was stretchered off, concussed, having suffered broken ribs and lost several teeth. The French players, supporters and millions of TV viewers expected a card for Schumacher. Instead, the Dutch referee, Charles Corver, pointed for a goal kick. Schumacher escaped without even a caution.

France kept their composure, kept pressing. Manuel Amoros hit the bar seven minutes from time. In the second minute of extra time, centre-back Marius Tresor – from the French Caribbean – swung a boot at a free kick and France led 2–1. Giresse scored again seven minutes later. Les Bleus had one foot in the final.

But the German coach Jupp Derwall had made an inspired substitution, replacing tired midfielder Hans-Peter Briegel with striker Karl-Heinz Rummenigge. Rummenigge pulled one back. Fischer conjured an equaliser with a brilliant bicycle kick.

Giresse, Amoros and Rocheteau scored for France in the penalty shootout. Manfred Kaltz and Paul Breitner replied for the Germans. Ettori saved Uli Stielike's kick. Six missed for France. Littbarski shot West Germany level. Platini and Rummenigge both netted. Bossis stepped up for France's final kick. Schumacher saved his shot. Horst Hrubesch kept his nerve and swept his kick past Ettori. West Germany's shootout hero was the goalkeeper who should never have been on the pitch.

French players, Platini included, shed tears. Years later, the France captain said, 'The referee stole the game from us. He failed to give a penalty and he failed to send off Schumacher after his foul on Battiston.'

Yet Platini insisted that the game had been one of the 'most thrilling and intense' occasions of his life. He said, 'No book, film or play could ever recapture the way I felt that night.'

Battiston and Schumacher were later reconciled. The Frenchman was even a guest at Schumacher's wedding. But the feeling of injustice raged throughout France. That the beneficiaries of such injustice were Germans increased the hurt. The German wartime occupation of France, which lasted four years, was still within painful living memory. The sports journalist Georges de Caunes said, 'The incident between Schumacher and Battiston revived in men of my generation the emotions felt during the war.'

The result also prompted soul-searching about French aspirations. Older fans remembered the 1958 World Cup semi-final – before substitutes – when French defender Robert Jonquet was injured and a Brazilian teenager called Pele scored a hat trick. Others pointed to the European Cup final of 1976, when Saint-Etienne hit the woodwork twice before Bayern Munich scored.

Would a French team ever win a major trophy? Or was it their fate to play with flair, yet always fall short? Platini and his teammates answered that question in the European Championship finals two years later.

In 1984, France were formidable: most of all their number 10, who towered over the tournament. Platini said, 'The number 10 shirt has always represented certain gifts in a player. He is the playmaker who can also score goals.'

He was both, deadly in open play and from wickedly curling free kicks. He had finished Serie A top scorer for three years running with Juventus. Now he applied that finishing touch for his country.

France hosted the finals, so they did not have to qualify. They entered the competition confident after four consecutive friendly wins, including a 2–0 victory over England when Platini scored with a free kick and a header.

Shootout defeat in Seville had made Hidalgo more of a realist. He included a midfield anchor now, the tough, industrious Luis Fernandez, the son of Spanish immigrants. He fielded two forwards, rather than two wingers and a central striker. He permed from Genghini, Bruno Bellone and Bernard Lacombe. None offered the penetration that Fontaine once supplied. But Fernandez's presence gave Giresse and Tigana licence to roam and released Platini to attack from the front of the midfield diamond.

The last eight were split into two groups of four. The top two in each group would contest the semi-finals.

Denmark were tough first opponents, despite losing winger Allan Simonsen with a broken leg. They resisted until late in the second half, when Platini struck to break the deadlock.

France moved up through the gears against Belgium. Platini scored a hat trick. Giresse and Fernandez netted, too, as Les Bleus romped to a 5–0 win. For an encore, Platini hit a hat trick in the space of 18 minutes against Yugoslavia, inspiring France's comeback after they trailed to Milos Sestic's goal at half-time. This time, there were no Germans to worry about in the semi-finals.

Spain had topped the other group from Portugal, on goals scored, after beating holders West Germany 1–0. It was stoppage time when Antonio Maceda headed home Juan Senor's cross to knock the Germans out.

Les Bleus never had to handle the psychological doubts the Germans might have implanted. Instead they had to dredge up their last reserves of character to beat Portugal in another thrilling semi-final.

Left-back Jean-Francois Domergue played his finest game for France, scored twice, then was eclipsed by Platini's sense of theatre. Domergue shot the French ahead from a 25th-minute free kick. Substitute Nene galvanised the Portuguese. Jordao levelled 16 minutes from time, then gave Portugal the lead in extra time with a weak shot that deceived keeper Joel Bats. Domergue bundled in an equaliser with five minutes left.

The nightmare of another penalty shootout grew closer and closer. The clock had ticked into the final minute. Tigana centred from the right. Platini scooped the ball out of the sky as if time had stood still, then shot the winner.

France's opponents in the final were Spain, who beat Denmark on penalties after a 1–1 draw. Maceda scored again and collected his second yellow card of the tournament, which ruled him out of the final. His midfield colleague Rafael Gordillo shared his fate.

Spain coach Miguel Munoz sent his team out to defend. France could not score an early goal. The players seemed to share the anxiety of the Parc des Princes crowd.

Platini broke the deadlock again, with some help from the Spanish keeper Luis Arconada.

Arconada had been one of Spain's stars – until the 57th minute of the final when he fumbled Platini's free kick and let the ball slip through his arms into the net.

France found their rhythm for 20 minutes. Then centre-back Yvon Le Roux was sent off for a second yellow card. Spain piled forward. They were caught out in the last minute. All their outfield players were in the French half when Tigana took possession and picked out Bellone's run. The striker waited for Arconada to commit himself, then chipped the killer goal.

It was France's 14th of the competition and their first scored by a forward. Platini had netted nine times, five more than Spain's total for the tournament. The French press dubbed him '*le goalois*'. The skipper lifted the Henri Delaunay trophy. Hidalgo retired as national coach, a delighted 51 year old, drenched in champagne. The nation celebrated. France *could* win the big matches.

Typically, Platini scored both goals when Les Bleus clinched qualification for the 1986 World Cup finals with a 2–0 win over Yugoslavia. By the time of the finals in Mexico, however, his candle was burning out. He had nursed a swollen ankle for months. He was struggling against tendonitis in his left heel. He was also haunted by the memories of the Heysel tragedy a year before and weighed down by the expectations placed on him.

France eased into the second round with a 1–0 win over Canada, a 1–1 draw against the Soviet Union and a 3–0 win over Hungary, all without a goal from Platini. They were drawn against holders Italy in the last 16. No one believed Platini when he said that 'this was just another match'.

He turned it France's way after 15 minutes when he controlled Rocheteau's pass and chipped keeper Giovanni Galli. A perfect through ball almost created a second for Giresse, before Tigana swayed into the box and found Rocheteau. Yannick Stopyra took the lay-off in his stride and drove in a low shot. The French coach Henri Michel said, 'I can still see Platini singing in the team bus, wearing a baseball cap that he'd swiped from the Italians.' It was Platini's last glory night for Les Bleus.

The young Platini had idolised Brazil's 1970 World Cup winners – Pele, Jairzinho, Tostao, Rivelino, Gerson. France were to face their successors in the quarter-final at Guadalajara, where Brazil had played all their group games in 1970.

The contest was fluid, exciting and full of skill. Platini scored France's equaliser, a tap-in after Stopyra's header rebounded off keeper Carlos. It was his 41st, and last, goal for Les Bleus.

The game finished 1–1. France won on penalties thanks to Fernandez's ice-cool dispatch of the deciding kick. But their 31-year-old skipper fired his shot over. It was his first miss in 68 internationals. He had been a peripheral figure, too.

This was the night when years of pressure and responsibility caught up with Platini. His marker, Alemao, said, 'The Platini I faced didn't cause me many problems.' Platini himself said, 'I felt destroyed after missing the penalty. My head was spinning. At that moment, I knew it was my last World Cup as a player.'

Careca, who had put Brazil ahead, and Muller both hit the

woodwork. Bats had saved a penalty from Zico. Michel admitted, 'If you look at the pattern of the game, Brazil should have won.'

France met West Germany again in the semi-final. This time there were no dramatic finales. The Germans squeezed the life out of the game after Andy Brehme gave them a ninth-minute lead. Rudi Voller hit the second with time running out. That 2–0 scoreline ended a glorious era in French football.

Platini retired a year later; Giresse followed in 1988. The French team broke up. France still produced flair players such as Eric Cantona and David Ginola, both to become heroes in England. But it would be a decade before Les Bleus touched the heights again.

French football in the early 1990s was rocked by a disaster and a bribe scandal. The disaster happened in Corsica in May 1992. Fifteen people died and more than 2,000 were injured when a temporary stand collapsed at Bastia's Furiani stadium before their French Cup semi-final against Marseille (see Chapter 13). The scandal involved Marseille, who in 1993 became the first French team to win the European Cup. Basile Boli headed the only goal of the game against Milan in Munich. It was a triumph for Marseille's controversial president, millionaire businessman and rising socialist politician Bernard Tapie.

All France celebrated their victory. At Marseille's last game before the final, at Valenciennes, the home club's juniors had welcomed them onto the pitch with a banner inscribed *Toute Valenciennes avec l'OM a Munich* (All of Valenciennes is with Marseille at Munich). Marseille won 1–0.

Then the allegations flew. The Valenciennes defender Jacques Glassmann claimed that Marseille's Jean-Jacques Eydelie had tried to bribe him, Jorge Burruchaga and Christophe Robert to 'take it easy'. Robert later admitted he had taken the bribe and police found 250,000 francs in a case buried in his in-laws' garden. Eydelie confessed that he had made the offer in a phone call to Robert. Glassmann and Burruchaga were with Robert at the time.

Eydelie said he had acted on the instructions of Marseille's managing director Jean-Pierre Bernes. Meanwhile, the Valenciennes coach Boro Primorac accused Tapie of trying to buy his silence. Another politician, Jack Mellick, first gave Tapie an alibi, then retracted his statement. Bernes and Tapie were charged with offering bribes. Tapie was charged with trying to suborn a witness. Bernes admitted the offence in court, and said he was acting on Tapie's instructions.

These were not the first rumours of bribery to swirl around Marseille, who had won five successive championships. This time there was hard evidence – followed by convictions. Tapie received a two-year jail term with one year suspended. Bernes, Eydelie, Burruchaga and Robert, and his wife Marie-Christine, received suspended sentences.

UEFA disqualified Marseille from the Champions League and the French authorities stripped them of the championship and relegated them to the second division for two seasons. The loss of European revenue, coupled with demotion, forced Marseille to sell their stars. Tapie complained, 'Forcing us out of Europe is like killing the club.'

Marseille have revived. They reached the UEFA Cup final in 2004 and they remain France's best-supported club. But a shadow has hung over them ever since the scandal.

Quietly, however, the French federation (FFF) had sown the seeds of future success, instituting a national youth development scheme far ahead of its European rivals.

Clubs such as Auxerre and Nantes had traditionally built their teams around home-grown youngsters. Coach Guy Roux, for instance, knew that Auxerre could never compete with the big clubs in the transfer market. So, for nearly 40 years, he made the youth scheme the focus of his planning.

The federation extended that policy across the country. The FFF created a national youth academy at Clairefontaine and youth academies at all the major clubs. There were two stages: *preformation* for 13 to 16 year olds, who went on to *centres de formation* at 16 and were expected to sign their first professional contract with the club that developed them. The academies offered a mixture of school subjects and specialist football coaching, with the emphasis on technique. The top 13 year olds attended Clairefontaine, then joined the clubs' centres.

Clairefontaine graduates include Thierry Henry, Nicolas Anelka, Louis Saha and William Gallas. The club *centres* have produced a succession of players, too. It is rare these days to find a senior French player who has not risen through the system. The Lyons and France midfielder Eric Carriere – spotted by Nantes playing in the third division – is the exception that proves the rule.

Boli and Cantona came through from Auxerre. World Cup winners Didier Deschamps, Marcel Desailly and Christian Karembeu developed at Nantes. Lilian Thuram, Manu Petit, Henry and David Trezeguet started with Monaco. Cannes produced Patrick Vieira and the most influential French player since Platini: Zidane.

Zidane – nicknamed 'Zizou' – was the mastermind of the sides that won the 1998 World Cup and Euro 2000. Like Platini, he could shape the play and score exhilarating goals. But his significance reached beyond football. His family is Algerian. In the 1950s and early '60s, the Algerians fought a bitter war of independence against France. The war had echoes in football. The leading Algerian player of the time, Rachid Mekloufi, turned his back on Les Bleus to support the fledgling Algerian state.

Zidane's story starts with his father Smail, who left the Algerian Berber village of Taguemoune to look for work in Paris. He settled in the northern suburb of Saint-Denis before moving to Marseilles. Saint-Denis is now the site of the Stade de France, scene of his son's greatest triumph.

Zidane grew up in the tough district of La Castellane, known in Marseilles as *un quartier difficil*. His father worked in a warehouse, usually on the night shift. Zidane said, 'I've been very inspired by him. It was my father who taught us that an immigrant must work twice as hard as anyone else and he must never give up.' Shades of Raymond Kopa.

Yet, like Platini, Zidane could wear several identities with comfort. He is 'a Kabyle [Berber] from La Castellane, an Algerian from Marseilles and a Frenchman'.

After the national euphoria of the World Cup victory, he said, 'It was a great thing for us. We were a family who'd come from nothing and now we had respect from French people of all kinds.'

Zidane, however, has never spoken out on political or racial issues, unlike his forthright colleague Thuram. Like Platini, his appeal cuts across various sections of French society. He is an example of integration. Maybe he has become too integrated for some disaffected young French Arabs.

Even the Boulogne Boys, the Paris Saint-Germain ultras who support the anti-immigrant National Front, respect him. One of their leaders, 'Patrice', was quoted before the 2002 World Cup finals, 'I don't have a problem with guys like him. He's French. He speaks like a Frenchman. I don't think of him as one of the immigrants. He's one of us.'

There is anger buried within Zidane, though. He was suspended during France's 1998 World Cup run for stamping on Saudi Arabia skipper Faoud Amin. At Juventus, he was banned from the Champions League for five games after head-butting Hamburg's Jochen Kientz.

His first coach at Cannes, Jean Varraud, said he had to channel his aggression towards football. Rolland Courbis was in charge at Bordeaux when Zidane broke into Les Bleus. He said, 'You could see Zidane was an extraordinary player straightaway, but it was a stage of his career when you couldn't just give him his head.'

By Euro 96 in England, Zidane had become France's playmaker. A team to challenge for the World Cup was taking shape: Thuram, Laurent Blanc and Desailly at the back; Deschamps and Youri Djorkaeff alongside Zidane in midfield; Christophe Dugarry in attack. Les Bleus beat Holland on penalties in the quarter-finals, then lost to the Czech Republic in another shootout.

Coach Aime Jacquet was under pressure, despite a record of only three defeats in four years heading into the World Cup finals. He stressed discipline and perseverance. Media and fans wanted to revive the glory days of Platini and Hidalgo, not watch goalless draws against the Dutch and the Czechs. Influential sports daily *L'Equipe* led the opposition to Jacquet, characterising him as a 'plodder'.

Jacquet was wounded. He said, 'In January 1998, I thought the knives would be shelved. I hoped that all the French people would get behind the team. Instead, the players were forced to prove themselves on the pitch, to show that they were the talented performers that I'd been telling everyone about.'

The FFF stood by Jacquet. So did Platini. On 12 July 1998 in the Stade de France, Jacquet answered his critics and Zidane scored twice, as Les Bleus beat Brazil to win the World Cup.

Jacquet's team – like Hidalgo's side – lacked a cutting edge. Henry and Trezeguet were promising but still raw. Les Bleus had an effective if eccentric keeper, Fabien Barthez, and an ironclad defence. For penetration, they looked to Zidane and Djorkaeff.

France opened the tournament with a 3–0 win over South Africa in Marseilles. They followed up with a 4–0 win over Saudi Arabia, marred by the red card for Zidane which ruled him out until the quarter-finals. They topped their group by beating Denmark 2–1 with a penalty by Djorkaeff on his home ground in Lyon and a second-half strike from Manu Petit.

They needed a 'golden goal' to break the resistance of Paraguay goalkeeper Jose Luis Chilavert in the last 16. Chilavert defied France for 114 minutes until Trezeguet headed down Robert Pires's cross and Blanc, striding forward, rifled the ball in.

Zidane was back for the quarter-final against Italy. He was one of five French starters who played for Serie A clubs. France virtually shut down for the 4.30 p.m. kick-off. There were no goals in 120 minutes. Gianluca Pagliuca saved Lizarazu's spot kick. Barthez saved from Demetrio Albertini. Les Bleus scored their next four, Italy three. Then Luigi di Baggio fired Italy's last penalty against the bar.

Davor Suker gave Croatia the lead in the semi-final. France were behind for the first time in the tournament. An unlikely marksman rescued them. Thuram scored twice from right-back. Unlucky Blanc was sent off after an innocuous challenge with Slaven Bilic. Frank Leboeuf took his place against Brazil in the final.

Brazil's top striker Ronaldo had been at the centre of a pre-match drama. He had been rushed to hospital earlier in the day, after suffering convulsions. Ronaldo arrived an hour before kick-off and played. He was a pale shadow of himself.

Jacquet had urged his team to test the Brazilian defence at dead ball kicks. Zidane administered the killer blows: two headers from corners to give Les Bleus a 2–0 half-time lead. Petit scored the third. Desailly's 68th-minute red card hardly seemed to matter.

Skipper Deschamps lifted the World Cup. Jacquet retired, happy and vindicated. Many of the messages of congratulation he received contained another word, 'Sorry'. *La toute France* went wild. The Champs-Elysees hosted Paris's biggest celebration since the liberation. The crowds chanted 'Zidane president!'

Zidane had been the star of the tournament. He had not towered over it like Platini towered over the 1984 European Championship. But the game had changed, as Platini noted, 'There are few footballers of Zidane's style left, a player who directs the team's play. Coaches have taken them out of teams. It's a shame. I'd like to see coaches encourage more players like him. It was easier to play that way 14, 15 years ago. I could still score goals as a number 10. Zidane is a goalscorer too, but his role is more difficult than mine was then.'

In the aftermath of victory, politicians and academics surveyed the team – Thuram from the French Caribbean, Desailly from Ghana, Karembeu from Polynesia, Zidane, the Senegal-born substitute Vieira – and talked of Europe's rainbow nation. But immigrants had long played a disproportionate role in French football. As *L'Equipe* pointed out a decade before, more than 30 per cent of Les Bleus down the years came from immigrant families or had been born outside metropolitan France.

World Cup victory changed public expectations of the team. So did the emergence of a generation of fine young strikers – Anelka, Henry, revitalised at Arsenal, and his old Monaco colleague Trezeguet. Vieira had become Zidane's midfield sidekick. The solid back line of 1998 had stayed together. The French public expected their team to win Euro 2000 in Belgium and Holland.

Les Bleus did just that, thus becoming only the second team to hold the World and European championships at the same time (West Germany were the first). It was a close-run thing, in the final most of all.

Zidane was at his peak in France's 3–0 opening win over Denmark. His pass sent Anelka through and Blanc slid in the rebound after Peter Schmeichel saved. Zidane made the second for Henry. Sylvain Wiltord added the third.

Djorkaeff hit the winner against the Czech Republic after Karel Poborsky's penalty cancelled out Henry's early goal. That win clinched France's quarter-final place. So coach Roger Lemerre fielded a virtual reserve side in the 3–2 defeat by Holland.

Zidane put France ahead with a free kick in the quarter-final against Spain. Gaizka Mendieta replied from the penalty spot but Djorkaeff finished off Vieira's pass to restore the French lead. In the final minute, Barthez hauled down Abelardo and referee Pierluigi Collina awarded a penalty. Mendieta had been substituted. Raul stepped forward instead – and shot over.

France fell behind after 19 minutes of the semi-final when Nuno Gomes scored for Portugal. They levelled six minutes after half-time when Anelka beat the Portuguese offside trap and Henry turned in his pass. Les Bleus turned up the pressure and dominated extra time. They won with a 117th-minute golden goal.

Abel Xavier was ruled to have handled Wiltord's shot and Austrian referee Gunter Benko awarded a penalty. The Portuguese were incensed. They surrounded the Slovak linesman Igor Sramka, who flagged for the offence. The Portuguese protests held up play for five minutes. Benko sent off Nuno Gomes. Zidane kept his nerve and his concentration to beat Vitor Baia with the spot kick.

Italy, shrewdly guided by Dino Zoff, defended deep in the final. They cut down the space for Henry to exploit and tight-marked Zidane. Henry hit a post but Italy slowly grew in confidence. They went ahead in the 55th minute when Marco Delvecchio volleyed in Gianluca Pessotto's centre. Four minutes later, Alessandro del Piero screwed wide from Francesco Totti's through ball.

Lemerre sent on Trezeguet as a third striker. Italy held out until the dying seconds. Wiltord wriggled clear on the left of the box and drove a low shot past Francesco Toldo.

France won with another golden goal, 13 minutes into extra time. Pires – of Portuguese immigrant descent – skipped his marker and crossed. Trezeguet fired into the roof of the net. Les Bleus had made history. Trezeguet joined his new, Italian, club, Juventus, a few days later.

The French team had become the expression of a confident nation, *La France qui gagne* (winning France). Les Bleus had reached the height of their achievements. Perhaps they had used up a store of luck, too.

Captain Deschamps and Blanc retired from international football. The team had lost its leaders. Blanc – nicknamed '*Le President*' – organised the back line and acted as a calming influence on younger colleagues.

Deschamps was steady and unspectacular. Platini said, 'He's done very well to achieve what he has, given his natural ability.' Cantona famously derided him as a 'water carrier'. But he was a natural leader and his coach's voice on the pitch. He was the voice of the team, too: the man who called on his countrymen to roar themselves hoarse for Les Bleus in 1998.

Deschamps skippered Nantes at the age of 19 and captained Marseille to European Cup final victory. He had the happy knack of making others around him play. He carried that quality into coaching and steered Monaco to the Champions League semi-finals in 2004.

As Platini pointed out, Zidane was too 'introverted' to lead the team. He shouldered enough responsibility as playmaker. Left-back Lizarazu said, 'When we don't know what to do, we give the ball to Zizou and he works something out.' Henry said, 'He's the man we can count on.'

France, the holders, did not have to qualify for the 2002 World Cup finals in Japan and South Korea. New skipper Desailly admitted, 'It's hard to keep your concentration at the very top when you only have friendlies to play.'

Perhaps the warning bells should have rung when they lost 2–0 to

Spain in 2001. The Spanish had a point to prove from Euro 2000. They were tough and physical. Lizarazu did not join in the media criticism of their tactics. He said, 'Maybe we need more games like this to prepare us for the competition that lies ahead.'

The friendly against Algeria in October 2001 – intended as a match of reconciliation – turned nasty in a different way. Zidane received death threats and his father was accused of being a French collaborator in the war of independence. The game was abandoned after young French Arabs invaded the pitch in the second half. The usually reticent Zidane went public, 'My father is Algerian. He's proud of who he is and he never fought against his country.'

Less than a year later, the National Front temporarily displaced the Socialists as the leading opposition party. Its leader, Jean-Marie Le Pen, ran off against the incumbent Jacques Chirac for the presidency. Le Pen lost heavily but his rise showed another side to the 'rainbow nation'.

Still France headed into the finals as one of the favourites. Zidane, by now the world's most expensive player at £46 million, had been in top form with Real Madrid. He had scored their European Cup winner against Bayer Leverkusen with a stinging left-foot volley. But Les Bleus were already without midfielder Pires, a cruciate ligament victim when he had been in the form of his life with Arsenal. The players, mainly drawn from the Premiership and Serie A, were tired, physically and mentally, after what Platini called 'more and more intense seasons'.

Soon they were without Zidane, too, sidelined for the first two games, against Senegal and Uruguay, by a thigh injury suffered in a warm-up friendly against South Korea. Senegal frustrated France and beat them 1–0. Uruguay defended in depth and held them to a 0–0 draw. Henry was sent off for a foul on Marcelo Romero and suspended for the final group game against Denmark.

France had no Henry, no Pires and the returning Zidane could play barely at half pace. Denmark won 2–0. France were eliminated without scoring a goal. Lemerre was attacked for not blooding younger players. France's system had become predictable and relied too much on Zidane, said the critics. They claimed that Lemerre had not made best use of Henry and added that Desailly lacked Deschamps' authority. Others criticised the FFF for involving the players in too many sponsorship deals when they should have been preparing for the competition.

Yet the criticism was relatively restrained. The writer Jean-Michel Normand said, 'We get ourselves worked up if we win but in defeat we think about other things because life goes on.'

Lyon's title-winning coach Jacques Santini succeeded Lemerre. Santini relied on most of the old guard, too, as France qualified to defend their European title with maximum points from eight matches. They headed to Euro 2004 in Portugal among the favourites again.

Zidane rescued them in stoppage time in their opening game against England. It was virtually a Premiership clash. Seven of Santini's starters played for English clubs.

England led through Frank Lampard. First, Barthez kept France in the game when he saved David Beckham's penalty. Then Les Bleus were awarded a free kick 20 yards out. Zidane lashed a curling shot past keeper David James to level. A minute later, James hauled down Henry and Zidane tucked away the penalty.

The French struggled against Croatia. They needed a Trezeguet equaliser to grab a 2–2 draw. They laboured against Switzerland until two Henry goals clinched a 3–1 win and booked a quarter-final meeting with Greece. Zidane was subdued, Vieira was injured. France lacked penetration. Angelos Charisteas headed the Greek winner.

This time the French media pulled no punches. *Le Parisien* claimed that France needed fresher, younger players. It said, 'This is the end of a team and the end of an era.' *Le Monde* said France deserved to be knocked out and added, 'The team were vulnerable in defence and disorganised in attack.' *Dernieres Nouvelles d'Alsace* said, 'Was this result really a surprise? In these championships, the team have lost their collective force, their imagination, their freshness.' *L'Equipe* added, 'They've fallen apart during the course of their matches.'

Lizarazu and Thuram retired from international football. So did Zidane at the age of 32. He said, 'This is the end of a cycle.'

Or was it? Zidane came out of international retirement in the summer of 2005 as France struggled to qualify for the 2006 World Cup finals. Thuram joined him. Zidane's presence inspired Les Bleus to three wins – including a crucial 1–0 victory over the Republic of Ireland in Dublin – and a draw, which gained them automatic entry to Germany 2006. He had become their talisman again.

CHAPTER 18

GO WEST, YOUNG MAN!

The great wing-half Josef Masopust was the first Czech to win the European Footballer of the Year award in 1962. Another great attacking midfielder, Pavel Nedved, became the second Czech winner in 2003. During the intervening 41 years, political and economic forces changed football in the countries of the old Soviet bloc beyond recognition.

Masopust played 16 seasons for the army team Dukla Praha (Prague), the leading club in the old Czechoslovakia. He was born in the northern Bohemian village of Strimice – later demolished to make way for a coal mine – began his career with the local club Most and made his name as a youngster with Teplice.

The almost inevitable move to Dukla followed. Conscription for young men was compulsory. It was also the means by which Dukla – in common with army clubs throughout eastern Europe – gathered up the pick of their country's young players, then handed them army ranks to stay on after their national service was done. The fans of other clubs heartily loathed Dukla because of this unfair advantage.

Masopust was Dukla's midfield general as they won eight Czechoslovak league titles, three cup finals and reached the European Cup semi-finals in 1967, when they lost to Celtic. He memorably likened his midfield role to 'a combination of playing the violin and doing the washing up'.

He tackled like an old-fashioned wing-half but his forte was attack. He was a two-footed dribbler who could 'go' either way. His trademark was the 'Masopust slalom' – jinking from foot to foot past tackles before finishing with a powerful shot.

He scored 79 goals for Dukla and ten in 63 appearances for Czechoslovakia. He skippered the team that reached the 1962 World Cup final. He even shot the Czechs ahead from Tomas Pospichal's pass before Brazil recovered to win 3–1.

Masopust was 37 with his best days behind him when he was finally allowed to move abroad to end his playing days with the modest Belgian club Molenbeek. As the Czech journalist Ladislav Josef wrote: 'In another age, Masopust might have been even more celebrated than Nedved. But conditions in communist Czechoslovakia meant that he spent virtually all his career with Dukla.'

Masopust was voted the best Czech player of the twentieth century. A replica Golden Ball stands on a shelf in his Prague flat. He remembers receiving the Golden Ball, the European Player of the Year trophy, before a European Cup tie against Benfica. He said, 'There was no ceremony. Eusebio shook hands with me, I put the trophy in my kit bag and went home later on the tram.'

How would Masopust have fared in Spain or Italy? How famous might he have become? What riches might he have earned? He said, 'They were not options when I played. I had a lot of good moments in football. Like every small boy, I dreamed of playing in a World Cup final and scoring in one. I lived that dream.'

Masopust is a great admirer of Nedved, five times Czech player of the year. He said, 'Pavel has been by far the best Czech player for several years now. He has great power and skill in attack and his movement is exceptional.'

Nedved played for Dukla while he did his army service in the early '90s. He also played for his country in a losing tournament final – Euro 96 against Germany. There the similarities with Masopust end.

Nedved made his name with Sparta, one of Prague's traditional top two. After Czechoslovakia's 'velvet revolution', the old clubs reasserted themselves, now backed by commercial sponsors. Those sponsors shunned Dukla. Supporting a team with Dukla's history would have been commercial suicide. Dukla had no fan base either, unlike Prague rivals Sparta, Slavia and Bohemians.

Without state backing, the club went into terminal decline. By 1993, they had slipped to the third division. They eventually left their ground at Juliska and amalgamated with provincial club Pribram, to be known as Dukla Pribram. The name is all that remains of Dukla's empire.

Czechoslovakia after the velvet revolution offered good players at knockdown prices to western clubs. Czechoslovak clubs – and the local economy – needed foreign currency. So the best Czech players started going abroad in their early 20s. The giant Sparta centre-forward Tomas Skuhravy led the way when he signed for Genoa after the 1990 World Cup finals.

Nedved followed that example after the Czechs' Euro 96 final defeat. But he had played for the Czech Republic, *not* Czechoslovakia. Slovak players had long played an important part in the national team. The side that Masopust skippered in the 1962 World Cup final included Slovak keeper Viliam Schroif, centre-back Jan Popluhar, inside-forward Adolf Scherer and striker Andrej Kvasnak.

Slovaks formed the majority of the squad that won the European Championship in 1976, when Czechoslovakia beat Holland 3–1 then overcame West Germany on penalties in the final. Czech keeper Ivo Viktor and midfielder Antonin Panenka – who scored the winning spot kick with an outrageous chip – grabbed the headlines. But, of the 13 who played that night, Karol Dobias, Jan Pivarnik, Anton Ondrus, Jozef Capkovic, Koloman Gogh, Jan Svehlik, Marian Masny and sub Ladislav Jurkemik all came from Slovakia.

In January 1993, less than four years after the velvet revolution, the Czechoslovak federation split into the Czech Republic and Slovakia in a 'velvet divorce'. Opinion polls at the time showed a majority in both countries wanted the federation to continue. But the collapse of communism had thrown into focus the imbalance between the more market-orientated Czech economy and the old-style heavy industry of Slovakia. The respective leaders, Vaclav Klaus for the Czechs and Vladimir Meciar for the Slovaks, spent months negotiating the disbanding of the federation.

At least it was an amicable separation, rather than the result of the old regime's implosion, as in the Soviet Union, or of internecine strife, as in the old Yugoslavia. But the effect was to weaken both the strength of the domestic leagues and that of the Slovakia national team, though the Czechs reached the final of Euro 96 and the semi-finals of Euro 2004. Nedved's injury, with the score 0–0 against Greece, almost certainly cost the Czech Republic a place in the final.

The Czech squad for that competition showed how much the game in their land had changed. In 1976, all the squad played in the domestic league. Even stars such as 90-times capped striker Zdenek Nehoda did not move abroad until they were in their 30s.

In 2004, all but three of the Czech 23 played for foreign clubs – and Tomas Hubschmann joined Shakhtar Donetsk soon after the finals.

The old Czechoslovak league provided tough competition, too, as shown by the performance of its clubs in Europe. As well as their semi-final appearance, Dukla reached the European Cup quarter-finals three times in the 1960s. Sparta reached the last eight in 1968. Slovan Bratislava became the first club from the old Soviet bloc to win a European trophy when they beat Barcelona in the 1969 Cup-Winners' Cup final.

Sparta and Slavia led the Czech challenge to Dukla, backed by provincial clubs such as Banik Ostrava and Zbrojovka Brno. Slovan Bratislava carried the Slovak banner with strong support from Spartak Trnava.

Popluhar recalled, 'When I was at my peak, the conditions for a footballer in Czechoslovakia were modest. But the spirit and support of the spectators was incredible.' He added, 'I'm not sure that modern players would want to return to my era, though!'

Now Sparta rule a league which has become a feeder competition for foreign clubs. Occasionally, Slavia – or a provincial club such as 2004 champions Banik Ostrava – will challenge their hegemony. Sparta can fill their Letna ground for Champions League matches but are lucky to attract 7,000 fans for most domestic league games.

Since 1999, Sparta have sold such international stars as Jan Koller, Tomas Rosicky, Zdenek Grygera, Petr Cech and Hubschmann – and used the cash to stay on top in domestic competition. They reached the closing stages of the first Champions League competition in 1992, before the player exodus reached full speed. Such progress is a pipe dream now.

Coach Frantisek Straka was sacked after their 5–0 Champions League defeat by Lyon in December 2004. Sparta failed to win a match in their group. Straka said, 'Advancing to the group stage itself is an achievement for Sparta nowadays. We can't compete financially with clubs in western Europe.'

Slavia's best side of the last decade, which reached the UEFA Cup semi-finals in 1996, was rapidly dismantled by western clubs. Karel Poborsky joined Manchester United, Patrik Berger went to Borussia Dortmund, Jan Suchoparek to Strasbourg and Radek Bejbl signed for Atletico Madrid.

The Czechs won the 2002 European Under-21 championship final, beating France on penalties. Two years earlier, they lost 2–1 to Italy in the final. Even for players of that age, the western clubs were hovering. The Czechs' Euro 2004 full-back Marek Jankulovski, for instance, was signed by Napoli straight after the 2000 final. The Czech Republic coach Karel Bruckner said, 'It's very difficult to build a club team here, because the best players move abroad every summer.'

With Dukla a memory, Czechs and Slovaks playing as separate nations, Czech players moving abroad by the planeload and the domestic league a much-weakened competition, no wonder Masopust said, 'Nothing much remains from my day.'

By Euro 2004, Nedved had proved himself one of the world's finest players, first with Lazio, then Juventus. He starred in the Lazio side that won the Serie A championship, the Coppa Italia and the last edition of the European Cup-Winners' Cup when he scored in their final victory over Mallorca. He was reputedly on £40,000 a week at Lazio and his salary rose even higher after a £20 million transfer to Juventus in the summer of 2001.

Masopust – and even later, the stars of 1976 – barely earned £40,000 in a career.

Nedved collects fine wines. A player who did that in the old Czechoslovakia would have quickly fallen foul of the communist cadres – who pried into every dressing-room – for exhibiting 'bourgeois tendencies'.

Nedved, who married his childhood sweetheart Ivana when they were 21, is a modest man, like Masopust. He talks of 'how hard I had to work to keep up with more talented players'. Zinedine Zidane, the former Juventus playmaker, tells a different story. He said, 'Nedved is a different type of player from me, but so very effective. When I left Juve, he stepped in and worked wonders.'

Nedved won a championship medal in his first season, then was inspirational, hitting nine goals from midfield, as Juve won a second successive title. (He added another title medal in 2005.)

Nedved struck a trademark goal to take Juventus to the 2003 European Cup final at Real Madrid's expense, surging into the box to strike home a 15-yard shot. It was his fifth goal of Juve's run. Afterwards, the Madrid defender Ivan Helguera said, 'Nedved is the complete player.'

Nedved also collected a yellow card in that second leg. That kept him out of the final. Juve lost on penalties to Milan. Coach Marcello Lippi admitted, 'He had been such an important player for us all season. We needed him on such a big occasion.'

Andriy Shevchenko scored the spot kick that won the European Cup for Milan that night – after he had a goal disallowed in normal time. The Ukraine striker – Nedved's successor as European Player of the Year – is another who went west to prove his greatness.

Nedved said, 'Defences in Serie A are very solid. It's probably harder to score here than in any other league. But that hasn't stopped Andriy finding the net regularly. Whenever Milan are in trouble, he usually gets them out of it.'

Shevchenko is acknowledged as Milan's best foreign signing since the heady days of Ruud Gullit, Marco van Basten and Frank Rijkaard. He made western clubs sit up when he scored a hat trick as Dynamo Kiev – now champions of independent Ukraine rather than the Soviet Union – won 4–0 at Barcelona in the 1998 Champions League. The following season, he powered Dynamo to the semi-finals with eight goals.

Milan paid Dynamo £16 million to sign him that summer. Shevchenko became the first foreigner to finish top scorer (*capocannoniere*) in his first season in Serie A. He netted 24 goals that season, 24 in 2000–01 and 24 again in 2003–04 when he finished league top scorer once more as Milan won the championship. He scored his 100th Serie A goal in a 2–1 win over Siena in November 2004 and finished the season with 17.

Milan coach Carlo Ancelotti said, 'He's simply awesome. He's not just a great finisher. He's become our leader on the pitch, a real team player.'

How different would Shevchenko's career have been if he had been born on 29 September 1956 instead of 20 years later? He would have spent his career with Dynamo in the old Soviet league. He would have played for the old Soviet Union. (At one time, in the 1980s, the Soviet international side was composed entirely of Dynamo Kiev players.) He would have been forbidden to play abroad until he was 28, at least.

Instead, he said, 'I was grateful to [Dynamo president] Hrihoriy Surkis and [coach] Valeriy Lobanovskyi for letting me move at the right time. It was a challenge for me. I wanted to prove that players from eastern Europe could succeed in Serie A.'

Earlier Soviet imports – such as Alexander Zavarov and Alexei Mikhailichenko – had flopped. The former title-winning Sampdoria coach Vujadin Boskov said, 'Mikhailichenko had the traits of a lot of players raised under socialism. When they signed a contract in the west, they thought their most cherished dream had come true. So he didn't play as if his career depended on it.'

Shevchenko, like Nedved and the Czech diaspora, was different. He was young and ambitious with his best years ahead of him. He had also grown up in a society that was evolving from a socialist economy to a partial free market.

Shevchenko has stayed close to his roots. He brought his parents, his sister Olena and her husband with him to Milan. After Milan's European Cup final victory, he wrapped himself in the Ukraine flag for the rossoneri's lap of honour. He said, 'By winning the Champions League, I fulfilled myself as a player. This was the outcome of all the work I've done since I was nine years old in Ukraine. I knew how many people in Ukraine had watched the final and supported me. I wanted to support them and my country in return.' He dedicated his winner's medal to Lobanovskyi, who died the previous year.

Lobanovskyi was a giant of Soviet and Ukrainian football, though relatively unknown in the west. He led Dynamo to become the first Soviet club to win a European trophy when they lifted the Cup-Winners' Cup in 1975. They repeated the feat 11 years later. He steered them to five Soviet titles and two European Cup semi-finals, and, in a later spell in charge, to five successive Ukraine championships. He was the guiding hand when Dynamo reached the Champions League semi-finals in 1999.

Shevchenko said, 'He was like a father to me. He taught me so much about football and about growing up.' Kakha Kaladze, the Georgian full-back who followed Shevchenko from Kiev to Milan, added, 'Any player who went through Lobanovskyi's football school could compete in the big leagues.'

Lobanovksyi never had the chance to prove himself in the west, nor to gain the rewards that accompanied success. Shevchenko has done both. His Champions League win bonuses with Dynamo brought his earnings for the 1998–99 season to an estimated £120,000. As the *Gazzetta dello Sport* pointed out, 'That's not much by Italian standards but it's a mind-boggling amount in Ukraine.'

Shevchenko remembered, 'As a small boy, I dreamed of riding a moped. Forget about a motor bike. My parents could only afford a bicycle.' Now he earns an estimated £5 million a season, is married to a model, drives top-of-the-range cars (Mercedes, apparently, is his favourite brand), has a series of sponsorship deals and is the public face of the Italian fashion house Armani in Ukraine.

Politics and football were entwined throughout the old Soviet bloc. Nowhere did they combine with such force as in the old East Germany (DDR). The government and the secret police, the *Stasi*, intervened in football as in all other walks of life. The best players were directed by the interior ministry to play for certain clubs – usually Stasi chief Erich Mielke's favourite team Dynamo Berlin.

The story of Dynamo Berlin's foundation is instructive. Berlin lacked a successful club. So, in 1954, Mielke ordered the players and staff of champions Dynamo Dresden to relocate there and henceforth to play as Dynamo Berlin. The Dresden club continued but was wrecked for a decade as a result.

Mielke also pressurised referees, who needed Stasi approval to leave the country to take charge of international contests. Dynamo Berlin won ten successive titles. Even their own players began to question their frequent good fortune and the number of decisions that favoured them at vital moments.

The Stasi had informers in every dressing-room. Dresden's star strikers in the late 1980s, Thorsten Gutschow and Ulf Kirsten, were both reputedly Stasi collaborators. Dresden player Gerd Weber was banned from football and imprisoned after it was discovered that he was considering an offer to join the Bundesliga club Cologne. The Dynamo Berlin player Lutz Eigendorf, who defected to play for Kaiserslautern in the west, was found dead after a mysterious car accident.

Sometimes, the Stasi did not even need informers, like the time they bugged Bayern Munich's dressing-room before a European Cup tie in Dresden.

But this surreal world came crashing down with the Berlin Wall. The 1990–91 season was the last for the East German league. Its top two clubs, Hansa Rostock and Dynamo Dresden, joined the Bundesliga. The next six went into the Bundesliga second division.

The top players inevitably voted with their feet, as the leading Bundesliga clubs cherry-picked the [eastern] '*Ossi*' teams. The most famous Ossi import was Matthias Sammer, who left Dresden for Stuttgart. He later inspired Germany's Euro 96-winning side and Borussia Dortmund's European Cup winners the following season.

Kirsten joined Bayer Leverkusen and became a regular in the Germany squad. Jorg Heinrich, Steffen Freund, Jens Jeremies, Thomas Linke and Alex Zickler – who had all grown up through the East Germany youth teams – became Bundesliga stars.

Clubs in the old DDR fell apart. Rostock, the only eastern team in the Bundesliga, were relegated at the end of the 2004–05 season after finishing one from bottom. There were just three other eastern clubs in the second division at the start of the 2005–06 season – Dresden, Energie Cottbus and Erzgebirge Aue.

Cities such as Leipzig and Magdeburg were without even a second-grade Bundesliga club. Dynamo Berlin, like Dukla, had fallen into disrepute and sunk into amateur football, shunned by sponsors and fans alike.

The decline of clubs linked to the old communist regimes was a feature of post-Soviet football. Of the old army clubs, only Partizan in Serbia and CSKA in Bulgaria maintained genuine support.

In Russia itself, Spartak Moscow were the most successful and best-supported club.

Dynamo Moscow had been linked to the interior ministry – and indirectly to the secret police. CSKA were the army club; Lokomotiv were still backed by the railway ministry. Torpedo had links with the Zil motor factory.

By contrast, Spartak were the 'people's team'. They won nine of the ten Russian championships between 1992 and 2001, including six in a row from 1996 – evidence of how their competition had diminished as the Soviet Union collapsed.

The Soviet league fell apart as the republics became independent nations. As Simon Kuper pointed out in *Football Against the Enemy*, football clubs in the republics filled the role of nationalist symbols in the old Soviet league, especially when they met Russian – particularly Moscow – clubs. When Zalgiris Vilnius finished third in 1988 for instance, local fans hailed their rise as a triumph for Lithuania. Dynamo Kiev, the leading non-Russian club of the Soviet era, have gone on to symbolise Ukrainian football, though they now face a strong challenge from oligarch-rich Shakhtar Donetsk.

The likes of Dynamo Tbilisi (Georgia), Ararat Erevan (Armenia), Dynamo Minsk (Belarus) once represented their republics in the federal arena. Now they dominate the leagues in their independent countries and act as feeders for the Russian and Ukrainian clubs as a conduit to the west.

The former president of the Soviet football federation Vyscheslav Koloskov said, 'Now each former republic has its own league and the standard in most of them is low.'

Russia were forced back to the drawing board as an international force, too. Many former Soviet internationals were non-Russian. Now they would play for their new states rather than their old one. Russia could no longer call on the likes of Maris Verpakovskis, whose goal against Turkey took Latvia to their first-ever championship finals (Euro 2004) and sparked celebrations on the streets of Riga, let alone Shevchenko and Kaladze.

The Yugoslav league fell apart in similar fashion. Once it was among the most competitive in eastern Europe. Belgrade rivals Red Star and Partizan were the top clubs in Serbia. Dynamo Zagreb and Hajduk Split inevitably mounted a strong Croatian challenge. Sarajevo and Vojvodina Novi Sad carried Bosnian hopes. Vardar Skopje played for Macedonia and Olimpia Ljubljana for Slovenia.

The break-up – and the bitter civil strife that followed – destroyed the league and the Yugoslav national team. The provinces became five independent states. Now one or two clubs dominate the league in each – and their best young players soon move to the west, like the Partizan striker Mateja Kezman, who joined Chelsea from PSV Eindhoven, then moved to Atletico Madrid. He is just one more example of the player exodus that has continued throughout eastern Europe.

Poland, under the influence of the Solidarity (*Solidarnosc*) opposition movement had taken nervous steps towards liberalisation in the early 1980s. One manifestation was the sale of the nation's star striker, Zbigniew Boniek, from Widzew Lodz to Juventus, while still at his peak in his mid-20s. Widzew reached the European Cup semi-finals in 1983, losing to Juve and Boniek. That was their high point, before the team broke up.

In August 2004, Boniek – now a successful businessman – reached for his own chequebook to rescue relegated Widzew from bankruptcy.

The Bulgarian striker Hristo Stoichkov became an icon in Johan Cruyff's dream team at Barcelona. Romanian stars such as Dan Petrescu, Gica Popescu, Florin Raducioiu and Ilie Dumitrache made their way to the Premiership. The greatest Romanian talent of all, midfielder Gheorghe Hagi, played for Real Madrid and Barcelona.

Emeric Ienei, who coached Steaua Bucharest to European Cup victory in 1986 said, 'After the 1990 World Cup finals, all our stars went abroad.'

Perhaps there were benefits for some national teams. Bulgaria reached the 1994 World Cup semi-finals with a side full of foreign-based players. Stoichkov finished joint top scorer in the finals with six goals. Goalkeeper Borislav Mihailov, now vice-president of the Bulgarian FA, said, 'Many of the players – such as Stoichkov, Emil Kostadinov, Krassimir Balakov and Lubo Penev – played for top European clubs and that helped Bulgaria.'

Ienei believes that the years between 1994 and 2000 were Romania's 'golden era'.

Nedved himself insists the Czechs have benefited from their players' experiences in western Europe. He said, 'We have a strong generation of players and we've had the advantage of playing for some of the best clubs in Europe.'

At the same time, the Slovaks have stagnated at international level. So have Hungary. So have Poland, once such a powerful force. The Poles won the 1972 Olympic tournament and finished third in the 1974 World Cup finals, despite the injury-enforced absence of their best player, Wlodzimierz Lubanski. They also finished third in the 1982 World Cup finals with a squad of home-based players.

The domestic result of the player exodus – coupled with the political changes – was the decline of competitive club football in the east. The international consequence was to massively weaken eastern teams in European club competition.

The leading teams from the old east stood their ground in the European Cup from its inception in 1955 to the early 1990s. Yugoslav champions Red Star were the first eastern club to reach the semi-finals in 1957, losing 1–0 on aggregate to Fiorentina. They illuminated the competition many times in the following 40 years. Their 1991 final win, over Marseille on penalties, was hardly their most entertaining performance, hiding the talents of Savicevic and Robert Prosinecki behind blanket defence. But Red Star had reached the 1971 semi-finals with a team including 'magic Dragan' Dzajic – and their win at Anfield in 1973–74 was the catalyst for Liverpool's change to a more measured style that came to dominate Europe. Their arch rivals, Partizan, reached the final in 1966, losing to Real Madrid.

Now the Serbian FA president, Dragan Stojkovic is full of

pessimism. He said, 'It will be very, very, difficult for our clubs to emulate what Red Star did in 1991. They lack money. In many cases, their budgets are tiny. Selling players is the only financial recourse that they have. The introduction of the Bosman rule [see Chapter 22] has practically ruined us, along with many other countries.'

Steaua, the Romanian club that became a plaything of the ruling Ceausescu family, won the European Cup in 1986, reached the semi-finals in 1988 and lost to Milan in the final a year later. Their city rivals, Dinamo, had reached the semi-finals in 1984. In 1986, only a handful of Romanian stars were allowed to play abroad. During the 1990s – after Nicolae Ceausescu's demise – Steaua alone sold players to western or Turkish clubs in deals totalling £25 million. By 2001, more than 400 Romanian pros were playing outside their homeland.

The Hungarian champions Vasas of Budapest emulated Red Star in 1958, reaching the semi-finals before they were eliminated by the great Real Madrid. Vasas Gyor (1965) and Ujpest Dosza (1974) were other Hungarian semi-finalists. Now most Hungarian clubs simply battle to survive varying degrees of financial hardship.

The Czechoslovak champions, Spartak Trnava, lost to Ajax in the 1969 semi-finals. In 2004–05, they narrowly escaped relegation from the Slovak top division. CSKA Sofia ended Nottingham Forest's run as European champions in 1980–81 and reached the semi-finals the following season, knocking out Liverpool in the last eight.

Mihailov said, 'In those days, our clubs had the advantage of quality players. Until the late 1980s, you could only go to play abroad when you were 28. That's changed now. The best players have the chance to play for top European clubs while in their early 20s. That's not good for our club sides. Nowadays it's very hard for the clubs to keep their best players.'

The odds against an eastern team even reaching the Champions League last 16 are immense. Kiev in 1999 were the only side from the old Soviet bloc to reach the last four since Red Star won the trophy.

In the days before the Champions League, the eastern champions were guaranteed entry to the European Cup first round. Now they are trapped in a vicious circle. The eastern clubs' standards have declined because their best players have gone abroad. So they can no longer make an impact in Europe and thus climb the UEFA rankings.

The Champions League – with its massive financial rewards – is heavily weighted towards the wealthy countries of western Europe (see

Chapter 20). UEFA is determined to keep the top clubs, the G-14 elite, on board. The Champions League offers the chance for up to four clubs from England, Italy and Spain to reach the group stage and up to three more from France and Germany.

(Greece were also given the chance to enter three clubs after their Euro 2004 victory.)

Meanwhile, the teams from the old east must pre-qualify even to compete in the group stage. Kiev, for instance, began their run to the 1999 semi-finals with an 8–0 win over League of Wales champions Barry Town in the first qualifying round.

Not one team from the old east was granted automatic entry into the 2004–05 Champions League group stage. Once-mighty Red Star began in the second qualifying round. So did Sparta Prague, Dinamo Bucharest, Ferencvaros (Hungary), Shakhtar Donetsk, CSKA Moscow and Lokomotiv Plovdiv (Bulgaria). Dynamo Kiev, Wisla Krakow and Banik Ostrava entered in the third qualifying round. Only Kiev, Shakhtar, CSKA Moscow and Sparta made it to the group stage.

In 2005–06, Sparta and Artmedia Bratislava – who started in the first qualifying round – were the only teams from the old east to play in the group stage. Both failed to reach the last 16. Kiev were eliminated in the second qualifying round. So were Dynamo Tblisi and Hajduk. Wisla, Debrecen (Hungary), Steaua, CSKA Sofia, Slavia, Shakhtar Donetsk and Lokomotiv Moscow all went out in the third qualifying round.

The evidence is compelling. The clubs of the old east have slid into serial decline. They are uncompetitive in the Champions League and the standard of their domestic leagues has plummeted. Their status now compares with the traditional role of the Scandinavian sides – to supply bargain buys to western Europe.

The collapse of the communist system has had huge consequences for football in the old Soviet bloc. Stars such as Nedved and Shevchenko have seized their chance to gain fame and fortune beyond the dreams of their predecessors. Meanwhile the eastern clubs – a handful of oligarch-backed teams apart – have grown ever poorer and weaker. If a third Czech is to follow Masopust and Nedved as European Footballer of the Year, it is almost certain that he will play for a western club.

CHAPTER 19

THE GENERALS OF THE CHAMPIONS LEAGUE

They are modern Europe's new generals, the victorious coaches of the Champions League: a diverse elite who have outwitted their opponents to win the European Cup.

By the time the Champions League began, coaches had become high-profile figures. Champions League competition raised their profiles even further. As more and more clubs from the big western leagues entered the competition, so the most famous coaches of the age were pitted against each other every season.

Not everyone who has coached a team to Champions League glory will be remembered as a great coach. Jupp Heynckes, for instance, who steered Real Madrid to victory in 1998, was promptly sacked because they 'only' finished fourth in La Liga. Raymond Goethals' 1993 triumph was tarnished by the Valenciennes bribe scandal (see Chapter 17), which led to Marseille being stripped of the trophy and relegated to the French second division.

But the aspiring greats know they need a European Cup victory on their CVs before they can really join the elite. Hector Cuper came within touching distance, steering Valencia to losing finals in 2000 and 2001. Yet the generals of the Champions League remain a select band.

The avuncular Vicente del Bosque won twice with one club, Real Madrid, while the brilliant man-manager Ottmar Hitzfeld was the first to win with different teams – Borussia Dortmund in 1997 and Bayern Munich four years later.

The group is completed by seven other members: the forceful pragmatist Fabio Capello; Arrigo Sacchi's disciple Carlo Ancelotti; the brusque Louis van Gaal, clipboard in hand, who built a winning team with Ajax and failed in his attempt to repeat the formula at Barcelona; the firebrand Sir Alex Ferguson; super-confident Jose Mourinho; and the cigar-smoking Marcello Lippi – though Juventus's achievements in the 1990s were later clouded by controversy. The latest was added to the band in May 2005: Liverpool's Rafa Benitez, who masterminded the greatest comeback in the history of the European Cup final.

Former Milan, Juventus and Italy midfielder Capello had been working for one of Silvio Berlusconi's media companies when the Milan president summoned him to succeed Sacchi. He had little experience of running a senior squad, beyond a brief spell as caretaker after Nils Liedholm left Milan in 1987. But Capello's achievements have vindicated Berlusconi's judgement. He is noted for his attention to detail and defensive organisation. Yet he can surprise opponents with unexpected tactics.

When Milan's lethal Dutch striker Marco van Basten was at his peak, Capello encouraged an expansive game. Van Basten played in the 1993 European Cup final against Marseille though clearly struggling with the ankle trouble that finished his career. Milan started favourites after winning all their ten games en route to the final. They missed first half chances – and lost 1–0 to Basile Boli's 43rd-minute header.

The following season, deprived of van Basten's goals, Capello emphasised solidity. Milan won Serie A by conceding just 15 goals – a league record – in 34 matches. He rotated his midfielders and strikers throughout the campaign, both in Serie A and the Champions League.

Milan were again unbeaten on their run to the final but they had only scored 17 goals in 11 matches. Two of their key defenders, skipper Franco Baresi and centre-back Alessandro Costacurta, were suspended for the final against Johan Cruyff's Barcelona. It was supposed to be a duel between Barcelona's attack and Milan's defence. Instead, Capello's side shocked Barca by sweeping forward. Daniele Massaro gave them a 22nd-minute lead. Massaro scored again and Dejan Savicevic made it three in the 47th minute. Marcel Desailly completed a 4–0 rout. Capello said, 'My team played an extraordinary game which demonstrated an enormous will to win.' They played with an intensity which matched that of their coach.

Milan had erred on the side of caution when they reached the final again in 1995. Capello had made the Champions League their priority after a poor start ruled them out of Serie A contention. Their opponents were van Gaal's Ajax. Patrick Kluivert became the youngest scorer in final history – at 18 years, 327 days – when he shot Ajax's 85th-minute winner.

Yet Capello was happy to attack again when he steered Real Madrid to the Spanish title in 1996–97. He oversaw a strike force – including Raul, Predrag Mijatovic and Davor Suker – that scored 85 goals in 42 games.

Clarence Seedorf, a European Cup winner with Ajax, Madrid and Milan, arrived at the Bernabeu that season. He said, 'That was an amazing year under Capello. He implanted a winning mentality in Madrid. Five or six players – including Roberto Carlos, Davor Suker, Predrag Mijatovic and myself – arrived along with the coach and created a great atmosphere. You could tell something positive was happening. That helped us beat Barcelona to the title, even though they had Ronaldo in their team.' The following season, the Madrid side that Capello had created won the European Cup with Mijatovic scoring the winning goal.

Capello, meanwhile, had left to breathe new life into Serie A's perennial underachievers, Roma. In 2001, he steered them to their first scudetto for 18 years. But they did not progress beyond the second-group stage in either of their two Champions League forays. He was linked with major jobs outside Italy, first as a possible successor to Sir Alex Ferguson at Old Trafford, then as a candidate for the Barcelona post after van Gaal's sacking in 2003. But, to date, that season at Madrid has been the only time that he has coached outside Serie A.

Capello – who succeeded Lippi at Juventus in the summer of 2004 – prefers to work on home ground and he insists on doing the job his own way. At Milan, he frequently left Berlusconi's favourite player, Savicevic, on the bench – much to the Serb's disgust. At Roma, he rowed with Italy playmaker Francesco Totti, whom he accused of lacking dedication, and striker Vincenzo Montella. Montella often played a cameo role, screaming at the coach as he was substituted.

Capello's Juve won Serie A in his first season. Summer signing Fabio Cannavaro lined up alongside Lilian Thuram to tighten the defence while Zlatan Ibrahimovic added variation in attack. Juventus led the table from virtually first to last and clinched the title with a 1–0 win over nearest challengers Milan at San Siro when David Trezeguet headed the only goal. Goalkeeper Gianluigi Buffon said, 'That game was like a cup final.' The intense Capello had instilled a winning mentality again. He said, 'We have a strong team spirit and that's been fundamental in going all the way.'

Yet Capello was outsmarted in the 2005 European Cup quarter-finals by Benitez, whose Liverpool side overwhelmed Juve in the early minutes at Anfield, then defended with huge discipline in Turin.

The financial contrast between the 1995 finalists could not have been starker. Milan's battle-hardened veterans were backed by Berlusconi's millions. Ajax were a young team of youth products and shrewd signings. Skipper Danny Blind and former Milan midfielder Frank Rijkaard were the only players over 25.

Van Gaal, a former teacher, had joined Ajax as a youth coach in 1987 and risen through their ranks. The club's flourishing youth academy and scouting network had unearthed a Dutch contingent of vast potential – Ronald and Frank de Boer, Seedorf, Edgar Davids, Kluivert, Michael Reiziger and Winston Bogarde. Forwards Finidi George and Nwankwo Kanu came from Nigeria. Another attacker, Jari Litmanen, had been signed from Finland.

Van Gaal emphasised quick passing and movement – and retaining possession. He ordered his players to keep the ball and move the opposition around until a gap opened up. His squad practised quick-fire triangles.

His approach divided former Ajax greats. Johan Cruyff, the greatest of them all, said, 'Ajax have their own style, a traditional way of playing. No one can ever change it and van Gaal didn't try to change it.' His old colleague, winger Sjaak Swart, disagreed. He lamented that van Gaal's players played the ball back to retain possession rather than take on opponents. He asked, 'Where's the creativity?'

But the Real Madrid coach Jorge Valdano was one of their biggest admirers. He said, 'Ajax are approaching football utopia. Their concept of the game is exquisite yet they have a physical superiority as well. They are Beauty and the Beast.'

Van Gaal was dedicated to the point of obsession. He also had an eye for a player, as he showed when he brought Ronald de Boer back from FC Twente in February 1993. He could be ruthless, too. He dispensed with popular goalkeeper Stanley Menzo after a costly mistake in the 1993 UEFA Cup semi-final and put his faith in the young Edwin van der Sar. He sold mercurial winger Bryan Roy to Foggia in Serie A and replaced him with a youngster called Marc Overmars.

Yet, even as skipper Blind lifted the European Cup in Vienna, van Gaal foresaw his side's disintegration. He had warned earlier that season, 'I'm afraid that players are about to leave us. We're playing well and the big Italian clubs are watching.'

The 1995 final represented a watershed. Benfica's 5–3 win over Real Madrid in the 1962 final had been the last of the flamboyant attacking contests between teams determined to outscore each other. Ajax's triumph 33 years later represented the last hurrah for home-grown teams which prospered through shrewd management. The future belonged to the big clubs, backed by pots of TV cash. They would come to monopolise the Champions League as UEFA conceded more and more places, to head off a possible breakaway Euro league backed by satellite TV. Only Porto in 2004, under Mourinho, would buck the trend. And even they are members of the G-14 group of leading western clubs.

The Bosman ruling, less than seven months after the 1995 final, heralded the end of the old transfer system. Ajax's stars were about to be cherry-picked by wealthy Italian clubs, who could sign them without a fee at the end of their contracts.

Ajax won the Dutch championship for the third year running in 1995–96. They reached the European Cup final again, after a thrilling semi-final comeback to beat Panathinaikos 3–0 in Athens. Overmars was injured and missed the final against Juventus in Belgrade. Reiziger was suspended.

Wealthy Juventus, historically backed by the Agnelli family, the owners of Fiat, presented another total contrast to Ajax. They won 4–2 on penalties after a 1–1 draw. Litmanen equalised Fabrizio Ravanelli's 12th-minute score. Juve keeper Angelo Peruzzi made crucial saves from Davids and Sonny Silooy in the shootout.

Ajax fell apart after the final. Davids went to Milan. Seedorf joined Sampdoria, then moved to Real Madrid. Kluivert signed for Milan and later went to Barcelona. Reiziger followed the same route. So did Bogarde.

Van Gaal himself took charge at Barcelona in 1997. Many of his old Ajax stars eventually joined him – the De Boers, Kluivert, Reiziger, Bogarde and Litmanen.

Barcelona players and fans resented the pervasive Dutch influence. The Catalan sports media dubbed the team 'Barc–Ajax' and – echoes of Swart – claimed that the coach was 'obsessed with systems'.

Yet Barcelona won the domestic double in 1998 and retained their title the following season. In 2000, they finished second to Deportivo La Coruna and reached the Champions League semi-finals. They crashed 4–1 in the first leg at Valencia.

That result spelled the end of van Gaal's first stay at the Nou Camp. It also signalled the beginning of his decline as a coaching icon. His Holland squad failed to qualify for the 2002 World Cup finals, despite the wealth of talent available. He spent a brief, unhappy second spell at Barcelona before rejoining Ajax as technical director but was sacked after they were eliminated at the 2004–05 Champions League group stage.

The winning Juventus coach in 1996 was Marcello Lippi. He was described by UEFA's own Champions League website thus: 'Lippi possesses a stubborn streak wider than the River Po, which many believe is the crucial ingredient in his success.' Indeed, Lippi had shown his leadership potential during 12 years with Sampdoria, where he rose to become club captain. He recalled, 'I worked hard for the squad, on and off the field, during my five years as skipper. At times, we didn't get paid. I had to confront the management and keep my colleagues on an even keel. It wasn't easy.'

Lippi finished top of the class in his coaching exams at the Italian federation academy at Coverciano, yet he had coached ten clubs in 11 years before his work with Atalanta, then Napoli brought him to the attention of Juventus in 1993.

He never stopped believing in himself, even after what he called a series of 'smacks in the mouth'. Lippi said, 'Whenever I was sacked, the club ended up worse than when I left them.'

Lippi stressed the need for super fitness and physical power and he imparted his own self-belief to his players. He said, 'We have a winning mentality and we make sure our new players are imbued with it. In my first season, Juve hadn't won the title for nearly ten years. Then we started working in a completely different way. We won several games in a row in different competitions and we acquired that winning mentality because we were convinced we were doing things right on the pitch. Everyone believed in the project.'

It was Lippi who rescued Gianluca Vialli's career after two unhappy years at Juve. 'He wanted to leave. He asked me if I could help him return to Sampdoria. I told him to lift his head up and insisted that he could be the strongest player in Europe if he tried.'

Lippi liked to build sides around talismanic players. Vialli was the talisman for the team that won the European Cup in 1996. Alessandro del Piero was the kingpin of the side that won successive titles in 1997 and 1998. Lippi had given the young signing from Padova his chance in Juve's 1994–95 championship campaign – usually at the expense of Roberto Baggio, who was sold to Milan that summer. When Lippi returned for a second spell in charge at Juve, he made Pavel Nedved, recently arrived from Lazio, the hub of the team in place of Madrid-bound Zinedine Zidane.

Juventus won the European Cup and three Serie A titles during Lippi's first spell. They also reached two more European Cup finals. In 1997, Juve were tactically outsmarted by Hitzfeld's Dortmund. A year later, Mijatovic scored the only goal of the game for Madrid in Amsterdam.

Juve's success under Lippi was clouded however by doping allegations, first made by the Roma coach Zdenek Zeman. Zeman noted 'unnaturally quick muscle development' in both Vialli and Del Piero – and claimed that Juve gave their players performance-enhancing drugs.

Investigating magistrates conducted a lengthy inquiry, leading to the prosecution of Juve doctor Riccardo Agricola and chief executive Antonio Giraudo. More than 280 different drugs – at least five containing banned substances – were found at Juve's training ground. Expert witness Professor Gianmartino Benzi testified, 'Either the players were always sick or they took drugs without justification . . . to improve performance.'

In November 2004, Agricola was sentenced to 22 months in prison for supplying illegal stimulants – including the blood-doping drug EPO – to the Juve players between 1994 and 1998. Giraudo was acquitted. No other action was taken against the club.

Lippi quit Juve after a 4–2 home defeat by Parma in February 1999. He spent a short, unsuccessful spell at Inter, ending in Champions League defeat by the Swedish club Helsingborg in 2000. He was sacked after just one game of the Serie A season.

It was as if he could only work his magic at Juventus. He returned in the summer of 2001 after Ancelotti had taken Juve to runners-up spot in both previous seasons. Juve sacked him. Ancelotti would take revenge later.

Lippi said, 'To go back was a hard decision to make. At first, my reaction was 'no'. Then, as time went by, I started to like the idea. Juventus is something special.' He promised, 'I'll give the team an extra push. We'll play with aggression and a rejuvenated Del Piero.'

Lippi's side overtook Cuper's Inter on the last day of the season to win the 2002 scudetto. They won the 2003 title in a canter and reached the European Cup final. Nedved scored the decisive goal of the semi-final, against Madrid in Turin. Then he picked up his second yellow card of the competition, which kept him out of the final against Ancelotti's Milan. Lippi's side could not cope with the loss of their talisman. At least there were no mutterings about illegal stimulants.

In 2003–04, Juve finished 12 points behind champions Milan. They were eliminated 2–0 on aggregate by Deportivo in the Champions League last 16. Lippi quit at the end of the season. He became Italy's national coach after Euro 2004.

Hitzfeld was a former mathematics teacher and amateur player. He had made his name as a coach by guiding the Zurich club Grasshoppers to Swiss championships in 1990 and 1991.

Dortmund had reaped rich financial rewards – boosted by around £10 million of TV income – from reaching the 1993 UEFA Cup final. They used the cash to bring back Stefan Reuter, Andy Moller, Jurgen Kohler and Matthias Sammer from Italy. Sammer would become Hitzfeld's leader on the pitch. Dortmund also signed the Brazilian Julio Cesar and the Portuguese midfielder Paulo Sousa. Dortmund had assembled a team of huge potential, organised by the shrewdest psychologist in the Bundesliga: Hitzfeld.

Uli Hesse-Lichtenberger, in *Tor!* wrote: 'Such a collection of egos would have resulted in chaos at a club like Bayern Munich. But Dortmund had Hitzfeld.' Daimler-Chrysler chief Jurgen Schremp described Hitzfeld as 'a role model for German business leaders'.

Dortmund won the Bundesliga in 1995 and 1996 but lost to Ajax in the 1996 Champions League quarter-finals. A year later, they knocked out Auxerre in the last eight, then beat Manchester United 1–0 home and away. Kohler held Dortmund's rearguard together at Old Trafford and midfielder Lars Ricken pinched the decisive goal.

Reuter, Moller, Kohler and Paulo Sousa had all been at Juventus. The Italian club – which included Zidane, Alen Boksic and Christian Vieri – started favourites. Juve pressed from the first whistle but Hitzfeld had noted their vulnerability at dead-ball kicks. In the 29th minute, they failed to clear Moller's corner. The Scottish midfielder Paul Lambert chipped the ball back and Karlheinz Riedle chested it down to shoot home. Five minutes later, another Moller corner found Riedle, who headed in at the near post.

Lippi sent on Del Piero for centre-back Sergio Porrini and the sub pulled a goal back in the 70th minute. Dortmund sub Ricken settled the game in a breakaway a minute later, racing onto Moller's pass to score with a 35-yard chip.

Dortmund's victory was a credit to Hitzfeld's tactical nous. At Grasshoppers, he stuck by 4–4–2. At Dortmund, he frequently varied formations and tactics, often in the same match. At times he even used three strikers in a 3–4–3 system.

Mentally drained by his exertions, Hitzfeld quit after the game and took a year off from football. Meanwhile, Bayern were struggling on the pitch and reeling from crisis to crisis off it. The German media dubbed them 'FC Hollywood'. In the summer of 1998, Bayern appointed Hitzfeld to sort them out. He said, 'I'm the boss – and I'm in charge.'

Hitzfeld showed Mario Basler the door in the autumn of 1999 after one nightclub incident too many. He fined Lothar Matthaus, Bixente Lizarazu, Thomas Helmer, Mehmet Scholl and Giovane Elber for indiscipline. But the players saw that Hitzfeld's approach paid off. The much-travelled Matthaus said, 'He can communicate what he wants more clearly than any coach I've played for. He's a terrific organiser who always has things under control.' Bayern vice-president Karl-Heinz Rummenigge agreed. He said, 'He's brought stability to the team. He has never let the smallest fire break out.'

Bayern won the Bundesliga in 1999. But that season will always be remembered for the sting in the tail – the dying minutes of the European Cup final against Manchester United in Barcelona.

It should have been another of Hitzfeld's glory nights. Bayern had controlled the game. They led through a Basler free kick with time running out. Scholl had lobbed against the bar.

In the 90th minute, Ryan Giggs drove a half-cleared corner back into the box and Teddy Sheringham touched it past Oliver Kahn for a shock equaliser. With seconds left of stoppage time, David Beckham swung in another corner. Sheringham flicked it on and Ole Gunnar Solskjaer poked the ball home. 'Who put the ball in the Germans' net? Ole Gunnar Solskjaer!' sang the United fans. The United boss Alex Ferguson admitted, 'It's like a fairy tale.'

Hitzfeld's Bayern went on to win the Champions League on a far less memorable occasion in 2001, when Kahn's penalty shootout heroics settled a drab final against Valencia after a 1–1 draw. They also had the satisfaction of beating their old bogey team, Madrid, home and away in the semi-finals.

The young Canadian-English midfielder Owen Hargreaves stood in for Stefan Effenberg in the 2001 European Cup semi-final second leg against Madrid and the final against Valencia. He said, 'Hitzfeld was a huge influence, a brilliant man. I remember how he let me know I was playing against Madrid. I never imagined I'd be playing. Then, two days before the game, he handed me one of the bibs in training. He did it so casually, like it was no big deal, like he trusted me.'

Hitzfeld led Bayern to two more Bundesliga titles. But the coach was rebuilding as his stars left for foreign clubs. Bayern did not advance beyond the quarter-finals in any of the next three seasons. In 2003–04, they finished second to Werder Bremen and gained automatic Champions League qualification only by beating Freiburg in their last Bundesliga game of the season. After a 3–1 home defeat by Bremen a fortnight before the end of the campaign, Bayern sacked Hitzfeld. Chief executive Uli Hoeness said, 'That game changed the world and the scales fell from my eyes. It just wasn't working.'

It seemed a harsh way to treat one of the greatest coaches in the history of German football. The national team was seeking a successor to Rudi Voller after their early exit from Euro 2004. The German federation turned to Hitzfeld but he had decided on another sabbatical, 'I need a break and I'm not in the right frame of mind to take on the Germany job.'

Alex (now Sir Alex) Ferguson's victory in Barcelona was the high point of his career and elevated him alongside the great Sir Matt Busby as a European Cup winner. In truth, it was not one of his sharpest tactical performances. United's attackers ran into cul-de-sacs for much of the game. Yet the finale was his reward for years of achievement, in Britain and in Europe.

Ferguson, once Rangers' centre-forward, began his working life in the Clyde shipyards. He became a trade union official and led a walk-out over a pay dispute. He has never been one to duck an argument.

Ferguson then developed into a bustling Scottish League centre-forward and spent three years with Rangers, the club he supported as a boy. That was until he was made the scapegoat for their 4–0 defeat against Celtic in the 1969 Scottish Cup final and sold to Falkirk.

Ferguson seems to have carried a burning sense of injustice throughout his managerial career. He started at the sharp end with East Stirling and St Mirren, before making his name at Aberdeen. There, he broke the Celtic–Rangers duopoly of Scotttish football. In his eight years in charge, Aberdeen won the championship three times, the Scottish Cup four times and beat Real Madrid in the 1983 Cup-Winners' Cup final.

Ferguson's biographer Hugh McIlvanney wrote: 'What he achieved at Aberdeen was incredible.' Aberdeen skipper Willie Miller concluded, 'He has been the best manager that Britain has ever produced.'

It was at Aberdeen, too, that he developed the traits that have characterised his years at Manchester United – nurturing talented youngsters, such as Scotland centre-back Alex McLeish, frightening players, opponents and media alike with a fiery temper, and creating the 'no one likes us, so let's stuff them' mentality.

In Scotland, the 'enemy' were Celtic, Rangers and the Glasgow media. When he moved to Old Trafford in 1986, it was everyone outside United, traditionally England's most glamorous club.

Guardian football writer Richard Williams shrewdly observed: 'No championship-winning manager has so assiduously and fruitfully cultivated a siege mentality. His genius is to make the biggest battalion of all seem outnumbered, outgunned and generally picked-on.' Sheringham said, 'He's a very intelligent man to be able to turn that hostility around so it worked in our favour. He drove it into us all the time. He said, "People want you to fail – show them you're not going to."'

United had not won a championship since 1967. Ferguson turned them into the dominant force in English football. They won the inaugural Premiership title in 1993 and carried on winning. Of the 13 Premiership competitions, they have won eight. Former United great Bobby Charlton said, 'Our fans have been in paradise for about 15 years and it might never be the same again. Alex has given them some magical moments.'

Ferguson had his doubters in his early years, never more than when United were crushed 5–1 by local rivals City in 1989. Victory in the FA Cup final replay against Crystal Palace a year later bought him time to build a team.

Ferguson is another workaholic, often at United's training ground by

7.30 a.m., prepared to put in 18-hour days. He has been a demanding boss who could lambast his players in private – but he always stood by them in public. Former United goalkeeper Peter Schmeichel said, 'He drives you on and on but he's also a very fair man. If you do a good job for him, he'll do anything for you.'

His most important early decision was to reorganise United's scouting system to ensure that they signed the cream of England's schoolboy talent. That decision led to the unearthing of Giggs, the Neville brothers, Beckham and Paul Scholes – the nucleus of the 1999 side that won the European Cup, the Premiership and the FA Cup.

Ferguson made inspired signings – Danish keeper Schmeichel; inspirational skipper Roy Keane; Eric Cantona, the French maverick who galvanised United in the mid-90s; and Ruud van Nistelrooy, the most prolific Dutch striker since van Basten. Furthermore, no one knows better than Ferguson how to pace the early stages of a Champions League campaign. That is why United's failure to qualify from their group in 2005–06 was such a shock.

Ferguson may be well into his 60s but a second European Cup remains a challenge that drives him on. It is one of his biggest regrets that United lost to Bayer Leverkusen on away goals in the semi-finals of 2002, when the final was staged in Glasgow.

Like Hitzfeld, former Real Madrid star and club retainer Del Bosque has won two European Cups. He became acting coach after John Toshack's acrimonious departure from the Bernabeu in 1999. He was confirmed in the job a few months later.

Like Hitzfeld, Del Bosque imposed calm on a potential hotbed of strife. He steered Madrid to European Cup success against Valencia, 3–0, in 2000, and a 2–0 victory over Bayer Leverkusen two years later. He was dumped by club president Florentino Perez after they won the Spanish championship in 2003, punishment for Madrid's Champions League semi-final defeat by Lippi's Juventus. Nevertheless, he stands as one of the most successful coaches in Champions League history – and Madrid endured two chaotic seasons after his departure. (Del Bosque's achievements are considered at length in Chapter 21.)

Former Milan playing hero Ancelotti was installed in November 2001 to restore stability after Fatih Terim's short, turbulent spell in charge. They finished fourth that season, 16 points behind Juventus. Ancelotti promised that his team would play in the style of Sacchi's great side of the late 1980s. They had the attacking flair of Portugal playmaker Rui Costa, the threat of Pippo Inzaghi and the lethal finishing of Ukraine striker Andriy Shevchenko.

Milan got off to a flying start in 2002–03. They led Serie A and scored impressive wins over Bayern and Deportivo in the Champions League but the winter break seemed to disrupt their rhythm. They slid down the table, to finish third, 11 points behind Juventus. Critics noted that Ancelotti had made a habit of missing out on major honours. He had already come second three times: once with Parma and twice with Juventus. The coach demanded a 'return to basics'. Milan's flowing game was placed on temporary hold while they chased the European Cup.

They topped their second-phase group, ahead of Madrid, then drew 0–0 with Ajax in the quarter-final first leg in Amsterdam. At San Siro, they came within minutes of elimination. Stephen Pienaar's 78th-minute equaliser made the score 2–2 on the night and put the Dutch side ahead on away goals. Ancelotti was mightily relieved when Jon Dahl Tomasson scored a stoppage-time winner.

In the semi-finals, they met Inter at San Siro. The first leg, designated Milan's home tie, ended 0–0. Shevchenko finished off Seedorf's pass to give Milan a 45th-minute lead in the away leg. Sub Obafemi Martins levelled but Milan went through on away goals.

The final, at Old Trafford, was a tense, cautious affair. As Lippi feared, Juve lacked their vital spark in Nedved's absence; Del Piero and David Trezeguet were shackled by Paolo Maldini and Alessandro Nesta.

Shevchenko settled the penalty shootout, 3–2 in Milan's favour after a 0–0 draw. It was Lippi's third defeat in four finals. He said, 'I don't think this means Milan are a better team than us, just that they were better tonight. We've just won the championship again and over the past two seasons we've been 27 points better than them.'

But this was Ancelotti's breakthrough. He had become only the second man to win the European Cup as player and coach with the same club. (The first was Miguel Munoz with Madrid.) He said, 'It's party time.'

Critics – led by Cruyff – complained about both teams' negative approach. Ancelotti replied, 'When Cruyff wants to be entertained, he should go to the cinema.' But the Milan coach returned to his roots in 2003–04. Milan played football reminiscent of the great days of Gullit, van Basten and Rijkaard. Cafu powered forward from right-back while Andrea Pirlo sprayed deft passes to set up attacks. The mercurial Kaka added an extra dimension in midfield. He was voted Serie A's Player of the Year while Shevchenko finished Serie A top scorer again with 24 goals as Milan won the title by 11 points from Roma.

Ancelotti's side were hot favourites to retain the European Cup. They eased into the last eight and beat Deportivo 4–1 at San Siro. Then their dream fell apart during an incredible first half in La Coruna. Walter Pandiani, Juan Carlos Valeron and Alberto Luque made it 3–0 at the interval. Fran added Deportivo's fourth.

Deportivo coach Javier Irureta said, 'It was almost mission impossible but we were sensational.' Ancelotti's response was, 'It's really hard to explain this defeat. They played to their very best. We didn't. We made too many errors.'

Were Milan over-confident and too complacent to fight back after Pandiani's early goal? Their coach insisted that they would never repeat the experience. But they did, against Liverpool in the second half of the 2005 European Cup final. All the old doubts about Ancelotti resurfaced after that game, which followed Milan's second-place finish behind Juventus in Serie A.

The 2003–04 competition threw up another Champions League general – Mourinho at Porto. Mourinho's father Felix had played in goal for Portugal. But Jose never played professionally. He was Bobby Robson's translator when the former England boss took charge of Sporting Lisbon in 1992. Robson soon came to appreciate Mourinho's tactical analyses and gave him increasing responsibility with the senior players. Robson said, 'He was very intelligent and very keen to learn. I had a feeling that he'd go a long way in the game. Even then, he had great confidence in his own ability.'

Mourinho helped Robson win two Portuguese titles at Porto and the Cup-Winners' Cup at Barcelona. His first attempt at going solo, with Benfica, ended after nine games because of boardroom conflicts.

Mourinho then guided cash-strapped Uniao de Leiria to fourth in the Portuguese table. Porto brought him back to take command after their poor start to the 2001–02 season. He built a side that won the Portuguese league and cup double and beat Celtic 3–2 in a dramatic UEFA Cup final.

Mourinho had an eye for a shrewd deal. Stars such as Paulo Ferreira, Ricardo Carvalho and Costinha were bargain buys by modern standards. He also managed the difficult trick of keeping his players happy even if they were not playing regularly.

He was, above all, flexible. He preferred to win with beautiful football, exemplified by Porto's creative force, Deco. If not, his team could defend with huge discipline, then break out to seize their chance. He was never afraid to change the formation or the personnel with bold substitutions. And he transmitted his confidence to his players.

Porto qualified for the Champions League last 16 from a group headed by Madrid. They had luck on their side in the last 16 second leg in Manchester. Benni McCarthy scored twice as Porto came from behind to win 2–1 at home. Scholes gave United the lead at Old Trafford, then had a goal mysteriously disallowed for offside. With time running out, United keeper Tim Howard failed to hold McCarthy's free kick and Costinha bundled in the equaliser to take Porto through to the last eight. Mourinho later pointedly contrasted Ferguson's transfer budget with his own modest outlay.

Porto beat Lyon and Deportivo to reach the final, against Monaco in Gelsenkirchen. Monaco were led by another remarkable character, Didier Deschamps, captain of France's World Cup and Euro 2000 winners and the Juventus side that lifted the trophy in 1996. They were short of cash yet Deschamps had made maximum use of his resources. In the quarter-finals, Monaco exploited Madrid's porous central defence to advance on away goals after losing 4–2 at the Bernabeu. They reached the final by winning 3–1 at home to moneybags Chelsea and drawing 2–2 in London.

Mourinho won the tactical battle. Porto lured Monaco forward, then ruthlessly exploited the gaps they left. Carlos Alberto scored after 39 minutes. Deco and Dimitri Aleinichev netted in the second half.

Porto had won the European Cup in 1987. But this was a far greater achievement, now that most of western Europe's top teams competed in the Champions League. The Portuguese magazine *O Jogo* commented, 'Mourinho's contribution to Porto's success can never be under-estimated.' The German magazine *kicker* said, 'Gelsenkirchen witnessed the demonstration of a tactical masterpiece.'

Chelsea came calling for Mourinho. Paulo Ferreira and Ricardo Carvalho followed him to London. Deco joined Barcleona. Pedro Mendes went to Tottenham. Typically, Mourinho arrived at Chelsea oozing self-belief, 'I'm not arrogant but I am the champion.'

Mourinho, as promised, led Chelsea to only the second championship in their history and their first for 50 years. Yet even he had to give way to Benitez in the European Cup semi-finals, when Luis Garcia scored the only goal of two tension-packed matches.

Benitez's record was already impressive before Liverpool's triumph in Istanbul. He served a nine-year coaching apprenticeship at Madrid, followed by brief spells at Valladolid and Osasuna. He led Extremadura to promotion in 1998, though they were relegated a year later. He won promotion again with Tenerife in 2001 and succeeded Cuper at Valencia that summer.

Benitez guided them to two titles, in 2002 and 2004, when they also won the UEFA Cup, but then turned down a two-year contract extension to join Liverpool. Dignified and tactically shrewd, Benitez emphasised the collective rather than the individual. He repeated his mantra from Valencia, 'Above all, we're a team which can depend on each other.'

He broke up the cliques in the Anfield dressing-room and began to instil a sense of unity that would come to fruition in the European Cup final. He brought in Spanish stars such as Xavi Alonso and Luis Garcia, while retaining local heroes Jamie Carragher and Steven Gerrard at the core of his project.

Benitez is another who has been influenced by Sacchi's pressing game. He said, 'My ideas are close to Sacchi's Milan. I like technical and aggressive teams that don't allow the opposition to play. I like teams that move the ball with speed.'

Liverpool did just that, twice, to Bayer Leverkusen in the last 16, winning 3–1 at Anfield and in Germany. They inflicted the same medicine on Juventus in the quarter-final first leg. Capello said after Liverpool's 2–1 win, 'They just came at us and never let us play in the first half.'

Liverpool, without the injured Gerrard, then showed great discipline to draw 0–0 in Turin. Benitez said, 'We had a plan to defend high up the pitch and the whole team carried it out.'

Benitez laughingly refers to himself as a 'loner with a laptop' and his preparation is legendary. The Valencia forward Mista said, 'He prepares like no one else, tells you everything you need to know. I've played in games where I found that what happened on the pitch was exactly what he said in his pre-match talk.'

But not even Benitez could have predicted what happened in Istanbul. Milan led 3–0 at half-time through Paolo Maldini's first-minute goal and two Hernan Crespo strikes. Gerrard, Vladimir Smicer and Xavi Alonso, from a penalty rebound, drew Liverpool level in the space of seven incredible minutes. Goalkeeper Jerzy Dudek was heroic in extra time and the shootout – and 300,000 turned out on the streets of Liverpool to welcome home the victors.

Benitez still has to fully impose himself on the Premiership. That is his next task. Fifth place in 2004–05, 37 points behind champions Chelsea, was a disappointing finish. But he is already a true general of the Champions League.

CHAPTER 20

THE G-14 AND THE 'EVOLUTION' OF THE EUROPEAN CUP

The G-14 group is an organisation of major western European clubs set up to lobby for their financial interests with UEFA. It began as a grouping of the eight most successful clubs in European football. Six more clubs joined later, hence the name G-14. By the 2004–05 season, the G-14 group comprised 18 clubs – Arsenal, Liverpool, Manchester United (England); Lyon, Marseille, Paris Saint-Germain (France); Bayer Leverkusen, Bayern Munich, Borussia Dortmund (Germany); Ajax, PSV Eindhoven (Holland); Internazionale, Juventus, Milan (Italy); Porto (Portugal); Barcelona, Real Madrid, Valencia (Spain).

Once upon a time, before the Champions League, there was the European Champions Cup. The competition format – devised by Gabriel Hanot, the editor of the French sports daily *L'Equipe* – was simplicity itself. The European Cup, as it was universally known, was a competition for the champions of each European country. They were joined by whoever had won the European Cup the previous season, who defended their title.

Each tie consisted of two legs, home and away, with a one match final as the climax of the competition. The last 16 featured clubs from 16 countries, or 15, if the holders had got that far.

In 2004–05, the last 16 of the Champions League featured four English clubs, three from Germany and Italy, two from France and Spain and one each from Portugal and Holland. Thirteen of those clubs were members of the G-14, a powerful lobby group that had wrung a series of concessions from UEFA.

The competition had become a 'Champions League' in name but hardly a league of champions. Not so much a European Cup either, rather a private battle among western Europe's leading clubs, unencumbered by unfashionable teams from the old Soviet bloc or hopeful outsiders from Scandinavia or the Balkans.

The 2005 winners, Liverpool, have not been English champions since 1990. They finished fifth in the Premiership in 2004–05, 37 points behind champions Chelsea. They had qualified for the Champions League preliminaries by finishing fourth in 2003–04, 30 points behind champions Arsenal.

UEFA's website says the competition 'has continued to evolve'. But Keir Radnedge, for many years editor of *World Soccer*, said, 'The present format is the price that UEFA has paid for keeping the big clubs on board. UEFA had always kept one step ahead of pressure from those big clubs and, by making concessions at the right time, it's been able to head off outright revolt.'

Hanot's concept of simple competition worked for more than 30 years – until the late 1980s, when the major western clubs began to want changes. The arrival of satellite TV, eager to build its subscriber base by screening live football, was about to drive the value of TV rights through the roof. As the Arsenal vice-chairman David Dein realised, 'There's going to be a revolution in football and it will be driven by television.'

The big clubs, who could deliver both television audiences and advertising, realised their commercial value in this new world. They would take the largest share of the new TV deals (see Chapter 22). They could also negotiate for much more lucrative club sponsorships because of their increased TV exposure.

There had been stage whispers for years about the possibility of a breakaway league of major clubs. Now there were media magnates – such as the Milan president Silvio Berlusconi – who might finance such a scheme and back it with TV coverage. But those clubs faced serious problems if they broke away from their domestic leagues.

To play professional football in the first place, a club had to be a member of its national association. It was that membership which entitled them to go and play other champions. Failure to secure membership of the domestic association meant no right to play in domestic competition let alone against top-class European opposition. If the big clubs broke out to play in richer circumstances, they faced being banned by their national associations.

There was some element of risk for the national associations. But given the power of national associations, backed up by UEFA, the greater risk lay with any breakaway clubs.

The issues they faced were boundless. Would they be able to go back if the breakaway group did not work? Were fans ready to lose traditional opponents, and particularly local derbies, to see super teams from abroad every week? If there could not be relegation to domestic leagues – and there could not, as that risked letting in less wealthy clubs and thus destroying the whole idea – would such a closed circuit not become tedious, for the players as much as for the fans? If national associations banned teams breaking away, how could those teams buy players from any of the clubs left behind in the national league? How could players in any breakaway clubs – who would tend to be the best players in any given country – continue to play for their national sides?

Yet the shrewder club officials recognised the international marketing potential of a redesigned European Cup, driven by television money, backed by multinational advertisers – and minus the economic minnows. Their aim was to advance their clubs' financial interests while avoiding an outright showdown with UEFA. They were helped by a power struggle at the top of FIFA's World Cup marketing company ISL, which led to the centralised marketing of the European Cup and began to open a path to riches for the major clubs.

Two of ISL's former leading figures, Jurgen Lenz and Klaus Hempel, formed a company called Team Marketing. In 1990, they approached UEFA with a scheme to maximise income from the competition. Team offered UEFA a deal to market the European Cup on the governing body's behalf. The clubs would hand the commercial rights to their home matches to UEFA in return for guaranteed – and increased – payments from the governing body.

Team would sell exclusive TV rights to one broadcaster in each country, plus exclusive stadia advertising rights and TV programming sponsorships, to a selection of rich multinational companies: a maximum of eight initially.

Team noted with satisfaction, 'By tying stadium advertising together with on-air sponsorship and programme advertising, it became almost impossible for non-sponsors to be associated with the competition.'

Team guaranteed UEFA a minimum £30 million in the first season of the agreement. Radnedge said, 'The income from TV and advertising revolutionised UEFA's finances, helped it subsidise its junior and women's competitions, gave early losers "parachute payments" and still left enough for UEFA to build its state-of-the-art headquarters at Nyon.'

The major western clubs, who paid big transfer fees and high wages, naturally welcomed increased payments from the centralised deal. But they still wanted more financial security from playing in Europe. Berlusconi set out their position. He said, 'It's nonsense that a club of Milan's standing should be eliminated in the first round of the European Cup.'

The alarm bells had started ringing for the big clubs in 1987–88. Real Madrid and the Italian champions, Diego Maradona's Napoli – both leading contenders – were paired in the first round. Napoli, making their first appearance in the competition, had not been seeded in the draw. Madrid won – but the major western clubs wanted to avoid such an 'accident' again, with the consequent loss of revenue for a big team.

Hanot's formula meant that only the champions of each country – plus the holders – could enter the European Cup. So, many of Europe's biggest clubs had to be content with playing in the less lucrative Cup-Winners' Cup or UEFA Cup. That rule would be swept away under a new dispensation that came to offer the major nations of western Europe up to four places in the Champions League each season and condemned the old east to picking at crumbs from the rich men's table.

Berlusconi was the driving force of the movement for change, supported by the Real Madrid president Ramon Mendoza. In May 1988, they suggested a new format for the competition. The 32 clubs would be drawn into eight groups of four. Each club would play six games on a home-and-away basis. The eight group winners would go into knockout quarter-finals. The financial attraction for the clubs was obvious: they were guaranteed income from a minimum of six matches rather than two. Big clubs such as Milan and Madrid could maximise their potential earnings.

UEFA reacted with scepticism. Yet, 16 years later, the format of the Champions League echoed the Berlusconi–Mendoza proposal, with two differences. The 32 teams in the competition proper were divided into eight groups of four. The top two in each group – virtually all from western Europe and G-14 members – went into the knockout stage. And many European countries were not represented at all.

In 1991, Berlusconi had used the PR agency Media Partners to bring together a group of major clubs to maximise their income from the competition and lobby UEFA. They were Milan, Internazionale, Juventus, Real Madrid, Barcelona, Bayern Munich, Liverpool and Ajax, invited on the basis that they had won at least five UEFA trophies. They were the forerunners of the G-14 group.

Ironically, when the Champions League began in 1991–92, Milan were banned from Europe for a year, for walking off at Marseille in the quarter-final second leg the previous season. UEFA did not accommodate the big clubs' demand for a group stage at the start of the competition either.

As Rab MacWilliam wrote in *The European Cup: An Illustrated History*: 'This was not exactly what the big clubs had in mind. Their idea was that the league system would replace the opening rounds, thereby ensuring that the big clubs would not be eliminated by some upstart in the early stages.'

The first two rounds were a knockout. Then the remaining eight teams were divided into two groups of four. The group winners contested the final. The advantage for the last eight was that they were guaranteed income from at least six league matches.

That formula, now known as the Champions League, continued in 1992–93. UEFA tinkered slightly with the format the following season. The top two from each group met in one-leg knockout semi-finals. The group winners had home advantage.

By now, though, UEFA had introduced a preliminary round. That was partly out of necessity, to accommodate the champions of the countries which had arisen after the collapse of the Soviet Union, and partly to weed out the weaker teams before the contest began in earnest.

UEFA came down heavily in favour of the major western clubs when it revised the format for the 1994–95 competition. Now there were four groups of four teams. Holders Milan and the other seven top clubs in UEFA's ranking system were guaranteed places and income from a minimum of six games. Spartak Moscow were the only club from outside western Europe.

The other participants came from preliminary ties between the clubs ranked between eight and 23. The top two in each group advanced to knockout quarter-finals. The finalists played 11 matches. Not perhaps enough for some of the bigger clubs but still an improvement on the nine games necessary to win the old European Cup.

In 1997–98, UEFA introduced the most dramatic change yet. No longer would entry be restricted to the holders and national champions. Now the runners-up from each of the top eight countries in the UEFA rankings would enter the Champions League in the second preliminary round. The first preliminary round became a knockout for the champions of the lowest-ranked countries. They would eliminate each other before they even caught sight of the big clubs.

Meanwhile, the top eight seeds went straight into the league stage, which was expanded to six groups of four. This was more like what Berlusconi and Mendoza had envisaged a decade before. They were joined by the 16 teams which had won through the preliminaries. The group winners, plus the two best losers, would contest the knockout quarter-finals. Suddenly, Germany had three entrants: holders Borussia Dortmund, champions Bayern Munich and Bundesliga runners-up Bayer Leverkusen.

UEFA had set a precedent and conceded a principle. No longer was the Champions League a league of champions. Soon, third- and fourth-placed teams from the major western leagues would be offered entry, too.

UEFA had offered concession after concession to appease the major western clubs. But the governing body was still caught off guard by Media Partners in the autumn of 1998. Media Partners suggested to the big clubs that they quit the Champions League for a new, TV-backed Super League, in which Berlusconi's media companies would be major players.

By now, the G-14 group was in place, in all but name. Manchester United, Borussia Dortmund, Paris Saint-Germain, Marseille, PSV Eindhoven and Porto had joined the original list of eight. (The clubs decided to register themselves officially as the 'G-14' in September 2000. They were later joined by Arsenal, Bayer Leverkusen, Valencia and Lyon to form an 18-club pressure group.)

By 1998, the G-14 included most of Europe's wealthiest and most famous clubs. Its members had won 21 of the 27 European Cups contested since 1971. The Champions League would lack credibility in their absence. Broadcasters and corporate sponsors would not support a competition shorn of its elite.

UEFA had expanded to more than 50 countries as a result of the collapse of the Soviet Union and the break-up of the old Yugoslavia. Its largely impoverished new members had little to offer in terms of commercial appeal. Radnedge summed up, 'UEFA had to do something – or watch someone else run off with their competition. UEFA basically had to buy them off.'

What UEFA did was bend over backwards to accommodate the new pressure group. It offered a whole tranche of extra matches and thus more opportunity to divide TV and commercial income among more big clubs from western Europe. For the 1999–2000 season, there were now no fewer than three qualifying rounds, to weed out the weaker teams.

The league stage would consist of 32 clubs, divided into eight groups of four. The top two in each advanced to the second group stage – four more groups of four. The top two in each group then contested the knockout quarter-finals.

The holders, plus the top 15 in the UEFA rankings, gained automatic entry. Those 15 comprised the champions of the top nine countries plus the runners-up from the top six. They were joined by 16 qualifiers from the preliminary rounds. Now the third- and fourth-placed clubs from Europe's major leagues entered the competition in the preliminaries, too.

Matches were played on Tuesday and Wednesday nights to ensure blanket media coverage and maximise TV revenue. UEFA president Lennart Johansson claimed, 'We've found a very good balance between sporting, political and commercial considerations.'

The embryo G-14 clubs could hardly have asked for more if they had written the rules themselves. It was as if they had gained acceptance for a breakaway-style league – without any club breaking away. The format offered income from up to 17 matches. It even went beyond the initial proposals championed by Berlusconi and Mendoza. Media Partners faded into the background again while the clubs from western Europe's major leagues licked their lips.

By the 2001–02 season, revenue from the Champions League amounted to around £1.4 billion. Most of the money had previously enriched UEFA. Now more than a third of the cash was handed over to the clubs. That was a huge increase on the £15 million distributed a decade earlier.

The western clubs who dominated the knockout stages of the competition obviously took the biggest portion. Radnedge said, 'It was the opportunity they'd been seeking to increase their share of the TV income and they grabbed it.'

Four German clubs reached the first group stage in 1999–2000: Bayern, Dortmund, Leverkusen and Hertha Berlin. There were three from England: Arsenal, Manchester United and Chelsea; three from Spain: Real Madrid, Barcelona and Valencia; and three from Italy: Milan, Lazio and Fiorentina.

The eastern Europeans were marginalised. Dynamo Kiev – who had reached the 1998–99 semi-finals after starting in the preliminaries – Spartak Moscow, Sparta Prague, Maribor and Croatia Zagreb were the only teams from the old east to reach the last 32. None survived until the last eight.

By the spring of 2002, G-14 was widely seen as the tail that wagged the dog of UEFA. Its general manager, Thomas Kurth, said, 'UEFA is a federation of national football associations. Its priorities are not the same as those of the clubs. The clubs are too distant from the power.' He justified the inclusion of third- and fourth-placed clubs from the major leagues, saying, 'G-14, as a general principle, wants fewer "weak" teams in the Champions League. We support the idea of having several teams from the strongest countries. These are the strongest leagues, with the best clubs and the best players.' He added, 'It doesn't make sense for the big clubs to go and play against teams from, say, Iceland or Belarus. They have to play in small stadiums, with small crowds and generally the result is imbalanced.'

Bayern Munich vice-president Karl-Heinz Rummenigge said, 'The big clubs have nothing to gain by playing against teams from small countries. The clubs from the big countries should limit themselves to playing in an elite competition, the Champions League.'

UEFA's then-spokesman Mike Lee responded, 'The Champions League is a huge success and already brings vast rewards for the most successful clubs. UEFA and European football in general has to account for a wide range of interests and needs, not just the immediate financial focus of any particular grouping.'

G-14's gripes provoked derision in the media. Duncan White wrote in *The Observer* in February 2002: 'G-14 are a band of oppressed clubs. They want to make the Champions League "better". But only for themselves. Their initial aim was to maximise profits from the European Cup. They achieved this by creating the Champions League – a similar tournament to the European Champions Cup, except that there was now no need to confine it to champions. Or to keep the cup format really, when two league stages could be just as exciting.'

White continued, with withering scorn: 'Apparently UEFA has been extorting vast sums of G-14's rightful money and siphoning it off to fat cats like the Andorra FA, who received a colossal £302,000. This dirty money seems to be directed towards a variety of suspect activities, with "grass roots development" being the most common of these unfortunate destinations. By contrast, the 2001 Champions League winners, Bayern Munich, took home a measly £31 million.'

Ordinary fans were angry, too – especially after the fancied European teams had failed to deliver at the 2002 World Cup finals. Fans' forums across the Internet blamed the G-14 for tiring out star players – or increasing the risk of injury to them – through such a protracted Champions League campaign.

Mike Gibbons wrote on www.planetworldcup.com: 'The rise of the G-14 has directly mirrored the decline in standards at the World Cup and this is no coincidence. France 98 and Japan/Korea 2002 were pale imitations of their predecessors.'

Others criticised the proliferation of 'meaningless' matches in the group stages. The English journalist Tony Pullein had identified the problem before the Champions League even started. He said: 'Under the old knockout system, virtually every game had a meaning to it. But, depending on early results, the group stages could end up with several meaningless matches in front of small crowds.'

(The problem remains. Juventus easily won their group in 2004–05. Their home attendances were: 6,494 v. Maccabi Tel-Aviv, 18,089 v. Bayern Munich and 6,875 v. Ajax. Bayern and Ajax are fellow G-14 members and former European Cup winners.)

In the summer of 2002, UEFA fought back. It overrode G-14's opposition and abolished the second group phase in favour of a knockout from the last 16 onwards.

It was a popular move. It eased the burden on the players. It reduced the number of meaningless matches at the second stage and it satisfied the fans' taste for the excitement of knockout football.

The G-14 clubs cited fears about lost revenue, because UEFA had reduced the number of possible fixtures from 17 to 13. There was brief speculation about a breakaway league backed by the Spanish media company Telefonica. Instead, the G-14 reluctantly accepted the governing body's decision.

G-14 vice-president Peter Kenyon (then with Manchester United) said, 'The clubs saw no reason to change the format. But, for various reasons, UEFA did. It never came to talk of a breakaway. It was always a question of living with the decision once it had been made but we were upset about the process.' Another G-14 vice-president, Ajax's Michael van Praag, said, 'G-14 is a very important group working closely with UEFA. The dialogue in future clearly has to be better.'

UEFA had won that little spat. Its (then) chief executive Gerhard Aigner said, 'We don't need advice from the G-14 about how to deal with the commercial market place. UEFA widely consulted all the parties concerned. We knew our decision wouldn't meet with unanimous approval but we were sure of its wisdom.

'As guardian of the overall interests of European football, UEFA hopes that clubs (read: G-14) will understand that longer-term strategy and the general interest must come before short-term concerns when important decisions are made.'

By then, UEFA had introduced its own Club Forum, comprising more than 100 clubs, as a counter-balance to G-14, who were a minority in the new grouping. But UEFA has made it clear that the old European Cup will never return. Johansson quickly slapped down Michel Platini, now a UEFA executive committee member, when he mused aloud about a more 'democratic' competition, including as many as 256 clubs in a knockout European Cup.

Platini said, 'The way the European Cup is today, it's a closed circus. It's become more and more certain that a big club will win the competition. But clubs like Bayern Munich should also play in Malta and in Georgia.'

G-14 were aghast: fancy one of its members losing in the first round of such an unstructured competition! Johansson provided instant reassurance. He said, 'This idea has not been accepted anywhere, by the bigger clubs, the smaller clubs, or UEFA's executive committee. It's not a practical idea. Who would back such an idea? What TV rights money would such a competition attract?'

The Media Partners episode gave UEFA a wake-up call. The governing body will not be caught unaware again. It knows it needs the G-14 clubs on board if the Champions League is to retain its credibility and its commercial appeal.

Broadcasting exclusivity was swept away in 2002, after the intervention of the European Union's competition commissioner Mario

Monti. TV rights were split into 14 separate categories, with Sky Sports, for instance, screening 14 of the 16 games on every group 'match day', while UEFA's previously exclusive English broadcasting partner ITV continued to show two major matches involving Premiership clubs.

UEFA vice-president Per Ravn Omdal said he was 'happy' with the outcome. Well he might be. An estimated 700 million around the globe watch the European Cup final annually. The latest TV deal – covering the seasons between 2003 and 2006 – ensures that Champions League action is shown live throughout Africa, on the Middle Eastern channel ART and the Far East satellite station ESPN Star, as well as on terrestrial TV in Australia, Hong Kong, Singapore, Vietnam and Indonesia. That audience – and the financial benefits that go with it – would be impossible without the G-14 clubs.

The G-14 know their limits, too. Their 'nuclear option' – pulling out of UEFA competitions to launch their own – is a threat that has worked once. But could it be used again without forcing UEFA into a showdown? And what would be the long-term financial consequences for the G-14 clubs if they were expelled from their domestic leagues and associations?

Anyway, the G-14 are doing very nicely out of the status quo. A survey of Europe's ten wealthiest clubs at the end of the 2003–04 season revealed that all had qualified for the 2004–05 Champions League, and – Chelsea apart – they were all G-14 members. Manchester United headed the list with an income of £171.5 million, followed by Real Madrid on £156.3 million. Then came Milan (£147.2 million), Chelsea (£143.7 million), Juventus (£142.4 milllion), Arsenal (£115 million), Barcelona (£112 million), Internazionale (£110.3 million), Bayern (£110.1 million) and Liverpool (£92.3 million).

Those Champions League riches have perpetuated and strengthened domestic elites, widening the financial gap between them and their rivals. The Champions League regulars have the cash to sign the best players and pay the highest wages, trumping their domestic competitors in the process. Manchester United's £27 million signing of England 'boy wonder' Wayne Rooney in 2004 was a prime example.

We can all predict with confidence which clubs will qualify from England (Arsenal, Chelsea, Manchester United and, usually, Liverpool), Italy (Juventus, Milan, Inter plus one) or Spain (in recent years, Madrid, Barcelona, Valencia and Deportivo).

Champions League revenue has distorted domestic competition further down the ladder, too. Sparta Prague lose their best players to western Europe every summer, then use their Champions League cash to dominate Czech football by buying up the best of the rest. Radnedge points to the best example of all – Rosenborg Trondheim. The Norwegian club have struggled in the Champions League since their surprise win at Milan in 1996–97 yet they have won 13 domestic championships in a row.

Aigner's successor as UEFA chief executive, Lars-Christer Olsson, is committed to encouraging competition, 'I don't think the [G-14] clubs are looking to start their own competitions. I think they're trying to get their views across, which is fine. But G-14 for me is just a lobbying group and nothing else.' He added, 'When we talk with the big clubs, some say they want even more of a closed shop. They're afraid of losing money if they don't play in the Champions League.

'UEFA's philosophy is that there must be no guarantees, that every year we must get the best teams. It could mean a different outcome each year. But that's how to develop the economic value of the game.'

The G-14 clubs' aim is to maximise the 'economic value of the game' for themselves. The result is that the European Cup has become unrecognisable from the simple competition that Hanot designed.

CHAPTER 21

BARCELONA AND MADRID –
THE STRUGGLE CONTINUES

On 20 May 1992, Barcelona stood at the height of their power. Ronald Koeman had scored the goal that beat Sampdoria at Wembley. Barcelona lifted the European Cup for the first time. Johan Cruyff had been the creative force behind the great Ajax side that won the trophy three times in a row, before joining Barca. After a glorious playing career, he returned to the Nou Camp as coach to assemble Barcelona's dream team.

Barca had played in an orange second strip that night. Their players quickly changed into their famous dark red and blue striped shirts for the presentation. They were to be crowned champions of Europe and they would wear the 'right' colours for the occasion.

Fast forward to 15 May 2002. Barca's bitter rivals Real Madrid had just won the European Cup for the ninth time by beating Bayer Leverkusen in Glasgow – while Barcelona were in turmoil. Their torment was worsened by the appearance of former Barca great Luis Figo in a Madrid shirt. Figo had been signed by Madrid's incoming president Florentino Perez in a transfer coup that Nou Camp fans have never forgiven. The balance of power had swung with a vengeance.

Cruyff the player had been hugely popular with the Nou Camp fans. Cruyff the coach delivered a team that won the European Cup, reached another final, won the European Cup-Winners' Cup, four successive Spanish titles and the Copa del Rey (King's Cup).

Cruyff had taken charge of his old club Ajax in July 1985. PSV Eindhoven dominated the Dutch league. They won four titles in a row and the European Cup in 1988. But Ajax won the Dutch cup in 1986, beating first division RBC 3–0 in the final. The following season, Cruyff delivered the Cup-Winners' Cup. It was Ajax's first European trophy for 14 years, since Cruyff himself lifted the European Cup after victory over Juventus in Belgrade.

Cruyff nurtured two young prodigies: midfielder Frank Rijkaard and striker Marco van Basten. They knocked out Bursapor (Turkey), Olympiakos and Malmo to reach the semi-finals. They lost 3–2 in Zaragoza and won the return 3–0 in Amsterdam. Rijkaard's stoppage-time goal was followed by a pitch invasion by delighted fans. Van Basten headed the only goal of the final against Lokomotiv Leipzig in Athens.

Van Basten scored twice as Ajax retained the Dutch cup with a 4–2 win over Den Haag. Then he joined Milan. Rijkaard, who had moved to Zaragoza after a fall-out with Cruyff, followed him to San Siro a year later. Cruyff had nursed van Basten through the end of the season, saving him for Ajax's major cup ties. The striker was already suffering the first throes of the ankle problems that eventually ended his career.

Cruyff went, too, in January 1988, after a succession of rows with club president Ton Harmsen. Cruyff was angry that Ajax had received only $750,000 for van Basten. He fell out with the president over transfers and players' contracts. He accused Harmsen of penny-pinching and having a 'grocer's mentality'.

Harmsen countered by claiming that Cruyff wanted to dictate every aspect of the club – even the training-ground lunch menu – and refused to listen to the board. Cruyff replied, 'That's why I asked for a job description.'

Ajax, with Barry Hulshoff in charge, reached the Cup-Winners' Cup final again and lost 1–0 to Belgian outsiders Mechelen.

Meanwhile, in Barcelona the fans were distressed. Madrid's legendary 'vulture squadron' – led by great striker Emilio Butragueno – won five successive titles between 1986 and 1990. Barca had won the championship under Terry Venables in 1985. But they lost the European Cup final to Steaua Bucharest on penalties the following year – and finished 1986–87 without a trophy.

In April 1988, the club were rocked by the 'mutiny of Hesperia'. The tax authorities found Barca guilty of tax evasion over players' contracts and ordered the club to pay back the money. Club president Josep Lluis Nunez said the players should pay. The bulk of the squad held a press conference at the Hotel Hesperia, calling on Nunez to resign. Caretaker coach Luis Aragones was caught in the middle.

Nunez removed ten of the 'mutineers' at the end of the season. But his position was precarious, with presidential elections a year away. One of Nunez's leading opponents, Ricardo Huguet, a businessman with links to the Catalan nationalist party, was already calling for Cruyff to return as coach. Nunez stole his opponent's clothes. He approached Cruyff first. The president needed the Dutch maestro to save him.

Cruyff, always one for taking charge, realised that he could dictate his own agenda. He noted the bad feeling between the players and the board. He solved it by establishing his own power base. The players – and the president – deferred to him. He said, 'I told the players that I was the boss in the dressing-room and I told the president not to come to the dressing-room.'

Cruyff's power seemed to suit both sides, though later it would lead to a major fall-out with Nunez. He said, 'In principle, the players do what I tell them.' He kept Alesanco as skipper, though he had been the spokesman for the 'mutineers'. Cruyff said, 'As the captain, he did what was necessary. I respect him for that. He was the messenger and usually the messenger gets shot. Not with me. He's a leader. When he says, "Let's go" – everyone goes.'

Cruyff's teams were based on key players in central areas: a constructive sweeper, a skilful holding midfielder, a creator who could swiftly turn defence into attack and a mobile goalscorer. He would find them in Ronald Koeman, Pep Guardiola, Michael Laudrup and Hristo Stoichkov.

Cruyff's early years in charge were marked by rapid changes in personnel. In his first season, he promoted five youngsters and introduced 11 signings – including Bakero and Julio Salinas – to the first-team squad. Whether he always fitted the right player to the right role was another matter. The England striker Gary Lineker left for Everton after Cruyff stuck him on the right wing. The Catalan winger Carrasco departed at the end of the season, baffled by the coach's tactics, too.

But Barcelona won the Cup-Winners' Cup. They had struggled against Lech Poznan and the Danish side Aarhus early in the competition but found their form to knock out the Bulgarian cup holders Sredetz Sofia 6–3 on aggregate in the semi-finals. Salinas, in the fourth minute, and sub Lopez Rekarte scored as Barca beat Sampdoria 2–0 in the final in Berne.

That summer, Barca made two vital signings. Koeman came from PSV Eindhoven and Laudrup arrived from Juventus after failing to shine in Serie A. Cruyff said of Koeman, 'He was a personality who made the other players feel secure. They knew they could count on him. He made other players play. And he likes the football that I preach about. He's ideal, a defender who's good for 15 goals a season.'

Laudrup said, 'I had a freedom that I'd never had before and the emphasis was always on attack.'

Barca finished behind Madrid and Valencia in the championship and lost to Anderlecht in the Cup-Winners' Cup. But they beat Madrid 2–0 in the Copa del Rey final. That defeat effectively ended John Toshack's first spell in charge at the Bernabeu.

Still players left, complaining they could not understand Cruyff's tactics. Roberto, who joined Valencia, was one of the more insistent. But the dream team was taking shape.

Guardiola, Catalan through and through, had joined Barca's youth section as a 13 year old. Like the young Cruyff at Ajax, he was effectively adopted by the club. He made his debut against Cadiz in December 1990 as a stand-in for the injured Koeman after Nunez had overruled Cruyff's plan to sign the Liverpool midfielder Jan Molby. Guardiola said, 'The circumstances helped. Koeman was injured, Guillermo Amor was suspended. But I owe Cruyff. He took a gamble on me and believed in me.'

Barcelona had also gambled on a fiery striker – Stoichkov, who had scored all three goals against them for Sredetz. Stoichkov came with a terrific goal record and a reputation for bust-ups. Both fitted into the coach's jigsaw. Cruyff said, 'Maybe we were too nice before. We need a player like Stoichkov. He's aggressive in a positive way and that will rub off on the others.'

Stoichkov was suspended when Barca beat Madrid 2–1 at the Nou Camp in January 1991. Laudrup scored the first goal with a brilliant aerial volley from Andoni Goikoetxea's cross, a finish reminiscent of Cruyff himself. At that moment, the balance of power in Spanish football symbolically shifted, from Madrid to Barcelona.

A month later, Cruyff, a heavy smoker, was rushed to hospital with a suspected heart attack. He needed a double by-pass operation and spent the rest of the season recovering.

Cruyff had turned Barcelona around. Now he turned himself around. He gave up smoking. He even became the vehicle for the Catalan government's anti-smoking campaign.

The team kept winning, under Cruyff's assistant, former Barca star Charly Rexach. Stoichkov scored four in one of the biggest triumphs, a 6–0 romp at Atletico Bilbao. Barca won the title by ten points from Atletico Madrid. Real were a point further back.

Barcelona reached the Cup-Winners' Cup final again but lost 2–1 to Manchester United. Cruyff's tactics were questionable. He started with Laudrup, a peripheral figure on the left wing. Bryan Robson set up both United's goals for Mark Hughes. A typical Koeman free kick came too late for Barca. Cruyff shrugged, 'When we won the championship, everyone was so happy that the Cup-Winners' Cup became unimportant.'

The European Cup was more than important. It was the unfulfilled dream of Barcelona's ambitions. They had lost finals in 1961 and 1986, after starting favourites against both Benfica and Steaua Bucharest.

Barca had reached the new group stage only thanks to Bakero's last-minute header that sent them through on away goals against Kaiserslautern. Then they saw off Sparta Prague, Dynamo Kiev and Benfica to reach the final. They won all three home games and lost only once on the road, to Sparta. Stoichkov and Julio Salinas shared the goals in an impressive 2–0 win in Kiev.

More than 35,000 Barca fans converged on Wembley for the final against Sampdoria.

Barcelona attacked from the start but could not score in 90 minutes. Stoichkov smashed a shot off an upright and fired another inches wide – but Barca keeper Andoni Zubizarreta had to make a brilliant save from Attilio Lombardo.

Koeman settled the issue in the 20th minute of extra time, running onto Bakero's free kick to blast a 20-yarder past Gianluca Pagliuca. Barcelona had laid those demons of dreams unfulfilled. Catalonia celebrated.

Cruyff said, 'It's been a great night because it's been such a long time coming.' A decade later, Koeman said, 'That was the most important goal of my life. Every year, on the anniversary of the match, I get phone calls and cards from fans around the world who have not forgotten.'

More than one million people turned out on the streets of Barcelona to welcome home Cruyff's European champions. The Catalan president

Jordi Puyol shouted to the crowds from his presidential balcony, '*Visca el Barca! Visca Catalunya!*' (Long live Barca, long live Catalonia!)

As Jimmy Burns wrote in *Barca: A People's Passion*: 'For the club's supporters, players, officials and coaching staff, Barca's victory at Wembley was the one that assumed legendary status. Catalans felt they had dealt with the bogyman.'

This was the greatest season in Barca's history. Cruyff had built their strongest-ever squad: Zubizarreta, the brilliant keeper; the other Basques, Bakero, Goikoetxea and Beguiristain; Guardiola; the defender Nadal, signed from Mallorca in the summer of 1991; the Spanish internationals Julio Salinas, Eusebio and Albert Ferrer; plus the three foreign superstars, Koeman, Laudrup and Stoichkov.

Weeks later, Barcelona clinched the championship on the last day of the season. They won 2–0 at home to Bilbao while Madrid lost 3–2 at Tenerife.

Barcelona's European Cup defence ended in swift disaster in the second round. They led 2–0 at home (3–1 on aggregate) against the Russian side CSKA after half an hour at the Nou Camp . . . then conceded three goals and crashed out of the competition. Nunez lamented how much that defeat would cost Barca in lost revenue.

Stoichkov scored the goal against Real Sociedad that clinched a third league title while Madrid lost 2–0 at Tenerife on the final day again. (Jorge Valdano, later to win the title with Madrid, was Tenerife's coach on both occasions.)

Now Barca had to restore their credibility in Europe. They had signed a new star – the Brazil striker Romario. He scored 30 goals in 33 games as Barcelona won a fourth consecutive title. But UEFA and Spanish league rules limited teams to three 'foreign' players. Cruyff played Romario and Stoichkov and rotated Koeman and Laudrup. When Laudrup was left out of the European Cup final against Milan, he decided it was time to leave. He said, 'I couldn't take any more.' He joined Madrid – and received a vicious 'welcome' on his return to the Nou Camp. Burns wrote: 'I have never seen such intensity of hate directed at one player.' A similar fate befell Figo years later.

Cruyff has always defended his decision to let Laudrup go. But the Dane continued to shine in Madrid colours while Romario proved a one-season wonder. The Brazilian was a disruptive influence in the dressing-room, partying before big games and forever wanting to make trips back to Rio de Janeiro. Cruyff said, 'He lacked discipline and that was one of the major problems we had to deal with. Each player has to respect his colleagues, otherwise everything ends in chaos.'

Barca knocked out Dynamo Kiev and FK Austria, then advanced unbeaten through the group stage to the semi-finals. Stoichkov scored twice and Koeman added a third in their 3–0 semi-final win over Porto at the Nou Camp.

The final against Milan was supposed to be a clash of contrasts – Barca's flowing attack against Milan's dogged defence. Cruyff said that the outcome 'could determine the tactical direction of the game for the next few years'.

Milan coach Fabio Capello surprised Barcelona. His side tore forward, ripped through Barca's defence and built a 3–0 lead by the 47th minute. Cruyff had been outmanoeuvred. Milan's 4–0 win was a watershed. Success was the currency that had kept Nunez out of the dressing-room. Now he began to think about interfering in Cruyff's domain. The dream team started to break up. Zubizarreta left for Valencia. Julio Salinas joined Deportivo. Goikoetxea returned to the Basque country with Bilbao.

In 1994–95, the balance of power swung again. Barca slipped to fourth, nine points behind champions Madrid. The link-up between Laudrup and the Chilean striker Ivan Zamorano was crucial to Real's success. A key date was 8 January 1995. Madrid crushed Barca 5–0 at the Bernabeu. Zamorano scored a hat trick. Real coach Valdano hailed their victory as 'the game of the century'.

Paris Saint-Germain eliminated Barca in the European Cup quarter-finals, after Cruyff's side led in the second leg at the Parc des Princes. Koeman, wanting regular starts, returned to Holland with Feyenoord at the end of the season. Romario departed to Rio de Janeiro, with Flamengo, after starting just 13 league games. Stoichkov went to spend a year with Parma. Beguiristain followed Julio Salinas to Deportivo.

Barcelona, finished third in 1995–96, ahead of Real Madrid but seven points behind champions Atletico Madrid. Cruyff insisted he was rebuilding after the dream-team era and was close to creating another successful side. But he had gone two seasons without delivering a title. Nunez felt it was time to step in. The emergence of Cruyff's son Jordi in the first team squad had added to the disquiet in the dressing-room.

Nunez turned down Cruyff's request to sign British stars such as Ryan Giggs, accusing the coach of 'wanting to waste money'. Cruyff's move for the Ajax pair, Edgar Davids and Michael Reiziger, was blocked too. Cruyff said, 'I'd always insisted that I had sole charge of the dressing-room, without interference from the president. I lost that freedom towards the end. Nunez was talking and drawing up contracts behind my back. Once that process began with one player, a sense began to spread among the others that the coach wasn't in control.'

Cruyff was sacked on 18 May 1996, a day before the penultimate league game of the season. The morning headlines said that Nunez and vice-president Joan Gaspart had already lined up Porto (and former England) coach Bobby Robson as Cruyff's successor.

Cruyff accused Nunez and Gaspart of going behind his back. Gaspart told Cruyff, 'You no longer belong here.' Nunez later told Burns, 'After spending two years without winning a title, and creating a lot of problems in the team, it was time for him to leave.'

Robson had a hard act to follow. He recognised that Cruyff had synchronised his own ideas with the old Ajax way of playing – and weaved his schemes around three of the world's best players: Koeman, Laudrup and Stoichkov.

The dream team had been the most successful in Barcelona's history. Cruyff's iconoclastic personality had made him its driving force – as he was at Ajax. But if his team failed to achieve what the directors wanted, then he was the man who had to pay the price.

Madrid had lurched from coach to coach during Cruyff's eight-year reign at Barca. Toshack, Alfredo Di Stefano, Radi Antic, Leo Beenhakker, Floro, Valdano and Arsenio all had spells in charge. Only Floro and Valdano lasted more than a year. Only Valdano delivered a championship – and he was sacked a few months later after Madrid lost to unfashionable city rivals Rayo Vallecano.

Yet Valdano had bequeathed one of the most devastating strikers in Europe to his successors: Raul. Real picked up the Madrid-born forward from Atletico's youth set-up during one of their rivals' financial crises. Valdano spotted his potential in a friendly against Karlsruhe. On 29 October 1994, he gave 17-year-old Raul his debut, against Zaragoza. The following week, Raul scored and set up two more goals in Real's derby win over Atletico.

A year later – with Zamorano gone and Butragueno retired – Raul was the new hero of the Bernabeu. The modest striker was one of the few constants at Madrid during their ups and downs of the next decade. He has scored more domestic goals than any other striker currently playing in Spain. He finished La Liga top scorer in 1999 and 2001. He heads the all-time Champions League scorers and the list of Spain's international strikers.

While Robson was taking over at Barca, Madrid were installing the man who had toppled Cruyff in the 1994 European Cup final: Capello.

Capello spent only one season at the Bernabeu before returning to Milan. But it was a memorable one. Madrid brought in Brazil left-back Roberto Carlos, Ajax midfielder Clarence Seedorf and two strikers: the Serb Predrag Mijatovic from Valencia and the Croat Davor Suker from Sevilla. Madrid pipped Barca to the title by two points. Perhaps Ronaldo's absence for Barca's shock defeat by Hercules was a crucial factor. But Raul dropped a little deeper and kept scoring. Barcelona had Ronaldo but Mijatovic scored 14 goals, Raul hit 21 and Suker netted 24.

Capello had also tightened Madrid's defence – only Deportivo conceded fewer goals – and toughened their mental approach, as they went head to head with Barca for almost nine months. Madrid would feel the benefits a year later in the European Cup.

Enter new coaches at both giants in 1997. Louis van Gaal, who had steered Ajax to European Cup victory in 1995, took over from Robson, whose side had *only* won the Cup-Winners' Cup and the Copa del Rey. Robson joined PSV Eindhoven for the second time. Jupp Heynckes arrived at Madrid from Benfica.

Both achieved instant success – and their clubs reacted in very different ways. Barcelona won the league and cup double and van Gaal was fêted by the directors. Ronaldo had joined Internazionale but Barcelona had new heroes – the Brazilian Rivaldo, signed from Deportivo, and the dazzling Portuguese winger Figo from Sporting Lisbon.

Rivaldo, a forward with a magical left foot, scored 19 goals in van Gaal's first title campaign and 24 the following season. In 1999, he was voted both World and European Player of the Year. Figo, whose 'assists' created so many goals, was voted European Player of the Year in 2000 and World Player of the Year a season later. But he won both honours while in the white strip of Madrid.

Madrid won the European Cup for the first time since 1966 – and Heynckes was sacked because they *only* finished fourth in the league. Barcelona's domestic double weighed heavily against the German.

Mijatovic scored the only goal of the final against Juventus in Amsterdam after Roberto Carlos's shot cannoned off defender Iuliano.

It was the high point of Heynckes' coaching career. But he stayed only a month afterwards and never enjoyed such success again, with Bilbao, Tenerife, or back in Germany. His successor, Jose Antonio Camacho, lasted 22 days after a row with the directors over transfer policy. Dutch coach Guus Hiddink followed for eight months. Toshack then returned for his second spell in charge.

At the Nou Camp, van Gaal took advantage of the Bosman ruling to draw together many of his former Ajax stars, trying almost to re-create Ajax in Catalonia. It was an unpopular policy with the fans. The coach's relations with the influential Catalan sports media were frosty, too. Only Nunez and the board seemed to support van Gaal, despite his achievements.

Yet Barcelona retained their title, finishing 11 points ahead of Madrid who were threatening to implode. Toshack was at loggerheads with Suker and the club president Lorenzo Sanz. Ivan Campo and Seedorf had a fight in training. Former Arsenal striker Nicolas Anelka was a sulking new presence in the dressing-room.

Toshack left and took (successful) action against the club for premature dismissal. By the end of the 1999–2000 season, however, Madrid had won the European Cup and van Gaal's tenure at the Nou Camp was over.

Madrid's salvation was an old retainer, Vicente del Bosque, a defensive midfielder in their teams of the late '70s and early '80s. He had been caretaker briefly before Valdano's arrival in 1994. Sanz turned to him to calm the storm created by Toshack's departure.

Del Bosque was mild-mannered, shrewd and avuncular, perhaps with echoes of Liverpool's Bob Paisley. He came from a trade unionist family in Salamanca and instilled those collective values in the dressing-room.

The players responded to his low-key approach. Midfielder Guti said, 'It's nice to play in an atmosphere where the players are not assumed to be naughty schoolboys in need of a regime of iron discipline.'

Del Bosque recognised the exceptional talent of young goalkeeper Iker Casillas. He acknowledged the influence of skipper Fernando Hierro, put his faith in Fernando Redondo as the midfield creator and encouraged the partnership between Raul and Fernando Morientes.

Madrid rose to sixth in the league and advanced on the European Cup again. They knocked out holders Manchester United, winning 3–2 at Old Trafford after a 0–0 draw at the Bernabeu. Redondo, another Valdano protégé, was outstanding. Raul scored twice.

Anelka netted in both legs of the semi-finals as Madrid ousted old rivals Bayern Munich 3–2 on aggregate. They met Valencia in Paris in the first all-Spanish final. Valencia had knocked out Barcelona in the other semi-final.

Argentine coach Hector Cuper had taken Mallorca from the second division to promotion and the last Cup-Winners' Cup final in 1999. That summer, he joined Valencia and turned them into contenders for all the major prizes. Cuper's style was based on a strong, experienced defence and swift counter-attacks. Gaizka Mendieta and Kily Gonzalez were the creative influences. Claudio Lopez supplied the cutting edge.

Some Valencia fans reckoned Cuper's tactics were too cautious. Still, they reached the European Cup final again the following season, losing to Bayern Munich on penalties. Cuper left for Internazionale in the summer of 2001. His successor, Rafa Benitez, turned Cuper's groundwork into trophies – the title in 2002 and a championship and UEFA Cup double in 2004. (This was followed by European Cup final glory for Liverpool in 2005.)

Madrid, in unfamiliar black strip, dominated the final. Morientes headed them in front from Michel Salgado's cross. Former Liverpool star Steve McManaman drove a weak clearance through a ruck of bodies for the second. Raul ran from inside his own half to dribble round keeper Santi Canizares to make it 3–0. It was Madrid's eighth European Cup success.

Now Del Bosque was head coach rather than caretaker. He had a new boss, too: Florentino Perez, who had beaten Sanz in the 2000 presidential election by promising to bring Figo from Barca. Redondo, who had publicly supported Sanz, was sold to Milan, where injury wrecked his career.

On the anniversary of his first year in charge, Del Bosque said, 'Nobody, least of all me, could imagine that I'd last this long. It's very difficult to last a year here. People try to undermine the coach's image, even if results are good.' Those words would come to describe his relationship with Perez.

Meanwhile, van Gaal had paid the penalty for a campaign that promised so much but ended in failure. By the start of the 1999–2000 season, he had assembled a Dutch legion at the Nou Camp – goalkeeper Ruud Hesp, midfielder Philip Cocu and winger Bodo Zenden – plus the old Ajax contingent of Reiziger, Frank de Boer, Patrick Kluivert and the Finnish forward Jari Litmanen.

But Barcleona finished second in La Liga, five points behind unfashionable champions Deportivo. They were knocked out by Atletico Madrid in the Copa del Rey semi-finals. And they crashed to Valencia in the European Cup.

Barca had a mountain to climb after losing the first leg 4–1 in Valencia. They had swept Chelsea aside 5–1 at the Nou Camp in the last eight after losing 3–1 in London. Van Gaal said, 'We can do it again.'

Instead, Valencia smothered Barca's stars. Mendieta scored an away goal to cement a 5–1 aggregate lead. De Boer and Cocu netted late goals to give Barca a 2–1 win on the night. By then, though, thousands of fans were calling for van Gaal's removal. Madrid's success heightened the pressure on president and coach. Construction magnate Nunez resigned after 22 years in his post. Van Gaal left, too. So did Figo, amid a furore in Catalonia.

Gaspart won the presidential elections and embarked on a spree, spending more than £50 million on the Arsenal pair Manu Petit and Marc Overmars, Valencia midfielder Gerard Lopez and Alfonso from Betis. Llorenc Serra Ferrer, the head of youth development, became coach. At least Barcelona did not sign Anelka, who returned to Paris Saint-Germain.

Barca struggled. Serra Ferrer was sacked. Cruyff's old assistant Rexach took over as caretaker after Barca's UEFA Cup defeat by Liverpool. Barcelona squeezed into the Champions League only thanks to Rivaldo's hat trick against Valencia on the last day of the season.

Gaspart made another raft of signings in the summer of 2001. Barcelona finished fourth again. Their Champions League campaign ended in disaster when they were beaten by Madrid in the semi-finals.

Meanwhile, Perez, a commercial property magnate, had a dream. *His* Madrid would not only be the most successful football club in Europe. They would also be the richest, eclipsing even Manchester United. He said, 'This club should have the best players in the world because they're the most profitable ones. Signing a world-class star means great international projection for Real Madrid and that translates into economic profit.'

Figo's £37 million transfer was Perez's first such signing. The deal was greeted with disbelief in Barcelona. Figo's move to the arch-enemy was viewed as treachery on a grand scale. When he returned with

Madrid, he was subjected to an outpouring of hate at the Nou Camp where he had been such an idol. Fans threw missiles, bottles, lighters and even mobile phones at him. Worse awaited Figo in the derby of November 2002. Roberto Carlos led the Madrid players off the field for ten minutes after Figo was pelted as he tried to take a corner.

Perez also managed to sell Madrid's old Ciudad Deportiva training complex to the city council, wiping out the club's debts at a stroke. Fans of other clubs – especially Barca – claimed that the Madrid municipality was effectively using taxpayers' money to subsidise Real. Conspiracy theorists pointed out that the conservative then-prime minister Jose Maria Aznar had been a member of Madrid since his youth. But it was a financial master stroke and freed Perez to pursue his dream of bringing the best attacking players in the world to the Bernabeu.

Every summer, Perez would sign one of these stars, now known as *galacticos*. In 2001, he brought France's World Cup and Euro 2000 playmaker Zinedine Zidane from Juventus for a world record £46 million fee. The following summer, he signed Brazil's World Cup-winning striker Ronaldo from Internazionale in a £29 milllion deal. Then, in 2003, he brought David Beckham from Manchester United.

Figo, Zidane and Ronaldo were all acknowledged as greats. Beckham was England captain but he had been troubled by injury throughout the 2002 World Cup finals and had shown only glimpses of his best. United boss Sir Alex Ferguson seemed relieved when he left Old Trafford, perhaps because of the constant hype surrounding Beckham's marriage to 'Posh Spice' Victoria Adams and his many off-field commitments.

But Beckham was a commercial icon, especially in the Far East market that Madrid were desperate to penetrate. Whether Beckham was a footballing success is a matter of debate. That he was a commercial success for Madrid is undoubted. Their income rose by 23 per cent in his first season. Madrid's club shops sold 8,000 'Beckham 23' shirts within four hours of going on sale. Beckham was a potent weapon as Madrid tried to reach commercial parity with Manchester United. Madrid's annual revenue rose from £134 million to more than £156 million. United, with £171 million, were the only club to earn more. Barcelona's income was £112 million.

Salgado assessed the side effects. He said, 'Beckham's arrival has opened us up to the gossip media. That's no good for us. They're hanging on our every move. It's a disaster.'

Perez wanted *galacticos*. Del Bosque wanted players who would fit in with his work ethic and make the squad stronger. He also wanted a central defender to play alongside the ageing Hierro. As McManaman and his co-author Sarah Edworthy say in *El Macca*: 'How many times would he fruitlessly request a centre-back from his president, only to be attacked later for his team's defensive frailties?' They quote one club insider: 'Florentino could not face spending a lot of money on a defender.'

Madrid won the title by seven points from Deportivo in 2001 – without Zidane, Ronaldo or Beckham. Barcelona finished 17 points behind.

Del Bosque's side finished behind Valencia and Deportivo the following season, the club's centenary. They lost the Copa del Rey final at home to Deportivo, too. 'It was a black day,' said Hierro. But they ended the centenary season with the European Cup. Second-half goals by Ivan Helguera and Guti saw off Bayern Munich in the quarter-final second leg at the Bernabeu.

Zidane and McManaman scored as they humiliated Barca 2–0 at the Nou Camp in the semi-final first leg. McManaman said, 'To lead 2–0 away against Barcelona was just crazy. In the dressing-room, the lads were absolutely thrilled. The Barca factor, how can an outsider truly understand it?'

Raul netted after 43 minutes at the Bernabeu. Madrid won 3–1 on aggregate and beat Bayer Leverkusen 2–1 in the final. Lucio levelled Raul's ninth-minute goal but Zidane conjured a winner of beauty, a crashing left-foot volley from the edge of the box. Casillas made a brilliant save in the dying seconds to preserve Madrid's lead.

Ronaldo scored 23 goals as Madrid won their 29th league title in 2002–03. He hit a hat trick against Manchester United in the European Cup quarter-finals and netted the first goal when Madrid beat Juventus 2–1 in the semi-final first leg. Then Madrid, lacking defensive cover, fell apart in Turin. David Trezeguet, Alessandro del Piero and Pavel Nedved gave Juve a 3–0 lead before Zidane scored a last-minute goal. Perez fired Del Bosque at the end of the campaign and released skipper Hierro along with 15 other players.

Madrid sources said that Hierro had been sacked after leading a players' delegation to protest at Del Bosque's sacking. Nearly two years later, Hierro reflected, 'We should have continued with Del Bosque and we should never have let Claude Makelele and Morientes go.

'Vicente had great qualities, as a coach and as a person. He knew how to deal with the players and he won seven trophies in four years. It was almost unique in such a short time.'

Del Bosque was replaced by a figure familiar to Beckham – Carlos Queiroz, the former assistant manager at Manchester United.

Now Madrid were a combination of *galacticos* and youngsters. They hardly had any squad players left. Perez's policy would cost them dear on the pitch.

Perez wanted a mixture of superstars – like Zidane – and Madrid youngsters, like centre-back Francisco Pavon. Defenders, holding midfielders and the experienced squad players were cast aside. Midfield anchor Makelele – unspectacular but hugely respected by his teammates – went to Chelsea. Morientes was loaned to Monaco.

Midfielder Santi Solari perceptively noted, 'The problem with the president's policy is that it tends towards the extinction of the middle class.' Helguera was more direct, 'If you don't sell lots and lots of shirts, then you're not a star. The club has to realise you don't just need individual talents who play wonderfully, you also need players who work a lot.'

The ex-Liverpool striker turned leading Spanish TV analyst Michael Robinson said, 'The club has become too Hollywood. Del Bosque had to go because he was fat and had a moustache.'

Barcelona's troubles were even greater. Van Gaal's return as coach in the summer of 2002 was met with incredulity in Catalonia. He immediately fell out with Rivaldo, who joined Milan. On 26 January 2003, Barca lost 2–0 at Celta Vigo and slipped to three points above the relegation zone. 'I've had a lot of criticism,' said van Gaal as he packed his bags again.

Antic lifted Barca to sixth in the final table but change was clearly on the agenda. Gaspart stepped down that summer. Lawyer Joan Laporta beat advertising mogul Lluis Bassat in the presidential elections. Laporta had promised to sign Beckham if he won. Beckham went to Madrid. Barca made an inspirational signing instead – £30 million Brazilian attacker Ronaldinho from Paris Saint-Germain. The former Holland coach – and Cruyff protégé – Rijkaard took charge.

Barca ended the season with a winning run that carried them into second place. Ronaldinho was inspirational. Now the Barcelona fans could laugh at Madrid who finished fourth, lost the Copa del Rey final to struggling Zaragoza and suffered a run of five successive defeats, an unwanted club record.

Madrid's defensive frailties also cost them dear in the European Cup. They were knocked out on away goals by Monaco after leading 4–1 at the Bernabeu with nine minutes left. Morientes – the man on loan from Madrid – made it 4–2 and scored in the return, which the French club won 3–1. Queiroz was sacked at the end of the season and returned to Manchester.

Barca fans began to believe the balance of power had swung in their favour once more. By the end of the 2004–05 season, it had.

Barcelona won the championship, by four points from Madrid. Ronaldinho was mesmeric. He was named FIFA World Player of the Year for the second time in succession. Cameroon striker Samuel Eto'o, who netted 24 league goals, finished third in the poll. Deco carried on where he left off at Porto. The Mexican midfield anchor Marquez had an outstanding season. So did the Catalans, skipper Carles Puyol and midfielder Xavi.

After Barca clinched the title with a draw at Levante, Jordi Cruyff said: 'Catalonia needed this. It's great credit to Rijkaard and Laporta. They've lots of good ideas and made several good signings.'

Madrid's season was chaotic by comparison. They lurched from crisis to crisis and coach to coach – Jose Antonio Camacho, caretaker Garcia Remon, then former Brazil boss Vanderlei Luxemburgo, who was sacked in December 2005 as Madrid trailed Barcelona again.

CHAPTER 22

SATELLITE TV, THE CHAMPIONS LEAGUE AND THE BOSMAN JUDGMENT

A generation brought up on satellite TV may find this hard to believe but, once upon a time in England, not one league match was televised live. The football authorities believed that live TV coverage would stop supporters going to the grounds. Armchair fans had to be content with live coverage of the FA Cup final plus selected England matches. The only live coverage came in the form of radio commentaries. And, until 1964, TV highlights were rare, too. So BBC TV's *Match of the Day* was a ground-breaking programme when it was first broadcast on the evening of 22 August 1964. The legendary commentator Kenneth Wolstenholme took the microphone for the game between champions Liverpool and Arsenal.

Match of the Day was the first regular show dedicated to football highlights and it was transmitted on a channel (BBC2) which had just been launched. The first programme was watched by just 20,000 viewers. But the BBC knew that a sure way to increase the audience for Britain's third free-to-air channel was to use it to screen football. Fans were soon queuing to have BBC2 installed. It was a portent of the tactics that companies like Sky would refine a generation or so later.

Match of the Day moved to BBC1 at the start of the 1966–67 season. In 1968, ITV launched a rival highlights show, *The Big Match*, screened on Sunday afternoons. But live coverage was still strictly limited.

By the mid-1980s, the leading clubs were eagerly seeking regular live TV exposure. Arsenal, Everton, Liverpool, Manchester United and

Tottenham – a group then known as 'the big five' – tried to force the issue. But the Football League limited the number of live matches to seven on each channel per season – and neither ITV nor BBC were prepared to enter a serious auction for TV football rights.

In 1983, the league allowed home clubs to keep their home gate money instead of having to give their opponents a share. This was a financial boon to big clubs with big crowds, such as Liverpool and Manchester United, and a serious financial blow to lesser clubs with small gates. It was also a symbolic step on the road to the consolidation of power within a wealthy elite.

The formation of the Premier League in 1992 was another significant step. One reason why the leading clubs decided to quit the Football League was their reluctance to hand over money from TV deals to subsidise lower league sides.

With the Premier League came Sky satellite TV – a new kind of coverage – and pots of cash, far more than the clubs could have hoped to extract from deals with terrestrial channels.

Sky was not the first satellite broadcaster to screen football on a subscription basis. Canal Plus in France broke that ground. But Sky has been the most successful, since it captured the Premier League TV rights in 1992.

Sky dominates in England, to the extent of virtually hand-picking the fixture list. The BBC must be content with selected England games, sharing FA Cup coverage and showing Premiership highlights on *Match of the Day*. Alex Fynn, one of Britain's leading experts on the relationship between TV and football, said, 'England has the highest number of pay-TV football subscribers in Europe, through Sky Sports. Live Premiership football coverage has been a key motivating factor in people taking out Sky subscriptions.

'Sky has penetrated in the UK far more than any other pay-TV football broadcaster in Europe. It's available in nearly 50 per cent of British homes. Compare that with Spain, Italy and Germany, where fewer than 3 million homes have paid-for access to satellite football.'

(Subscriber figures at the end of 2004 showed 7.6 million homes in the UK have access to Sky, compared with 4.9 million for Canal Plus, 3 million for Premiere in Germany, 2.8 million for Sky Italia and 2.1 million for Sogecable in Spain.)

Sky's presence created a bonanza for the clubs. No longer could the terrestrial broadcasters, BBC and ITV, tacitly hold down the bill for TV football rights. Suddenly they were faced by an aggressive competitor. Fynn said, 'Sky's participation was the crucial factor in driving up the price of TV rights in England. Sky was prepared to pay much more than terrestrial TV, because it gambled on football hugely increasing its subscriber base. Sky's TV deals in England have set the benchmark for the rest of Europe.'

He added, 'Pay TV has driven up the price of football TV rights throughout Europe, because the pay-TV companies must have football if they're to build a subscriber base. I'd say that all European pay-TV companies, except perhaps Sky, have overpaid for those rights and some have found themselves in financial difficulties as a consequence.'

The German channel Premiere is an example. When its parent media company, Kirch, collapsed and went into receivership in 2002, Premiere was reckoned to be losing £1 million a day. (It is now run by the private investment group Permira, which reduced losses by 38 per cent in its first year in charge.)

There are variations in TV coverage throughout the five major western leagues – England, France, Germany, Italy and Spain. But only in Spain is there still a terrestrial TV presence at league matches, through the FORTA network – and the satellite broadcaster Sogecable is also a major player.

Even so, the start of the 2003–04 season was in doubt for weeks because of a row over the division of TV revenue between a group of 12 major clubs, led by Real Madrid and Barcelona, and the other first- and second-division clubs. The smaller clubs wanted a centralised TV deal. A compromise was eventually agreed. The big clubs could hold their own TV rights. The other 30 clubs in the top divisions agreed a collective deal with Sogecable.

In France, in 2004, Canal Plus outbid satellite rival TPS and signed a £1.28 billion three-year deal to screen L1 (first division) in France exclusively again, after sharing coverage with TPS since 1999. It was the biggest TV deal in French league history. League president Frederic Thiriez said, 'Our league is going to reap its true worth. Our football has been undervalued but it's beginning to catch up.'

Canal Plus became France's first pay-TV broadcaster in 1984, when the Mitterand government ended the state's TV monopoly. Three years later, the most popular state terrestrial channel, TF1, was privatised. A bidding war between Canal Plus and TF1 – eventually won by Canal

Plus – drove up the value of TV football rights. As Geoff Hare wrote in *Football in France: A Cultural History*: 'In France as in England, the commercialisation of football took place in close symbiosis with changes in how television was distributed and sold.'

The French TV deal was centralised so that every club in the top two divisions benefited. Hare noted: 'The income from TV rights shared among the L1 and L2 [second division] clubs quadrupled between 1991 and 1996. Television rapidly became a principal source of income for French clubs.'

In December 1996, Canal Plus – then about to start digital transmission – began to broadcast every L1 match on pay-per-view TV. French Cup and League Cup games are the only domestic matches screened on terrestrial TV.

Helmut Kohl's government changed West Germany's media laws in 1983 to allow the introduction of satellite TV. Two major players soon emerged. Sat Eins, backed by the Kirch group, and RTL Plus, owned by Bertelsmann, both challenged the traditional broadcasters for TV football rights. Between 1988 and 1991, the value of Bundesliga TV rights doubled from DM40 million to DM80 million.

Premiere won the Bundesliga TV rights in 1991. In 2000, it introduced a pay-per-view package offering live coverage of every Bundesliga game. The cost was estimated at around DM700 million a season. But Premiere has yet to match the success of Sky in England. Unlike *Match of the Day* – which is screened after the start of Sky's Saturday highlights show – Bundesliga highlights programmes still attract audiences of around 8 million on terrestrial TV.

In Italy, pay TV rules. Silvio Berlusconi's government has been friendly to satellite TV. The Italian prime minister himself held shares in the country's first pay-TV company, Telepiu, until 'conflict of interest' legislation forced him to sell 90 per cent of his stake.

Now armchair fans can only watch live Serie A matches on Sky Italia's *Sky Calcio* package. Sky Italia also offers dedicated channels for Milan, Internazionale and Roma. Only Italy's internationals and the Coppa Italia are screened on free-to-air TV.

Satellite TV coverage has made the old terrestrial version look sedate. Uli Hesse-Lichtenberger in *Tor!* summed up the difference brilliantly: 'The presenters [on pay TV] were not reporters, they were entertainers. They didn't present programmes but "shows". They were not merely following the games, they were selling them.'

He was analysing the German experience, but he could just as easily have been talking about England.

Sky made every live game an event, with scores of new camera angles, instant replays, expert analysis and talking heads before the game, at half-time and after. Technically, it was superb. Sky had learned fast from Canal Plus, the German stations and from Australia, where Sky owner Rupert Murdoch's TV stations had breathed fresh life into cricket coverage. (Sky's interactive service would revolutionise coverage even further by offering viewers a choice of eight different screens to view aspects of the same match.)

Suddenly, all was breathless enthusiasm. Premiership football was hyped into the greatest sporting contest in history. Trained journalists made way for ex-players chosen for their celebrity value. It worked. Sky developed its four subscription sports channels: first, through covering England's overseas cricket tours and then – most effectively – by dragging football into a new era. That had a financial knock-on and the clubs enjoyed the commercial benefits.

Fynn said, 'Sky changed the nature of the game by their presentation. They turned football into showbiz, creating massive hype which in turn has brought sports goods and leisurewear companies into the game and created all sorts of opportunities for commercial deals and sponsorship. Sky's coverage has made football trendy.'

The Europe-wide effect of satellite TV – led by Sky – combined with the explosion of cash in the Champions League to make the rich clubs even richer and more dominant.

In Italy, the Milan clubs, Juventus and Roma have entered into lucrative deals for their home TV rights. They feature frequently in live games screened by the multi-language satellite broadcaster Eurosport.

In Spain, Real Madrid and Barcelona have reaped huge rewards from selling the TV rights to their home games. Every match at the Bernabeu or the Nou Camp has become a satellite TV event throughout Europe. According to Fynn, 'These deals put money into the pockets of the big clubs. They can call the shots – though they still need the lesser clubs to provide the opposition for televised matches.'

Even in England, France and Germany, which operate centralised TV deals, the big teams collect the most money because they appear most often. Canal Plus (which rescued Paris Saint-Germain from bankruptcy in the early 1990s) quickly discovered that its two biggest draws were

PSG and Marseille. Bayern Munich and Borussia Dortmund predominate in Germany.

The TV cash statistics for the 2004–05 Premiership season make interesting reading. Fifty per cent of the money was divided equally among the clubs, who received £8.8 million each. Of the remaining cash, 25 per cent was divided in facility payments for appearances and 25 per cent in merit payments, according to final league position. (The current deal is worth £1.03 billion over three years, slightly less than the £1.1 billion that Sky paid to secure the rights between 2001 and 2004. Between 2000 and the end of 2004, Sky increased its subscriber base from 3.5 million households to 7.6 million.)

Inevitably, the leading clubs – Manchester United, Arsenal and Chelsea – were screened most often and collected the highest rewards for filling the top three positions. According to a table in the *Mail on Sunday*, Chelsea earned a total of £16.17 million – £6.67 million from TV appearances plus £9.5 million for winning the championship. Runners-up Arsenal received £16.215 million – £7.19 million from TV games and £9.025 million as merit money. United, third, were the biggest benficiaries of all with £16.51 million. They topped the list of TV earners with £7.96 million and collected £8.55 million in merit payments.

Contrast those figures with the cash earned by the relegated teams. Bottom club Southampton totted up little more than £4 million from TV appearances and merit money. Norwich, one place above them, collected £4.58 million. The other relegated club, Crystal Palace, earned £4.305 million.

Even the gap between the top clubs and their mid-table rivals is vast. Eleventh-placed Charlton, for instance, earned a total of £7.97 million from TV appearances and merit money.

TV cash has become a crucial part of those big clubs' income. Professors Jonathan Michie and Christine Oughton, in *Competitive Balance in Football*, show the proportion of revenue the leading five English clubs derived from TV in the 2002–03 season. Only Manchester United – who sell out Old Trafford's 67,000-capacity for every home game – took significantly more in gate receipts than they received from TV. (The figures are for TV and broadcast revenue from all sources, including the Champions League.)

United's income amounted to £53.5 million from TV, £65 million from gate receipts and £42.5 million from commercial activities. By contrast, Arsenal collected £47.9 million from broadcast revenue, as much as their gate receipts and commercial income combined. Liverpool earned £42 million from TV, £26.4 million from gate receipts and £27.2 million from commercial activities. Newcastle received £38.5 million from broadcasting revenue, £30.1 million from gate receipts and £20.3 million from commercial activities. Chelsea, in their last season before Roman Abramovich's takeover, collected £27.6 million from TV money, £26 million at the gate and £30 million from commercial activities.

The extra revenue from the Champions League further widens the gap between the haves and the have-nots. As sports business analyst Peter Sharkey pointed out, 'It's the Champions League where the massive difference lies.'

The wealthiest clubs with the largest domestic TV income play regularly in the Champions League and reap even bigger rewards, from TV revenue and related commercial activities. Michie and Oughton estimate the value of a run to the European Cup final at 'up to £30 million'. They detail the cash that the top English clubs earned from Champions League competition in the 2003–04 season. Manchester United (last 16) received £18.3 million from broadcasting revenue alone, never mind the other commercial benefits. Arsenal (quarter-finalists) received £18.6 million simply from broadcasting revenue and semi-finalists Chelsea £19 million. No wonder there is a frantic scramble for England's fourth Champions League place after the usual suspects have qualified. Michie and Oughton concluded, 'Given that these revenues are only attainable by the top clubs in the league, the growth in Champions League revenue streams is a significant factor in the growing inequality in the distribution of income between the top clubs and the rest.' They also conclude that the effect has been a 'decline in competitive balance' as a result.

Fynn said, 'The Champions League has widened the gap between the rich and poor even further. That extra cash gives the wealthy clubs even more clout to sign the best players and dominate their domestic competitions. It's like a snowball that's increasing at an alarming rate.'

The Coventry chairman Bryan Richardson proved an accurate forecaster when he said in March 2001, 'It will soon be impossible for more than two or three clubs to win the Premiership. That's not good for the game, because if you remove that hope from, say, 17 clubs, where's the incentive to go and support them?'

Fynn said, 'There's less competition throughout *all* the major leagues because the leading clubs are so much wealthier than the rest. You can be pretty sure of the Champions League qualifiers before the season starts. Take England: Arsenal, Chelsea and Manchester United have filled the top three places, in whatever order, then there has been a huge scrap for the fourth Champions League slot.

'The richest clubs buy the best, as Chelsea have shown under Abramovich. There's no way that a smaller club could be promoted and surprise the big clubs now – like Ipswich in the 1960s and Derby and Nottingham Forest in the 1970s, who all won the championship.' (Forest also won the European Cup twice. They were relegated from the Championship at the end of the 2004–05 season.)

Yet centralised TV deals along Premiership lines may become an anachronism if the European Union's competition commissioner Mario Monti has his way. The EU is resolutely opposed to TV contracts that guarantee exclusivity to one broadcaster. It probed the latest Sky deal at length and is expected to challenge Sky's leading role when the Premiership TV contract is renegotiated later in 2006.

That might suit the big clubs in England (and France and Germany) – if they could hold their own rights and negotiate direct with TV like their Spanish and Italian counterparts. Imagine the cash that could be generated from a game like Arsenal's Premiership clash with Manchester United on 1 February 2005 which was screened live – via Sky's cameras – in 130 countries.

The big western European clubs – 18 of them now members of the G-14 pressure group – have another card to play, too: the threat of a breakaway league, backed by a satellite broadcaster (see Chapter 20). Long-term, that may prove a risky game but UEFA has been very careful to keep them on board in the Champions League after the breakaway threatened by the Media Partners group in 1998.

The coming of both satellite TV and the modern Champions League has caused massive changes in football's finance and organisation. So has the impact of a verdict reached in a Luxembourg courtroom – the Bosman judgment. By the late 1980s, UEFA was already concerned at the prospect of the big clubs buying up the best players from around the world. National associations had their own, varying, rules about the number of foreign players whom teams could field in domestic competitions.

UEFA then introduced the 'three foreigners rule' for its own competitions – the European Cup, Cup-Winners' Cup and UEFA Cup. Clubs were only permitted to field three foreign players plus two assimilated players – foreigners who had spent at least five years in their club's country. The scheme was known as the '3+2 rule'.

The major losers were the English clubs on their return to European competition. Players from Scotland, Wales and Northern Ireland were classified as foreigners. The effect was to inflate domestic transfer fees for the best English players, exemplified by the £7.5 million that Manchester United paid Newcastle for striker Andy Cole in January 1995. Eleven months later, both the transfer system and the foreigners rule were swept away by a landmark court verdict.

The Belgian player Jean-Marc Bosman was an unlikely revolutionary. He had played for RFC Liege between 1988 and 1990. At the end of his contract, Liege offered him a one-year extension but at a quarter of his previous wages. Bosman turned down the offer. He lined up a move to the French side Dunkerque, who agreed a transfer fee with Liege.

Liege were worried about possible financial problems at Dunkerque and did not ask the Belgian federation to issue the transfer certificate that would have completed Bosman's move. So Bosman was without a club and unable to make his living as a footballer.

He sued UEFA and the Belgian federation, claiming that the transfer system was a restriction on his freedom to choose a place of work and therefore incompatible with European Union competition laws and provisions for the free movement of labour in member states.

The case went before the Belgian court of appeal, which referred the issue to the European Court of Justice. Bosman argued that, under Article 39 of the European Union charter, he was a 'worker' who should be free to change employers (clubs) when his contract expired – without his club demanding a transfer fee.

UEFA and the Belgian federation – supported by other associations – argued that the end of the traditional transfer system would lead to the big clubs snapping up all the best players without compensation for the less wealthy clubs. They also argued that ending the restrictions on foreign players would lead to clubs importing players from all over the world, thus diluting the character of national leagues.

On 15 December 1995, the European Court of Justice ruled in Bosman's favour. The transfer system for out-of-contract players was abolished. So were UEFA's restrictions on foreign players.

The judgment initially applied only to the member states of the European Union. That left FIFA with a problem: the world body could hardly have two different sets of rules for countries inside and outside the EU. It implemented the European Court of Justice ruling worldwide.

The UEFA president Lennart Johansson said, 'We had to blame ourselves. We had lived with the same rules and regulations for 100 years and we were taken by surprise by the Bosman judgment. It left us in a mess.'

It was as if UEFA had not grasped the significance of the case until it was too late.

The distinguished lawyer, Robert Reid QC, said, 'The way the European Union treated UEFA after the judgment reflected its dissatisfaction with the way that UEFA tried to pretend it was above the law.' He also forecast, correctly, 'The top of the various leagues will grow more elitist according to who can afford the best players.'

The outgoing UEFA chief executive, Gerhard Aigner, said in January 2004, 'I think we could have revised the transfer system in a coherent way and kept the rule which limits the movement of players.' He added, 'The Bosman ruling was a disaster for football. All of the excesses that we know now and many of the problems in the game go back to that decision.'

But Bosman's case was stark. Either the transfer system and player quotas were upheld or they were abolished. There was no halfway house. The Bosman judgment established the primacy of European Union labour and competition law over UEFA's regulations.

UEFA found that out when it tried, unsuccessfully, to reintroduce player quotas. In April 2000, the European Union's sports commissioner Viviane Reding vetoed Johansson's proposals, based on a variation of the old foreigners rule.

However, the beneficiaries from the Bosman judgment were not ordinary footballers like Bosman himself but the big clubs, the star players and their agents. A new system evolved. The stars signed a contract, then began negotiations on a new deal hardly before the ink was dry. They knew that they could get more or less whatever they wanted – at their current club or a new one.

If a club could not agree a new deal with a player, it would sell him a year before the end of his contract, rather than risk him leaving on a free transfer – known as 'a Bosman free'. The Holland midfielder

Edgar Davids became the first big star to move on a Bosman free when he left Ajax for Milan in 1996.

Clubs which did not sell before the end of a contract could find themselves burned financially. For instance, the Liverpool and England midfielder Steve McManaman joined Real Madrid on a Bosman free in 1998. Three years later, England centre-half Sol Campbell left Tottenham when his contract expired and joined their arch rivals Arsenal, without a transfer fee.

The big clubs, buoyed by their new wealth from TV income and the Champions League, had the cash to buy players and offer them huge wages. Salaries of £1 million-plus a year became common throughout the upper reaches of the Premiership. The sky was the limit for others, such as the Manchester United defender Rio Ferdinand, who in 2005 signed a new deal reputedly worth £100,000 a week.

Smaller clubs were deprived of income from the transfer market. They became resigned to selling their best players – for whatever they could get – before their contracts expired or receiving no fee at all. Agents grew in importance because they could deliver players to clubs, from all around the globe. Fynn said, 'The only way to get players now is through agents. That puts them in a very powerful position. Often they act with huge conflicts of interest, representing both a player and a buying or selling club, but these people lubricate the wheels of commerce.'

FIFA's decision to implement the Bosman judgment worldwide had further consequences. The clubs and leagues of eastern Europe were denuded as their best players headed west for fatter contracts. The Yugoslav federation president Dragan Stojkovic spoke for the old east when he said, 'The introduction of the Bosman rule has practically ruined us.'

The rest of the world became feeder competitions for western Europe's leagues of dreams. Scandinavians headed to England and Germany by the score. The exodus of South American stars grew ever more hurried. Not just to their traditional destinations of Italy or Spain either. Brazilians Edu and Silvinho, then Gilberto, arrived at Arsenal. Lucio and Ze Roberto starred for Bayer Leverkusen. Edmilson won French title medals with Lyon.

French clubs scooped up the brightest talent from Africa. When Senegal beat France 1–0 in the opening match of the 2002 World Cup finals, their team contained more players from French league clubs than France. The top Japanese player, midfielder Hidetoshi Nakata, went to Perugia in Serie A, then on to Roma and Parma.

England was once among the most insular of football nations. Manchester United, Liverpool, Nottingham Forest and Aston Villa had won the European Cup with virtually all-British teams. Now English became a minority language in many dressing-rooms.

The process was speeded by the arrival of foreign coaches and one in particular: Arsene Wenger at Arsenal. The Slovak coach Jozef Venglos spent a mediocre season in charge at Aston Villa in 1990–91. Six years later, Wenger was a ground breaker. He was articulate, professorial and he won matches. The Frenchman introduced revolutionary ideas on diet, training, fitness and medicine, and steered Arsenal to the league and FA Cup double in his second season at Highbury.

Other clubs turned to foreign coaches, hoping to emulate Wenger's success. Liverpool appointed the Frenchman Gerard Houllier. Then, in the summer of 2004, they replaced him with Spanish coach Rafa Benitez, who guided them to European Cup victory in his first season.

Chelsea appointed Ruud Gullit, followed by Gianluca Vialli and Claudio Ranieri. Then they brought in Porto's European Cup-winning coach Jose Mourinho to succeed Ranieri – and won the 2004–05 championship. Tottenham appointed former Lyon and France coach Jacques Santini. When he quit suddenly, they promoted the Dutchman Martin Jol.

Such coaches brought in players they knew and trusted from abroad. Arsenal usually play with only two Englishmen, Campbell and Ashley Cole. John Terry, Frank Lampard and Joe Cole are the only Englishmen who start regularly for Chelsea. Liverpool are full of imports from France and Spain. Of England's leading clubs, only Manchester United, under Sir Alex Ferguson, have retained a British core. Aston Villa were the last Premiership side to field an all-English 11. That was in 1999. Now England's (Swedish) coach Sven-Goran Eriksson has less than 50 Premiership players to pick from.

Other national coaches face the same problem. More than 60 per cent of Bundesliga players come from outside Germany. The German federation president Gerhard Mayer-Vorfelder said in 2003, 'More than 60 per cent is simply too many. It has nothing to do with racism. But it's bad for the national team. If the national coach can only pick from a crop of 40 players from a nation of 80 million, it's just not enough.'

The same complaint is heard in Spain and Italy: that too many of the most important players are ineligible for the national team. Real Madrid have made a habit of collecting foreign galacticos – the Brazilians Roberto Carlos and Ronaldo, and the French playmaker Zinedine Zidane – who overshadow Spanish talent such as Raul and Iker Casillas. At Barcelona in 2004–05, midfielder Xavi apart, all the key attacking players were foreigners: World Player of the Year Ronaldinho (Brazil); his compatriot, the marauding full-back Belletti; Ludovic Giuly (France); Henrik Larsson (Sweden) and Samuel Eto'o (Cameroon).

The Czech midfielder Pavel Nedved and his Brazilian colleague Emerson provided the inspiration for Italian champions Juventus. Milan relied heavily on the Brazilians Cafu and Kaka, the Dutchman Clarence Seedorf and the 2004 European Footballer of the Year, Ukraine striker Andriy Shevchenko.

Perhaps the big clubs are not much concerned about national sides, though. Bayern Munich chief executive Uli Hoeness replied to Mayer-Vorfelder, wondering if there was a 'need for national teams any more'. Milan president Adriano Galliani said, 'If we want to play 11 foreign players, no one should [be able to] stop us.'

UEFA's answer is to try to run a more sophisticated quota system past the European Union. Johansson said, 'If young people see three foreigners sitting on a bench and all the players in the team are foreigners, that can have a negative effect on their will to dedicate themselves to football. In the long run, this is dangerous for the future of the game.'

UEFA vice-president Per Ravn Omdal unveiled the plans in 2004. Clubs would be ordered to carry squads of no more than 25 players. Of the 25, four must be products of the club's youth system and four more must have been 'trained in that country'. The wording is deliberately framed to get round EU labour laws which bar discrimination on the basis of nationality.

The big clubs – and especially the G-14 group of leading western clubs – are bound to fight the proposal, even before the European Union steps in. The Premiership clubs, meeting in January 2005, unanimously opposed the scheme, citing restraint of trade. Arsenal vice-chairman David Dein said, 'It's misguided and it will be challenged.'

Meanwhile, the big clubs want to make even more money. Manchester United had stolen a march on their European rivals by expanding their commercial activities into the vast markets of the Far East. Real Madrid wanted to match United in sales of replica shirts and souvenirs. It was widely assumed that one reason they signed David Beckham in the summer of 2003 was because of his popularity in markets such as China and South-east Asia. Madrid's income duly increased by more than £22 million during the 2003–04 season.

But not all can keep up. Roma and Lazio, both recent Serie A champions, have been forced to sell several stars to stave off financial crises caused by overstretching themselves. Leeds reached the Champions League semi-finals in 2001, then crashed out of the Premiership in 2004 with huge debts after committing themselves to vast transfer and salary expenditure. Borussia Dortmund – the first German club to float on the stock market – posted record losses last year. They spent the 2004–05 season teetering on the brink of bankruptcy, despite being the Bundesliga's best-supported club with home gates of more than 65,000.

Fynn said, 'I can see two major problems ahead. One is that clubs could stretch themselves to the point of bankruptcy or beyond by trying to keep up with the elite and falling short.

'The other is the concentration of too much money in too few hands – leading to a decline in fair competition and, eventually, a fall-off in interest by the fans who don't want to watch uncompetitive matches.'

He concluded, 'The effect of satellite TV deals, the Champions League and the Bosman judgment has been to concentrate the best players from around the world in a few clubs in a few western European leagues. Players naturally go where the money and the opportunities are.

'The result though is that football now is not about fair competition. It's about maximising revenue for the major clubs who have the most expensive squads.'

PART TWO

EUROPEAN COMPETITIONS

THE STORY OF THE UEFA CUP

The European Cup was not the only competition inaugurated in 1955. On 18 April, the Inter Cities Fairs Cup (renamed the UEFA Cup in 1971) was established and was open to European cities which had hosted trade fairs. If a city had more than one club, then it had to send a representative side.

The first tournament, which kicked off in 1955, had representatives from Barcelona, Basle, Birmingham, Copenhagen, Frankfurt, Lausanne, Leipzig, London, Milan and Zagreb. The first final – which was not held until 1958 – was between London and Barcelona. A 2–2 draw at Stamford Bridge was followed by a comprehensive 6–0 win by Barcelona at the Nou Camp, Luis Suarez and Evaristo both scoring twice. The second tournament, now comprising 16 clubs, was held over 1958–60 and was again won by Barcelona, who beat Birmingham 4–1 on aggregate, Zoltan Czibor scoring twice.

With the competition now held on an annual basis, Birmingham reached the final again in 1961, losing to Roma. For the 1961–62 tournament, UEFA decided to allow three teams to enter from each country. Valencia won the following two competitions but it was another Spanish side, Real Zaragoza, who claimed victory in 1964, beating Valencia 2–1 in a one-off final. The last single-leg final until 1998 was in 1965, when Ferencvaros eliminated the likes of Atletico Bilbao and Manchester United en route to beating Juventus 1–0 in Turin.

Although Barcelona won again the following year in an all-Spanish final, beating Real Zaragoza 4–3 (Pujol scoring three in the away leg for Barca), no Spanish club would reach the final for almost another 20 years. An emergent Leeds were about to spearhead the dominance of English clubs in the tournament.

Although Don Revie's side were beaten 2–0 by Dynamo Zagreb in 1967, they won the following year thanks to a Mick Jones goal against Ferencvaros in the home leg at Elland Road, having gone through the competition unbeaten.

Newcastle maintained English supremacy in 1969 with a 6–2 final win over Ujpest Dozsa, three of the Geordies' goals coming from Bobby Moncur. In 1970, Arsenal magnificently overturned a 3–1 defeat in Brussels by beating Anderlecht 3–0 at Highbury, the winner coming from Jon Sammels.

Leeds were back in 1971 to play Juventus, having beaten Liverpool over two games in the semi-final. The first game was abandoned after 55 minutes because of rain in Turin but they forced a 2–2 draw in the replay, with goals from Paul Madeley and substitute Mick Bates. A 1–1 result at Elland Road gave a resolute Leeds the trophy on away goals.

Now formally known as the UEFA Cup, the 1972 competition saw the first all-English final, between Tottenham Hotspur and Wolves. Martin Chivers scored two breakaway goals in the first leg at Molineux, finishing 2–1, and an Alan Mullery header at White Hart Lane was equalled by a David Wagstaffe strike. Spurs held on to win 3–2 on aggregate and become the first English club to have won two European titles (the first being their 1963 Cup-Winners' Cup).

It was Liverpool's turn the following season, when two goals from Kevin Keegan and one from Larry Lloyd gave them a 3–0 first-leg lead at Anfield against Borussia Monchengladbach. Two goals from Juup Heynckes in Monchengladbach were not enough to prevent Liverpool lifting the trophy.

Tottenham were beaten 4–2 on aggregate by Feyenoord in the 1974 final, with their fans running riot in Rotterdam. Seventy Spurs fans were arrested and over 200 people injured.

Small Dutch club Twente Enschede faced Borussia Monchengladbach in 1975 and, although they surprisingly drew 0–0 in Germany, they were overwhelmed 5–1 in Holland, Heynckes scoring a hat trick and Alan Simonsen claiming two.

Liverpool had eliminated mighty Barcelona 2–1 on their way to the 1976 final against Club Brugge. In the first leg at Anfield, Brugge were 2–0 ahead after 20 minutes, until two goals from Ray Kennedy and a

Keegan penalty gave Liverpool a 3–2 advantage. In the away leg, Brugge took another early lead, giving them the advantage on away goals, but Keegan bent a free kick into the net. Liverpool retreated into defence and required a great save from Ray Clemence at the last to win the title.

The next four UEFA Cups remained on the European continent: Juventus winning on away goals against Atletico Bilbao in 1977; PSV Eindhoven beating France's Bastia in 1978; victory for Borussia Monchengladbach again against Red Star Belgrade, thanks to a penalty and an own goal in 1979; and Borussia appearing again against Eintracht Frankfurt in 1980 but losing on away goals.

The English were back in 1981. Bobby Robson's Ipswich side knocked out Cologne and Saint-Etienne before beating AZ67 Alkmaar 5–4 in the final, with John Wark and Frans Thijssen both scoring twice, bringing Wark's goal tally in that year's competition to 14.

IFK Gothenburg became the first Swedish side to win a European trophy in 1982, beating Hamburg 4–0, and the Swedes won again in 1987 when they defeated Dundee United, the first Scottish side to reach the UEFA Cup final. United had defeated Barcelona 2–1 at the Nou Camp and Borussia Monchengladbach 2–0 to get there but lost 2–1 to Gothenburg.

Anderlecht beat Benfica 2–1 in 1983 and reached the final again in 1984 against Tottenham. The two legs ended 2–2 after extra time and Spurs won the penalty shootout at White Hart Lane, helped by two brilliant saves from reserve keeper Tony Parks.

Real Madrid won in 1985 and 1986, 3–1 against Videoton and 5–3 over Cologne. The cup returned to Germany in 1988, when Bayer Leverkusen beat Espanol on penalties, but for the next seven years the trophy remained in Italy – Juventus and Inter both winning twice – with the exception of 1992 when Ajax beat Torino.

Germany then reclaimed the cup in 1996 and 1997, through Bayern Munich and Schalke, but the following year, in a re-introduced single leg final, goals from Zamorano, Zanetti and Ronaldo gave Inter a 3–0 win over Lazio in an all-Italian final. The trophy remained in Serie A in 1999 when Parma beat an under-strength Marseille 3–0, helped by two errors from Laurent Blanc in a snowy Moscow.

The Cup-Winners' Cup was abandoned from season 1999–2000, and domestic cup winners now qualified for the increasingly expanding tournament. Also, qualification was awarded to the clubs eliminated from the third qualifying round of the Champions League and the eight third-placed finishers in the same competition's group stage.

That season, another British club – Arsenal – won through to the final, having been eliminated from the Champions League. Their run in the tournament included a magnificent 5–1 defeat of Deportivo La Coruna at Highbury and a Ray Parlour hat trick in the 4–2 win against Werder Bremen in Germany. They met a Gheorghe Hagi-led Galatasaray in Copenhagen in the final, against a backdrop of street battles between opposing fans. The game was goalless at the end of normal time and, although Hagi was sent off early in extra time, the Gunners could still not score. In the shootout, both Davor Suker and Patrick Vieira missed, and Gheorghe Popescu's successful kick gave the trophy to the Turkish side.

Liverpool went one better the following season. Small Spanish club Alaves had fought their way to the final, beating Inter Milan 5–3 on aggregate and Kaiserslautern 9–2 in their impressive route to meeting the Merseysiders. In a spirited game of attacking football, the score was 4–4 at the end of normal time, Alaves' Jordi Cruyff heading in the equaliser with one minute remaining. Two Alaves players were sent off in extra time and the game was won by a golden goal when Gary McAllister's shot was deflected into his own net by Delfi Geli. Liverpool became the first English club to win the FA Cup, League Cup and UEFA Cup in the same season.

In 2002, two goals from Pierre van Hooijdonk helped Feyenoord to a 3–2 win over Borussia Dortmund in another exciting final. Borussia's cause was not helped by the sending-off of Jurgen Kohler on the half-hour mark.

Season 2002–03 was Celtic's turn to reach the final. Having defeated Blackburn 3–0 and proceeding on away goals against Celta Vigo and Stuttgart, they beat Liverpool 3–1 in the 'Battle of Britain' quarter-final. A soporific semi-final victory over Boavista in Portugal, Larsson scoring the winner with ten minutes left, set them against Porto in the final in Seville. Celtic twice came from behind, both through Larsson, to leave the score 2–2 at the end of normal time against Porto, inspired by the skills of Deco. A valiant performance by Celtic ended in defeat when Derlei scored the 'silver goal' winner in the 115th minute but the Bhoys could hold their heads up after a magnificent run in the competition.

The 2004 final was held in Gothenburg between Valencia and

Marseille. French keeper Fabien Barthez was sent off on the interval for fouling Mista, Vicente scoring from the penalty. Mista scored another in the second half as the Spaniards claimed the trophy with a 2–0 victory.

This ever-expanding competition changed format again in 2004–05 when, after two qualifying rounds, 80 clubs played in the first round proper. The winning 40 then moved into eight groups of five teams each, both playing two home and two away matches. The top three from each group then joined the eight third-placed clubs in the Champions League to contest a 32-club, home-and-away knockout tournament.

Critics of the competition complain that the format is now too unwieldy and all-embracing, and that having so many teams devalues the tournament. However, for smaller clubs without the resources to compete in the Champions League against the likes of Real Madrid and Milan, the UEFA Cup remains their only real chance of fame and riches in Europe.

CSKA Moscow won the trophy in 2005, coming from behind to beat Sporting Lisbon 3–1 in their own Alvalade Stadium. Rogerio gave Sporting a 29th-minute lead but they wasted a series of chances. CSKA replied with second-half goals from Aleksei Berezoutski, Yuri Zhirkov and Brazilian striker Vagner Love.

THE STORY OF THE CUP-WINNERS' CUP

As a result of the success of the European Cup, UEFA inaugurated the European Cup-Winners' Cup competition at the start of season 1960–61. The competition was open to Europe's domestic cup winners but, as many countries did not have knockout cup competitions, the initial field comprised clubs from only ten countries.

Rangers, who had been embarrassingly beaten 12–4 by Eintracht Frankfurt in the previous year's European Cup semi-finals, reached the semi-final after a narrow 5–4 win over Ferencvaros and an 11–0 trouncing of Borussia Monchengladbach.

In the semi-final, the Gers beat Wolves 2–0 at Ibrox and held on to a 1–1 draw at Molineux, to reach the final. In the only two-leg final in the competition's history, they met Fiorentina at Ibrox and went down 2–0, both goals coming from Aurelio Milani. In Italy, Milani put Fiorentina further ahead early on and, although right-winger Alec Scott equalised, Fiorentina's Kurt Hamrin scored near the end for a 4–1 aggregate win for the Italian side.

As was the case with the European Cup, the success of the first competition attracted more entries – 23 – for the 1961–62 tournament. Fiorentina again reached the final, drawing 1–1 with Atletico Madrid but losing the replay 3–0 four months later.

In 1963, Tottenham Hotspur became the first British team to win a European trophy. Managed by Billy Nicholson and led by inspirational captain Danny Blanchflower, Spurs had beaten Rangers 8–4 on their way to the final in Rotterdam against holders Atletico Madrid. Without influential Scottish wing-half Dave Mackay in the side, Spurs were nonetheless 2–0 ahead at half-time through striker Jimmy Greaves and inside-forward John White. Atletico scored a penalty early in the second half but little left-winger Terry Dyson lobbed the Spanish keeper for Spurs' third 20 minutes later. Greaves added another, and Dyson wrapped it up near the end with a virtuoso run and 25-yard shot for a final score of 5–1 to Spurs and a great deal of rejoicing down Tottenham High Road.

The trophy moved to Portugal in 1964, when Sporting Lisbon beat MTK Budapest 1–0 in a replay, but came back to Britain in 1965. West Ham, skippered by Bobby Moore, eliminated Ghent, Sparta Prague, Lausanne and Real Zaragoza on their way to the final at Wembley against Munich 1860. Without regular forwards Johnny Byrne and Peter Brabrook, West Ham fielded young Martin Peters and reserve winger Alan Sealey. Two goals in two minutes midway through the second half from Sealey decided the game, and West Ham, with a 2–0 victory, collected their only European trophy.

Britain was again represented in the 1966 final, when Liverpool, who had knocked out Juventus, Standard Liege and Honved, met Celtic in the semi-final. One–nil down after the first leg at Parkhead, Liverpool equalised at Anfield through a Tommy Smith free kick and qualified for the final with a Geoff Strong header. Siggi Held put Borussia Dortmund ahead in the final at Hampden but Roger Hunt levelled the score. The game went into extra time, and winger 'Stan' Libuda's 40-yard shot won the trophy for the Germans.

Scotland were represented in the 1967 final, with Rangers facing Bayern Munich in Nuremberg. Still suffering from their first-round Scottish Cup shock exit at the hands of lowly Berwick Rangers, a nervy performance from the Gers, with a makeshift forward line, allowed Bayern to score the only goal of the match, through Franz Roth in extra time.

Two goals from Kurt Hamrin gave Milan a 2–0 win over Hamburg the following year, and Slovan Bratislava became the first eastern European winners of the competition in 1969, beating favourites Barcelona 3–2 in the final.

For the next three seasons, the cup was in British hands. In 1970, Manchester City met Gornik in the final in Vienna, and goals from Neil Young and Francis Lee gave City victory, despite a Gornik late strike.

In 1971, Chelsea beat Manchester City 2–0 to reach the final against

Real Madrid in Athens. Centre-forward Peter Osgood gave Chelsea the lead but Zoco equalised and Chelsea were lucky to hang on for a draw. In the replay two days later, John Dempsey fired Chelsea ahead and then Osgood extended the scoreline. Real pulled a goal back but the final result was 2–1 in Chelsea's favour.

Rangers were back in the final in 1972, facing Dynamo Moscow in Barcelona. Early in the second half, Rangers were 3–0 ahead through two goals from the prolific Colin Stein and one from winger Willie Johnston, and although Dynamo replied twice, Rangers held on for a 3–2 victory. The success was marred by a series of crowd invasions by their fans during the match, and by a pitched battle after the game with the Spanish police, with over 150 injured and one person killed. 'The Battle of Barcelona' led to Rangers being barred from Europe by UEFA for a season.

Don Revie's Leeds were the fourth British club in a row to reach the final when they met Milan in 1973 in Salonika. Luciano Chiarugi gave Milan the lead in the fourth minute from a free kick and although Leeds outplayed the Italian side, a combination of dubious refereeing, cynical Italian defending and inspired goalkeeping kept the score at 1–0.

The following two seasons, the trophy remained behind the Iron Curtain, with Magdeburg defeating Milan 2–0 and then Dynamo Kiev beating Ferencvaros 3–0. West Ham reached the final for the second time in 1976 but despite equalising twice, they went down 4–2 to Anderlecht, two of the goals coming from Rob Rensenbrink. On-form Anderlecht were in the next two finals, losing 2–0 in 1977 to Hamburg but winning again in 1978, 4–0 against FK Austria in Paris.

Barcelona and Fortuna Dusseldorf served up seven goals in the 1979 final, the winner coming from Barca striker Hans Krankl in extra time.

Arsenal lined up against Valencia, managed by Alfredo Di Stefano, in Brussels in the 1980 final. In spite of the presence of Argentinian striker and World Cup winner Mario Kempes in the Spanish side, the game was a tense one and remained goalless after extra time. Kempes took the first penalty and missed. Liam Brady missed the next. With the score 5–4, Arsenal's Graham Rix had to score. The keeper saved, Rix was devastated and Arsenal had lost.

The 1981 winners were Dinamo Tbilisi, defeating Carl Zeiss Jena 2–1, while Barcelona claimed their second victory in four years the following season with a 2–1 win over Standard Liege. Alex Ferguson's Aberdeen had recently been rivalling the Old Firm for mastery in

Scotland, and they met Real Madrid in the 1983 final in Gothenburg, having earlier dismissed Bayern Munich 3–2 and losing only one game in the competition. In the pouring rain, in front of a small crowd, Aberdeen went ahead in the seventh minute when Eric Black hammered in a goal but Juanito levelled from the penalty spot. With eight minutes remaining of extra time, John Hewitt headed in Aberdeen's winner, only the third time a Scottish club had won a European trophy.

Juventus won the tournament for the first time in 1984, with Polish star Zbigniew Boniek scoring the winner in the 2–1 defeat of Porto. The following season, a 3–1 semi-final home win over Bayern Munich saw Everton face Rapid Vienna in the final in Rotterdam. Goals from Andy Gray, Trevor Steven and Kevin Sheedy secured the trophy for the Merseysiders in the 3–1 defeat of the Austrians. English clubs were now banned from the tournament, post-Heysel, and Dynamo Kiev emphatically beat Atletico Madrid 3–0 in 1986. A Marco van Basten goal gave victory to Ajax over Lokomotiv Leipzig in 1987, while Ajax surprisingly lost 1–0 to Belgian underdogs Mechelen in 1988. Barcelona won for the third time in 1989, defeating Sampdoria 2–0, but Sampdoria triumphed in 1990, when two extra-time goals from Gianluca Vialli gave the Italian side a 2–0 win over Anderlecht.

English clubs were now back in Europe, and Manchester United celebrated their reappearance by reaching the 1991 final against Barcelona in Rotterdam. Mark Hughes, who had been regarded as a failure when he played for Barcelona, tapped in the opening goal from a Steve Bruce header and also scored the second, smashing the ball into the net from a tight angle. A Ronald Koeman free kick in the 89th minute reduced the deficit but United held on to win 2–1 and claim their, and manager Alex Ferguson's, second European trophy.

Werder Bremen won their only European trophy in 1992 with a 2–0 defeat of Monaco and the following season newly emerged top Italian side Parma claimed the title, beating Antwerp 3–1.

George Graham's Arsenal were back in the tournament in 1994, and defeated Standard Liege, Torino and Paris Saint-Germain to meet Parma in the final. With star striker Ian Wright suspended, Arsenal's Alan Smith latched on to a poor overhead clearance in the 20th minute and volleyed the ball into the net with his left foot. Arsenal defended their lead doggedly and held onto their advantage until the final whistle.

The next season, Arsenal were back in the final. A late semi-final goal from Gunners' Swedish midfielder Stefan Schwarz had forced a 5–5 aggregate result against Sampdoria after extra time. David Seaman heroically saved a penalty from Attillio Lombardo in the shootout to ensure the Gunners' presence in the final.

They faced Real Zaragoza in Paris, and Real's Argentine striker Juan Esnaider opened the scoring in the 75th minute with a left-foot volley. Five minutes later, John Hartson equalised. With only seconds of extra time remaining, Nayim spotted Seaman off his line and lofted the ball towards the Arsenal goal from 50 yards. A frantically back-pedalling Seaman could not stop the ball falling into the net and Zaragoza won 2–1 in the most dramatic fashion.

In 1996, Paris Saint-Germain eliminated Celtic, Parma and Deportivo La Coruna on their way to the final, where a 28th-minute goal from defender Bruno N'Gotty gave them a 1–0 win over Rapid Vienna. In 1997, a penalty goal from Ronaldo was the only score as Barcelona beat PSG in Rotterdam in the final.

New Chelsea manager Gianluca Vialli guided his club to the final in 1998 against Stuttgart, and Gianfranco Zola scored a beautiful goal within seconds of coming on as a substitute to give Chelsea a 1–0 victory.

The last ever European Cup-Winners' Cup final was held at Villa Park, Birmingham, in May 1999, when Lazio beat Real Mallorca 2–1. Christian Vieri scored for Lazio in the seventh minute, with Mallorca's Dani levelling four minutes later. Ten minutes from time Pavel Nedved scored Lazio's winner. The final whistle went and the competition which had provided some of the most exciting and attractive football in European history was no more.

EUROPE UNITES: THE EUROPEAN CHAMPIONSHIP 1958–68

Designed to bring together the various smaller, regional international tournaments – such as the British Home Championship, the Mitropa Cup and the Nordic Cup – the European Championship was proposed in the mid-1950s by Henri Delaunay, secretary of the French football federation. Delaunay died before the tournament proper began, but the trophy still bears his name. Although a competition of this nature had been talked about for years, the tournament only got off the ground in 1958, when invitations were sent out to the 33 European national football associations.

The tournament was to be organised on a straight home-and-away knockout basis, with the semi-finals and final taking place in one country. Many nations – including the British countries, West Germany, Italy and Sweden – declined to enter, as they were not convinced of the potential of the competition, or the need for it. Indeed, the invitation was accepted by fewer than 16 countries, and frantic behind-the-scenes negotiations were required in order to make the tournament at all viable. In the event, 17 finally entered. The contenders for what was then called the European Nations Cup were whittled down to the necessary 16 when Czechoslovakia defeated the Republic of Ireland 4–2 on aggregate in a qualifying round.

Triumph for the Soviet Union (1958–60)

The first game was between the USSR and Hungary, at Moscow's recently completed Central Stadium. The vast crowd of over 100,000 must have gladdened the organisers' hearts. Hungary, not the all-conquering side they had been a few years previously, and missing the 'defectors' Puskas, Kocsis and Czibor, found themselves 3–0 down by half-time to a rampaging Soviet side, led by Torpedo Moscow striker Valentin Ivanov. Hungary pulled one back in the second half. In the second leg – almost a year later – 78,000 spectators in Budapest saw Soviet captain Yuriy Voinov claim another goal to eliminate the Hungarians.

France – still basking in their high-scoring third place in the 1958 World Cup finals – knocked out Greece, then ran up a 9–4 aggregate win over Austria to reach the semi-finals. Czechoslovakia, led by Dukla Prague captain and legendary midfielder Josef Masopust, had easy wins over Denmark and Romania to reach the semis. Yugoslavia joined them after a narrow win over Bulgaria and a 5–1 home defeat of Portugal. The fourth semi-finalists, the Soviet Union, had been due to play Spain. The dictator Francisco Franco, remembering Russian participation on the Republican side in the Spanish Civil War, refused to allow Spain to travel to Moscow. So the Soviets had a walkover into the last four.

Both semis took place on 6 July 1960. In Paris, France, missing the injured Raymond Kopa and Just Fontaine, were 4–2 ahead of Yugoslavia midway through the second half. But, inspired by two late goals from Croatian striker Drazen Jerkovic, the Yugoslavs won 5–4 to reach the final and knock out the home side. Meanwhile in Marseilles an unlucky Czech side succumbed to two goals from Ivanov in a 3–0 defeat. The Soviets were saved on numerous occasions by the brilliance of their famed keeper Lev Yashin, 'the black spider'.

The final was played on 10 July at the Parc des Princes in front of a disappointing 18,000 crowd. Yugoslavia went on the attack and were 1–0 ahead just before half-time, through a header from Partizan Belgrade centre-forward Milan Galic – his tenth goal in consecutive internationals. Without Yashin's heroics, the score would again have been higher.

In the second half, the roles were reversed with the Soviets taking the game to the Yugoslavs. Winger Slava Metreveli equalised, and the match went into extra time. The Soviets continued to press and scored again through Viktor Ponedelnik in the 113th minute. Yugoslavia could not respond and the first Henri Delaunay trophy went to the USSR, who, to a degree, had General Franco as much as Yashin to thank for their relatively easy progress in the competition.

Spain Reign at Home (1962–64)

The interest aroused across Europe in the first tournament led to an entry of 29 countries for the 1962–64 competition, with the semi-finals and final to be held in Spain. Only West Germany, Scotland, Finland and Cyprus stayed at home.

With no seeding yet in place, the first round drew England against France and the French travelled to Sheffield in October 1962. A Raymond Kopa-inspired first half saw France take the lead, and their fluid 4–2–4 formation bamboozled the English defence with its rigid man-marking system. Wolves' Ron Flowers equalised from the penalty spot, much against the run of play, to give England a fortunate 1–1 draw. An unfit Ron Springett was in goal for England in the second match and his errors helped France to secure a 5–2 victory and send England and Alf Ramsey back to the drawing board to prepare for the 1966 World Cup finals.

Greece had been drawn against Albania, with whom they had been technically at war since 1912. The Greeks refused to play, allowing Albania the nod through to the second round.

The biggest shock of the round was Northern Ireland's 2–0 win in Poland, and they showed it was no fluke by winning 2–0 again at home, the goals coming from Johnny Crossan and Billy Bingham.

Another shock was the elimination of Czechoslovakia by East Germany. The Czechs were beaten 2–1 in East Germany. In the return in Prague in March 1963, the Czech attack pounded the German defence throughout the match. They finally scored in the second half but Carl Zeiss Jena midfielder Roland Ducke equalised near the end. The Czechs were out.

The big game of the second round featured Italy against the Soviet Union. In an ill-tempered game in Moscow in October 1963 – with at one time only nine Italians on the pitch – the Soviets achieved a 2–0 win. In Italy, Yashin was again their hero, deflecting and absorbing the Italian attacks, and the Soviets went ahead through Gusarov. In the second half, Yashin saved a weak Sandro Mazzola penalty, although young Milan inside-forward Gianni Rivera equalised in the final minute. Too little too late for Italy.

A huge upset occurred when Holland (who normally sent their reserve side to play the Duchy) were beaten 3–2 on aggregate by minnows Luxembourg. Denmark, France, Hungary, Spain and Sweden, the last with a hard-fought 3–2 win over the previous runners-up Yugoslavia, progressed safely to the quarter-finals.

Plucky Luxembourg took Denmark to a play-off in Amsterdam after two draws, 3–3 and 1–1. Denmark eliminated the Duchy through Ole Madsen, who had scored all their previous four goals in the clash. Spain and Hungary eased their way through to the semis against, respectively, the Republic of Ireland and France, while the Soviet Union required two late goals, from Ivanov and Voronin, to beat Sweden 4–2 on aggregate.

With national pride at stake – and the chance of a European title – Franco allowed the Soviets to travel to Spain for the finals. The first semi-final – between the USSR and Denmark – was held in Barcelona, where goals from Voronin, Ponedelnik and Ivanov gave the USSR an easy victory over the Danish amateurs. The other semi-final was between Spain and Hungary, the countries' first meeting for 38 years, in Madrid.

Spain's neat, speedy play upset the more ponderous Hungarians, although charismatic Ferencvaros centre-forward Florian Albert had the first real shot of the game. Jesus Maria Pereda headed Spain in front late in the first half but striker Ferenc Bene levelled the score with five minutes remaining. Real Madrid winger Amancio ensured Spain's place in the final with an extra-time goal.

The final, in front of around 100,000 at Madrid's Bernabeu stadium, was attended by Franco, who must have winced at the prospect of seeing the trophy being presented to the Soviet communists. Spain took a sixth-minute lead when Pereda neatly converted a pass from Luis Suarez, Internazionale playmaker and man of the match. A minute later, Spanish keeper Jose Angel Iribar fluffed a hopeful shot from Galmizyan Khusainov to level the score. The heavens then opened and, in the slippery conditions, the game deteriorated in quality, although both Iribar and Yashin produced excellent saves.

With six minutes remaining, Pereda crossed for Marcelino Martinez to score the winner from a diving header. Jose Villalonga's Spain celebrated their first and, to date, only international trophy, while for the Soviet Union it was their first defeat in the European Nations Championship. Franco could permit himself a smile of triumph.

Italy Win Final Replay (1968)

Before the 1966–68 tournament, the competition's name was formally changed by UEFA to 'the European Championship' and the knockout system was abandoned and replaced by one of groups, which for the first time would be seeded in the early stages. With 31 countries entered, eight groups were formed, with the eight winners playing home-and-away leg ties. One group comprised the four home countries – Scotland, England, Wales and Northern Ireland. The semi-finals and final would be held in Italy.

The first group was seen as a straight fight between Spain and Czechoslovakia, with Turkey and the Republic of Ireland the makeweights. Czechoslovakia met Spain in Prague, winning 1–0 after Iribar failed to hold a simple shot from Horvath. Three weeks later, they met again in Madrid. Young forwards Jose Pirri and Atletico's Jose Garate both scored in the first half, with Garate picking up another in the second period. The Czechs came back through Ladislav Kuna but they were beaten 3–1.

After a goalless match against Turkey, they faced the Irish in Prague needing only one point to qualify over Spain. Perhaps feeling over-confident, Czechoslovakia strolled through the first half and were handed an own goal in the 15th minute of the second half. With 20 minutes left, Ray Treacy headed in an Eamon Dunphy cross and, with Czechoslovakia down to ten men, Ireland scored another. The team of essentially English lower division players held on to win 2–1, thereby enabling Spain to qualify at the last moment.

Eusebio's Portugal, third-placed in the 1966 World Cup, were expected to qualify from Group Two but a home defeat by Sweden and a draw against Norway meant they had to beat Bulgaria twice in order to qualify. A 1–0 win in Sofia saw Bulgaria go through.

In the third group, the Soviet Union easily qualified despite two defeats by Austria. With only three teams in Group Four, West Germany seemed certain to qualify over Yugoslavia and Albania, until their 0–0 draw in Tirana against a defensively-minded Albania enabled Yugoslavia to go through.

In Group Five, Hungary had to beat East Germany in Budapest to proceed in the tournament. A sparkling display from the Magyars, and a hat trick from Janos Farkas, guaranteed them a quarter-final place.

After a humiliating exit in the World Cup, Italy cruised through Group Six, clinching qualification with a 4–0 defeat of Romania in Bucharest.

Group Seven was a tighter affair. In the last game of the group, France had to draw at home with Luxembourg to qualify ahead of Poland and Belgium, and a Loubet hat trick squeezed the French through.

The eighth group was decided at Hampden Park, Glasgow, in February 1968, watched by the highest-ever attendance at a European Championship tie: 130,711. Although Scotland had thrillingly beaten World Champions England 3–2 at Wembley in April 1967, the Scots had faltered in Belfast and needed a victory at Hampden to qualify. Without the architects of the April game, Denis Law and Jim Baxter, Scotland could only draw 1–1, in spite of a virtuoso display by Chelsea's Charlie Cooke. England were through.

England reached the semi-finals with two wins over Spain, 1–0 at Wembley and 2–1 (the scorers being Martin Peters and Norman Hunter) in Madrid.

Three–two down after their visit to Sofia, Italy met Bulgaria again in Naples. A cracking shot from Milan's Pierino Prati in the 14th minute and a rocket from Angelo Domenghini in the second half secured Italy's place in the semis.

In the third quarter-final, Yugoslavia atoned for a 1–1 draw in Marseilles to go 4–0 ahead after 30 minutes in Belgrade, finishing the game 5–1 victors. In the final game, Hungary travelled to Moscow carrying a 2–0 lead but three goals from the Soviets without reply ended their interest in the tournament.

Both semi-finals took place on 5 June 1968. In Naples, the Soviet Union contained the Italian forwards for a scrappy goalless draw after extra time. The result was decided by the toss of a coin. Captain Giacinto Facchetti had to come out of the dressing-room to inform the fans that Italy had guessed correctly.

Geoff Hurst and Nobby Stiles – two of England's World Cup heroes – had been omitted from the line-up against Yugoslavia in Florence. The lively Yugoslavs had England on the back foot for most of the match – an intimidating affair with 49 fouls recorded. Alan Mullery became the first Englishman ever to be sent off in an international when he retaliated against Yugoslavia's Dobrivoje Trivic. In the closing minutes, Red Star Belgrade left-winger Dragan Dzajic, regarded as the country's greatest-ever player, sealed the game for Yugoslavia for a 1–0 win.

The final was played in Rome on 8 June. Yugoslavia tore into Italy's defence from the kick-off, and the bewildered Italians, without the presence of playmaker Rivera and creative forward Mazzola, were in tatters. Dzajic was in spellbinding form and scored in the 40th minute. The acrobatics of keeper Dino Zoff were all that kept Italy in the game. With nine minutes to go, Domenghini scored from a free kick while the Yugoslav wall was still being organised and the referee allowed the goal to stand. The game went into extra time. There were no more goals.

Mazzola was back for the replay against the tired Yugoslavs and Italy took the initiative. Luigi Riva, also back in the side, scored within the first 20 minutes and then Pietro Anastasi added another and the game petered out, Yugoslavia seemingly content to allow Italy victory. A 2–0 score was the inevitable result and Italian captain Facchetti collected the Henri Delaunay trophy on behalf of a somewhat fortunate Italian team.

WEST GERMANY SET THE STANDARD: THE EUROPEAN CHAMPIONSHIP 1970-92

The previous three tournaments had revealed the footballing excellence of a number of European nations but, until now, no one country had clearly and emphatically dominated the competition. This was to change in 1970–72 with the appearance of West Germany and, in particular, the artistry and technical excellence of Bayern Munich captain and sweeper Franz Beckenbauer, Borussia Monchengladbach playmaker Gunter Netzer and stocky little Bayern striker Gerd Muller. West Germany were developing into Europe's top team and had given clear notice of their winning potential in the 1970 World Cup where they were eliminated by Italy in the semi-finals. This European Championship was to reveal them at their imperious best.

Again, there were eight qualifying groups, with four teams in each, and the knockouts began at the quarter-finals. For this tournament, the home countries were dispersed across four groups. In the first group, Czechoslovakia and Romania slugged it out for qualification. With two games remaining, Romania had to win both to qualify, as they had an inferior goal difference to Czechoslovakia. They first beat the Czechs 2–1 in Bucharest, with 100,000 watching, and a 2–0 defeat of Wales saw them through to the last eight.

The leadership of Group Two oscillated between Hungary, France and Bulgaria but, with Hungary's games finished, France and Bulgaria had to overhaul each other twice to beat Hungary. Neither side could do this, and Hungary went through.

Group Three appeared a stroll for England but Switzerland proved a surprise obstacle. A 3–2 win in Basle for England, an own-goal clinching victory, moved them to the top of the table. At Wembley, Switzerland gave England a fright, causing all sorts of problems in the home defence and opening the scoring, but Mike Summerbee's equaliser all but mathematically ensured a quarter-final place. A 2–0 defeat of Greece made sure. The Soviet Union finished top of Group Four, taking three points off rivals Spain.

In the fifth group, Scotland's victories over Belgium and Portugal in Glasgow ensured that the final match between Belgium and Portugal (in Portugal) was the qualifying decider. Ageing Benfica forwards Eusebio and Jose Torres were back in the Portuguese side, who had to win by three goals. Belgium went ahead early in the second half when a pass from Anderlecht star Paul van Himst was turned into the net by Brugge centre-forward Raoul Lambert but, although Portugal equalised with a penalty, Belgium qualified. With one game remaining, Italy had secured qualification in Group Six, having defeated Austria and the Republic of Ireland twice and drawn with Sweden. In Group Seven, Yugoslavia drew 0–0 with East Germany in their penultimate game to qualify, although they could only achieve a goalless draw with Luxembourg in the last, albeit meaningless, match.

In Group Eight, West Germany, who should have strolled through against Albania, Poland and Turkey, faltered in their first match, with Muller levelling for a 1–1 draw against Turkey in Cologne. In the return game in Istanbul, Muller scored twice and West Germany turned on the style, with Horst Koppel grabbing a third. In Poland, the Germans were kept in the game through the brilliance of keeper Sepp Maier but Muller claimed another two, and powerful Frankfurt winger Jurgen Grabowski a third in the 3–1 win. A dour 0–0 draw ensured the Germans' place in the last eight.

All the quarter-finals kicked off on 29 April 1972. West Germany travelled to Wembley for an eagerly anticipated match and the Germans took immediate control, with Beckenbauer and the vision of Netzer inspiring five-man attacks against an outclassed England. Bayern's Uli Hoeness opened the scoring in the first half and, although Francis Lee made it 1–1 after the interval, Netzer scored another from the penalty spot. A goal from Muller sealed a 3–1 win for West Germany.

In the return at the Olympic Stadium, Beckenbauer again superbly controlled his defence, and an inept England could not find a way through. A tedious game ended 0–0.

Belgium defended well against Italy and came away with a 0–0 draw. In the Parc Astrid in Brussels, Wilfried van Moer put Belgium ahead midway through the first half, only to have his leg broken by a vicious Mario Bertini tackle in the 45th minute. In spite of an increasingly brutal performance from the Italians, van Himst increased Belgium's lead with 20 minutes remaining. Italy scored a penalty through Luigi Riva but Belgium advanced to the semi-finals.

In the other two ties, the Soviet Union beat Yugoslavia 3–0 while Romania scored in the 83rd minute at home against Hungary to take the game to a play-off in Belgrade, where Hungary triumphed 2–1.

Belgium was selected as the venue for the semi-finals and final. In front of a tiny crowd, the USSR opened the scoring against Hungary in the 52nd minute with a deflection from an Anatoli Konkov shot. Near the end, Hungary missed a penalty and the Soviets moved into their third final in four competitions.

In the second semi-final, Belgium played West Germany in Antwerp, the home crowd dwarfed by the German support. In the 20th minute, a beautifully flighted pass from Netzer was finished by Muller with the Belgian keeper Christian Piot rooted to the spot. Belgium then pushed forward but keeper Maier was equal to their shots, making a number of excellent saves. Muller scored Germany's second from another Netzer pass and, although Odilon Polleunis scored past an unsighted Maier, Germany won 2–1.

The final at the Heysel Stadium in Brussels was a one-sided affair. Yet again Beckenbauer and Netzer controlled the game, with Germany launching attack after attack against the Russian defence, saved only by the agility of Evgeni Rudakov in the Russian goal. At one point, the Germans strung together 30 consecutive passes.

On half-time, Muller breached the defence, chesting down a cross and slipping the ball past Rudakov. In the second half, midfielder Herbert Wimmer scored another, torpedoing the ball into the roof of the net. Five minutes later, Muller added a third, sending Rudakov the wrong way. The game ended 3–0 and West Germany had proven themselves by some distance the best team in Europe. Two years later they were to claim the title of best team in the world by defeating Holland in the final of the World Cup. And it was little surprise that

Beckenbauer, Netzer and Muller won the top three places in 1972's European Footballer of the Year poll.

The Underdogs Have Their Day (1974–76)

The 1974 World Cup final had been played between West Germany and Holland. Both countries were in this championship, along with another four countries in the last eight of the World Cup, making it one of the strongest competitions yet. Under the guiding genius of Johan Cruyff, Holland had players of the calibre of visionary yet hard-tackling Johan Neeskens, defender Ruud Krol, and forwards Johnny Rep and winger Rob Rensenbrink. They were expected to shine in the tournament.

Curiously, one of the strongest groups was Group One – England, Czechoslovakia, Cyprus and Portugal – none of whom had qualified for the World Cup finals. Don Revie's England started brightly, beating Czechoslovakia 3–0 at Wembley and then Cyprus 5–0 (all coming from Malcolm 'Supermac' Macdonald). However, they stumbled at home to Portugal, whose packed midfield denied an aimless England a goal, and then lost 2–1 to the Czechs.

Czechoslovakia, who had thrashed Portugal 5–0, beat an increasingly inept England 2–1 in Bratislava, despite Mick Channon's opening goal. England then required a win over Portugal to have any chance of qualification but could only draw 1–1. An easy 3–0 stroll over Cyprus saw Czechoslovakia through and England out.

Wales, with their powerful centre-forward John Toshack and imposing midfielder Terry Yorath, were the surprise qualifiers from Group Two, with two wins over Hungary and Luxembourg. Their first-ever qualification was ensured in their last game against Austria at Wrexham, when local favourite Arfon Griffiths scored the only goal of the match.

In Group Three, favourites Yugoslavia duly qualified, with victories over Sweden, Norway and Northern Ireland. In the last game, Northern Ireland needed to win by two clear goals in Yugoslavia. Branko Oblak scored the only goal of the game, and Pat Jennings had to produce a superb display of goalkeeping to prevent an embarrassing result.

Spain – attempting to atone for their elimination from the World Cup qualifiers by Yugoslavia – were favourites to win Group Four and began with two away victories against Denmark and Scotland. However, the Scots, as was often their custom in away matches, scored in the first minute in Valencia and outplayed the Spanish – until a scrambled 67th minute goal saved Spain's blushes. With Scotland defeating Denmark 3–1, their chance of qualification depended on Romania defeating Spain in Bucharest in their last game. A 2–2 draw meant that Spain qualified.

Group Five was unquestionably the toughest group, containing Holland, Italy and Poland, with Finland making up the numbers. A shameful, goalless game at home against Finland virtually ended Italy's hopes, while Holland crumbled in Poland to a 4–1 defeat. A magical Cruyff performance demolished the Poles 3–0 in the return. Poland's 0–0 draw against defensive Italy put Holland at the top and in an almost unassailable position. Although defeated 1–0 by Italy, Holland were through to the next round.

In Group Six, the Soviet Union – fielding virtually the entire Dynamo Kiev team – held off the challenge of the Republic of Ireland to qualify, despite losing 3–0 in Dublin. QPR forward Don Givens scored a hat trick.

The seventh group was a nervy affair, with the lead changing between France, East Germany and Belgium. The Belgians' 0–0 draw with France in their last game gave them qualification over East Germany in second place.

Group Eight was equally tense. World champions West Germany were two points behind Greece with two games to play against Bulgaria and Malta. Juup Heynckes scored the only goal against the Bulgarians, and the Germans' 8–0 win over Malta secured their place in the last eight.

In the quarter-finals, West Germany had a fairly easy 3–1 aggregate win over Spain. Wales, 2–0 down to Yugoslavia, could only draw 1–1 at Ninian Park, with the game coming close to abandonment due to crowd invasion in the second half. Rob Rensenbrink scored a magnificent hat trick in Holland's 5–1 home defeat of Belgium and Dutch superiority was confirmed with a 2–0 win in the return, the goals scored by Cruyff and Rep. Czechoslovakia reached the semi-finals with a 2–0 win against the Soviet Union in Prague and a 2–2 draw in Kiev.

The semi-finals and final were to be held in Yugoslavia. With Czechoslovakia playing Holland and West Germany lining up against Yugoslavia, the prospect of a re-run of the 1974 World Cup final seemed more than a possibility. In Zagreb, the Czechs defended well against the probing elegance of Holland. They went ahead through Anton Ondrus in the first half but he then deflected a Dutch shot into his own net. Jaroslav Pollak was sent off for Czechoslovakia and Neeskens and Wim van Hanegem were also red-carded. With their numerical advantage, the Czechs scored early in extra time through Zdenek Nehoda and Jozef Moder claimed another just before the final whistle.

West Germany faced Yugoslavia in Belgrade the following day. Yugoslavia immediately went on the attack, rattling the German defence and going close on several occasions. Branko Oblak crossed a high ball over the German defence and Danilo Popivoda ran on to head past Maier. Yugoslavia scored another when Maier palmed away a Stevo Zungul cross and Dragan Dzajic scored from close range. At half-time, the score was 2–0, which flattered the Germans. In the second half, the Yugoslavs pulled back into defence and allowed West Germany the initiative. Substitute Heinz Flohe's shot cannoned off Bernd Holzenbein's chest and into the net to make it 2–1, and Dieter Muller then levelled. Muller added another two in extra time and West Germany were to meet Czechoslovakia in the final.

In the final in Belgrade, Czechoslovakia piled on the pressure and were rewarded early on with a Jan Svehlik goal. Karol Dobias doubled the total when he seized on a Beckenbauer clearance from little winger Marian Masny's free kick. Muller scored with an acrobatic volley for Germany and the score was 2–1 at half-time. A tiring Czech defence was saved by the brilliance of keeper Ivo Viktor (later voted Player of the Tournament), before Holzenbein headed in a last-minute equaliser. The game went into extra time but the score remained 2–2 and a penalty shootout began.

Seven successive penalties were converted until Uli Hoeness blazed his attempt over the bar. Antonin Panenka stepped up and lofted a beautiful chip over Maier, who had guessed the direction correctly but had not counted on Panenka's guile.

Czechoslovakia, regarded as underdogs at the start of the tournament, were now champions of Europe and deservedly so.

West Germany Again (1978–80)

Major changes were put into force for this, the sixth European Championship. The eight quarter-finalists were now arranged into two league groups of four and the finals were now all to be played in one country, in this case Italy. Although 32 countries again competed at the earlier group stage, Italy as hosts were automatically allocated a place in the finals, leaving 31 countries unevenly divided into seven groups. Semi-finals were discarded. Instead, the two group winners would play each other in the final.

In the qualifying stages, there were surprises for some of the fancied countries with, among others, Yugoslavia, Poland, the Soviet Union, France, East Germany and Austria eliminated, while Belgium and Greece made it through to the finals in Italy. The tournament, by and large, was a collection of drab and uninspiring games, with the exception of the final itself.

The first two games in final Group One kicked off on 11 June 1980, with Czechoslovakia playing West Germany in Rome and Holland against Greece in Naples. West Germany were again favourites to win the trophy and had a strong side, with Karl-Heinz Rummenigge and Horst Hrubesch in attack.

In the Olympic Stadium, in front of only 15,000 spectators, the first half was a disappointing, disjointed affair. The Germans, however, scored in the 55th minute through Rummenigge and they retreated into defence, increasingly besieged by the Czech forwards, in particular the dangerous Ladislav Jurkemik. Masny came on during the second half but Germany held on for both points.

In Naples, the tournament's surprise package Greece outplayed Holland in the first half but Greek keeper Konstantinou unaccountably tripped Holland's Ajax forward Dick Naninga with no danger threatening in the box. Kees Kist scored the penalty and, although Greece frantically mounted waves of attacks, the Dutch held on to win.

The next game, West Germany against Holland, was at last an exciting game of attacking football. Striker Klaus Allofs opened the scoring in the 15th minute, and he ended up with a hat trick midway through the second half. Germany put on young substitute Lothar Matthaus in the 73rd minute but he gave away a penalty, which was converted by Johnny Rep. Holland's Willy van der Kerkhof brought the score back to 3–2 with four minutes remaining but the Germans finished again with two points. Czechoslovakia beat Greece 3–0 on the same day.

Holland met Czechoslovakia in Milan three days later and were subjected to tough Czech tackling, with Rene van der Kerkhof and Naninga being substituted through injury. Nehoda scored for Czechoslovakia and Kist equalised in the 60th minute but the Dutch attack could not capitalise further on their superiority. This result confirmed West Germany as one of the finalists and they played out a meaningless, non-scoring game with Greece.

The other group began with England playing Belgium in Turin. Ray Wilkins sprung Belgium's offside trap to score in the 32nd minute and Jan Ceulemans levelled within six minutes. A large section of the crowd were English supporters somewhat the worse for drink and this goal was the signal for fighting to break out on the terraces between them and Italian fans who had been taunting them. The Italian police stepped in and broke up the fighting with batons and tear gas. Unfortunately, the gas floated onto the pitch and affected the players, some of whom were having difficulty drawing breath. The game was held up for five minutes as the players recovered.

Tony Woodcock appeared to have scored the winner in the 73rd minute but it was ruled offside. More than 70 fans were taken to hospital and the next day UEFA fined the English FA £8,000. This was, however, a problem which was not going to go away.

Italy faced up to Spain in Milan and a tedious game ended in a goalless draw, the Italian fans reserving their ire for the home side, some of whom had been involved in a domestic bribery scandal.

Three days later, Spain went down to an early Erik Gerets goal but equalised through Quini. The second half was all Belgium, and Julien Cools scored the winner in the 65th minute.

The same day, England met Italy in Turin. With playmaker Giancarlo Antognoni in superb form, the Italians created several good chances but it was not until ten minutes from time that they went ahead, Inter's Marco Tardelli scoring from a Francisco Graziani cross. England were now out, although they beat Spain 2–1 in their last match.

The other finalists were now to be Belgium or Italy, playing in Rome later that day. In a terrible match of defensive brawling and cynical play, the Belgians took on Italy at their own game and emerged with a 0–0 draw which did neither side any credit. It did however mean that Belgium had reached the final.

Belgium and West Germany met in the final on 22 June in the Olympic Stadium, Rome, and a tense, attacking game finally lived up to expectations, after much of the sterile, defensive play which had preceded it. Within four minutes, Belgian keeper Jean-Marie Pfaff dived to turn away a Hansi Muller shot for a corner. Six minutes later, young midfielder Bernd Schuster, soon to move to Spain, played a one–two with Allofs, and found Hrubesch, who smashed the ball into the net. Hans-Peter Briegel, another new recruit to the German team, was having an influential game in midfield but was injured early in the second half and replaced by Bernd Cullman. The German midfield began to lose its rhythm and Belgium exploited Briegel's absence. A disputed penalty was awarded to Belgium in the 71st minute, when Uli Stielike was adjudged to have fouled Frankie van der Elst in the box, and Rene van der Eycken converted from the spot. With play switching from end to end, the game appeared to be moving to extra time but Hrubesch headed in a near-post corner in the 89th minute and was swamped by his teammates. His two goals had won the championship for West Germany for the second time.

Platini Stars as France Win (1982–84)

For this tournament, held in France, there were several top countries surprisingly conspicuous by their absence, including England, Italy, Czechoslovakia, the Soviet Union and Holland. None of these countries made it through the qualifying rounds, although the Dutch non-qualification from Group Seven aroused suspicion. Holland and Spain were on the same number of points, although the Dutch had a far higher goal difference. Spain played Malta at home on their last game and had to win by 11 goals to overtake Holland. Spain, who had not scored more than four goals in a game since 1978, beat the Maltese 12–1, with three coming in the last ten minutes. UEFA studied a tape of the match and allowed the result to stand.

The only fundamental change to this tournament was that semi-finals were reintroduced and the top two teams in each group would go through.

Managed by Michel Hidalgo, France had reached the semi-final of the 1982 World Cup finals only to lose unluckily to West Germany in a penalty shootout. At the hub of the team was Michel Platini, the reigning European Footballer of the Year: a brilliant, visionary playmaker with a powerful shot. He was supported in midfield by the elegant Jean Tigana and his Bordeaux teammate, the busy little Alain Giresse. These three were to be the creative force behind France's dominance of the championship.

They played their first game in final Group One against Denmark on 12 June 1984 at the Parc des Princes Stadium in Paris. Both sides produced a thrilling contest of open, attacking football, although some of the tackles were questionable. Towards the end of the first half,

French centre-half Yvon Le Roux lunged at Alan Simonsen, leaving the Dane with a badly broken leg. With Simonsen gone, France grabbed the initiative and Platini opened his account with the only goal of the game in the 77th minute.

In game two, Belgium, fielding 18-year-old creative midfielder Enzo Scifo, met Yugoslavia and the Belgians won 2–0. Three days later, France played Belgium and were 3–0 up by half-time. Two more late goals from Platini completed his hat trick and confirmed his position as France's highest-ever goalscorer. The same day, Denmark played Yugoslavia and although the Danes won 5–0, this was a misleading scoreline as a skilful and determined Yugoslavia could and should have scored on several occasions.

With France now assured of a semi-final place, and Yugoslavia eliminated, the two countries met at Saint-Etienne three days later. Yugoslavia went ahead through Milos Sestic but an unhurried France bided their time. Early in the second half, Platini took over and scored another hat trick in a blistering 18-minute spell.

On the same day, Denmark and Belgium met to decide the other semi-final place. It was another top-quality, dramatic match, with Denmark needing only to draw to proceed into the semi-finals. With seven minutes remaining, the score was 2–2, until Preben Elkjaer scored from a tight angle to give Denmark a 3–2 win.

The opening games in the other group, by comparison, were boring affairs, West Germany drawing 0–0 with Portugal, and Spain sharing a 1–1 result with Romania. The Germans moved up a gear in their next match, striker Rudi Voller scoring both goals in the 2–1 win over Romania. A 1–1 draw between Spain and Portugal the same day meant that all four countries went into their last games with a chance of qualifying. With the score 0–0 midway through the second half between Portugal and Romania in Marseilles, the Portuguese brought on veteran striker Nene who repaid his coach's confidence in his experience by blasting the winner from the edge of the box. At the same time in Paris, West Germany were in command over Spain and threatening to score. Spain, however, fought back, and in injury time Senor crossed for Maceda to head into the net.

The semi-final between France and Portugal was a splendid game of football, combining goals, skill and excitement. With the majestic Platini again dominating the match, France went ahead through Jean-Francois Domergue but Jordao equalised in the 73rd minute and a thrilling game went into extra time. Jordao scored again but the fighting French equalised with Domergue's second goal. In the last minute, Platini met Tigana's cross and fired the ball firmly into the Portuguese net for a 3–2 victory to France. The following day, Denmark and Spain contested another heart-stopping semi-final. Soren Lerby put Denmark ahead in the sixth minute but Maceda equalised midway through the second half. A toughly fought game went into extra time and, although it finished goalless, Denmark's Berggren was sent off in the 106th minute. The tie went to a penalty shootout, won 5–4 by Spain.

On 27 June, France met Spain at the Parc des Princes in the final. The play was fluid from both sides and buzzed from end to end but by half-time the score remained goalless. The game, however, was determined in the 57th minute. Platini curled a free kick around the Spanish defensive wall and Spain's captain and goalkeeper Luis Arconada held the ball but bizarrely allowed it to squeeze out of his grasp and over the goal line. A demoralised Spain were then sent reeling by the French attack until Le Roux was sent off for a second bookable offence in the 84th minute. Spain rallied, but seconds before the final whistle, with virtually the entire Spanish team in the French half, Tigana cleared the ball to Monaco's Bruno Bellone who ran on to it and chipped it neatly over Arconada for a 2–0 win for Les Bleus.

Platini's performances confirmed him as the Player of the Tournament and his nine-goal tally in the finals remains a record. The tournament was France's first major international trophy but it was also a triumph for skilful, attacking football.

Van Basten and Holland Triumph in Germany (1986–88)

The eighth European Championship was held in West Germany. Non-attendees included Romania, Portugal, Poland, Czechoslovakia, and reigning champions France (from whom Platini had recently retired). The Republic of Ireland had qualified for the first time, as Scotland's win over Bulgaria in Sofia in the qualifying stages had handed them victory in Group Seven. West Germany were seeded, in final Group One, as were England, in Group Two.

Group One comprised West Germany, Denmark, Italy and Spain. The opening game was between West Germany, now managed by Franz Beckenbauer, and Italy in Dusseldorf on 10 June 1988. The Italians penned the Germans into their own half for much of the first half, although Jurgen Klinsmann narrowly headed over the bar on a counter-attack. In the 51st minute, Milan's Roberto Donadoni pounced on a misunderstanding between Matthaus and defender Matthias Herget to make a goal for Roberto Mancini, his first for his country. However, only four minutes later, Italian keeper Walter Zenga was penalised for taking too many steps in the box. Cologne's Pierre Littbarski passed the ball to Andreas Brehme who smacked it into the corner of the net. The game ended 1–1. The next day, Denmark and Spain were 1–1 until early in the second half when Real Madrid's star striker Emilio Butragueno scored from what seemed an offside position. Rafael Gordillo scored a third and although Denmark pulled one back, they were well beaten 3–2 by an impressive Spanish side.

In the next match, West Germany were 1–0 ahead thanks to an early Klinsmann goal. Although the Danes came back into the game in the second half, in the 85th minute Littbarski sent in a perfectly judged corner which was headed in by Olaf Thon from the back of the box.

In the Italy v. Spain match the same day, Gianluca Vialli missed several chances before he scored the only goal of the game in the 73rd minute. Three days later, West Germany took on Spain and, with Matthaus controlling midfield, Voller scored in the 30th minute. Five minutes into the second half, Matthaus scampered half the length of the pitch, backheeled to Voller, and the blond striker scored Germany's second. The match finished 2–0. Italy played Denmark in Cologne, with the Italians aware that a draw would see them through to the semi-finals. The Danish keeper, Peter Schmeichel, had a nervy match but kept the Italians out until the 65th minute when Inter's Alessandro Altobelli found the net. Another substitute, midfielder Luigi de Agostini, scored a second goal towards the end.

The second group began with a game between England and Ireland in Stuttgart. Underdogs Ireland, managed by Jack Charlton, went ahead against a shocked England as early as the fifth minute, Ray Houghton's header beating keeper Peter Shilton. The Irish defence stood firm against an inept English attack, with John Barnes and Gary Lineker particularly to blame, and, with keeper Pat Bonner in splendid form, held on to their lead until the final whistle.

Holland, coached by Rinus Michels, were the team to watch. Inspired by the dreadlocked Ruud Gullit, a powerful and abundantly talented player, and his Milan teammate and deep midfield creator Frank Rijkaard, with the long-passing Ronald Koeman in defence, and Arnold Muhren and the lethal Marco van Basten, also with Milan, up front, they were the team of all the talents, and drew comparisons with Johan Cruyff's Total Football side of the 1970s. In their first game, Holland put the USSR under almost continual pressure but it was the Russians who scored on a counter-attack, full-back Vasily Rats finding the net in the 53rd minute from a cross from Igor Belanov. Although technically superior, Holland had to settle for a 1–0 defeat. Holland then had to beat England. In Dusseldorf, England were rather unlucky to be 1–0 down at half-time, the goal coming from van Basten. In the 53rd minute, Bryan Robson equalised, following a one–two with Gary Lineker. Van Basten took full advantage of a Gullit pass in the 72nd minute to grab his second, and four minutes later he touched in a ball from Wim Kieft for his hat trick.

In the penultimate group game, Ronnie Whelan expertly volleyed in a long throw from Mick McCarthy to open the scoring against the Soviets, who equalised in the second half – meaning that Ireland needed only a point from their last game to reach the semi-finals. They played Holland, and a somewhat fortuitous header from Kieft with nine minutes left knocked the Irish out 1–0. Meanwhile England had played dismally against the Soviets and were beaten 3–1, leaving Bobby Robson's side with no points and a lot of explaining to do when they arrived home.

Holland lined up against West Germany in Hamburg for the first semi-final, in what was a historic game for the men in orange. They had not beaten West Germany, their bitter rivals, for 32 years, and the time was also right to avenge their 2–1 defeat in the 1974 World Cup final. In front of a crowd packed with singing Dutch supporters, Holland spurned a number of first-half chances. In the 54th minute, Klinsmann, as was his habit, fell over Rijkaard's legs in the box and Matthaus scored from the resultant penalty. An incensed Holland fought back, and in the 74th minute they were also awarded a dubious penalty, when van Basten tumbled over Jurgen Kohler's outstretched leg. With two minutes remaining, Jan Wouters' defence-splitting pass found van Basten, and the Dutch striker slid the ball past German keeper Eike Immel for the winner. The next day in Stuttgart, Sergei Litovchenko and Oleg Protasov each scored for the USSR to beat an increasingly demoralised Italian side 2–0, and they were to face Holland in the final.

The final kicked off on 25 June in the Olympic Stadium in Munich. The USSR were without central defender Oleg Kuznetsov, suspended after the Italy game, and the side contained seven Dynamo Kiev players. Holland took advantage of Kuznetsov's absence, and Koeman blasted a typical thunderbolt free kick over the bar in the sixth minute. In the 32nd minute, the Dutch went ahead, when Erwin Koeman crossed to van Basten who headed on to Gullit who, in turn, powerfully headed past keeper Renat Dasayev. In the 53rd minute, Holland went further ahead with a goal which was certainly the best of the tournament, and probably the finest in the history of the European Nations Championship. Adri van Tiggelen picked up a loose ball in midfield and passed to Arnold Muhren on the left. Muhren sent in a perfect cross to van Basten at the back of the penalty area, and van Basten volleyed in a superb dipping shot from a tight angle with his right foot past an amazed Dasayev. Dutch keeper Hans van Breukelen gave away a stupid penalty six minutes later but managed to push Belanov's spot kick clear. The Russians now seemed to know they were beaten, and Rijkaard came close to making the score 3–0 at the end. The whistle blew and the popular Dutch had won their first-ever major international championship. For the second tournament in succession, joyful, attacking football was also the winner.

Denmark Fail to Qualify but Win (1990–92)

The tournament was played out against the background of momentous events across Europe. The Soviet Union had not intervened as the Soviet bloc nations of Poland, East Germany, Czechoslovakia, Bulgaria, Romania, and Hungary all abandoned Communist rule by 1990. In 1991, powered by growing nationalistic movements in many of the republics and with the economy in freefall, the Soviet Union dissolved and Mikhail Gorbachev resigned as president. Republics such as Ukraine, Latvia, Azerbaijan and Estonia re-emerged as sovereign states but they were to play no part in this competition. The collapse of the Berlin Wall was the end of the last symbol of a divided Germany, which became one nation again.

With the increasing footballing parity between European countries, several of the more fancied sides failed to qualify. These included Czechoslovakia, Spain, Romania, Italy, Portugal and Poland. Austria's attempt to qualify was not helped by their visit to the Faroe Islands in Group Four when, even with Atletico Madrid striker Toni Polster in the side, they were beaten 1–0 by the part-timers, playing their first European Championship match. The Austrian manager Josef Hickersberger resigned immediately after the game, with the result generally regarded as the biggest shock in the history of the tournament.

A bitter war was raging in the Balkans between Serbians, Croats and Bosnians and although Yugoslavia qualified for the final stages, they were disqualified from the tournament as the United Nations Security Council imposed sanctions on Serbia. At 11 days' notice, the Yugoslav spot in the final groups went to Denmark, who had finished second to Yugoslavia in their qualifying group. The Danes were to prove the revelation of the tournament. Scotland, who had finished above Switzerland and Romania in their group, reached the final stage of the tournament for the first time.

Played in Sweden, the Group One games kicked off on 10 June 1992 with the first game between Sweden and France ending in a 1–1 draw. Next day in Malmo, Denmark faced England. Graham Taylor's makeshift team struggled against the lively Danes, who almost scored when a John Jensen shot hit the inside of the post in the second half, but the game petered out goalless.

A defensively minded France met England three days later in Malmo. Stuart Pearce, his face bloodied by a head-butt from Basile Boli, smashed a free kick against the bar in the later stages but a dour and unappealing game ended with no goals.

A much more entertaining match was played on the same day between Denmark and Sweden in Malmo. Both sides went close in a goalless first half but Sweden struck early in the second period when Jonas Thern passed to Martin Dahlin who crossed to Tomas Brolin, and the Swedish striker walloped the ball into the net. Winger Anders Limpar's attempt to add another was thwarted by the imposing Danish keeper Schmeichel. The match ended 1–0 to Sweden and all four countries were still in with a chance of progressing.

England met Sweden in their final game in Stockholm, and were 1–0 ahead by the interval from a third-minute David Platt volley. In the 51st minute, Sweden drew level. Graham Taylor then unaccountably replaced the dangerous striker Gary Lineker with Arsenal's Alan Smith, much to the dismay of English players and supporters, and Sweden dominated from there on in, scoring the winner through Brolin with eight minutes remaining. Lineker's baffling substitution, and his subsequent retirement from international football, prevented him from catching up with Bobby Charlton's record of 49 goals for his country. He retired with 48 and, one suspects, a healthy disregard for Taylor's judgement.

In Malmo, a lacklustre and defensive France went 1–0 down to an eighth-minute goal from Preben Larsen and had three players booked in the first half. Striker Jean-Pierre Papin equalised in the second period but the Danes were in control, scoring the winner through Lars Elstrup twelve minutes from time.

In the other group, Scotland met Holland in Gothenburg and produced a spirited, robust performance. They ably contained the star-studded Dutch attack, with Richard Gough superbly marking van Basten, but succumbed to the pressure in the 75th minute when Dennis Bergkamp struck Gullit's corner into the net. Germany played out a physical contest with the CIS (formerly the Soviet Union) in Norrkoping the same day, with Voller suffering a broken arm after a collision with Kuznetsov in the first half. The CIS opened the scoring with an Igor Dobrovolski penalty but a convenient stumble by substitute Klinsmann on the edge of the box in the final minute won a free kick, curled into the net by Thomas Hassler for a 1–1 draw. In the next game, a positive Scotland took the game to Germany in Norrkoping. Although 1–0 down to a Karl-Heinz Riedle rocket in the 28th minute, Scotland went close on several occasions. Early in the second period Scotland's Maurice Malpas deflected a Stefan Effenberg cross over a stranded Andy Goram in the Scottish goal to make the final score 2–0, although Germany could count themselves lucky. Meanwhile, in Gothenburg, Holland and the CIS played out a 0–0 draw.

There were now two games left in the group. Germany were completely outplayed by Holland in Gothenburg, going 1–0 down from a Rijkaard header in the second minute and 2–0 down twelve minutes later when Rob Witschge hit a low shot inside the post. With the news that Scotland were 2–0 ahead of the CIS at half-time, Germany scented survival and reduced the score to 2–1 through Klinsmann. Aron Winter came on to bolster the Dutch midfield and Bergkamp scored to make the final result 3–1. Meanwhile, in Norrkoping Scotland had scored two early goals from Paul McStay and Brian McClair against a tired-looking CIS. A Gary McAllister penalty in the 83rd minute gave Scotland a well-deserved 3–0 win but Holland and Germany went through to the semi-finals.

Sweden played Germany in Stockholm in the first semi-final. Without the influential Stefan Schwarz, the Swedish midfield looked nervous, and the Swedes went behind to an early Hassler free kick. Germany went further ahead early in the second half, when Riedle scored from a Matthias Sammer cross but, with little winger Limpar now on the pitch, the Swedes reduced the deficit to 2–1 thanks to a Brolin penalty. Germany ensured their appearance in the Final when Riedle added his second in the 84th minute.

The other semi-final was held in Gothenburg. Within five minutes, Denmark were one ahead of Holland from a Henrik Larsen header, although Bergkamp equalised in the 23rd minute. Ten minutes later Larsen scored his second, taking advantage of a mis-timed clearance from Koeman. In the second period, Holland went on the attack and five minutes from time Rijkaard scored from a corner. The Danes were now on the rack but held on until the end of extra time to move to a penalty shootout. Van Basten (without a single goal in the finals) was the only player not to score, and Denmark moved into the final.

Favourites and World Champions Germany met Denmark on 26 June 1992 in the final in Gothenburg. Denmark were without their suspended midfielder Henrik Andersen and started the game under pressure from the Germans. However, the Danes took the lead in the 18th minute when Christian Poulson cut the ball back for Arsenal-bound Jensen to smash the ball into the net, despite Effenberg's full-length dive to prevent it going in. Germany became increasingly edgy and Effenberg and Hassler were both booked before half-time. Stefan Reuter followed them into the referee's book shortly after the interval. With 12 minutes remaining, Denmark scored another, substitute Claus Christiansen heading back a bad clearance to Kim Vilfort who despatched the ball into the net. Two more Germans – Thomas Doll and Klinsmann – were booked, as they realised that their hopes of another championship had disappeared. When the final whistle blew, the most unlikely winners in the history of the championship to date were Denmark, who were certainly fortunate to qualify but, once there, showed that they deserved their victory. Keeper Peter Schmeichel summed up the mood in the Danish camp when he said, 'We still don't understand what we have done.'

Interest in the European Championships across the continent was now massive. From relatively humble beginnings in 1960, the tournament had become the biggest footballing event in the world, after the World Cup. And in 1996, football was going home . . .

FOOTBALL'S COMING HOME: THE EUROPEAN CHAMPIONSHIP 1994-2004

Euro 96: Germany Win With Golden Goal (1994–96)

The refrain 'Three Lions on my Shirt' echoed across England in the summer of 1996 as the country – 'the home of football' – prepared to host the European Championship. The red cross of St George – previously appropriated by far-right groups – was now increasingly a valid symbol of a gentler and less xenophobic English sense of collective belonging, with the nation keen to atone for '30 years of hurt' and, above all, to witness at least a decent showing by the English team in the forthcoming tournament. During June, English cities were vivid kaleidoscopes of colour, as Dutch fans decked in orange mingled with the Scottish Tartan Army, the Danish Vikings and the blue of Italy, as the party continued.

Given that membership had now expanded to more than 40 countries, UEFA had decided to enlarge the final group stage to sixteen countries, organised into four groups. The rival claims to host the tournament – from Austria, Holland, Portugal and England – had been assessed, and England had won. English clubs had been re-admitted into Europe in 1990 and Manchester United had won the European Cup-Winners' Cup in 1991 without any major hooligan problems. The award of the tournament to England was a recognition of the country's welcome back to full participation in European football – and recognition of the changes wrought by the Taylor Report.

Forty-eight countries had entered the qualifying stages, and the finals kicked off at Wembley when England met Switzerland on 8 June 1996 in Group A. Bustling striker Alan Shearer put England ahead in the 22nd minute (his first international goal in his last twelve appearances) but England faded in the second half and Kubilay Turkilmaz equalised from the penalty spot – a questionable decision against Stuart Pearce – with 10 minutes remaining. The other two teams in Group A – Holland and surprise qualifiers Scotland – faced each other at Villa Park, and Scotland demonstrated their resilience by securing a 0–0 draw against the likes of Clarence Seedorf, Dennis Bergkamp and Edgar Davids. For Holland's next game, against Switzerland, Davids had returned home following an argument with coach Gus Hiddink (shades of Ruud Gullit in the 1994 World Cup finals). In the second half, a tremendous strike by Jordi Cruyff (son of Johan) and a Dennis Bergkamp goal gave the Dutch a 2–0 victory.

The next game was the eagerly awaited clash between England and Scotland at Wembley. Scotland had the better of the first half, with captain Gary McAllister going close twice. England, prompted by substitute Jamie Redknapp, came back strongly in the second period, and in the 51st minute Shearer headed in from a Gary Neville cross. Scotland, however, still threatened, and were awarded a penalty in the 77th minute for a Tony Adams foul. McAllister struck the spot kick well but David Seaman saved it with his trailing arm. Within a minute Paul Gascoigne flicked the ball over Scotland centre-half Colin Hendry, accelerated into the box and slammed the ball past helpless keeper Andy Goram. The final 2–0 scoreline was harsh on the Scots, and manager Craig Brown spoke for many Scots when he said they were 'unluckily beaten'.

Before the last two games, all four countries were in with a chance of qualification, with England and Holland the favourites. England turned on the style against Holland at Wembley. With Shearer a constant threat, Paul Ince was tripped in the box in the 22nd minute and Shearer converted the penalty. By half-time, England's midfield were dominant. In the opening quarter of an hour of the second period, England rocked Holland with three well-taken goals. Teddy Sheringham headed in the first from a Gascoigne corner, Shearer scored another, and Sheringham grabbed the third. Patrick Kluivert slotted the ball under Seaman in the 77th minute to give a final score of 4–1. Holland's fate was now determined by what was going on at Villa Park, where Scotland were playing Switzerland.

Scotland striker Ally McCoist missed two good first half chances but finally scored in the 37th minute. Without the injured forward Duncan Ferguson, however, Scotland lacked the scoring touch and the game finished 1–0. Kluivert's goal at Wembley meant that Holland went through with England and that Scotland were eliminated, although the Tartan Army have never forgiven Seaman for not saving Kluivert's shot.

Group B opened with a match between Spain and Bulgaria at Elland Road. Bulgarian star player Hristo Stoichkov controlled the game and scored from the spot in the 64th minute. Spain equalised ten minutes later when substitute Alfonso scored with a deflected free kick with his first touch of the ball. At St James' Park, a Christophe Dugarry first half header for France against Romania was the only goal in what was a rather scrappy performance. Again inspired by Stoichkov, Bulgaria went ahead in the third minute when he smashed an unstoppable shot into the Romanian net. A 1–0 win meant Romania were eliminated.

France and Spain played out a 1–1 draw at St James' Park, a second-half strike from Youri Djorkaeff cancelled out by a late goal from substitute Jose Caminero. In the last games of the group, Spain went ahead in the 11th minute through Javier Manjarin but Romania, under the guiding genius of Gheorghe Hagi, playing in his 100th international, equalised in the 29th minute. Spain won the game with five minutes remaining when Amor headed in an Alfonso cross. With Marcel Desailly tightly marking Stoichkov (and being booked in the process), France scored in the 20th minute with a header from centre-back Laurent Blanc. They went two ahead in the second half when Dimitar Penev headed an own goal and, although Stoichkov scored with a superbly taken free kick, France won 3–1 when substitute Patrice Loko scored in the last minute. France and Spain both qualified.

In what was to be a rehearsal for the final, Germany and the Czech Republic met in the first game of Group C – christened the 'Group of Death' – at Old Trafford. Jurgen Kohler, captain in place of the injured Jurgen Klinsmann, was badly injured and was to miss the remainder of the tournament. Full-back Christian Ziege shot in off the post to open Germany's account in the 26th minute, and minutes later Andreas Moller scored another for an easy 2–0 win. Meanwhile, Italy beat Russia 2–1 at Anfield, both goals coming from Pierluigi Casiraghi, although a 2–1 defeat by a Karel Poborsky-inspired Czech Republic in the next match meant that Italy had to beat Germany in their final group match to progress to the quarter-finals. Germany, who had comprehensively beaten Russia 3–0, met Italy at Old Trafford. German keeper Andreas Kopke brilliantly saved an Italian penalty in the first half and the game remained goalless.

If the Czech Republic lost to Russia in the last group game, Italy would be through. By half-time, a ruthless, attacking display ensured the Czechs were two ahead. Russia re-organised themselves in the second half and pulled two back. With five minutes left, they took the lead through substitute Vladimir Beshastnykh's long-range effort. With under a minute to play Vladimir Smicer scored the vital goal. Germany and the Czech Republic were through. Italy were out.

Group D began with a 1–1 draw between reigning champions Denmark and Portugal at Hillsborough. The marauding Portuguese attack pinned down the Danish defence, ably marshalled by keeper Peter Schmeichel. The other two teams in the group – Croatia and Turkey – played the next game. Croatia, with goalscoring winger Alen Boksic, striker Davor Suker, captain Zvonimir Boban and midfield supremo Robert Prosinecki, were third favourites to win the tournament. Substitute Goran Vlaovic claimed the only goal in the 85th minute, running the length of the pitch to score. A goal from defender Fernando Couto gave Portugal the three points in their next game against Turkey.

Croatia then took on Denmark, with the score 0–0 after a disappointing first half. Eight minutes into the second half Suker opened the scoring from the penalty spot after Schmeichel was deemed to have fouled midfielder Mario Stanic. Ten minutes from time Boban finished off a Suker move. Then Suker attempted a lofted shot over Schmeichel but the big keeper scrambled back to prevent the goal. With one minute left, and Schmeichel charging into the centre circle, Suker did it again, cheekily and exquisitely biding his time and chipping the ball over the big keeper into the net as he rushed fruitlessly back into position.

Croatia had now qualified and fielded seven reserves in their final game against Portugal, losing 3–0. Denmark beat Turkey 3–0, with two from Brian Laudrup, but Portugal and Croatia both qualified for the quarter-finals.

To encourage attacking football, UEFA had decided to adopt the golden goal rule, i.e. the game ends when a team scores first in extra time – sudden death overtime. However, the experience in the quarter-

and semi-finals indicated that the golden goal rule meant that, rather than go on the attack, teams became even more defensive.

England and Spain met at Wembley in the first quarter-final, with England fortunate to reach extra time against the lively Spaniards, who had two goals disallowed in the first half. Seaman had to be on his best form to keep the scoreline blank. Extra time was sterile and, in the penalty shootout, with the score 4–2 in England's favour, Seaman dived to his left to punch away Miguel Angel Nadal's effort, and England were through.

The same day France took on Holland at Anfield, a disappointing match which ended in another penalty shootout. Clarence Seedorf missed the fourth Dutch penalty, and when Blanc scored France's fifth Les Bleus had reached the semis. The following day Croatia and Germany played their quarter-final at Old Trafford. Croatia's game plan appeared to be to kick the Germans off the pitch, reserving Klinsmann for special attention. Klinsmann scored from a penalty in the first half after a foul on Sammer but Suker equalised early in the second half. In the intervening period, Croatia's Igor Stimac had been sent off for a second bookable offence. Sammer gave the lead back to Germany, and Croatia became even more hot-headed and aggressive. Germany won 2–1. Later in the day, the last quarter-final was contested between Portugal and the Czech Republic. The first half was goalless but the Czechs won the game in the 52nd minute with Poborsky's sensational scooped goal over the keeper.

In the first semi-final, England lined up against Germany at Wembley. In the second minute, Shearer scored his fifth goal of the tournament but Stefan Kuntz levelled 13 minutes later. The rest of normal time saw no further goals. In the first eight minutes of extra time, Darren Anderton hit the post, Seaman made an acrobatic save from Moller, the referee disallowed a Kuntz goal and Gascoigne was inches away from scoring. The match went to penalties. Each side scored their first five penalties, with Stuart Pearce atoning for his miss in the shootout against West Germany in the 1990 World Cup semi-final. Up stepped Gareth Southgate, who had never scored a penalty in senior football, and his shot was saved by Kopke. Moller converted and took Germany to where they usually end up, the final.

The other semi was a boring, defensive game, which inevitably led to another shoot-out. France and the Czech Republic both successfully converted their first five attempts, and Reynard Pedros missed France's sixth. Czech captain Miroslav Kadlec smashed the ball into the net and the Czechs were to meet Germany.

On 30 June, the two teams met at Wembley in the final. In the 59th minute, Kuntz felled Poborsky and, although television replays proved that this was outside the box, Patrik Berger, back from injury, made no mistake with the penalty. Then Germany coach Berti Vogts brought on Oliver Bierhoff for Mehmet Scholl in the 68th minute. This inspired substitution was to make all the difference, as four minutes later the tall striker rose at the far post to head Germany back into the game from a Ziege free kick, and Germany began to dominate. Just before the end of normal time Smicer replaced Poborsky, and almost immediately he hit a fierce shot, only for Kopke to tip the ball round the post. In the fifth minute of extra time, Bierhoff scored his second, latching onto a Klinsmann ball and firing a shot which was deflected into the net by Czech defender Michal Hornak. Germany had become the first team to win the championship with a golden goal and also the first country to win the tournament three times.

Euro 2000: France Win Through

The 11th European Championship was held in Belgium and Holland. The tournament was a feast of goals and attacking football, with world-class individual performances and boundless skill coming from such teams as Holland and France. The event was marred by outbreaks of hooliganism, mainly from England supporters, but even this mindless violence could not detract from the general bonhomie and excitement of the tournament.

England, who had beaten Scotland in the two-leg play-off for the last place, opened their tournament with a game against Portugal in Eindhoven in Group A. Manager Kevin Keegan had opted for an attacking line-up with Steve McManaman in midfield. Paul Scholes and McManaman put England 2–0 in the lead by the 17th minute but then the Portuguese, led by the creative, speedy winger Luis Figo and playmaker Rui Costa, took over. Figo and Joao Pinto levelled by half-time and striker Nuno Gomes scored a deserved winner in the 59th minute.

The other two teams in Group A – Germany and Romania – played out a 1–1 draw in Liege. Romania took the lead through Viorel Moldovan in the fifth minute and the Germans were fortunate to equalise with a Mehmet Scholl screamer 20 minutes later. In Charleroi,

England took on Germany, and a Shearer header from a David Beckham cross early in the second half was the only goal of the game. Although not a spectacle for the footballing purist, this was England's first competitive win over Germany for 34 years.

Romania then met Portugal in Arnhem, where a last-minute header from Costinha, who had come off the bench minutes before, gave the Portuguese a 1–0 victory and guaranteed their ticket to the quarter-finals. In the following games, Portugal, fielding a virtual reserve team, nonetheless humbled the dour Germans and sent them out of the championship. Lothar Matthaus was playing his 150th game for Germany, but his team could not match the flair and invention of the Portuguese, who won 3–0 thanks to a hat trick from the little Lazio forward Sergio Conceicao.

England also crashed out of the tournament the same day in Charleroi. With Seaman injured in the warm-up, Nigel Martyn took over in goal and, although they were 2–1 ahead at the interval against a lively Romania, Dorinel Munteanu equalised with a volley early in the second half. With three minutes to play, Phil Neville needlessly fouled Moldovan in the box and substitute Ion Ganea made the final score 3–2 from the spot.

Group B contained co-hosts Belgium, Sweden, Italy and Turkey, with the first two countries meeting in the opening game of the tournament in Brussels. In a fast, exciting match, Belgium took the lead through Bart Goor in the first half and doubled it early in the second period when Emile Mpenza smashed an unstoppable volley into the roof of the net. A bizarre error by Belgian keeper Filip de Wilde, when he allowed the ball to roll under his foot, was converted by Johan Mjallby for a final score of 2–1.

Dino Zoff's Italy went ahead early in the second half against Turkey, courtesy of a spectacular overhead kick by Antonio Conte, but the Turks levelled shortly after with an Okan Buruk header. Juventus striker Filippo Inzaghi scored the winner from the penalty spot.

In the third game, Italy met Belgium and took the lead in the fifth minute when Roma captain Francesco Totti headed in from Demetrio Albertini's cross. A stung Belgium went on the attack and the Italians were saved only by the woodwork and the acrobatic goalkeeping of Francesco Toldo. Stefano Fiore scored Italy's winner in the 65th minute, playing a one–two with Inzaghi and scoring from twenty yards.

After a boring 0–0 game between Sweden and Turkey, Italy became the first team to qualify for the quarter-finals. Turkey joined them after game five, when two goals from Hakan Sukur eliminated Belgium from the competition. Belgium were the first host nation not to reach the second round. A goal apiece from Luigi di Baggio and Alessandro del Piero in Italy's 2–1 defeat of Sweden also sent the Swedes home.

The third favourites for the tournament, Spain, confirmed their reputation as perennial underachievers when a second half looping header from Norway's Steffen Iversen was the only goal in the opening game of Group C. Striker Raul was particularly culpable, missing several chances. One of the competition's supposed minnows, Slovenia, were 3–0 ahead, two coming from Zlatko Zahovic, against Yugoslavia early in the second half of game two. Substitute Slavo Milosevic, however, claimed two and Lubinko Drulovic another in Yugoslavia's fight back, to end the game 3–3.

Against Slovenia in Amsterdam, Spain took the lead in the fourth minute from a beautiful goal by Raul. Zahovic equalised in the second half but one minute later Joseba Etxeberria scored the Spanish winner. Another Milosevic strike was the only goal in Yugoslavia's 1–0 win over Norway, a crucial result as events unfolded.

The last two games in Group C – played at the same time – had an astonishing conclusion. Norway had dragged out a goalless draw against Slovenia in Arnhem and, with the score 3–2 to Yugoslavia against Spain with 90 minutes played in Brugge, had assumed they were through to the quarter-finals along with the Yugoslavs. In a pulsating game in Brugge, a Milosevic header was answered with a goal from Alfonso in the first half. Early in the second period, substitute Dejan Govedarica drilled in a lovely goal from the edge of the box but Spain came back again, through a curling shot from another substitute, Pedro Munitis. Slobodan Komljenovic scrambled in Yugoslavia's third and, as stoppage time began, the score remained 3–2 in Yugoslavia's favour.

Suddenly, however, the referee awarded a penalty for a foul on Abelardo and Gaizka Mendieta tucked it away: 3–3. Seconds later, Alfonso volleyed into the net with his left foot and the whistle blew for full-time. Spain had dramatically won 4–3. The Yugoslav fans' despair turned to joy as they realised that their win over Norway meant that Yugoslavia went through with Spain and that Norway were eliminated.

The two favourites – France and Holland – were in Group D, along with Denmark and the Czech Republic. Denmark were almost immediately under pressure against France, tormented by the pace of Thierry Henry and Nicolas Anelka.

Blanc opened the scoring in the 16th minute. In the 64th minute, Henry surged down the left, cut in and clipped a shot past Schmeichel for the second. Sylvain Wiltord added a third in the last minutes.

In the game between Holland and the Czech Republic, the Dutch controlled the first half with their fluid, precise movement. However, in a breathtaking second period, the Czechs bombarded the Dutch goal, hitting the woodwork twice and bringing out a brilliant save from Edwin van der Sar. Poborsky missed a sitter early on and, against the run of play, Holland scored with a minute to go through a hotly disputed Frank de Boer penalty.

Henry was again outstanding in France's 2–1 win over the Czechs in Brugge, scoring the opener and making the second for Youri Djorkaeff.

Despite a stuttering start against Denmark, they gradually assumed control, beating the Danes 3–0 and eliminating them from the tournament. The Czechs won 2–0 against Denmark, both goals coming from Smicer, in a meaningless match.

A thrilling contest ensued in Amsterdam between what were now regarded as the best sides in the competition, France and Holland. France rested several key players, including Zinedine Zidane, Henry and Anelka, while Holland fielded virtually an unchanged side.

In the eighth minute, Christophe Dugarry headed France ahead from a Johan Micoud corner and six minutes later, Kluivert buried a Bergkamp pass past Bernard Lama in the French goal. On the half-hour, Wiltord fired in another goal, the ball taking a deflection off Dugarry.

In the second half, Frank de Boer flashed a thunderous, 25-yard free kick past Lama, and Bodo Zenden ran into the penalty area to rasp a shot into the net for a final score of 3–2 to Holland.

In the quarter-finals, Italy, assisted by the sending off of Hagi in the 60th minute, made sure of their passage to the semis with Totti and Inzaghi scoring two goals within the first ten minutes against Romania. At the same time, Portugal, who had come through their group with a 100 per cent record, were defeating Turkey 2–0 in Amsterdam.

Figo, in scintillating form, sent in a perfect cross in the 44th minute for Nuno Gomes to score with a diving header. Turkey defender Alpay Ozalan had been sent off in the 29th minute for throwing a punch at Couto. Portuguese keeper Vitor Baia saved an Arif penalty early in the second half and five minutes later Figo crossed again for Gomes to score, this time with a simple tap-in. Portugal progressed 2–1.

In Rotterdam, a dominant display from Kluivert saw the tall Dutch striker net four goals in 30 minutes either side of the interval against Yugoslavia. Marc Overmars scored two more as Holland swamped Yugoslavia 6–1. In the last quarter-final, France played Spain in Brugge. Player of the Tournament Zidane blasted in the first goal in the 32nd minute with a ferocious free kick from 25 yards. Mendieta levelled from the spot five minutes later but Djorkaeff lashed in France's second from a tight angle before half-time. The game saw no more goals but Raul missed a great chance to equalise in the last minute, blazing his penalty over.

In the first semi-final in Brussels, between Portugal and France, a much-anticipated match between two of the most attractive sides in European football degenerated into undignified scenes.

Portugal scored first through a stunning 18th-minute volley from Nuno Gomes. With Zidane in sparkling form, it was no surprise that France equalised just after half-time, through Henry. The game moved into extra time, with the players becoming tired and tempers fraying. With only minutes left and a shootout looming, Abel Xavier handled a Wiltord shot in the box and a penalty was given. The incensed Portuguese harangued the referee and linesman, having to be dragged away by their coach, Humberto Coelho. Figo walked off the pitch in disgust but returned. Zidane, the coolest player on the pitch, calmly scored from the spot and France were through to the final.

The following day, Italy faced Holland in Amsterdam. The sending off of Gianluca Zambrotta in the 33rd minute served to draw the Italians further back into defence, with only Inzaghi up front. Incredibly, however, Holland missed two penalties: the first when Toldo made an excellent save from Frank de Boer in the 35th minute and the second when Kluivert's effort sent Toldo the wrong way but hit the base of the post 12 minutes later. Italy, although criticised for stifling the game, actually produced an organised and composed performance, and Holland could not find a way through. The match went into extra time and then penalties. Holland missed a further three in the shootout and Italy went through 3–1 to the final.

The final between France (who had scored 11 goals in the tournament) and Italy (who had conceded only two) was held in Rotterdam on 2 July. Clearly, the game was going to reflect different footballing philosophies. In a largely cat-and-mouse first half, the Italian defence determinedly snuffed out the predictable French attack. Zidane was well shackled by the industrious Di Baggio and Albertini.

Italy scored on a breakaway when Marco Delvecchio volleyed home a Gianluca Pessotto cross from close range in the 54th minute. In the third minute of injury time, France dramatically equalised when Wiltord shot under Toldo. Thirteen minutes into extra time, David Trezeguet rifled a Robert Pires cross into the corner of the net. France had won on the golden goal. Captain Didier Deschamps, flanked by his teammates, paraded the Henri Delaunay trophy in the centre of Paris the following day as thousands of French supporters celebrated their triumph, with echoes of the World Cup homecoming in 1998.

Euro 2004: Triumph of the Underdogs

Portugal was the venue for the championship, with the stadiums having been renovated and the country's infrastructure modernised for the tournament. Benfica's Stadium of Light had been rebuilt to accommodate 65,000 and Porto's old neo-brutalist ground had also been rebuilt, while one end of the new stadium at Braga had been carved out of a massive granite quarry. Portugal was clearly intent on joining the elite footballing countries, a membership more than justified by the abundant talent of their national team, now ageing but resolutely determined to make this competition their triumphant swansong.

The home nation drew Greece, Spain and Russia in Group A. At the opening match against Greece in Porto on 12 June, the Portuguese received a shock as early as the sixth minute, when Georgios Karagounis scored from 25 yards. Angelos Basinas added another from the penalty spot and the Portuguese were reeling. Although the Greek defence were solid and organised, this was not supposed to be happening. Tricky young winger Cristiano Ronaldo made the score 2–1 at the end but Portugal now had to fight for survival in the group.

Spain's opening match was against Russia in the Algarve. With Raul and Morientes in particularly menacing form, backed up by Valencia's Reuben Baraja and left-winger Vicente, Spain could reasonably expect to overcome their tendency to implode in major competitions. They launched waves of attacks on the Russian defence and finally scored in the 60th minute, when sub Juan Carlos Valeron struck the only goal of the game with his first touch.

In their next game, against Greece, Raul craftily back-heeled for Morientes to score with a 12-yard shot in the 27th minute. In the 65th minute, with the Spanish defence dithering over a long ball, Angelos Charisteas levelled the score and stubborn Greek defending kept the final result at 1–1.

Maniche gave a much-improved Portugal an early lead against Russia but it was not until the last minute that Rui Costa scored another. Russian keeper Sergei Ovchinnikov had been sent off on the stroke of half-time. Now out of the competition and playing for pride, Russia took on Greece, claiming their opener after just 68 seconds and adding another a few minutes later. Zisis Vryzas' chip over the Russian keeper just on half-time gave the Greeks a critical goal in the 2–1 result.

Portugal achieved their first win over Spain since 1981, 1–0, in an end-to-end match. A brilliant flick from Figo in the 57th minute found Nuno Gomes in space and the striker made no mistake from 20 yards. Greece qualified by virtue of a goal scored ahead of Spain and the Spanish once again left early from a major tournament.

Group B began with a tightly contested 0–0 draw between Switzerland and Croatia. France played England the same day at the Stadium of Light.

Spurs' Ledley King made an impressive debut at centre back alongside Arsenal's Sol Campbell as England went ahead with a 38th-minute Lampard header from a Beckham cross. Eighteen-year-old Everton forward Wayne Rooney was in superb form and won a penalty when he was fouled by Mikael Silvestre midway through the second half. Barthez, however, produced a fine save from Beckham's resulting spot kick. In the 90th minute, Zidane curled a magnificent free kick past a helpless David James to equalise. Three minutes later, with the referee about to blow for full time, Henry was dragged to the ground by James and Zidane scored from the spot for a 2–1 win to France.

England restored some of their reputation and secured all the points in their 3–0 defeat of Switzerland four days later. Switzerland started well, with set pieces from Stuttgart's Hakan Yakin causing the English defence problems. England took the lead against the run of play when Rooney headed in powerfully from a Beckham cross, becoming the youngest player ever to score in the championship. In the 60th minute, Bernt Haas was sent off and Switzerland's challenge evaporated. Rooney scored a second 15 minutes later and Steven Gerrard made it 3–0 towards the end.

The same evening, France's run of 14 straight wins was ended by Croatia, who held them to a 2–2 draw.

A 4–2 defeat of Croatia then set up England to play Portugal in the quarter-finals. Rooney, again their star performer, scored twice to bring his tournament tally to four. Scholes equalised Niko Kovac's sixth-minute goal and Lampard wrapped it up with ten minutes remaining.

A confident France strolled to the quarter-finals with a 3–1 win over Switzerland. Zidane opened the scoring with a 20th-minute header, but 18-year-old forward Johann Volathen levelled six minutes later, beating Rooney's record as the youngest player to score in the tournament. In the last 15 minutes, Henry showed why he is among the world's best strikers by scoring twice.

Denmark and Italy played out a disappointing 0–0 draw in the first game of Group C. Although the Danes were dominant, they could not penetrate the Italian defence and keepers Thomas Sorensen and Gianluigi Buffon were in inspired form. Italy's Totti, the player from whom so much had been expected, was subsequently banned for three games for spitting at Denmark's Christian Poulsen. 'Totti's madness' screamed *La Gazzetta dello Sport*, although Italy's form improved without him.

Bulgaria began well but gradually succumbed to Sweden, for whom tall Ajax striker Zlatan Ibrahimovic was particularly menacing. His cross to Arsenal's Freddie Ljungberg midway through the first half led to the little Swede opening the scoring. In the 57th minute, Henrik Larsson scored one of the goals of the tournament when he produced a stunning, full-length diving header to power the ball into the net from Erik Edman's cross. A minute later, Larsson scored his second, volleying into the roof of the net. Ibrahimovic scored a penalty with twelve minutes remaining and Marcus Allback completed the 5–0 rout with an injury-time volley, although the score was perhaps an unfair reflection on Bulgaria's spirited contribution to the game.

Bulgaria were then eliminated 2–0 by Denmark. Italy had to avoid defeat to stay in the tournament and they untypically piled into attack against Sweden. Their persistence was rewarded when Christian Panucci crossed for Antonio Cassano to head in the opener in the 36th minute. Ibrahimovic, however, gave Sweden a lifeline with the equaliser with six minutes remaining, flicking the ball over Buffon and into the corner of the net.

Martin Petrov put Bulgaria ahead on half-time with a controversial penalty but Italy scored twice in the second half, through Simone Perrotta and a brilliant strike from Cassano in injury time.

Meanwhile, a superb dipping volley from Jon Dahl Tomasson gave Denmark the lead in the 28th minute against Sweden. Larsson levelled from the spot just after the interval and a second Tomasson strike midway through the second half put the Danes back in the lead. With two minutes to go, Matthias Jonson hooked in the equaliser and the game ended 2–2. Italy, Sweden and Denmark all finished on five points but the draw meant that Italy were eliminated, having scored fewer goals than Sweden and Denmark. Coach Giovanni Trapattoni said, 'We leave with our heads held high.' But a more adventurous policy, and the ability to finish off moves, could well have meant their progress to the knockouts.

Group D comprised the Czech Republic, Latvia, Germany and Holland. The first two met in Aveiro and unheralded newcomers to the tournament Latvia surprised the Czechs by going ahead through Maris Verpakovskis on half-time. Milan Baros brought the Czechs back into the game from ten yards and Marek Heinze won it with a volley five minutes from time.

Germany went ahead against Holland with a Torsten Frings curled free kick, but in the 80th minute Ruud van Nistelrooy's acrobatic close-range shot sealed the draw.

Latvia's robust and speedy play, combined with solid defending, deserved more than a 0–0 draw against Germany in Porto. The game between the Czech Republic and Holland – featuring the incisive wing play of young Dutchman Arjen Robben – was much more exciting. A Wilfred Bouma header put Holland ahead within three minutes, with van Nistelrooy doubling the Dutch lead in the 19th minute from a Robben cross. Giant striker Jan Koller replied for the Czechs four minutes later, after an error by Dutch captain Phillip Cocu, and the game was levelled by Baros's stunning half volley lashed home. Smicer's winning goal with two minutes left on the clock ensured the Czech's progress to the quarter-finals.

In the last of the Group D games, another influential display from Robben, two goals from van Nistelrooy and a third from substitute Roy Makaay gave Holland a comfortable 3–0 win over Latvia, although they had to hope that the Czech Republic beat Germany in the other game.

Fielding a near-reserve side, the Czechs did just that. Although

Michael Ballack thundered a left-foot screamer in the 21st minute to give Germany the lead, a spectacular free kick from Heinze levelled the score and Baros won the game for the Czechs with his 75th-minute goal. Germany were out of the tournament for the second championship in a row and a delighted Holland moved into the quarter-finals.

Portugal played England in the Stadium of Light in the first quarter-final and England made a dream start. Costinha headed backwards a long clearance from David James in the third minute and Michael Owen ran on to flick the first goal past Ricardo. The Portuguese came back strongly, with Figo, Ronaldo and Maniche making chances, but they were kept out by Campbell, John Terry and the assured Ashley Cole. England's talisman Wayne Rooney went off injured in the 27th minute and they were lucky to go in at the interval with their lead intact.

Simao and Helder Postiga came on during the second half and it was these two who drew Portugal level, Postiga heading in a Simao cross in the 83rd minute. A Campbell goal was disallowed at the end of normal time for Terry's push on keeper Ricardo. In extra time, Rui Costa rocketed in an excellent strike in the 100th minute and Lampard equalised five minutes later. In the shootout, Beckham missed for England while Rui Costa was the only Portuguese not to score. Substitute Darius Vassell missed the sixth attempt while Ricardo took Portugal's sixth and found the net. Portugal were through to the semis 6–5 on penalties.

The following day, in the most sensational result of the tournament yet, France were eliminated by underdogs Greece. In the first half, the lively Greeks outplayed the sluggish French. In the second period, the French were more dangerous, until captain Theo Zagorakis crossed to Charisteas who powered in an unstoppable header in the 65th minute. The organisation and work rate of the Greeks contained the French attack until the final whistle.

In game three, Holland had the bulk of the possession against Sweden, with Robben and van der Meyde switching wings at will but making no impact on the Swedish defence. Extra time came and went without a goal. Van der Sar saved Olof Mellberg's attempt and when Robben's turn arrived, he sent Andreas Isaksson the wrong way for a 5–4 penalty win to Holland.

The last game saw an accomplished display from the Czech Republic and particularly Baros, whose two goals helped send Denmark out of the competition. With Baros partnering Koller up front and the creative Pavel Nedved organising from midfield, it was a surprise that the Czechs had not scored by half-time. However, in the 49th minute Koller headed in a Poborsky corner. Then Baros's two goals in two minutes knocked the stuffing out of the Danes. In the 63rd minute, he received a delightful through-ball from Poborsky and neatly chipped keeper Sorensen in Denmark's goal. Two minutes later, Nedved supplied him with a defence-splitting pass and Baros lashed the ball into the net for his fifth goal of the tournament. He ended the competition as top scorer.

On 30 June, Portugal met Holland in Lisbon in the first semi-final. With Luis Figo, substituted against England, at his electric best, Portugal went on the offensive. Deco created the opening goal in the 26th minute, sending in an inswinging corner for Ronaldo to score with a downward header. Five minutes before the interval, van Nistelrooy had a goal disallowed for offside and then Figo's sublime curling left-foot shot beat keeper van der Sar but hit the post.

Early in the second half, Ronaldo took a short corner to Nuno Maniche who hit a stunning, swerving right-foot shot past van der Sar for Portugal's second and a sure candidate for goal of the tournament. Portuguese defender Jorge Andrade reduced the deficit in the 63rd minute when he miskicked into his own goal from a Gio van Bronckhorst cross. The final whistle blew and Portugal were through to the final. The car horns in Lisbon sounded well into the night.

The following day in Porto, Greece and the Czech Republic contested the second semi-final. The Czechs immediately took to the attack, with Rosicky thumping a volley against the crossbar in the second minute. The well-drilled Greeks grew in confidence as the game went on, with keeper Antonis Nikopodolis and defender Trainos Dellas particularly impressive. The Czechs suffered a major blow in the 40th minute when playmaker Nedved limped off to be replaced by Smicer, and the attack made little headway against Greece in normal time. In the 106th minute, Dellas headed in from a Vassilis Tsiartas free kick and the Greeks had won through to the final with a 'silver goal'.

The final was held in Lisbon on 4 July and was to prove one of the greatest shocks in the history of the competition. The Greeks, coached by Otto Rehhagel, had come this far as a result of their organised and committed defending and their ability to punish opponents' errors. They packed in defence in the first half – often with ten men around the penalty area – but went ahead in the second period when Charisteas climbed to head in from their first corner. Greece then successfully contained the Portuguese attack, although Ronaldo and Figo almost scored, and held on to their one-goal lead until the final whistle, much to the ecstatic delight of their 15,000 fans chanting '*Hellas ole*' in the Stadium of Light.

Rehhagel said, 'The Greeks have made football history. It's a sensation.' Thirty-two-year-old captain Theo Zagarakis, possessor of 95 caps, was also voted Player of the Tournament.

The next day, the team, who had started the championships as 80–1 outsiders, were given a heroes' welcome home by over 100,000 fans in Athens, providing the perfect curtain-raiser for the following month's Olympic Games and immeasurably raising the prestige of Greek football in Europe.

Appendices

EUROPEAN CUP FINALS 1956–2005

Year	Winners	Runners-up	Score	Venue
1956	Real Madrid	Reims	4–3	Paris
1957	Real Madrid	Fiorentina	2–0	Madrid
1958	Real Madrid	Milan	3–2	Brussels
1959	Real Madrid	Reims	2–0	Stuttgart
1960	Real Madrid	Eintracht Frankfurt	7–3	Glasgow
1961	Benfica	Barcelona	3–2	Berne
1962	Benfica	Real Madrid	5–3	Amsterdam
1963	Milan	Benfica	2–1	Wembley
1964	Internazionale	Real Madrid	3–1	Vienna
1965	Internazionale	Benfica	1–0	Milan
1966	Real Madrid	Partizan Belgrade	2–1	Brussels
1967	Celtic	Internazionale	2–1	Lisbon
1968	Manchester United	Benfica	4–1	Wembley
1969	Milan	Ajax	4–1	Madrid
1970	Feyenoord	Celtic	2–1	Milan
1971	Ajax	Panathinaikos	2–0	Wembley
1972	Ajax	Internazionale	2–0	Rotterdam
1973	Ajax	Juventus	1–0	Belgrade
1974	Bayern Munich	Atletico Madrid	4–0	Brussels
	(replay following 1–1 draw in Brussels)			
1975	Bayern Munich	Leeds	2–0	Paris
1976	Bayern Munich	Saint-Etienne	1–0	Glasgow
1977	Liverpool	Borussia Monchengladbach	3–1	Rome
1978	Liverpool	Brugge	1–0	Wembley
1979	Nottingham Forest	Malmo	1–0	Munich
1980	Nottingham Forest	Hamburg	1–0	Madrid

Fields of Glory, Paths of Gold

1981	Liverpool	Real Madrid	1–0	Paris
1982	Aston Villa	Bayern Munich	1–0	Rotterdam
1983	Hamburg	Juventus	1–0	Athens
1984	Liverpool	Roma	1–1	Rome
	Liverpool won 4–2 on penalties			
1985	Juventus	Liverpool	1–0	Brussels
1986	Steaua Bucharest	Barcelona	0–0	Seville
	Steaua Bucharest won 2–0 on penalties			
1987	Porto	Bayern Munich	2–1	Vienna
1988	PSV Eindhoven	Benfica	0–0	Stuttgart
	PSV Eindhoven won 6–5 on penalties			
1989	Milan	Steaua Bucharest	4–0	Barcelona
1990	Milan	Benfica	1–0	Vienna
1991	Red Star Belgrade	Marseille	0–0	Bari
	Red Star Belgrade won 5–3 on penalties			
1992	Barcelona	Sampdoria	1–0	Wembley
1993	Marseille	Milan	1–0	Munich
1994	Milan	Barcelona	4–0	Athens
1995	Ajax	Milan	1–0	Vienna
1996	Juventus	Ajax	1–1	Rome
	Juventus won 4–2 on penalties			
1997	Borussia Dortmund	Juventus	3–1	Munich
1998	Real Madrid	Juventus	1–0	Amsterdam
1999	Manchester United	Bayern Munich	2–1	Barcelona
2000	Real Madrid	Valencia	3–0	Paris
2001	Bayern Munich	Valencia	1–1	Milan
	Bayern Munich won 5–4 on penalties			
2002	Real Madrid	Bayer Leverkusen	2–1	Glasgow
2003	Milan	Juventus	0–0	Manchester
	Milan won 3–2 on penalties			
2004	Porto	Monaco	3–0	Gelsenkirchen
2005	Liverpool	Milan	3–3	Istanbul
	Liverpool won 3–2 on penalties			

APPENDIX II

FAIRS CUP AND UEFA CUP FINALS 1958–2005

FAIRS CUP

Year	Winners	Runners-up	Score	Venue
1958	Barcelona	London XI	2–2 (a), 6–0 (h)	home and away
1960	Barcelona	Birmingham	0–0 (a), 4–1 (h)	home and away
1961	Roma	Birmingham	2–2 (a), 2–0 (h)	home and away
1962	Valencia	Barcelona	6–2 (h), 1–1 (a)	home and away
1963	Valencia	Dynamo Zagreb	2–1 (a), 2–0 (h)	home and away
1964	Zaragoza	Valencia	2–1	Barcelona
1965	Ferencvaros	Juventus	1–0	Turin
1966	Barcelona	Zaragoza	0–1 (h), 4–2 (a)	home and away
1967	Dynamo Zagreb	Leeds	2–0 (h), 0–0 (a)	home and away
1968	Leeds	Ferencvaros	1–0 (h), 0–0 (a)	home and away
1969	Newcastle	Ujpest Dozsa	3–0 (h), 3–2 (a)	home and away
1970	Arsenal	Anderlecht	1–3 (a), 3–0 (h)	home and away
1971	Leeds	Juventus	2–2 (a), 1–1 (h)	home and away
	Leeds won on away goals			
1972	Tottenham	Wolverhampton	2–1 (a), 1–1 (h)	home and away
1973	Liverpool	Borussia Monchengladbach	3–0 (h), 0–2 (a)	home and away
1974	Feyenoord	Tottenham	2–2 (a), 2–0 (h)	home and away
1975	Borussia Monchengladbach	FC Twente	0–0 (h), 5–1 (a)	home and away
1976	Liverpool	Brugge	3–2 (h), 1–1 (a)	home and away
1977	Juventus	Atletico Bilbao	1–0 (h), 1–2 (a)	home and away
	Juventus won on away goals			
1978	PSV Eindhoven	Bastia	0–0 (a), 3–0 (h)	home and away
1979	Borussia Monchengladbach	Red Star Belgrade	1–1 (a), 1–0 (h)	home and away

1980	Eintracht Frankfurt	Borussia Monchengladbach	2–3 (a), 1–0 (h)	home and away
	Eintracht won on away goals			
1981	Ipswich	AZ67 Alkmaar	3–0 (h), 2–4 (a)	home and away
1982	Gothenburg	Hamburg	1–0 (h), 3–0 (a)	home and away
1983	Anderlecht	Benfica	1–0 (h), 1–1 (a)	home and away
1984	Tottenham	Anderlecht	1–1 (a), 1–1 (h)	home and away
	Tottenham won 4–3 on penalties			
1985	Real Madrid	Videoton	3–0 (a), 0–1 (h)	home and away
1986	Real Madrid	Koln	5–1 (h), 0–2 (a)	home and away
1987	Gothenburg	Dundee United	1–0 (h), 1–1 (a)	home and away
1988	Bayer Leverkusen	Espanol	0–3 (a), 3–0 (h)	home and away
	Leverkusen won 3–2 on penalties			
1989	Napoli	Stuttgart	2–1 (h), 3–3 (a)	home and away
1990	Juventus	Fiorentina	3–1 (h), 0–0 (a)	home and away
1991	Internazionale	Roma	2–0 (h), 0–1 (a)	home and away
1992	Ajax	Torino	2–2 (a), 0–0 (h)	home and away
	Ajax won on away goals			
1993	Juventus	Borussia Dortmund	3–1 (a), 3–0 (h)	home and away
1994	Internazionale	Salzburg	1–0 (a), 1–0 (h)	home and away
1995	Parma	Juventus	1–0 (h), 1–1 (a)	home and away
1996	Bayern Munich	Bordeaux	2–0 (h), 3–1 (a)	home and away
1997	Schalke	Internazionale	1–0 (h), 0–1 (a)	home and away
	Schalke won 4–1 on penalties			
1998	Internazionale	Lazio	3–0	Paris
1999	Parma	Marseille	3–0	Moscow
2000	Galatasaray	Arsenal	0–0	Copenhagen
	Galatasaray won 4–1 on penalities			
2001	Liverpool	Alaves	5–4	Dortmund
		(with golden goal)		
2002	Feyenoord	Borussia Dortmund	3–2	Rotterdam
2003	Porto	Celtic	3–2	Seville
2004	Valencia	Marseille	2–0	Gothenburg
2005	CSKA Moscow	Sporting Lisbon	3–1	Lisbon

Note: Since 1997–98, the final has been decided in one match and not over two legs

EUROPEAN CHAMPIONSHIPS 1960–2004

Year	Winners
1960	USSR
1964	Spain
1968	Italy
1972	West Germany
1976	Czechoslovakia
1980	West Germany
1984	France
1988	Holland
1992	Denmark
1996	Germany
2000	France
2004	Greece

APPENDIX IV

EUROPEAN CUP-WINNERS' CUP FINALS 1961-99

Year	Winners	Runners-up	Score	Venue
1961	Fiorentina	Rangers	2–0 (a), 2–1 (h)	home and away
1962	Atletico Madrid	Fiorentina	3–0	Stuttgart
	after 1–1 draw in Glasgow			
1963	Tottenham	Atletico Madrid	5–1	Rotterdam
1964	Sporting Lisbon	MTK Budapest	1–0	Antwerp
	after 3–3 draw in Brussels			
1965	West Ham	Munich 1860	2–0	Wembley
1966	Borussia Dortmund	Liverpool	2–1	Glasgow
1967	Bayern Munich	Rangers	1–0	Nurnberg
1968	Milan	Hamburg	2–0	Rotterdam
1969	Slovan Bratislava	Barcelona	3–2	Basle
1970	Manchester City	Gornik Zabrze	2–1	Vienna
1971	Chelsea	Real Madrid	2–1	Athens
	after 1–1 draw in Athens			
1972	Rangers	Dynamo Moscow	3–2	Barcelona
1973	Milan	Leeds	1–0	Salonika
1974	Magdeburg	Milan	2–0	Rotterdam
1975	Dynamo Kiev	Ferencvaros	3–0	Basle
1976	Anderlecht	West Ham	4–2	Brussels
1977	Hamburg	Anderlecht	2–0	Amsterdam
1978	Anderlecht	FK Austria	4–0	Paris
1979	Barcelona	Fortuna Dusseldorf	4–3	Basle

1980	Valencia	Arsenal	0–0	Brussels
	Valencia won 5–4 on penalties			
1981	Dinamo Tbilisi	Carl Zeiss Jena	2–1	Dusseldorf
1982	Barcelona	Standard Liege	2–1	Barcelona
1983	Aberdeen	Real Madrid	2–1	Gothenburg
1984	Juventus	Porto	2–1	Basle
1985	Everton	Rapid Vienna	3–1	Rotterdam
1986	Dynamo Kiev	Atletico Madrid	3–0	Lyon
1987	Ajax	Lokomotiv Leipzig	1–0	Athens
1988	Mechelen	Ajax	1–0	Strasbourg
1989	Barcelona	Sampdoria	2–0	Berne
1990	Sampdoria	Anderlecht	2–0	Gothenburg
1991	Manchester United	Barcelona	2–1	Rotterdam
1992	Werder Bremen	Monaco	2–0	Lisbon
1993	Parma	Antwerp	3–1	Wembley
1994	Arsenal	Parma	1–0	Copenhagen
1995	Zaragoza	Arsenal	2–1	Paris
1996	Paris Saint-Germain	Rapid Vienna	1–0	Brussels
1997	Barcelona	Paris Saint-Germain	1–0	Rotterdam
1998	Chelsea	Stuttgart	1–0	Stockholm
1999	Lazio	Mallorca	2–1	Birmingham

BIBLIOGRAPHY/SOURCES

NEWSPAPERS/PERIODICALS
Archived and library material from the main British newspapers plus material from these specialist football magazines:
A Bola (Portugal)
France Football (France)
Gol (Czech Republic)
kicker (Germany)
Marca (Spain)
O Jogo (Portugal)
Rothman's Football Yearbook (1972–2003)
World Soccer

BOOKS
Arnold, Peter, Connolly, Kevin and MacWilliam, Rab *Great Football Moments of the 20th Century* (Hamlyn, London, 1999)

Ball, Phil, *An Englishman Abroad* (Ebury Press, London, 2004)

Ball, Phil, *White Storm: 100 Years of Real Madrid* (Mainstream, Edinburgh, 2003)

Barend, Frits, and van Dorp, Henk, *Ajax, Barcelona, Cruyff: The ABC of an Obstinate Maestro* (Bloomsbury, London, 1998)

Burns, Jimmy, *Barca: A People's Passion* (Bloomsbury, London, 1999)

Carlin, John, *White Angels* (Bloomsbury, London, 2004)

Glanville, Brian, *Champions of Europe* (Guinness Publishing, London, 1991)

Glanville, Brian, *The Story of the World Cup* (Faber & Faber, London, 2001)

Hare, Geoff, *Football in France* (Berg, Oxford, 2003)

Hesse-Lichtenberger, Uli, *Tor! The Story of German Football* (WSC Books, London, 2003)

Kuper, Simon, *Football Against the Enemy* (Phoenix, London, 1994)

MacWilliam, Rab, *The European Cup: An Illustrated History* (Aurum, London, 2000)

McManaman, Steve, with Sarah Edworthy, *El Macca* (Simon and Schuster, London, 2004)

Michie, Jonathan and Oughton, Christine, *Competitive Balance in Football*, (Football Governance Research Centre, London, 2004)

Rees, Jasper, *Wenger, The Making of a Legend* (Short Books, London, 2003)

Ruhn, Christov, ed., *Le Foot* (Abacus, London, 2000)

Sharpe, Ivan, *Forty Years in Football* (Sportsman's Book Club, London, 1954)

Wall, Bob, *Arsenal from the Heart* (Souvenir Press, London, 1969)

Winner, David, *Brilliant Orange: The Neurotic Genius of Dutch Football* (Bloomsbury, London, 2000)

WEBSITES

The websites of the major European clubs, associations and broadcasting organisations, plus:

for statistics:
www.rsssf.com

for social issues relating to football:
www.le.ac.uk (The Sir Norman Chester Centre for Football Research, University of Leicester)
www.sirc.org (Social Issues Research Centre)

357

INDEX